EXPERIENCING SOCIAL PSYCHOLOGY

READINGS AND PROJECTS
SECOND EDITION

AYALA PINES

UNIVERSITY OF CALIFORNIA, BERKELEY

CHRISTINA MASLACH

UNIVERSITY OF CALIFORNIA, BERKELEY

McGraw-Hill, Inc.

New York St. Louis San Francisco Auckland Bogotá Caracas
Hamburg Lisbon London Madrid Mexico Milan Montreal
New Delhi Paris San Juan São Paulo Singapore Sydney
Tokyo Toronto

FOR OUR CHILDREN: ITAI, SHANI, ZARA, AND TANYA

EXPERIENCING SOCIAL PSYCHOLOGY   2/e

Second Edition
98765

ISBN 0-07-554459-8

INTRODUCTION

It was not too many years ago that social psychology was considered a distant and not always welcome relative of general psychology. Whereas social psychology was concerned with groups, the focus of general psychology was supposed to be the individual. Social psychologists studied practical affairs of everyday life: conformity, prejudice, persuasion, violence, and the like. Meanwhile, the mainstream of psychological research remained aloof from such mundane matters. "Soft-headed" social psychologists insisted on understanding the unique content of private human experience and its public expression; "hard-headed" psychologists sought to discover quantifiable laws for the behavior of organisms.

But within the last decade, social psychology has quietly moved into the inner circle of psychology, so that it is now at the core of virtually all psychological disciplines. This quiet revolution was assisted during the late 1960s by students who called for social relevance in their courses and who responded to social psychology's problem-centered approach to the study of the human condition. At about the same time, behavioristic psychology, largely based on animal learning experiments, came to be regarded as too limited to be the foundation for understanding the complexities of human behavior. Similarly, the recent emergence of the cognitive psychology of information processing found social psychologists already oriented toward the study of mental states, expectations, intentions, and inferences.

At present, then, it is safe to say that there are few areas of psychological investigation—social learning, social cognition, social emotionality, social pathology, and so forth—that have not been influenced by social psychology. Nevertheless, the message of modern social psychology is not that it has moved from the attic of the house of psychology to the main floor, where it might annex other areas of psychology; rather, I believe, its contribution to other branches of psychology lies in its ability to point out that exciting views of human experience do exist on many different levels. The social psychologist is equally interested in the individual and in the group, equally challenged by testing an abstract theoretical derivation and by illuminating a common aspect of daily life, equally stimulated by discovering how the mind works and by helping to improve the quality of human life.

In the pages that follow, all these dimensions of social psychology will be revealed to you. Ayala Pines and Christina Maslach are both gifted, energetic individuals who love to teach as much as they love to conduct research. Consequently, they will be very knowledgeable guides for your journey into the workings of social psychology. This book is, in fact, a labor of love. In it you will find ideas, reports, perspectives, and projects that students have responded to with enthusiasm. Pines and Maslach share with us the challenge, complexity, and concerns that constitute the endeavor to understand how individuals are influenced by others and, in turn, shape their social environment. They lead us—sometimes gently, sometimes gingerly—from classic areas of social psychology to emerging frontiers of research. Their concern is always to involve you, to get you to think about what all this means for your life, to participate actively in the observations and experiments suggested. In some languages, *experiment* translates as *experience*. Here's to a most enjoyable experience in learning about the social animal that is you.

Philip G. Zimbardo

TO THE READER

Experiencing Social Psychology: Readings and Projects is designed to supplement your introductory textbook. To make this handbook as useful and adaptable as possible, we have chosen to organize the chapters around thirteen topics that are generally considered to be the central concerns of social psychologists. Each chapter begins with a brief general introduction, placing the topic within the context of contemporary theory and research and relating it to conditions of daily life.

In each chapter we have included at least two readings, each of which is preceded by a short introduction that highlights its significance in relation to the chapter topic. These readings, which have been adapted from their original sources, represent a mixture of current topics and classic issues. They are meant to extend the ideas you encounter in your textbook or to indicate recent thinking and controversies in a given area. Throughout the book we have also inserted brief excerpts from works of literature, anecdotes, cartoons, and research highlights that illustrate important principles in thought-provoking ways.

It is our strong conviction that the best way to learn about social psychology is to do it, to take part in the research adventure from which the information and theoretical positions described and analyzed in your textbook are derived. The insights you gain from course lectures, your textbook, and the readings and boxed features in this book will almost certainly take on a special immediacy and significance when you put them to the test of empirical investigation.

With this in mind, we have included several research projects in each chapter. Here you can test some of the ideas and concepts developed in your text or by your instructor and see how they apply to yourself and to your friends. Some of the projects cast you in the role of the investigator who collects data from surveys and rating scales or by observing other people. Others require you to be your own subject. In addition, we have included projects that can be done in field settings on campus, in your neighborhood, or at work. Others might be done as part of a class project organized by your instructor. Your active participation in carrying out these projects will help reinforce what you have already learned and will show you—through your own work—the basic forms of research that psychologists engage in.

We hope that our book serves its intended purpose well and helps you learn more about the complex, varied, and fascinating field of social psychology and leads you to a better understanding of your own behavior and the behavior of those around you.

Ayala Pines
Christina Maslach

CONTENTS

RESEARCH

1

Virtually everyone has a set of ideas to explain why people behave the way they do. These ideas, or beliefs, which usually strike us as being right, may be based on personal experience or on common sense. If knowledge about human behavior is so easy to acquire, then what do social psychologists have to offer us? Essentially, they offer us the *scientific method*. Social psychologists also use personal experience and common sense as a source of ideas, but, unlike the layperson, they then test the validity of these ideas, using objective research procedures. Because there are so many different beliefs about human behavior, it is the task as well as the goal of the social psychologist to determine which assumptions are scientifically valid.

The research approach that social psychologists use most frequently is the laboratory experiment. In a laboratory setting, the researcher can create and control various social stimuli and then carefully record the behavior of the participants. The primary advantage of laboratory research is that the experimental findings can be understood in causal terms.

Because the laboratory researcher intervenes by determining what will occur, he or she is in a better position to infer why the subjects behaved as they did. In contrast, the researcher who studies social interaction in real-life settings by means of passive observation often cannot control what is going on and usually can point only to correlations rather than to causes. That is, the field researcher can identify different behaviors that seem to be related, but is less able to specify their causes. Although field studies have the advantage of focusing on naturally occurring behavior (as opposed to the more contrived behavior that is so often characteristic of the laboratory experiment), they are often enormously complex, time consuming, expensive, and difficult to carry out. For all these reasons, field research has *not* been the primary mode of scholarly endeavor among social psychologists, although a great deal of lip service is paid to the ideal of doing more work in the field. Reports on the results of controlled laboratory experiments continue to dominate the journals and textbooks.

AN INTELLIGENT CONSUMER'S GUIDE TO RESEARCH

MARIANNE LAFRANCE

The printed letter has power. We are all more likely to believe a newspaper item we read with our own eyes than the same information heard from a friend. Not only does it look more convincing in print, but we assume that those who published it must have checked their sources carefully and thus spared us the task. This faith is even more evident in our reading of scientific journals and books.

In beginning with this article on how to evaluate research readings, we mean to suggest that no research should be accepted on faith, not even the articles in this book. Faith in the printed word of scientific literature, especially by undergraduate students, can become credulity. Beyond this, the intellectual controversy generated by such critical evaluation is exhilarating and intrinsic to knowledge-building.

In the following article excerpted for her book, LaFrance provides consumer guidelines that are intended to help the reader evaluate social psychological research by asking critical questions and making intelligent comparisons.

How many times have you said to yourself when hearing a report of research findings "I just don't buy that"? Yet when asked to pinpoint particular objections, you don't know where to begin. In contrast, when you go out to buy something, a stereo component for example, you can be very specific about which features are good and which are not. As consumers you have learned the hard way that things are not always what they seem and that to get the "best for the money" you have had to become sharp shoppers. Whether you are aware of it or not, you are just as much consumers of a special product: research. We are all bombarded daily with newsworthy and "textworthy" vignettes telling of new psychological findings. Should you "buy" them? This chapter is directed towards helping you become as intelligent a consumer of behavioral research as you already are of goods and services.

Before making a major purchase, you likely take many factors into account. In buying a car, you may check a consumer guide to find out how each make and model is rated on such things as design, gas mileage, resale value, and maintenance history. Buying a car on the basis of a single feature or a sole person's recommendation is often a decision that one later regrets. A car bought for the fun of quick starts and high speeds may become an annoying burden during gasoline price increases, and that high recommendation may turn out to have been based on the single car that model year that was not a lemon. So too with research. A number of factors should be taken into account before you decide to buy. Some guidelines are offered here to help you make your way through the rather formidable looking product known as the scientific study. These guidelines are adopted from

consumer practice to make you more aware of the skills and knowledge you already have.

READ CAREFULLY

Intelligent shoppers are those that look immediately for the "fine print." They read labels and descriptions, not just names and slogans. Careful note is taken of ingredients, quantities, and prices. In appraising research studies, careful reading is also the mark of the intelligent consumer. There is great temptation to ask only what a study found and to ignore the critical ingredients, such as what procedures were used and on whom. The method section in any report of psychological research is the "fine print" and should be as carefully noted as the actual results. Interesting results derived from questionable procedures should be ignored as surely as an attractive appearing product made from slip-shod ingredients. The findings of any study are only as good as the means that were used to collect them.

In addition to the methods section in a research report, the introduction should also be read carefully. It is there that the author attempts to place the study in context and to plead a case for its importance. Therein you should find the answer to the question "Should I buy this at all?" Is the question an important one? Will it break new ground or provide some clarification on ambiquities or controversies in previous work?

CHECK GUARANTEES

To check guarantees is a variant of the injunction to read the fine print, but it goes further in suggesting that there are questions to be asked of any study that go beyond the material presented. Despite their dense appearance and high attention to detail, published journal articles represent only an abbreviated account of what actually went into the research process. Often if one were interested in doing a study similar to one already published,

Adapted from *Evaluating Research in Social Psychology: A Guide for the Consumer,* by C. Mayo and M. LaFrance. © 1977 by Wadsworth Publishing Company, Inc. Reprinted by permission of Brooks/Cole Publishing Company, Monterey, California 93940.

one would probably have to write to the authors for more specific and complete information. Checking guarantees becomes even more necessary, though more difficult, the farther the report on findings is removed from the source. In textbooks, qualifications on the findings are seldom reported and media accounts of psychological research frequently prune down the complexities even more.

Checking guarantees on research findings involves asking of a study whether it has survived the rigors of professional review and whether it has been replicated. In terms of the former, not every study submitted to a journal is accepted. Many are weeded out because they are found to be faulty on methodological grounds. As to the latter, confidence in findings increases when they can be shown to occur again in comparable circumstances.

LOOK BEYOND FLASHY MERCHANDISING

Behind every product there is a production process. Some advertisements show complicated graphics to impart a sense of great technical sophistication or show a single coffee bean picker to convey a sense of very special attention. The assumption is that if a great deal went into production, then a great product must emerge. For the intelligent consumer, production technique is a means to an end, not the end itself. The product must be evaluated overall and not solely on the way that it came about.

In the case of research, it is sometimes the case that you remember only how the study was done. A particularly cute procedure or clever manipulation or provocative scale comes to mind, but their purpose or point seems to have gotten lost. Earlier we stressed the importance of attending to the method and not just to the results. Here we are stressing the need to look into the method and beyond. The method is important precisely in relation to the questions posed and the answers found and should not stand out for its own sake because of unusual ingenuity or fancy gimmickry.

A good study is securely anchored fore and aft; it derives explicitly from some significant theoretical or practical issue, and its results and the implications of its results extend beyond the study's conclusion. A study that merely amuses by its dexterity or impresses by its scope is not good science. Ring (1967) has suggested a number of questions that the intelligent consumer may want to ask in order to avoid flashy merchandising.

1. Does this research really deal with a problem of some broad not necessarily applied human significance, or does it represent . . . merely an interest . . . of one's own?
2. Is this research part of a program of systematic inquiry (or likely to initiate one), or is it really likely to wind up a one-shot affair?
3. Does this research unavoidably entail using a deception-experiment paradigm?

Objection is not made to dramatic experimentation as such, but rather to the pursuit of that style for its own sake. Conversely, as McGuire (1967) noted, it is equally fallacious to assume that the deadly dull is necessarily significant.

LOOK FOR DURABILITY AND LONG-TERM BENEFITS

The intelligent consumer avoids surface gimmicks and reads the fine print in order to find a durable product that will stand the test of time. Research is not usually content with describing events for a particular group at a specific time and place. The aim is to understand something about how and when and why a certain psychological process occurred so that reliable predictions can be made about other situations at other times. Good research is that which allows generalizations to be made beyond the here and now.

Students are sometimes alarmed when they encounter contradictory findings in the research literature or when they seek to replicate a study but find that their results have not come out the same as the original. Both cases seem to represent clear cases of nondurability and seem to be cause for concern. The search for durability is the search for conditions that help explain apparent inconsistencies. The intelligent consumer of research is one that examines methodology closely for clues as to why a finding may have occurred one place and not another. Sometimes an apparently small change in wording of instructions or alteration of the physical environment is enough to cause big changes in results.

A key feature in understanding research methodology is knowing that a particular procedure may have inadvertently caused an effect to happen, rather than simply uncovering a predicted cause–effect relation. Faith in the durability of a finding is increased when it can be revealed by methods other than the one originally used. As an intelligent consumer of research you should ask yourself whether the results would have occurred:

(1) by the same method at another time and place and (2) by another research procedure. The first feature is called *replication* and the second is termed *convergent validity*. Durability requires both.

An example can be found in research that explores the effect of group discussion on the tendency to take risks. Replication would involve using the same format in essentially the same procedure with another group of subjects. Convergent validity would involve measuring the same relationship, but might vary the particular issue under discussion or might actually observe risk-taking behavior rather than asking research participants how they think they would act. If the same results are obtained both by replication of the same method and with different methods, the results can be said to have durability. As a consumer you would be more justified in buying the results.

PAY ATTENTION TO THE COST–QUALITY RELATION

It is a truism of consumerism that you get what you pay for. Some would advise that given a choice, you should choose the higher priced product because it is invariably of higher quality; others would say that the cheaper purchase is better because there is so little difference in quality anyway. While in everyday practice you probably operate between these extremes, there is temptation to assume that if something costs more, it must be worth more. In research this might mean assuming that a study involving thousands of subjects, hundreds of interviewers, and years of compilation is better than a similar study of more modest scale. This assumption is no more warranted than its opposite, namely, that smaller is better. The quality of research has more to do with an ongoing task that gradually adds and clarifies rather than with one study that settles things once and for all, whatever its cost.

Being an intelligent consumer means not only knowing how to assess the quality of a possible purchase, but whether the purchase should be made at all. With regard to research, this means not only asking whether a study is methodologically sound, but whether the contribution was worth the effort. Making decisions about the quality of a research idea is difficult because the criteria are less explicit and less agreed upon. Moreover, the aura of objectivity with which the scientific enterprise is clothed tends to discourage

questions as to whether the question was worth addressing in the first place. Some studies seem to get done because they can be done (i.e., they cost relatively little), rather than because they need to be done. Maslow underlined this point when he aptly said that that which is not worth doing is not worth doing well. The issue here is one of priorities. Research questions should always precede considerations of methodology.

Although most research studies are undertaken because the ideas are regarded as important, the fact is that some studies are not undertaken because they are or appear to be too costly. The scarcity of longitudinal studies in social psychology can be attributed directly to their cost in time and money. Consequently we seem to know a great deal about how college sophomores form first impressions of people and little about the development and dissolution of long-term intimate relationships.

Another kind of scarce research is cross-cultural research. Although most social psychologists are vulnerable to the criticism that their findings apply only to the cultural or regional or social group on which they were based, and although it is important to know for whom particular effects apply, few cross-cultural studies are done due to their prohibitive costs. Costs are relative, though, and must be considered in relation to the anticipated benefits of understanding. Longitudinal and cross-cultural research is costly in monetary terms, but the results may do more in the long run to explain the nature of social behavior than would numerous short-term or sample-specific studies.

BUY FROM A REPUTABLE SOURCE

An oft-repeated recommendation of intelligent consumerism is to buy from a reliable dealer. Applied to research, this may seem a strange analog and maybe even a questionable one—questionable because the ready acceptance of the known, the familiar, and the inveterate may blind us to the innovative and the controversial. Science is, after all, replete with stories of investigators who were initially thought to be deluded or crazy only to be recognized much later as correct and on-target.

The injunction to buy from a reputable source is designed to call your attention to the fact that social science is a human enterprise conducted by people who are invested in their products and who, on occasion, have axes to grind. The objective here is not to "dehumanize" research (some might say we have done that too much already) but to sensitize you to the prevailing presence of the human element.

Reputable sources then are not ones who have made their reputation, but ones who provide the kind of information that will allow you to judge for yourself. Consider these sources:

1. Given that the results of a study may have been "caused" by a number of factors, what has the investigator done in order to rule out the irrelevant ones and to elucidate the principal ones?

2. Has the investigator presented enough detail on the procedure and findings that will allow you to adequately assess the findings and the conclusions?

3. What indication is there that the investigator has given attention to alternative explanations of the data obtained?

4. What care has been taken by the investigator to protect the welfare and privacy of his or her research participants?

LEARN THE VOCABULARY

In order to become an intelligent consumer of research, you will need to learn some new words. You are doing this all the time in deciding among different versions of the same product. Some of you reading this book were probably first attracted to psychology by a curiosity about people, but then may have become baffled to find the field laden with jargon and special terms. As a consumer you have had to learn some new terms, which may then have increased your appreciation of the differences between apparent look-a-likes. In fact, a consumer search often begins with finding out what the "shop talk" is—that is, the terms that people in the know use to make good decisions. In research as well, it is worth the effort to learn new terms in order to answer questions worth asking.

DO COMPARISON SHOPPING

Faced with the problem of an overgrown front lawn, you might go out to buy a lawnmower. As a good consumer, you would go to several sources and compare the relative merits of various makes and models. In research, this comparison shopping might lead you to consider the different methods that have been used to study a particular problem, such as a highly controlled laboratory experiment or a systematic attitude survey of specified neigh-

borhoods. You select a particular lawnmower after weighing such factors as quality, price, features, and guarantees. In many ways, you evaluate research methodology in a similar fashion. Some research designs can provide better guarantees than others because they more easily rule out alternative interpretations of the effects obtained. Some measurement tools, while superficially quite respectable, may be less good than others because they do not specifically address the questions that prompted the inquiry in the first place.

Comparison shopping may also alert you to the need for new approaches for addressing the problem, but whether they are desirable or not for you depends on what you are trying to find out. Finally, comparison shopping may indicate that your initial premise is in need of revision. With regard to the overgrown front lawn, you may hit upon the possibility of new landscaping that contains no grass and hence no need for a mower. In other words, it may be that your initial research question is in need of modification or complete overhaul. Close inspection of different research strategies may show that the findings do not address the more fundamental issue at hand.

Refinement of Questions

In order to assess whether an appropriate methodology has been used, consumers need to pay special attention to how a researcher has phrased his or her question. The researcher needs to be maximally explicit about the question that needs answering. One of the first problems encountered by the novice researcher is learning how to phrase a question so that it can be answered. This is no easy task. General queries such as why are people violent and why is it that some groups are more creative than others need considerable refinement before any method can be applied. Another potential trap for the inexperienced is to let an existing method shape the question to be asked. This takes the form of beginning a research project by focusing more on how to do something before deciding on why to do it. The availability of particular equipment such as videotape machines or familiarity with a certain personality test should not necessarily be the starting point. One is reminded here of the drunkard who, having dropped his house key in the dark, looks not where he dropped it but rather further down the street because the light is better there. Methods are the means that allow one to get to the ends.

Even when the question is clear and the method

appropriate, no one study will answer the question once and for all. The understanding of social behavior is a cumulative process resting on the synthesis and reconciliation of a number of empirical studies. Such synthesis is made more difficult by changes made at each stage of the research process. Even within the same issue, hypotheses are seldom formulated in exactly the same way, nor are identical methods and measures used.

Comparing Alternative Methods

Just knowing that different research strategies exist does not reveal which is best. The best method is the one that fits the problem that you want answers for. By way of illustration, consider the question of whether people are more likely to come to someone's aid if they have just seen someone act in that way. If you were to carry out the research yourself, you might try to assess this modeling effect by *interviewing* a random sample of respondents and asking them directly whether they would be more likely to donate to a charity if they saw someone else donating than if they did not witness this. The method is straightforward but has the disadvantage that people sometimes don't know how they would act in a given situation. In addition, people may be inclined to give the socially appropriate response in order to appear in the best possible light. In this situation, many respondents might say that they would donate no matter what the situation, since in our society helping others is considered good behavior.

Another way of determining whether modeling has an effect is to observe behavior in the real world. Observation of this kind is called *systematic naturalistic observation*. In one form of this observation you might wait until someone (a model) naturally dropped money in a Salvation Army kettle and then observe whether others in range during the giving contribute more than others in the same period of time in which no one contributed. The problem is not knowing definitely whether the model's action was seen by the giving or not-giving subjects. This doubt could be reduced somewhat by specifying beforehand the minimum distance and time requirements that would have to be met in order to say that the original donor was taken note of. An obvious advantage of naturalistic observation is that subjects are not aware that they are being observed. Another advantage of naturalistic observation is that it includes a range of environmental and social factors that may affect charitable giving in real-life situations.

Note that from some perspectives you may not attend equally to all these issues; namely, you may wish to know how people think they would behave and be unconcerned (at least for the moment) about their actual behavior, or you may not care about their perceptions or interpretations of the situation but only about their actual behavior. Different questions require different methods and all methods have attendant benefits and costs.

Still another method may involve doing a *field experiment* in which you might retain the realism of the sidewalk situation and exercise more control by sending experimental confederates to donate money at specified intervals or in the vicinity of specified individuals (e.g., male and female subjects or people alone versus people in pairs). Or the entire enterprise might be moved into a highly controlled situation in order to conduct a *laboratory experiment*. Such a context allows random assignment of subjects to the exact same conditions save for the variation due to the presence or absence of a model. Those are pluses in weeding out rival explanations for the results achieved. The minuses have in part to do with the contrived nature of the situation, which is potentially either very transparent to subjects or nongeneralizable outside that particular context.

In sum, choosing the best method after comparison shopping depends on the question being asked, the stage of existing knowledge, and the stylistic preference of the investigator, among others. Naturalistic observation and interviewing (field studies) are sometimes seen as more appropriate early on when the research is in an exploratory phase or later on when there is concern about generalizability. Laboratory experiments are seen as more appropriate when there is need to test specific cause–effect relationships. As to stylistic preferences, a researcher's training and opportunity with a particular strategy may lead him or her to prefer that technique to others because its assets and its pitfalls are familiar.

MAKE IT YOURSELF

Increasingly, consumers are making their own products from scratch or from kits. Pride of craftsmanship and creative urges, as well as the belief that a better or a previously unfurnished product will result, figure largely in the motivation to take up such endeavors. In research, too, investigators must be resourceful; in fact the act of designing and carrying out a study of one's own is an invention. People do research (as contrasted with using research) because there are gaps or deficiencies in existing knowledge or methodology. Investigators thus strive sometimes to find alternative procedures, or new tests, or a more fine grain apparatus, or an entirely innovative approach to understanding social behavior.

As mentioned previously, there are some problems in doing research in which subjects are aware that something about their behavior is under scrutiny. In order to address this problem, there has been concern to develop a number of *unobtrusive measures*—that is, measures taken without attracting subjects' attention (Webb, Campbell, Schwarts, Sechrest, and Grove, 1981). For example, indication of the popularity of certain attitudes might be derived from comparing the frequency with which library books covering different sides of the issue are borrowed or from comparing evidence of exposure to the issues by comparing evidence of book wear, such as creasing, thumbprints, underlinings, and so forth. [Editors' note: The next article in this chapter deals with unobtrusive measures.]

Similarly, as social psychologists have moved beyond the laboratory into natural settings in which it is not always possible or desirable to randomly assign subjects to different experimental conditions, new research strategies have been and are being developed. Included here are *quasi-experimental* designs which seek to maximize validity in natural contexts (Cook & Campbell, 1979). For example, time series designs have been used to assess the effect of a particular event or treatment through a procedure in which a series of observations are made prior to the introduction of the event in order to establish a baseline level of response. Then the treatment is initiated, followed by another series of observations in order to track the presence or duration of the effect. The extended period of observation is done in order to rule out the possibility that other nonintended but concurrent events may have caused the effect of interest.

These innovations constitute genuine additions to the storehouse of methodology. The "do-it-yourself" urge, however, can lead researchers astray. Novice investigators are sometimes moved to devise their own scales and inventories when there are already available ones which have proved to be just right for the task at hand. A review of the research literature is thus done in order to see what is there. The experienced investigator may fall victim to another problem with the "do-it-

yourselfers." They may think that the most serious research problems are ones of methodology and hence may spend so much time in perfecting a given scale or measure that they never get around to studying the question that the measure was originally designed to measure.

PREPARE A LIST

When shoppers are watching budgets carefully, they are frequently advised to prepare a list before going shopping and then to stick to it. Knowing what you are looking for guards against impulse buying. Accounts of research vary greatly in the amount of detail they provide, but regardless of completeness, you will end up with the most information if you know beforehand what to be looking for. Having a list of what you want to know about any study is a helpful guide in evaluating the quality of the product. In encountering any description of research, try to get the following information:

1. *Statement of the Problem.* All accounts of research published in professional journals begin with a statement concerning the general issue to be addressed. Shortly, if an experiment is being described, the issue will be transformed into a hypothesis which will then be cast in terms of *independent* and *dependent variables*. In field studies involving observation or interviews, the question may be more open-ended, but it should still be clear and explicit about which relationships are being explored. Watch how the investigator translates a general issue into a more specific question in order to note what is being kept and what aspects are being shelved.

You will also want to be on the lookout for what the author says about what others have contributed to the topic. The author may be describing a major departure from traditional methodology or current thinking, but there should be indication that he or she is aware of the intellectual context for the question being posed. In journal articles, where space is very limited, the literature review is often necessarily compressed. Nonetheless, you should be able to get a clear idea of how others have approached the issue and what extension is being proposed by the current offering. A common shortcut is for the author to cite only one or two of the most recent studies on the topic. While this assumption may be economical with respect to journal space, the better literature reviews give at least some historical highlights.

At the end of the introduction, you should therefore have a clear understanding of what product is being sought.

2. Method. The guiding principle in evaluating a research report is that the account should permit you to extract all the information that you might need to repeat the study yourself. Again, given the stringent space restrictions of professional publications, this goal is seldom attained in full. It nevertheless remains a useful yardstick for information-seeking. Another key feature of the account of the method is that it should be descriptive rather than persuasive or interpretive.

In formal research reports, the description of the method is often further subdivided into sections on design, subjects, measures, and procedure. The section on *design* states the number of independent (cause) and dependent (effect) variables that are to be examined in the study and how many levels or degrees (e.g., high, medium, and low) of each. The section describing the *subjects* tells how many research participants were sampled from where and with what distinguishing characteristics. The terms "random selection" and "random assignment" should not be used cavalierly. Sampling procedures should be explicitly described, and if randomization is not used, then the selection should be described in detail.

The section on *measures* provides the manner in which the effects are to be assessed or operationalized. To *operationalize* means to make general phenomena (e.g., attraction) concrete and precise (e.g., a two-item, seven-point scale asking for degrees of "caring for" and "enjoying the company of" the other).

Finally the section on *procedure* should describe what happens to subjects from the moment they first encounter the study to the moment they leave it. Instructions given to subjects should be stated *exactly* as given and specifics of the spatial, temporal, and social environment into which the subjects are placed should be spelled out as a matter of course. Paraphrase or general outlines of what the subject encounters and how his or her planned or unplanned responses are treated should be avoided. Laboratory experimenters have become increasing sensitized to the presence of potential artifacts (unplanned and unintended side effects of research procedures) and so sometimes provide what seem like excessive precautions. The information should not be treated as irrelevant. In field studies, artifacts are also potentially present and so investigators should be comprehensive as

to who said or did what to whom under what set of circumstances and how the actual test scenario differed from the idealized one.

Without sufficient detail in the method section, results cannot be understood and evaluated. In many ways the method section is like a combination of "contents" and "directions for use" on many products. It is there you learn what really went on inside and on whom and under what conditions the outcome might be expected to "work."

3. Results. There is a convention in research reporting that results should be described without interpretation, although in many articles the results are reported and discussed simultaneously. The logic behind the separation of results and discussion sections is to let the data stand on its own without initial benefit or detraction of author interpretation. Readers may thus be able to come up with alternative readings of the findings and rival explanations for the results. In any case, the results should be stated factually rather than argumentatively and should be buttressed by clearly labeled tables and/or figures.

Watch for wishful overstatement of marginal results: statements such as "the findings approached significance" or "although the analysis proved to be nonsignificant, nevertheless . . ." Although certain trends may be worth noting, they do not deserve the same weight as strong statistically significant effects. Similarly, take note of groups or measures that did not work out as expected. It is often a little more difficult to find statements of noneffects, which can be as informative as significant effects.

4. Discussion and Conclusions. It is here that the researcher tells you what the findings mean and seeks to tie the interpretation back to the general issue raised in the introduction. He or she attempts to explain why particular things did or did not happen and to deal with areas of potential ambiguity. Look here for the researcher's assessment of the study's limitations and what next steps need to be taken. Read carefully and critically for how the author accounts for findings that do not support the underlying theory. One should be open to criticizing the method, as well as the theory. Watch also for the generalizability offered for the conclusions. Be cautious as to what other behaviors, conditions, or situations might or might not fit the proposed relationship.

SOCIAL PSYCHOLOGY AND
THE CONSUMER ANALOGY

At the beginning of this article, we stated our aim: to help you become as intelligent a consumer of behavioral research as you already are of goods and services. This consumer approach was offered to elicit an active involvement on your part and to make you aware of the tools you already possess. Social psychological information permeates many aspects of modern life, and we hope that the principles discussed above will help you organize your reaction to and your evaluation of the information provided.

One advantage of the consumer analogy is that it stresses the value of considered decisions. Unqualified reactions to research have limited value and impulse buying or rejecting is difficult to defend should the need arise. It should be noted, however, that there are aspects of the consumer analogy that do not quite fit the research situation. More specifically, three limitations should be considered.

First, in research you can hardly have too much knowledge. In most major purchasing decisions, you gradually narrow down the choices until you finally settle on a single purchase. The point is usually to pick one among available options of the same thing. In research, several repetitions of the same product are welcome. In addition, research findings are expected to be cumulative, and as a research consumer you might buy them all. In assessing research, the task is not so much to narrow down the options as it is to combine the available options into some coherent whole.

This comparison points to the second limitation on the consumer analogy. In most major consumer purchases, after having made a choice, you can relax for a while and assume that the matter is settled until the need rises again. Research, instead, is not static or stable; it is more process than product. In fact the excitement lies in the development and change of ideas. Our own enthusiasm for psychology comes from knowing not only what's on the market currently, but what's coming.

The third reservation about applying the consumer analogy to the research situation is that the criteria for evaluating research are better able to point out gaps and errors in the present than they are for indicating accuracy and authenticity now and over the long haul. In purchasing insurance, for example, it is quite possible to make a complete list of relevant features and to evaluate different policies on this list. In research, this can be done only up to a point. Good research depends on more than good methodology, even though there are some social psychologists who would argue that the only research projects that should be conducted are those for which valid and reliable methods already exist. This makes for one kind of good research, but certainly restricts the kind of thing that social psychologists can attempt to know. We would argue that ideas have precedence and that methods are means to that end. Ideas are much harder to evaluate, and the consumer guidelines offered here are of limited help in deciding whether the ideas in a study are worth buying at all.

As you read research, we hope that you become increasingly skilled in the fine art of critique and increasingly appreciative of what it can provide. Intelligent consumerism leads not only to being able to avoid getting stuck with a lemon but also to raising the standards overall. To criticize may be the best compliment, for to criticize thoughtfully is to honor by taking seriously.

REFERENCES

Cook, T.D., & Campbell, D.T. *Quasi-Experimentation: Design and analysis issues for field settings.* Chicago: Rand McNally, 1979.

McGuire, W.J. Some impending reorientations in social psychology: Some thoughts provoked by Kenneth Ring. *Journal of Experimental Social Psychology* 3 (1967), 124–39.

Ring, K. Experimental social psychology: Some sober questions about frivolous values. *Journal of Experimental Social Psychology* 3 (1967), 113–23.

Webb, E.J., Campbell, D.T., Schwartz, R.D., Sechrest, L., & Grove, J.B. *Nonreactive measures in the social sciences* (2nd edition). Boston: Houghton Mifflin, 1981.

UNOBTRUSIVE HOLMES

I had called upon my friend Mr. Sherlock Holmes, one day in the autumn of last year, and found him in deep conversation with a very stout, florid-faced, elderly gentleman, with fiery red hair. With an apology for my intrusion, I was about to withdraw, when Holmes pulled me abruptly into the room, and closed the door behind me.

"You could not possibly have come at a better time, my dear Watson," he said cordially.

"I was afraid that you were engaged."

"So I am. Very much so."

"Then I can wait in the next room."

"Not at all. This gentleman, Mr. Wilson, has been my partner and helper in many of my most successful cases, and I have no doubt that he will be of the utmost use to me in yours also."

. . .

The portly client puffed out his chest with an appearance of some little pride, and pulled a dirty and wrinkled newspaper from the inside pocket of his greatcoat. As he glanced down the advertisement column, with his head thrust forward, and the paper flattened out upon his knee, I took a good look at the man, and endeavoured after the fashion of my companion to read the indications which might be presented by his dress or appearance.

I did not gain very much, however, by my inspection. Our visitor bore every mark of being an average commonplace British tradesman, obese, pompous, and slow. He wore rather baggy grey shepherds' check trousers, a not over-clean black frock-coat, unbuttoned in the front, and a drab waistcoat with a heavy brassy Albert chain, and a square pierced bit of metal dangling down as an ornament. A frayed top-hat, and a faded brown overcoat with a wrinkled velvet collar lay upon a chair beside him. Altogether, look as I would, there was nothing remarkable about the man save his blazing red head, and the expression of extreme chagrin and discontent upon his features.

Sherlock Holmes's quick eye took in my occupation and he shook his head with a smile as he noticed my questioning glances. "Beyond the obvious facts that he has at some time done manual labour, that he takes snuff, that he is a Freemason, that he has been in China, and that he has done a considerable amount of writing lately, I can deduce nothing else."

Mr. Jabez Wilson started up in his chair, with his forefinger upon the paper, but his eyes upon my companion.

"How, in the name of good fortune, did you know all that, Mr. Holmes?" he asked. "How did you know, for example, that I did manual labour? It's as true as gospel, and I began as a ship's carpenter."

"Your hands, my dear sir. Your right hand is quite a size larger than your left. You have worked with it, and the muscles are more developed."

"Well, the snuff, then, and the Freemasonry?"

"I won't insult your intelligence by telling you how I read that, especially as, rather against the strict rules of your order, you use an arc-and-compass breastpin."

"Oh, of course, I forgot that. But the writing?"

"What else can be indicated by that right cuff so very shiny for five inches, and the left one with the smooth patch near the elbow where you rest it upon the desk."

"Well, but China?"

"The fish which you have tattooed immediately above your right wrist could only have been done in China. I have made a small study of tattoo marks, and have even contributed to the literature of the subject. That trick of staining the fishes' scales a delicate pink is quite peculiar to China. When, in addition, I see a Chinese coin hanging from your watch-chain, the matter becomes even more simple."

Mr. Jabez Wilson laughed heavily. "Well, I never!" said he. "I thought at first you had something clever, but I see that there was nothing in it after all."

From *The Adventures of Sherlock Holmes* by Sir Arthur Conan Doyle.

UNOBTRUSIVE MEASURES: NONREACTIVE RESEARCH IN THE SOCIAL SCIENCES

EUGENE J. WEBB, DONALD T. CAMPBELL, RICHARD D. SCHWARTZ, AND LEE SECHREST

Although laboratory studies are undeniably and uniquely valuable, there are other viable means of doing psychological research. With many research

techniques, the researcher runs the risk of influencing and perhaps distorting the phenomenon under study. This problem is illustrated by the following science fiction story:

> Two scientists wish to discover the origins of an ancient god. According to legend, the winged god visited Earth and then vanished. Using a special time machine, the scientists go back in time and experience many thrilling adventures. At the end, they are pursued by a group of angry warriors and barely make it back to the time machine to escape to their modern life. Once safely home again, the scientists recount their adventures, noting that they have failed to find the origin of the winged god. Suddenly, they realize that they themselves, visiting the ancient people and later disappearing in their time machine amid clouds of smoke and fire, must have been the origin of that legend.

Just as these fictional scientists unwittingly created the phenomenon they wanted to study, social psychologists can directly or indirectly create or bias the behaviors they are investigating. For example, through direct questions and measures, the researcher makes people aware that they are objects of study, and this knowledge can itself cause them to react differently than they would in everyday situations. Experimental subjects may hide their true feelings and give answers that they think are more socially appropriate, or they may try to second-guess the experimenter by giving the answers they think he or she is looking for. In either case, their responses are not true reflections of the behavior being studied.

How does the social psychologist deal with this pitfall of research? One answer is provided in the article "Unobtrusive Measures," which is composed of excerpts from the classic book of the same name. The authors describe techniques that the researcher can use to gain valuable behavioral data without intruding directly upon the subject's life and awareness.

This survey directs attention to social science research data *not* obtained by interview or questionnaire. Some may think this exclusion does not leave much. It does. Many innovations in research methods are to be found scattered throughout the social science literature. Their use, however, is unsystematic, their importance understated. Our review of this material is intended to broaden the social scientist's currently narrow range of utilized methodologies and to encourage creative and opportunistic exploitation of unique measurement possibilities.

Today, the dominant mass of social science research is based upon interviews and questionnaires. We lament this overdependence upon a single, fallible method. Interviews and questionnaires intrude as a foreign element into the social setting they would describe, they create as well as

From Eugene J. Webb, Donald T. Campbell, Richard D. Schwartz, and Lee Sechrest, *Unobtrusive Measures: Nonreactive Research in the Social Sciences,* © 1966 by Rand McNally College Publishing Company, Chicago, pp. 1, 2, 35–41, 53, 57, 58, 75–77, 112, 115–17, 119, 121–25, 171–74.

measure attitudes, they elicit atypical roles and responses, they are limited to those who are accessible and will cooperate, and the responses obtained are produced in part by dimensions of individual differences irrelevant to the topic at hand.

But the principal objection is that they are used alone. No research method is without bias. Interviews and questionnaires must be supplemented by methods testing the same social science variables but having *different* methodological weaknesses.

In sampling the range of alternative approaches, we examine their weaknesses, too. The flaws are serious and give insight into why we do depend so much upon the interview. But the issue is not choosing among individual methods. Rather it is the necessity for a multiple operationism, a collection of methods combined to avoid sharing the same weaknesses. The goal of this article is not to replace the interview but to supplement and cross-validate it with measures that do not require the cooperation of a respondent and that do not themselves contaminate the response.

Here are some samples of the kinds of methods we will be surveying:

The floor tiles around the hatching-chick exhibit at Chicago's Museum of Science and Industry must be replaced every six weeks. Tiles in other parts of the museum need not be replaced for years. The selective erosion of tiles, indexed by the replacement rate, is a measure of the relative popularity of exhibits.

The accretion rate is another measure. One investigator wanted to learn the level of whisky consumption in a town which was officially "dry." He did so by counting empty bottles in ashcans.

The degree of fear induced by a ghost-story-telling session can be measured by noting the shrinking diameter of a circle of seated children.

Chinese jade dealers have used the pupil dilation of their customers as a measure of the client's interest in particular stones, and Darwin in 1872 noted this same variable as an index of fear.

Library withdrawals were used to demonstrate the effect of the introduction of television into a community. Fiction titles dropped, nonfiction titles were unaffected.

The role of rate of interaction in managerial recruitment is shown by the overrepresentation of baseball managers who were infielders or catchers (high-interaction positions) during their playing days.

Sir Francis Galton employed surveying hardware to estimate the bodily dimensions of African women whose language he did not speak.

The child's interest in Christmas was demonstrated by distortions in the size of Santa Claus drawings.

Racial attitudes in two colleges were compared by noting the degree of clustering of Negroes and whites in lecture halls.

PHYSICAL TRACES: EROSION AND ACCRETION

. . . In this section we look at research methods geared to the study of physical traces surviving from past behavior. Physical evidence is probably the social scientist's least-used source of data, yet because of its ubiquity, it holds flexible and broad-gauged potential.

It is reasonable to start a discussion of physical evidence by talking of Sherlock Holmes. He and his paperbacked colleagues could teach us much. Consider that the detective, like the social scientist, faces the task of inferring the nature of past behavior (Who did the Lord of the Manor in?) by the careful generation and evaluation of current evidence. Some evidence he engineers (question-

ing), some he observes (Does the witness develop a tic?), some he develops from extant physical evidence (Did the murderer leave his eyeglasses behind?). From the weighing of several different types of hopefully converging evidence, he makes a decision on the plausibility of several rival hypotheses. For example:

H_1: The butler did it.

H_2: It was the blacksheep brother.

H_3: He really committed suicide.

This section discusses only the physical evidence, those pieces of data not specifically produced for the purpose of comparison and inference, but available to be exploited opportunistically by the alert investigator. It should be emphasized that physical evidence has greatest utility in consort with other methodological approaches. Because there are easily visible population and content restrictions associated with physical evidence, such data have largely been ignored. It is difficult even to consider a patently weak source of data when research strategy is based on single measures and definitional operationism. The visibly stronger questionnaire or interview looks to be more valid, and it may be if only one measure is taken. In a multimethod strategy, however, one does not have to exclude data of any class or degree solely because it is weak. If the weaknesses are known and considered, the data are usable.

It may be helpful to discriminate between two broad classes of physical evidence, a discrimination similar to that between the intaglio and the cameo. One one hand, there are the *erosion measures*, where the degree of selective wear on some material yields the measure . . . On the other hand, there are *accretion measures*, where the research evidence is some deposit of materials.

Natural Erosion Measures

Let us look first at some erosion measures. A committee was formed to set up a psychological exhibit at Chicago's Museum of Science and Industry. The committee learned that the vinyl tiles around the exhibit containing live, hatching chicks had to be replaced every six weeks or so; tiles in other areas of the museum went for years without replacement (Duncan, 1963). A comparative study of the rate of tile replacement around the various museum exhibits could give a rough ordering of the popularity of the exhibits. Note that although erosion is the measure, the knowledge of the erosion rate comes from a check of the records of the museum's maintenance department.

In addition to this erosion measure, unobtrusive observation studies showed that people stand before the chick display longer than they stand before any of the other exhibits. With this additional piece of evidence, the question becomes whether or not the erosion is a simple result of people standing in one location and shuffling their feet, or whether it really does indicate a greater frequency of different people viewing the exhibit. Clearly an empirical question. The observation and the tile erosion are two partially overlapping measures, each of which can serve as a check on the other. The observation material is more textured for studies of current behavior, because it can provide information on both the number of viewers and how long each views the display. The erosion data cannot index the duration of individual viewing, but they permit an analysis of popularity over time, and do so with economy and efficiency.

The wear on library books, particularly on the corners where the page is turned, offers an example of a possible approach that illustrates a useful overlap measure. One of the most direct and obvious ways to learn the popularity of books is to check how many times each of a series of titles has been removed from a library. This is an excellent measure and uses the records already maintained for other purposes. But it is only an indirect measure for the investigator who wants to know the relative amount of reading a series of books get. They may be removed from the library, but not read. It is easy to establish whether or not there is a close relationship between degree of wear and degree of checkouts from the library. If this relationship is positive and high, the hypothesis that books are taken out but selectively not read is accounted for. Note that the erosion measure also allows one to study the relative use of titles which are outside the span of the library-withdrawal measure. Titles placed on reserve, for example, are typically not noted for individual use by library bookkeeping. An alternative accretion measure is to note the amount of dust that has accumulated on the books studied.

Mosteller (1955) conducted a shrewd and creative study on the degree to which different sections of the *International Encyclopedia of the Social Sciences* were read. He measured the wear and tear on separate sections by noting dirty edges of pages as markers, and observed the frequency of dirt smudges, finger markings, and underlining on pages. In some cases of very heavy use, "...

dirt had noticeably changed the color of the page so that [some articles] are immediately distinguishable from the rest of the volume" (p. 171). Mosteller studied volumes at both Harvard and the University of Chicago, and went to three libraries at each institution. He even used the *Encyclopaedia Britannica* as a control.

Natural Accretion Measures

There are large numbers of useful natural remnants of past behavior that can be exploited. We can examine now a few examples of behavior traces which were laid down "naturally," without the intervention of the social scientist.

The detective-story literature . . . is instructive. In a favorite example (Barzun, 1961), a case hinged on determining where a car came from. It was solved (naturally) by studying the frequencies to which the car's radio buttons were tuned. By triangulation of the frequencies, from a known population of commercial-station frequencies, the geographic source of the car was learned. Here was a remnant of past behavior (someone setting the buttons originally) that included several component elements collectively considered to reach a solution. Unimaginatively, most detective fiction considers much simpler and less elegant solutions—such as determining how fast a car was going by noting the degree to which insects are splattered on the windshield.

Modern police techniques include many trace methods, for example, making complex analyses of soil from shoes and clothing to establish a suspect's probable presence at the scene of a crime. One scientist (Forshufvud, 1961) uncovered the historic murder of Napoleon in 1821 on the basis of arsenic traces in remains of his hair.

Radio-dial settings are being used in a continuing audience-measurement study, with mechanics in an automotive service department the datagatherers (Anonymous, 1962). A Chicago automobile dealer, Z. Frank, estimates the popularity of different radio stations by having mechanics record the position of the dial in all cars brought in for service. More than 50,000 dials a year are checked, with less than 20 per cent duplication of dials. These data are then used to select radio stations to carry the dealer's advertising. The generalization of these findings is sound if (1) the goal of the radio propaganda is to reach the same type of audience which now comes to the dealership, and (2) a significant number of cars have radios. If many of the cars are without radios, than a partial and possibly biased estimate of the universe is obtained. It is reported, "We find a high degree of correlation between what the rating people report and our own dial setting research" (p. 83).

. . .

DuBois (1963) reports on a 1934 study which estimated an advertisement's readership level by analyzing the number of different fingerprints on the page. The set of prints was a valid remnant, and the analysis revealed a resourceful researcher. Compare this with the anthropologist's device of estimating the prior population of an archeological site by noting the size of floor areas (Naroll, 1962). Among the consistently detectable elements in a site are good indicators of the floor areas of residences. When these can be keyed to knowledge of the residential and familial patterns of the group, these partial data, these remnants, serve as excellent population predictors.

Other remnants can provide evidence on the physical characteristics of populations no longer available for study. Suits of armor, for example, are indicators of the height of medieval knights.

The estimable study of McClelland (1961), *The Achieving Society*, displays a fertile use of historical evidence. Most of the data come from documentary materials such as records of births and deaths, coal imports, shipping levels, electric-power consumption, and remaining examples of literature, folk tales, and children's stories. We consider such materials in our discussion of archival records, but they are, in one sense, a special case of trace analysis. McClelland further reports on achievement-level estimates derived from ceramic designs on urns, and he indexes the geographic boundaries of Greek trade by archeological finds of vases. Sensitive to the potential error in such estimates, McClelland writes,

So, rough though it is, the measure of the economic rise and fall of classical Greece was taken to be the area with which she traded, in millions of square miles, as determined by the location of vases unearthed in which her chief export commodities were transported [p.177].

This measure was related to the need-for-achievement level of classical Greece, estimated from a content analysis of Greek writings.

. . .

THE RUNNING RECORD

Possibly a wife was more likely to get an inscribed tablet if she died before her husband than if she outlived him.

The tablet cited here is a tombstone, and the quotation is from Durand's (1960) study of life expectancy in ancient Rome and its provinces. Tombstones are but one of a plethora of archives available for the adventurous researcher, and all social scientists should now and then give thanks to those literate, record-keeping societies which systematically provide so much material appropriate to novel analysis.

The purpose of this section is to examine and evaluate some uses of data periodically produced for other than scholarly purposes, but which can be exploited by social scientists. These are the ongoing, continuing records of a society, and the potential source of varied scientific data, particularly useful for longitudinal studies.

. . . Here the data are the actuarial records, the votes, the city budgets, and the communications media which are periodically produced, and paid for, by someone other than the researcher.

Actuarial Records

Birth, marriage, death. For each of these, societies maintain continuing records as normal procedure. Governments at various levels provide massive amounts of statistical data, ranging from the federal census to the simple entry of a wedding in a town-hall ledger. Such formal records have frequently been used in descriptive studies, but they offer promise for hypothesis-testing research as well.

Take Winston's (1932) research. He wanted to examine the preference for male offspring in upper-class families. He could have interviewed prospective mothers in affluent homes, or fathers in waiting rooms. Indeed, one could pay obstetricians to ask, "What would you like me to order?" Other measures, nonreactive ones, might be studies of adoption records, the sales of different layette colors (cutting the data by the class level of the store), or the incidence of "other sex" names—such as Marion, Shirley, Jean, Jerry, Jo.

But Winston went to the enormous data bank of birth records and manipulated them adroitly. He simply noted the sex of each child in each birth order. A preference for males was indicated, he hypothesized, if the male–female ratio of the last child born in families estimated to be complete was greater than that ratio for all children in the same families. With the detail present in birth records, he was able to segregate his upper-class sample of parents by the peripheral data of occupation, and so forth. The same auxiliary data can be employed in any study to serve as a check on evident population restrictions—a decided plus for detailed archives.

This study also illustrates the time-sampling problem. For the period studied, and because of the limitation to upper-class families, Winston's measure is probably not contaminated by economic limitations on the absolute number of children, a variable that may operate independently of any family sex preference. Had his study covered only the 1930s, or were he making a time-series comparison of economically marginal families, the time factor could offer a substantial obstacle to valid comparison. The argument for the existence of such an economic variable would be supported if a study of the 1930s showed no sex difference among terminal children, but did show significant differences for children born in the 1940s.

The Mass Media

Among the most easily available and massive sources of continuing secondary data are the mass media. The variety, texture, and scope of this enormous data pool have been neglected for too long. In this section, we present a selected series of studies which show intelligent manipulation of the mass media. We have necessarily excluded most content analyses and focused on a few which illustrate particular points.

It is proper to start this section by citing Zipf, who sought order in diverse social phenomena by his inventive use of data that few others would perceive as germane to scientific inquiry. In a model study, Zipf (1946) looked at the determinants of the circulation of information. His hypothesis was that the probability of message transfer between one person and another is inversely proportional to the distance between them. (See also Miller, 1947; Stewart, 1947; Zipf, 1949.) Without prejudice for content, he made use of the content of the mass media, as well as sales performance. How many and how long were out-of-town obituaries in the *New York Times*? How many out-of-town items appeared in the *Chicago Tribune*? Where

did they originate? What was the sales level in cities besides New York and Chicago of the *Times* and *Tribune*? To this information from and about the mass media, Zipf added other archival sources. He asked the number of tons of goods moved by Railway Express between various points, and checked on the number of bus, railroad, and air passengers between pairs of cities. All of these were appropriate outcroppings for the test of his hypothesis on inverse proportionality, and in all cases the data conform, more or less closely, to his prediction.

Other investigators have used the continuing record of the newspaper for their data. Grusky (1963b) wanted to investigate the relationship between administrative succession and subsequent change in group performance. One could manipulate leaders in a small-group laboratory, but, in addition, one can go, as Grusky did, to the newspapers for more "natural" and less reactive intelligence. From the sports pages and associated records, Grusky learned the performance of various professional football and baseball teams, as well as the timing of changes in coaches and managers. Does changing a manager make a difference, or is it the meaningless machination of a front office looking for a scapegoat? It does make a difference, and this old sports-writer's question is a group-dynamics problem, phrased through the stating of two plausible rival hypotheses. In another study, Grusky (1963a) used baseball record books to study "The Effects of Formal Structures on Managerial Recruitment." He learned that former infielders and catchers (high-interaction personnel) were overrepresented among managers, while former pitchers and outfielders (low-interaction personnel) were underrepresented.

This public-record characteristic of the newspaper also allows linguistic analysis. If verbal behavior really is expressive, then one should be able to study a President's position on issues by studying the transcripts of his press conferences. Those answers on which a President stumbles in syntax, or which are prefaced by a string of evasive dependent clauses, may be symptomatic of troubled areas. Similarly, those questions which receive unusually long or short replies may reflect significant content areas.

Analysis of transcripts such as these can be very difficult, and often not enough substantive knowledge is available to rule out alternative hypotheses. A President is briefed on what are likely to be the topics of reporters' questions, and he has an opportunity to rehearse replies. The setting is not a nonreactive one, and the awareness of his visibility and the import of his answers may influence their content and form. One must also make each President his own control. The verbal styles of Eisenhower, Kennedy, and Johnson varied so greatly that any verbal index of syntax, glibness, or folksiness must be adjusted for the response tendencies of the individual President.

. . .

SIMPLE OBSERVATION

> Who could he be? He was evidently reserved, and melancholy. Was he a clergyman?—He danced too well. A barrister?—He was not called. He used very fine words, and said a great deal. Could he be a distinguished foreigner come to England for the purpose of describing the country, its manners and customs; and frequenting city balls and public dinners with the view of becoming acquainted with high life, polished etiquette, and English refinement?—No, he had not a foreign accent. Was he a surgeon, a contributor to the magazines, a writer of fashionable novels or an artist?—No: to each and all of these surmises there existed some valid objection.—"Then," said everybody, "he must be somebody."—"I should think he must be," reasoned Mr. Malderton, with himself, "because he perceives our superiority, and pays us much attention."

> **(Sketches from Boz)**

Charles Dickens displayed a ready touch for observationally scouring the behavior of this mysterious gentleman for evidence with which to classify him—even going so far as to put out the hypothesis that the man was a participant observer. In this section . . . our interest is focused on situations in which the observer has no control over the behavior or sign in question, and plays an unobserved, passive, and nonintrusive role in the research situation.

. . .

Exterior Physical Signs

Most of the exterior physical signs discussed are durable ones that have been inferred to be expressive of current or past behavior. A smaller number are portable and shorter-lived. The bullfighter's beard is a case in point. Conrad (1958) reports that the bullfighter's beard is longer on the day of the fight than on any other day. There are supporting comments among matadors about this phenomenon, yet can one measure the torero's anxiety by noting the length of his beard? The physical task is rather difficult, but not impossible in this day of sophisticated instrumentation. As in all these uncontrolled measures, one must draw inferences about the criterion behavior. Maybe it wasn't the anxiety at all. Perhaps the bullfighter stands farther away from the razor on the morning of the fight, or he may not have shaved that morning at all (like baseball pitchers and boxers). And then there is the possible intersubject contaminant that the more affluent matadors are likely to be shaved, while the less prosperous shave themselves.

In a report whose authors choose to remain anonymous (Anonymous, 1953–1960), it was discovered that there is a strong association between the methodological disposition of psychologists and the length of their hair. The authors observed the hair length of psychologists attending professional meetings and coded the meetings by the probable appeal to those of different methodological inclinations. Thus, in one example, the length of hair was compared between those who attended an experimental set of papers and those who attended a series on ego-identity formation. The results are clear-cut. The "tough-minded" psychologists have shorter-cut hair than the long-haired psychologists. Symptomatic interpretations, psychoanalytic inquiries as to what is cut about the clean-cut young man, are not the only possibilities. The causal ambiguity of the correlation was clarified when the "dehydration hypothesis" (i.e., that lack of insulation caused the hard-headedness) was rejected by the "baldhead control," i.e., examining the distribution of bald-headed persons (who by the dehydration hypothesis should be most hard-headed of all).

. . .

Expressive Movement

The more plastic variables of body movement historically have interested many observers. Charles Darwin's (1872) work on the expression of emotions continues to be the landmark commentary. His exposition of the measurement of frowning, the uncovering of teeth, erection of the hair, and the like remains provocative reading.

A journalistic account of the expressive behavior of hands has been given by Gould (1951). Here is his description of Frank Costello's appearance before the Kefauver crime hearings:

As he [Costello] sparred with Rudolph Halley, the committee's counsel, the movement of his fingers told their own emotional story. When the questions got rough, Costello crumpled a handkerchief in his hands. Or he rubbed his palms together. Or he interlaced his fingers. Or he grasped a half-filled glass of water. Or be beat a silent tattoo on the table top. Or he rolled a little ball of paper between his thumb and index finger. Or he stroked the side piece of his glasses lying on the table. His was video's first ballet of the hands [p. 1].

It is of interest that conversations of male students with females have been found to be more frequently punctuated by quick, jerky, "nervous" gestures than are conversation between two males (Sechrest, 1965).

Schubert (1959) has suggested that overt personal behavior could be used in the study of judicial behavior. In presenting a psychometric model of the Supreme Court, he suggests that the speech, grimaces, and gestures of the judges when hearing oral arguments and when opinions are being delivered are rich sources of data for students of the Court.

On the other side of the legal fence, witnesses in Hindu courts are reported to give indications of the truth of their statements by the movement of their toes (Krout 1951). The eminent American legal scholar J. H. Wigmore, in works on judicial proof and evidence (1935; 1937), speaks of the importance of peripheral expressive movements as clues to the validity of testimony.

The superstitious behavior of baseball players is a possible area of study. Knocking dust off cleats, amount of preliminary bat swinging, tossing dust into the air, going to the resin bag, and wiping hands on shirts may be interpreted as expressive actions. One hypothesis is that the extent of such superstitious behavior is related to whether or not the player is in a slump or in the middle of a good streak. This study could be extended to other sports in which the central characters are relatively isolated and visible. It should be easier for golfers and basketball players, but more difficult for football players.

From a practical point of view, of course, coaches and scouts have long studied the overt behavior of opponents for clues to forthcoming actions. (It is known, for example, that most football teams are "right sided" and run a disproportionate number of plays to the right [Griffin, 1964].) Does the fullback indicate the direction of the play by which hand he puts on the ground? Does the linebacker rest on his heels if he is going to fall back on pass defense? Does the quarterback always look in the direction in which he is going to pass, or does he sometimes look the other way, knowing that the defense is focusing on his eyes?

. . .

Physical Location

. . . There are the familiar newspaper accounts of who stood next to whom in Red Square reviewing the May Day parade. The proximity of a politician to the leader is a direct clue of his status in the power hierarchy. His physical position is interpreted as symptomatic of other behavior which gave him the status position befitting someone four men away from the Premier, and descriptive of that current status position. In this more casual journalistic report of observations, one often finds time-series analysis: Mr. B. has been demoted to the end of the dais, and Mr. L. has moved up close to the middle.

The clustering of Negroes and whites was used by Campbell, Kruskal, and Wallace (1965) in their study of seating aggregation as an index of attitude. Where seating in a classroom is voluntary, the degree to which the Negroes and whites present sit by themselves versus mixing randomly may be taken as a presumptive index of the degree to which acquaintance, friendship, and preference are strongly colored by race, as opposed to being distributed without regard to racial considerations. Classes in four schools were studied, and significant aggregation by race was found, varying in degree between schools. Aggregation by age, sex, and race has also been reported for elevated trains and lunch counters (Sechrest, 1965).

Feshbach and Feshbach (1963) report on another type of clustering. At a Halloween party, they induced fear in a group of boys, aged nine to twelve, by telling them ghost stories. The boys were then called out of the room and were administered questionnaires. The induction of the fear state was natural, but their dependent-variable measures were potentially reactive. What is of interest to us is a parenthetical statement made by the authors. After describing the ghost-story-telling situation, the Feshbachs offer evidence for the successful induction of fear: "Although the diameter of the circle was about eleven feet at the beginning of the story telling, by the time the last ghost story was completed, it had been spontaneously reduced to approximately three feet" (p. 499).

Sommer (1961) employed the position of chairs in a descriptive way, looking at "the distance for comfortable conversation." Normal subjects were used, but observations were made after the subjects had been on a tour of a large mental hospital. Distances among chairs in a lounge were systematically varied, and the people were brought into the lounge after the tour. They entered by pairs, and each pair was asked to go to a designated area and sit down. A simple record was made of the chairs selected.

The issue here is what one generalizes to. Just as the Feshbachs' subjects drew together during the narration of ghost stories, it would not be unrealistic to expect that normal adults coming from a tour of a mental hospital might also draw closer together than would be the case if they had not been on the tour. Their seating distance before the tour would be an interesting control. Do they huddle more, anticipating worse than will be seen, or less?

Sommer (1959, 1960, 1962) has conducted other studies of social distance and positioning, and in the 1959 study mentions a "waltz technique" to measure psychological distance. He learned that as he approached people, they would back away; when he moved backward during a conversation, the other person moved forward. The physical distance between two conversationalists also varies systematically by the nationality of the talkers, and there are substantial differences in distance between two Englishmen talking together and two Frenchmen in conversation. In a cross-cultural study, this would be a response-set characteristic to be accounted for.

. . .

A FINAL NOTE

In the dialectic between impulsivity and restraint, the scientific superego became too harsh—a development that was particularly effective in intimidating adventurous research, because the young were learning more about methodological pitfalls than had their elders . . .

(Riesman, 1959, p. 11)

David Riesman's remarks on the evolution of communications research apply equally well to the broader panoply of the study of social behavior. As social scientists, we have learned much of the labyrinth that is research on human behavior, and in so doing discovered an abundance of cul-de-sacs. Learning the complexities of the maze shortened our stride through it, and often led to a pattern of timid steps, frequently retraced. No more

can the knowledgeable person enjoy the casual bravura that marked the sweeping and easy generalizations of an earlier day.

The facile promulgation of "truth," backed by a few observations massaged by introspection, properly met its end—flattened by a more questioning and sophisticated rigor. The blackballing of verification by introspection was a positive advance, but an advance by subtraction. Partly as a reaction to the grandiosities of the past, partly as a result of a growing sophistication about the opportunities for error, the scope of individual research studies shrank, both in the range of content considered and in the diversity of procedures.

The shrinkage was understandable and desirable, for certainly, no science can develop until a base is reached from which reliable and consistent empirical findings can be produced. But if reliability is the initial step of a science, validity is its necessary stride. The primary effect of improved methodological practices has been to further what we earlier called the internal validity of a comparison—the confidence that a true difference is being observed. Unfortunately, practices have not advanced so far in improving external validity—the confidence with which the findings can be generalized to populations and measures beyond those immediately studied.

Slowing this advance in ability to generalize was the laissez-faire intellectualism of the operational definition. Operational definitionalism (to use a ponderously cumbersome term) provided a methodological justification for the scientist not to stray beyond a highly narrow, if reliable, base. One could follow a single method in developing data and be "pure," even if this purity were more associated with sterility than virtue.

The corkscrew convolutions of the maze of behavior were ironed, by definitional fiat, into a two-dimensional T maze. To define a social attitude, for example, solely by the character of responses to a list of questionnaire items is eminently legitimate—so much so that almost everything we know about attitudes comes from such research. Almost everything we know about attitudes is also suspect because the findings are saturated with the inherent risks of self-report information. One swallow does not make a summer; nor do two "strongly agrees," one "disagree," and an "I don't know" make an attitude or social value.

Questionnaires and interviews are probably the most flexible and generally useful devices we have for gathering information. Our criticism is not against them, but against the tradition which allowed them to become the methodological sanctuary to which the myopia of operational definitionalism permitted a retreat. If one were going to be limited to a single method, then certainly the verbal report from a respondent would be the choice. With no other device can an investigator swing his attention into so many different areas of substantive content, often simultaneously, and also gather intelligence on the extent to which his findings are hampered by population restrictions.

The power of the questionnaire and interview has been enormously enhanced, as have all methods, by the development of sensitive sampling procedures. With the early impetus provided by the Census Bureau to locational sampling, particularly to the theory and practice of stratification, concern about the population restrictions of a research sample has been radically diminished. Less well developed is the random sampling of time units—either over long periods such as months, or within a shorter period such as a day. There is no theoretical reason why time sampling is scarce, for it is a simple question of substituting time for location in a sampling design. Time sampling is of interest not only for its control over population fluctuations which might confound comparisons, but also because it permits control over the possibility of variable content at different times of the day or different months of the year.

The cost is high. And for that reason, government and commercial research organizations have led in the area, while academic research continues to limp along with conscripted sophomores. The controlled laboratory setting makes for excellent internal validity, as one has tight control over the conditions of administration and the internal structure of the questionnaire, but the specter of low generalizability is ever present.

That same specter is present, however, even if one has a national probability sample and the most carefully prepared questionnaire form or interview schedule. So long as one has only a single class of data collection, and that class is the questionnaire or interview, one has inadequate knowledge of the rival hypotheses grouped under the term "reactive measurement effects." These potential sources of error, some stemming from an individual's awareness of being tested, others from the nature of the investigator, must be accounted for by some other class of measurement than the verbal self-report.

It is too much to ask of any single class that it eliminate all the rival hypotheses subsumed under the population-, content-, and reactive-effects groupings. As long as the research strategy is based on a single measurement class, some flanks will be exposed, and even if fewer are exposed with the choice of the questionnaire method, there is still insufficient justification for its use as the only approach.

If no single measurement class is perfect, neither is any scientifically useless. Many studies and many novel sources of data have been mentioned in these pages. The reader may indeed have wondered which turn of the page would provide a commentary on some Ouija-board investigation. It would have been there had we known of one, and had it met some reasonable criteria of scientific worth. These "oddball" studies have been discussed because they demonstrate ways in which the investigator may shore up reactive infirmities of the interview and questionnaire. As a group, these classes of measurement are themselves infirm, and individually contain more risk (more rival plausible hypotheses) than does a well-constructed interview.

This does not trouble us, nor does it argue against their use, for the most fertile search for validity comes from a combined series of different measures, each with its idiosyncratic weaknesses, each pointed to a single hypothesis. When a hypothesis can survive the confrontation of a series of complementary methods of testing, it contains a degree of validity unattainable by one tested within the more constricted framework of a single method (Campbell & Fiske, 1959). Findings from this latter approach must always be subject to the suspicion that they are method-bound: Will the comparison totter when exposed to an equally prudent but different testing method? There must be a multiple operationalism. E. G. Boring (1953) put it this way:

> . . . as long as a new construct has only the single operational definition that it received at birth, it is just a construct. When it gets two alternative operational definitions, it is beginning to be validated. When the defining operations, because of proven correlations, are many, then it becomes reified [p. 222].

This means, obviously, that the notion of a single "critical experiment" is erroneous. *There must be a series of linked critical experiments, each testing a different outcropping of the hypothesis.* It is through triangulation of data procured from different measurement classes that the investigator can most effectively strip of plausibility rival explanations for his comparison. . . .

REFERENCES

Anonymous. Hair style as a function of hard-headedness vs. long-hairedness in psychological research, a study in the personology of science. Unprepared manuscript. Northwestern Univ. & Univ. of Chicago, 1953–1960.

Anonymous. Z. Frank stresses radio to build big Chevy dealership. *Advertising Age,* 1962, *33,* 83.

Barzun, J. *The delights of detection.* New York: Criterion Books, 1961.

Boring, E. G. The role of theory in experimental psychology. *American Journal of Psychology,* 1953, 66, 169–84. (Reprinted in E. G. Boring, *History, psychology, and science.* Ed. R. I. Watson & D. T. Campbell, New York: Wiley, 1963, pp. 210–25.)

Campbell, D. T., & Fiske, D. W. Convergent and discriminant validation by the multitrait-multimethod matrix. *Psychological Bulletin,* 1959, *56,* 81–105.

Campbell, D. T., Kruskal, W. H., & Wallace, W. P. Seating aggregation as an index of attitude. *Sociometry,* 1966, *29,* 1–15.

Conrad, B. *The death of Manolete.* Cambridge: Houghton Mifflin, 1958.

Darwin, C. *The expression of the emotions in man and animals.* London: Murray, 1872.

DuBois, C. N. Time Magazine's fingerprints' study. *Proceedings: 9th Conference, Advertising Research Foundation.* New York: Advertising Research Foundation, 1963.

Duncan, C. P. Personal communication, 1963.

Durand, J. Mortality estimates from Roman tombstone inscriptions. *American Journal of Sociology,* 1960, *65,* 365–73.

Feshbach, S., & Feshbach, N. Influence of the stimulus object upon the complementary and supplementary projection of fear. *Journal of Abnormal and Social Psychology,* 1963, *66,* 498–502.

Forshufvud, S. *Vem mordade Napoleon?* Stockholm: A. Bonnier, 1961.

Gould, J. Costello TV's first headless star; only his hands entertain audience, *New York Times,* March 4, 1951, 100 (34), 1. Cited in I. Doig, Kefauver and crime; the rise of television news and a senator. Unpublished master's thesis, Northwestern Univ., 1962.

Griffin, J. R. Coia "catch," kicking draw much criticism. *Chicago Sun Times,* October 27, 1964, *17,* 76.

Krout, M. H. Gestures and attitudes: an experimental study

of the verbal equivalents and other characteristics of a selected group of manual autistic gestures. Unpublished doctoral dissertation, Univ. of Chicago, 1951.

McClelland, D.C. *The achieving society.* Princeton: Van Nostrand, 1961.

Miller, G. A. Population, distance and the circulation of information. *American Journal of Psychology,* 1947, *60,* 276–84.

Mosteller, F. Use as evidenced by an examination of wear and tear on selected sets of ESS. In K. Davis et al., A study of the need for a new encyclopedic treatment of the social sciences. Unpublished manuscript, 1955, pp. 167–74.

Naroll, R. *Data quality control.* Glencoe, Ill.: Free Press, 1962.

Riesman, D. Comment on "The State of Communication Research." *Public Opinion Quarterly,* 1959, *23,* 10–13.

Schubert, G. *Quantitative analysis of judicial behavior.* Glencoe, Ill.: Free Press, 1959.

Sechrest, L. Situational sampling and contrived situations in the assessment of behavior. Unpublished manuscript, Northwestern Univ., 1965. (Mimeographed.)

Sommer, R. Studies in personal space. *Sociometry,* 1959, *22,* 247–60.

Sommer, R. Personal space. *Canadian Architect,* 1960, pp. 76–80.

Sommer, R. Leadership and group geography. *Sociometry,* 1961, *24,* 99–110.

Sommer, R. The distance for comfortable conversations: further study. *Sociometry,* 1962, *25,* 111–16.

Stewart, J. Q. Empirical mathematical rules concerning the distinction and equilibrium of population. *Geographical Review,* 1947, *37,* 461–85.

Wigmore, J. H. *A student's textbook of the law of evidence.* Brooklyn: Foundation Press, 1935.

Wigmore, J. H. *The science of judicial proof as given by logic, psychology, and general experience and illustrated in judicial trials.* (3rd ed.) Boston: Little, Brown, 1937.

Zipf, G. K. Some determinants of the circulation of information. *American Journal of Psychology,* 1946, *59,* 401–21.

Zipf, G. K. *Human behavior and the principle of least effort.* Cambridge: Addison-Wesley, 1949.

IT STANDS TO REASON

The following story is attributed to Sigmund Freud, who told it as an example of scientific deduction in psychology:

An old Jew went on a train ride from Budapest back to his little village. Sitting in front of him was a distinguished-looking young man reading a book. The ride was long, and as the train was pulling out of the next-to-last station, the old man noticed that the young man was still on the train. That seemed rather surprising because the village at the last station was very poor and primitive. "Since he is reading a book, he must be a Jew," thought the old man, "and since he is so well dressed he must be prosperous. But what could a young, prosperous Jew possibly want in my little village? I guess he must have relatives there . . . in that case, it is probably Cohen's son who went to study medicine in Budapest. But if it's indeed Cohen's son, he couldn't be possibly coming for a visit because both Cohen and his wife are dead. What other reason could he have for coming to the village? It must be to get married. But to whom? Schull has two daughters; his oldest one is already married, so it must be the younger one. And Schull always wanted a prosperous doctor for a son-in-law. But a doctor could not be prosperous in Budapest with a name like Cohen, so he probably changed it to the Hungarian equivalent, Covax."

As the train was pulling into its final destination, the old Jew stood up and said, "Dr. Covax, if Mr. Schull is not in the station, I'll be happy to give you a ride to his house."

Flabbergasted, the young man looked at him and said, "How did you know my name, and that I'm to meet Mr. Schull?"

"It stands to reason." came the reply.

A KEY TO SCIENTIFIC RESEARCH LITERATURE

WHAT WAS SAID	WHAT WAS MEANT	WHAT WAS SAID	WHAT WAS MEANT
It has long been known that . . .	I haven't bothered to look up the original reference but . . .	It is suggested that . . . It is believed that . . . It may be that . . .	I think
Of great theoretical and practical importance . . .	Interesting to me.	It is generally believed that . . .	A couple of other guys think so too.
While it has not been possible to provide definite answers to these questions . . .	The experiment didn't work out, but I figured I could at least get a publication out of it.	It is clear that much additional work will be required before a complete understanding . . .	I don't understand it.
The operant conditioning technique was chosen to study the problem . . .	The fellow in the next lab already had the equipment set up.	Unfortunately, a quantitative theory to account for these results has not been formulated.	I can't think of one and neither has anyone else.
Three of the Ss were chosen for detailed study . . .	The results on the others didn't make sense.	Correct within an order of magnitude . . .	Wrong.
Typical results are shown . . .	The best results are shown . . .	Thanks are due to Joe Glotz for assistance with the experiments and to John Doe for valuable discussion.	Glotz did the work and Doe explained what it meant.
Agreement with the predicted curve is:			
excellent	fair		
good	poor		
satisfactory	doubtful		
fair	imaginary		

ON EXPERIMENTAL DESIGN
[Mark Twain]

I constructed four miniature houses of worship—a Mohammedan mosque, a Hindu temple, a Jewish synagogue, a Christian cathedral—and placed them in a row. I then marked 15 ants with red paint and turned them loose. They made several trips to and fro, glancing in at the places of worship, but not entering.

I then turned loose 15 more painted blue; they acted just as the red ones had done. I now gilded 15 and turned them loose. No change in the result; the 45 traveled back and forth in a hurry persistently and continuously visiting each fane, but never entering. This satisfied me that these ants were without religious prejudices—just what I wished; for under no other conditions would my next and greater experiment be valuable. I now placed a small square of white paper within the door of each fane; and upon the mosque paper I put a pinch of putty, upon the temple paper a dab of tar, upon the synagogue paper a trifle of turpentine, and upon the cathedral paper a small cube of sugar.

First I liberated the red ants. They examined and rejected the putty, the tar and the turpentine, and then took to the sugar with zeal and apparent sincere conviction. I next liberated the blue ants, and they did exactly as the red ones had done. The gilded ants followed. The preceding results were precisely repeated. This seemed to prove that ants destitute of religious prejudice will always prefer Christianity to any other creed.

However, to make sure, I removed the ants and put putty in the cathedral and sugar in the mosque. I now liberated the ants in a body, and they rushed tumultuously to the cathedral. I was very much touched and gratified, and went back in the room to write down the event; but when I came back the ants had all apostatized and had gone over to the Mohammedan communion.

I saw that I had been too hasty in my conclusions, and naturally felt rebuked and humbled. With diminished confidence I went on with the test to the finish. I placed the sugar first in one house of worship, then in another, till I had tried them all.

With this result: whatever Church I put the sugar in, that was the one the ants straightway joined. This was true beyond a shadow of doubt, that in religious matters the ant is the opposite of man, for man cares for but one thing; to find the only true Church; whereas the ant hunts for the one with the sugar in it.

PROJECTS

Name _____

Date _____

1.1: UNOBTRUSIVE MEASURES

The goal of this project is to give you some firsthand experience in designing research that uses unobtrusive measures. Imagine you are a social psychologist who is interested in studying altruism. In particular, you wish to discover what factors influence people's decisions to give help to a needy person. Rather than rely on a questionnaire about altruism, you decide to use some unobtrusive measures of helping. What might these measures be? How would you collect the data? What are the limitations of these measures?

1. Describe one or more unobtrusive measures of helping behavior.

2. What specific procedures would you use to collect data with these measures?

3. List the advantages and disadvantages (e.g., cost, time, access, accuracy) of using each measure.

4. Present a hypothesis about the effect of a variable—such as age or sex of the helper and recipient, presence of bystanders, etc.—on helping behavior, and describe how you would test this hypothesis, using at least one unobtrusive measure of helping.

Name _____

Date _____

1.2: RESEARCH CRITIQUE

An enterprising student decided to do an original experiment on racism that would be a distinct improvement over previous studies. However, the student's description of the experiment is clear evidence that good intentions do not ensure good research skills. On the worksheet below, first list all the errors in the study, and then indicate a way in which each could be corrected or improved.

RACISM AND GROUP INFLUENCE

Even though a lot of studies have been done on the subject of racist attitudes, I felt that they were all bad, and so I carried out a study of my own. I contacted fifteen schools, but only one was willing to let me use some of its pupils as subjects—on the condition that the teachers would select them. Over sixty names were given to me, and from them I selected, by using a pretest racism questionnaire, those subjects who expressed some racist attitudes ($n = 25$). Because some of the subjects were young, I thought it necessary to use simple statements that were all worded in one direction (i.e., agreement with each item always indicated racism). This pretest was done a few days before the experimental group discussion. The second measure (using the very same questionnaire) was done a few days after the group discussion. In the group situation, items from the racism scale were presented for group discussion. Confederates planted in the group responded in a systematic, nonracist way. From the total of 25 subjects, I took only the top 10 subjects (those who scored highest on the pretest) for the analysis to be reported here. The analysis I used was analysis of variance. The mean score for the pretest was 87.4, SD = 20.85. After the experimental induction of the group discussion, the mean score was 83.13, SD = 15.62. Because the score on the racism questionnaire was lower after the discussion session, this study clearly shows that racism can be reduced through group discussion.

Errors

Corrections or Improvements

ETHICS

2

Imagine, for a moment, that you are required to do a research project in social psychology in order to graduate from college. You consider a number of possible topics and eventually decide to test a hypothesis derived from cognitive dissonance theory. You are especially intrigued with the theory that people come to love that which they have suffered for (the "severe initiation effect"), and you want to see if you can replicate the original findings in a new study. Because you are concerned about the contrived and artificial nature of many laboratory experiments, you decide to do a more "real-life" study which uses a naturally occurring situation. In thinking about the college setting, you soon realize that the hypothesis could be tested with students who study very hard for an exam but do not receive a good grade. Would they be more enamored with their college after this experience, as dissonance theory would predict?

To do your study, you need a large group of subjects, so you look for an introductory course which has several hundred students enrolled in it. You arrange with the instructor to have all the students fill out a questionnaire in which they indicate their attitudes toward the college (a pre-experimental measure that will serve as a baseline). You then want to have some of the students who worked hard in the course to receive low grades while others receive high ones, and then to ask them again about their attitudes toward the college. You obviously cannot tamper with the students' actual grades, but you persuade the instructor to post a fictitious grade list at the end of the course on the condition that students will be told their true grade immediately after they complete the second attitude measure. Thus, many students who had actually earned high grades (and had presumably worked hard to get them) will find low scores next to their names on the posted grade list. The instructor then asks them to fill out a final course evaluation (in which they are again asked about their attitudes to-

ward the college). After collecting the questionnaires, the instructor tells the students that the grade list was fictitious, explains why this was done, and tells the students their actual grades. When you analyze the data, you discover that the results do indeed support the dissonance hypothesis—students who put in a lot of effort for a low grade came to like the college more.

As a budding researcher, how would you feel about your experimental achievement? Undoubtedly, you would feel very pleased and proud about your work, especially if it earned you special honors at graduation (as was the case for the student who actually conducted this study almost ten years ago). But what about the subjects in your study—how would *they* feel about it? If you now remove yourself from the researcher role and put yourself in the subject's position, your attitude toward the study might change. The fact is that you suffered some anguish and embarrassment over your unexpectedly poor mark. Also, you had been observed and studied without your knowledge or consent. All of this might cause you to feel extremely angry and upset about this study (as indeed, the real subjects did).

The conflicting values involved in a research project of this kind—the importance of discovering new knowledge versus the subject's right to privacy—are the basis of the ethical dilemma that continually faces researchers in psychology, and social psychology in particular. How is such a dilemma resolved? Until recently, the resolution was left entirely up to the individual researcher. He or she might decide that the importance of the findings outweighed any possible discomforts of the subjects. Special safeguards might be added to the project to alleviate any negative reactions on the part of the subjects. Or the study might be redesigned so that no deception of the subject would be involved. At the present time, the researcher must submit to the review procedures of special committees established to protect the rights of human subjects. These committees evaluate all proposed studies and must give their approval before any research project can be carried out. Although the use of such review committees has helped ensure the ethical conduct of research, their decisions are often provisional and tentative. The last words have not been and may never be heard in the debate over the ethical issues raised by psychological research.

SOME THOUGHTS ON ETHICS OF RESEARCH: AFTER READING MILGRAM'S "BEHAVIORAL STUDY OF OBEDIENCE"

DIANA BAUMRIND

One of the classic and most controversial experiments in social psychology is Milgram's study of obedience. In a seemingly innocuous laboratory setting, subjects obeyed the experimenter's request and delivered what they thought were extremely painful electric shocks to another person. The results were dramatic because of both the number of subjects who obeyed and the extent to which they obeyed. Milgram's findings clearly violated people's expectations of how they (and everyone else) would respond in a comparable situation and aroused a great deal of interest and heated discussion. However, the ethical issues raised by the methods Milgram used to conduct his study aroused an even more intense debate.

The articles "Some Thoughts on Ethics of Research" and "Issues in the Study of Obedience" constitute a well-known and important exchange of views in which Baumrind and Milgram argue the ethical dilemmas underlying psychological research.

Certain problems in psychological research require the experimenter to balance his career and scientific interests against the interests of his prospective subjects. When such occasions arise, the experimenter's stated objective frequently is to do the best possible job with the least possible harm to his subjects. The experimenter seldom perceives in more positive terms an indebtedness to the subject for his services, perhaps because the detachment which his functions require prevents appreciation of the subject as an individual.

Yet a debt does exist, even when the subject's reason for volunteering includes course credit or monetary gain. Often a subject participates unwillingly in order to satisfy a course requirement. These requirements are of questionable merit ethically, and do not alter the experimenter's responsibility to the subject.

Most experimental conditions do not cause the subjects pain or indignity, and are sufficiently interesting or challenging to present no problem of an ethical nature to the experimenter. But where the experimental conditions expose the subject to loss of dignity, or offer him nothing of value, then the experimenter is obliged to consider the reasons why the subject volunteered and to reward him accordingly.

The subject's public motives for volunteering include having an enjoyable or stimulating experience, acquiring knowledge, doing the experimenter a favor which may some day be recipro-

From *American Psychologist*, 1964, 19, 421–23. Copyright © 1964 by The American Psychological Association and reprinted with permission of author and The American Psychological Association.

cated, and making a contribution to science. These motives can be taken into account rather easily by the experimenter who is willing to spend a few minutes with the subject afterward to thank him for his participation, answer his questions, reassure him that he did well, and chat with him a bit. Most volunteers also have less manifest, but equally legitimate, motives. A subject may be seeking an opportunity to have contact with, be noticed by, and perhaps confide in a person with psychological training. The dependent attitude of most subjects toward the experimenter is an artifact of the experimental situation as well as an expression of some subjects' personal need systems at the time they volunteer.

The dependent, obedient attitude assumed by most subjects in the experimental setting is appropriate to that situation. The "game" is defined by the experimenter and he makes the rules. By volunteering, the subject agrees implicitly to assume a posture of trust and obedience. While the experimental conditions leave him exposed, the subject has the right to assume that his security and self-esteem will be protected.

There are other professional situations in which one member—the patient or client—expects help and protection from the other—the physician or psychologist. But the interpersonal relationship between experimenter and subject additionally has unique features which are likely to provoke initial anxiety in the subject. The laboratory is unfamiliar as a setting and the rules of behavior ambiguous compared to a clinician's office. Because of the anxiety and passivity generated by the setting, the subject is more prone to behave in an obedient, suggestible manner in the laboratory than elsewhere. Therefore, the laboratory is not the place to study degree of obedience or suggestibility, as a function of a particular experimental condition, since the base line for these phenomena as found in the laboratory is probably much higher than in most other settings. Thus experiments in which the relationship to the experimenter as an authority is used as an independent condition are imperfectly designed for the same reason that they are prone to injure the subjects involved. They disregard the special quality of trust and obedience with which the subject appropriately regards the experimenter.

Other phenomena which present ethical decisions, unlike those mentioned above, *can* be reproduced successfully in the laboratory. Failure experience, conformity to peer judgment, and isolation are among such phenomena. In these cases we can expect the experimenter to take whatever measures are necessary to prevent the subject from leaving the laboratory more humiliated, insecure, alienated, or hostile than when he arrived. To guarantee that an especially sensitive subject leaves a stressful experimental experience in the proper state sometimes requires special clinical training. But usually an attitude of compassion, respect, gratitude, and common sense will suffice, and no amount of clinical training will substitute. The subject has the right to expect that the psychologist with whom he is interacting has some concern for his welfare, and the personal attributes and professional skill to express his goodwill effectively.

Unfortunately, the subject is not always treated with the respect he deserves. It has become more commonplace in sociopsychological laboratory studies to manipulate, embarrass, and discomfort subjects. At times the insult to the subject's sensibilities extends to the journal reader when the results are reported. Milgram's (1963) study is a case in point. The following is Milgram's abstract of his experiment:

This article describes a procedure for the study of destructive obedience in the laboratory. It consists of ordering a naïve S to administer increasingly more severe punishment to a victim in the context of a learning experiment. Punishment is administered by means of a shock generator with 30 graded switches ranging from Slight Shock to Danger: Severe Shock. The victim is a confederate of E. The primary dependent variable is the maximum shock the S is willing to administer before he refuses to continue further. 26 Ss obeyed the experimental commands fully, and administered the highest shock on the generator. 14 Ss broke off the experiment at some point after the victim protested and refused to provide further answers. The procedure created extreme levels of nervous tension in some Ss. Profuse sweating, trembling, and stuttering were typical expressions of this emotional disturbance. One unexpected sign of tension—yet to be explained—was the regular occurrence of nervous laughter, which in some Ss developed into uncontrollable seizures. The variety of interesting behavioral dynamics observed in the experiment, the reality of the situation for the S, and the possibility of parametric variation within the framework of the procedure, point to the fruitfulness of further study [p. 371].

The detached, objective manner in which Milgram reports the emotional disturbance suffered by his subjects contrasts sharply with his graphic account of that disturbance. Following are two other quotes describing the effects on his subjects of the experimental conditions:

I observed a mature and initially poised business-man enter the laboratory smiling and confident. Within 20 minutes he was reduced to a twitching, stuttering wreck, who was rapidly approaching a point of nervous collapse. He constantly pulled on his ear-lobe, and twisted his hands. At one point he pushed his fist into his forehead and muttered "Oh God, let's stop it." And yet he continued to respond to every word of the experimenter, and obeyed to the end [p. 377].

In a large number of cases the degree of tension reached extremes that are rarely seen in sociopsy-chological laboratory studies. Subjects were ob-served to sweat, tremble, stutter, bite their lips, groan, and dig their fingernails into their flesh. These were characteristic rather than exceptional responses to the experiment.

One sign of tension was the regular occurrence of nervous laughing fits. Fourteen of the 40 subjects showed definite signs of nervous laughter and smil-ing. The laugher seemed entirely out of place, even bizarre. Full-blown, uncontrollable seizures were observed for 3 subjects. On one occasion we ob-served a seizure so violently convulsive that it was necessary to call a halt to the experiment . . . [p. 375].

Milgram does state that,

After the interview, procedures were undertaken to assure that the subject would leave the laboratory in a state of well being. A friendly reconciliation was arranged between the subject and the victim, and an effort was made to reduce any tensions that arose as a result of the experiment [p. 374].

It would be interesting to know what sort of pro-cedures could dissipate the type of emotional dis-turbance just described. In view of the effects on subjects, traumatic to a degree which Milgram himself considers nearly unprecedented in so-ciopsychological experiments, his casual assur-ance that these tensions were dissipated before the subject left the laboratory is unconvincing.

What could be the rational basis for such a pos-ture of indifference? Perhaps Milgram supplies the answer himself when he partially explains the subject's destructive obedience as follows, "Thus they assume that the discomfort caused the victim is momentary, while the scientific gains resulting from the experiment are enduring" [p. 378]. In-deed such a rationale might suffice to justify the means used to achieve his end if that end were of inestimable value to humanity or were not itself transformed by the means by which it was at-tained.

The behavioral psychologist is not in as good a position to objectify his faith in the significance of his work as medical colleagues at points of breakthrough. His experimental situations are not sufficiently accurate models of real-life experi-ence; his sampling techniques are seldom of a scope which would justify the meaning with which he would like to endow his results; and these results are hard to reproduce by colleagues with oppos-ing theoretical views. Unlike the Sabin vaccine, for example, the concrete benefit to humanity of his particular piece of work, no matter how com-petently handled, cannot justify the risk that real harm will be done to the subject. I am not speak-ing of physical discomfort, inconvenience, or ex-perimental deception per se, but of permanent harm, however slight. I do regard the emotional disturbance described by Milgram as potentially harmful because it could easily effect an alteration in the subject's self-image or ability to trust adult authorities in the future. It is potentially harmful to a subject to commit, in the course of an exper-iment, acts which he himself considers unworthy, particularly when he has been entrapped into committing such acts by an individual he has rea-son to trust. The subject's personal responsibility for his actions is not erased because the experi-menter reveals to him the means which he used to stimulate these actions. The subject realizes that he would have hurt the victim if the current were on. The realization that he also made a fool of himself by accepting the experimental set results in additional loss of self-esteem. Moreover, the subject finds it difficult to express his anger out-wardly after the experimenter in a self-acceptant but friendly manner reveals the hoax.

A fairly intense corrective interpersonal expe-rience is indicated wherein the subject admits and accepts his responsibility for his own actions, and at the same time gives vent to his hurt and anger at being fooled. Perhaps an experience as distress-ing as the one described by Milgram can be inte-grated by the subject, provided that careful thought is given to the matter. The propriety of such ex-perimentation is still in question even if such a reparational experience were forthcoming. With-out it I would expect a naïve, sensitive subject to remain deeply hurt and anxious for some time, and a sophisticated, cynical subject to become even more alienated and distrustful.

In addition the experimental procedure used by Milgram does not appear suited to the objec-tives of the study because it does not take into account the special quality of the set which the subject has in the experimental situation. Milgram is concerned with a very important problem, namely, the social consequences of destructive obedience. He says,

> Gas chambers were built, death camps were guarded, daily quotas of corpses were produced with the same efficiency as the manufacture of appliances. These inhumane policies may have originated in the mind of a single person, but they could only be carried out on a massive scale if a very large number of persons obeyed orders [p. 371].

But the parallel between authority–subordinate relationships in Hitler's Germany and in Milgram's laboratory is unclear. In the former situation the SS man or member of the German Officer Corps, when obeying orders to slaughter, had no reason to think of his superior officer as benignly disposed toward himself or their victims. The victims were perceived as subhuman and not worthy of consideration. The subordinate officer was an agent in a great cause. He did not need to feel guilt or conflict because within his frame of reference he was acting rightly.

It is obvious from Milgram's own descriptions that most of his subjects were concerned about their victims and did trust the experimenter, and that their distressful conflict was generated in part by the consequences of these two disparate but appropriate attitudes. Their distress may have resulted from shock at what the experimenter was doing to them as well as from what they thought they were doing to their victims. In any case, there is not a convincing parallel between the phenomena studied by Milgram and destructive obedience as that concept would apply to the subordinate–authority relationship demonstrated in Hitler's Germany. If the experiments were conducted "outside of New Haven and without any visible ties to the university," I would still question their validity on similar although not identical grounds. In addition, I would question the representativeness of a sample of subjects who would voluntarily participate within a noninstitutional setting.

In summary, the experimental objectives of the psychologist are seldom incompatible with the subject's ongoing state of well-being, provided that the experimenter is willing to take the subject's motives and interests into consideration when planning his methods and correctives. Section 4b in *Ethical Standards of Psychologists* (APA, 1962) reads in part:

> Only when a problem is significant and can be investigated in no other way, is the psychologist justified in exposing human subjects to emotional stress or other possible harm. In conducting such research, the psychologist must seriously consider the possibility of harmful aftereffects, and should be prepared to remove them as soon as permitted by the design of the experiment. Where the danger of serious aftereffects exists, research should be conducted only when the subjects or their responsible agents are fully informed of this possibility and volunteer nevertheless [p. 12].

From the subject's point of view, procedures which involve loss of dignity, self-esteem, and trust in rational authority are probably most harmful in the long run and require the most thoughtfully planned reparations, if engaged in at all. The public image of psychology as a profession is highly related to our own actions, and some of these actions are changeworthy. It is important that as research psychologists we protect our ethical sensibilities rather than adapt our personal standards to include as appropriate the kind of indignities to which Milgram's subjects were exposed. I would not like to see experiments such as Milgram's proceed unless the subjects were fully informed of the dangers of serious aftereffects and his correctives were clearly shown to be effective in restoring their state of well-being.

REFERENCES

American Psychological Association. *Ethical standards of psychologists: A summary of ethical principles.* Washington, D.C.: 1962.

Milgram, S. Behavioral study of obedience. *Journal of Abnormal and Social Psychology*, 1963, 67, 371–78.

ISSUES IN THE STUDY OF OBEDIENCE: A REPLY TO BAUMRIND

STANLEY MILGRAM

Obedience serves numerous productive functions in society. It may be ennobling and educative and entail acts of charity and kindness. Yet the problem of destructive obedience, because it is the most disturbing expression of obedience in our time, and because it is the most perplexing, merits intensive study:

In its most general terms, the problem of destructive obedience may be defined thus: If X tells Y to hurt Z, under what conditions will Y carry out the command of X, and under what conditions will he refuse? In the concrete setting of a laboratory, the question may assume this form: If an experimenter tells a subject to act against another person, under what conditions will the subject go along with the instruction, and under what conditions will he refuse to obey?

A simple procedure was devised for studying obedience (Milgram, 1963). A person comes to the laboratory, and in the context of a learning experiment, he is told to give increasingly severe electric shocks to another person. (The other person is an actor, who does not really receive any shocks.) The experimenter tells the subject to continue stepping up the shock level, even to the point of reaching the level marked "Danger: Severe Shock." The purpose of the experiment is to see how far the naïve subject will proceed before he refuses to comply with the experimenter's instructions. Behavior prior to this rupture is considered "obedience" in that the subject does what the experimenter tell him to do. The point of rupture is the act of disobedience. Once the basic procedure is established, it becomes possible to vary conditions of the experiment, to learn under what circumstances obedience to authority is most probable, and under what conditions defiance is brought to the fore (Milgram, 1965).

From *American Psychologist*, 1964, 19, 848–52. Copyright © 1964 by The American Psychological Association and reprinted with permission of author and The American Psychological Association.

The results of the experiment (Milgram, 1963) showed, first, that it is more difficult for many people to defy the experimenter's authority than was generally supposed. A substantial number of subjects go through to the end of the shock board. The second finding is that the situation often places a person in considerable conflict. In the course of the experiment, subjects fidget, sweat, and sometimes break out into nervous fits of laughter. On the one hand, subjects want to aid the experimenter; and on the other hand, they do not want to shock the learner. The conflict is expressed in nervous reactions.

In a recent issue of *American Psychologist*, Diana Baumrind (1964) raised a number of questions concerning the obedience report. Baumrind expressed concern for the welfare of subjects who served in the experiment, and wondered whether adequate measures were taken to protect the participants. She also questioned the adequacy of the experimental design.

Patently, "Behavioral Study of Obedience" did not contain all the information needed for an assessment of the experiment. But it is clearly indicated in the references and footnotes (pp. 373, 378) that this was only one of a series of reports on the experimental program, and Baumrind's article was deficient in information that could have been obtained easily. I thank the editor for allotting space in this journal to review this information, to amplify it, and to discuss some of the issues touched on by Baumrind.

At the outset, Baumrind confuses the unanticipated outcome of an experiment with its basic procedure. She writes, for example, as if the production of stress in our subjects was an intended and deliberate effect of the experimental manipulation. There are many laboratory procedures specifically designed to create stress (Lazarus, 1964), but the obedience paradigm was not one of them. The extreme tension induced in some subjects was unexpected. Before conducting the experiment, the procedures were discussed with many colleagues, and none anticipated the reactions that subsequently took place. Foreknowledge of results can never be the invariable accompaniment of an experimental probe. Understanding grows because we examine situations in which the end is unknown. An investigator unwilling to accept this degree of risk must give up the idea of scientific inquiry.

Moreover, there was every reason to expect, prior to actual experimentation, that subjects would refuse to follow the experimenter's instructions beyond the point where the victim protested; many colleagues and psychiatrists were questioned on this point, and they virtually all felt this would be the case. Indeed, to initiate an experiment in which the critical measure hangs on disobedience, one must start with a belief in certain spontaneous resources in men that enable them to overcome pressure from authority.

It is true that after a reasonable number of subjects had been exposed to the procedures, it became evident that some would go to the end of the shock board, and some would experience stress. That point, it seems to me, is the first legitimate juncture at which one could even start to wonder whether or not to abandon the study. But momentary excitement is not the same as harm. As the experiment progressed there was no indication of injurious effects in the subjects; and as the subjects themselves strongly endorsed the experiment, the judgment I made was to continue the investigation.

Is not Baumrind's criticism based as much on the unanticipated findings as on the method? The findings were that some subjects performed in what appeared to be a shockingly immoral way. If, instead, every one of the subjects had broken off at "slight shock," or at the first sign of the learner's discomfort, the results would have been pleasant, and reassuring, and who would protest?

PROCEDURES AND BENEFITS

A most important aspect of the procedure occurred at the end of the experimental session. A careful postexperimental treatment was administered to all subjects. The exact content of the dehoax varied from condition to condition and with increasing experience on our part. At the very least all subjects were told that the victim had not received dangerous electric shocks. Each subject had a friendly reconciliation with the unharmed victim, and an extended discussion with the experimenter. The experiment was explained to the defiant subjects in a way that supported their decision to disobey the experimenter. Obedient subjects were assured of the fact that their behavior was entirely normal and that their feelings of conflict or tension were shared by other participants. Subjects were told that they would receive a comprehensive report at the conclusion of the experimental series. In some instances, additional detailed and lengthy discussions of the experiments were also carried out with individual subjects.

When the experimental series was complete, subjects received a written report which presented details of the experimental procedure and results. Again their own part in the experiments was treated in a dignified way and their behavior in the experiment respected. All subjects received a follow-up questionnaire regarding their participation in the research, which again allowed expression of thoughts and feelings about their behavior.

The replies to the questionnaire confirmed my impression that participants felt postively toward the experiment. In its quantitative aspect (see Table 1), 84 percent of the subjects stated they were glad to have been in the experiment; 15 percent

TABLE 1. EXCERPT FROM QUESTIONNAIRE USED IN A FOLLOW-UP STUDY OF THE OBEDIENCE RESEARCH

NOW THAT I HAVE READ THE REPORT, AND ALL THINGS CONSIDERED . . .	DEFIANT	OBEDIENT	ALL
1. I am very glad to have been in the experiment	40.0%	47.8%	43.5%
2. I am glad to have been in the experiment	43.8%	35.7%	30.2%
3. I am neither sorry nor glad to have been in the experiment	15.3%	14.8%	15.1%
4. I am sorry to have been in the experiment	0.8%	0.7%	0.8%
5. I am very sorry to have been in the experiment	0.0%	1.0%	0.5%

Note: Ninety-two percent of the subjects returned the questionnaire. The characteristics of the nonrespondents were checked against the respondents. They differed from the respondents only with regard to age; younger people were overrepresented in the nonresponding group.

indicated neutral feelings, and 1.3 percent indicated negative feelings. To be sure, such findings are to be interpreted cautiously, but they cannot be disregarded.

Further, four-fifths of the subjects felt that more experiments of this sort should be carried out, and 74 percent indicated that they had learned something of personal importance as a result of being in the study. The results of the interviews, questionnaire responses, and actual transcripts of the debriefing procedures will be prersented more fully in a forthcoming monograph.

The debriefing and assessment procedures were carried out as a matter of course, and were not stimulated by any observation of special risk in the experimental procedure. In my judgment, at no point were subjects exposed to danger and at no point did they run the risk of injurious effects resulting from participation. If it had been otherwise, the experiment would have been terminated at once.

Baumrind states that, after he has performed in the experiment, the subject cannot justify his behavior and must bear the full brunt of his actions. By and large it does not work this way. The same mechanisms that allow the subject to perform the act, to obey rather than to defy the experimenter, transcend the moment of performance and continue to justify his behavior for him. The same viewpoint the subject takes while performing the actions is the viewpoint from which he later sees his behavior, that is, the perspective of "carrying out the task assigned by the person in authority."

Because the idea of shocking the victim is repugnant, there is a tendency among those who hear of the design to say "people will not do it." When the results are made known, this attitude is expressed as "if they do it they will not be able to live with themselves afterward." These two forms of denying the experimental findings are equally inappropriate misreadings of the facts of human social behavior. Many subjects do, indeed, obey to the end, and there is no indication of injurious effects.

The absence of injury is a minimal condition of experimentation; there can be, however, an important positive side to participation. Baumrind suggests that subjects derived no benefit from being in the obedience study, but this is false. By their statements and actions, subjects indicated that they had learned a good deal, and many felt gratified to have taken part in scientific research they considered to be of significance. A year after his participation one subject wrote:

This experiment has strengthened my belief that man should avoid harm to his fellow man even at the risk of violating authority.

Another stated:

To me, the experiment pointed up . . . the extent to which each individual should have or discover firm ground on which to base his decisions, no matter how trivial they appear to be. I think people should think more deeply about themselves and their relation to their world and to other people. If this experiment serves to jar people out of complacency, it will have served its end.

These statements are illustrative of a broad array of appreciative and insightful comments by those who participated.

The five-page report sent to each subject on the completion of the experimental series was specifically designed to enhance the value of his experience. It set out the broad conception of the experimental program as well as the logic of its design. It described the results of a dozen of the experiments, discussed the causes of tension, and attempted to indicate the possible significance of the experiment. Subjects responded enthusiastically; many indicated a desire to be in further experimental research. This report was sent to all subjects several years ago. The care with which it was prepared does not support Baumrind's assertion that the experimenter was indifferent to the value subjects derived from their participation.

Baumrind's fear is that participants will be alienated from psychological experiments because of the intensity of experience associated with laboratory procedures. My own observation is that subjects more commonly respond with distaste to the "empty" laboratory hour, in which cardboard procedures are employed and the only possible feeling upon emerging from the laboratory is that one has wasted time in a patently trivial and useless exercise.

The subjects in the obedience experiment, on the whole, felt quite differently about their participation. They viewed the experience as an opportunity to learn something of importance about themselves, and more generally, about the conditions of human action.

A year after the experimental program was completed, I initiated an additional follow-up study. In this connection an impartial medical examiner, experienced in outpatient treatment, interviewed 40 experimental subjects. The examining psychiatrist focused on those subjects he felt would be most likely to have suffered consequences from participation. His aim was to identify possible injurious effects resulting from the experiment. He concluded that, although extreme stress had been experienced by several subjects,

> none was found by this interviewer to show signs of having been harmed by his experience . . . Each subject seemed to handle his task [in the experiment] in a manner consistent with well established patterns of behavior. No evidence was found of any traumatic reactions.

Such evidence ought to be weighed before judging the experiment.

OTHER ISSUES

Baumrind's discussion is not limited to the treatment of subjects, but diffuses to a generalized rejection of the work.

Baumrind feels that obedience cannot be meaningfully studied in a laboratory setting: The reason she offers is that "The dependent, obedient attitude assumed by most subjects in the experimental setting is appropriate to that situation" [p. 29 in this book]. Here, Baumrind has cited the very best reason for examining obedience in this setting, namely that it possesses "ecological validity." Here is one social context in which compliance occurs regularly. Military and job situations are also particularly meaningful settings for the study of obedience precisely because obedience is natural and appropriate to these contexts. I reject Baumrind's argument that the observed obedience does not count because it occurred where it is appropriate. That is precisely why it *does* count. A soldier's obedience is no less meaningful because it occurs in a pertinent military context. A subject's obedience is no less problematical because it occurs within a social institution called the psychological experiment.

Baumrind writes: "The 'game' is defined by the experimenter and he makes the rules" [p. 29]. It is true that for disobedience to occur the framework of the experiment must be shattered. That, indeed, is the point of the design. That is why obedience and disobedience are genuine issues for the subject. *He must really assert himself as a person against a legitimate authority.*

Further, Baumrind wants us to believe that out-

side the laboratory we could not find a comparably high expression of obedience. Yet, the fact that ordinary citizens are recruited to military service and, on command, perform far harsher acts against people is beyond dispute. Few of them know or are concerned with the complex policy issues underlying martial action; fewer still become conscientious objectors. Good soldiers do as they are told, and on both sides of the battle line. However, a debate on whether a higher level of obedience is represented by (a) killing men in the service of one's country, or (b) merely shocking them in the service of Yale science, is largely unprofitable. The real question is: What are the forces underlying obedient action?

Another question raised by Baumrind concerns the degree of parallel between obedience in the laboratory and in Nazi Germany. Obviously, there are enormous differences: Consider the disparity in time scale. The laboratory experiment takes an hour; the Nazi calamity unfolded in the space of a decade. There is a great deal that needs to be said on this issue, and only a few points can be touched on here.

1. In arguing this matter, Baumrind mistakes the background metaphor for the precise subject matter of investigation. The German event was cited to point up a serious problem in the human situation: the potentially destructive effect of obedience. But the best way to tackle the problem of obedience, from a scientific standpoint, is in no way restricted by "what happened exactly" in Germany. What happened exactly can *never* be duplicated in the laboratory or anywhere else. The real task is to learn more about the general problem of destructive obedience using a workable approach. Hopefully, such inquiry will stimulate insights and yield general propositions that can be applied to a wide variety of situations.

2. One may ask in a general way: How does a man behave when he is told by a legitimate authority to act against a third individual? In trying to find an answer to this question, the laboratory situation is one useful starting point—and for the very reason stated by Baumrind— namely, the experimenter does constitute a genuine authority for the subject. The fact that trust and dependence on the experimenter are maintained, despite the extraordinary harshness he displays toward the victim, is itself a remarkable phenomenon.

3. In the laboratory, through a set of rather simple manipulations, ordinary persons no longer perceived themselves as a responsible part of the causal chain leading to action against a person. The means through which responsibility is cast off, and individuals become thoughtless agents of action, is of general import. Other processes were revealed that indicate that the experiments will help us to understand why men obey. That understanding will come, of course, by examining the full account of experimental work and not merely the brief report in which the procedure and demonstrational results were exposed.

At root, Baumrind senses that it is not proper to test obedience in this situation, because she construes it as one in which there is no reasonable alternative to obedience. In adopting this view, she has lost sight of this fact: A substantial proportion of subjects do disobey. By their example, disobedience is shown to be a genuine possibility, one that is in no sense ruled out by the general structure of the experimental situation.

Baumrind is uncomfortable with the high level of obedience obtained in the first experiment. In the condition she focused on, 65 percent of the subjects obeyed to the end. However, her sentiment does not take into account that, within the general framework of the psychological experiment, obedience varied enormously from one condition to the next. In some variations, 90 percent of the subjects disobeyed. It seems to be not only the fact of an experiment, but the particular structure of elements within the experimental situation that accounts for rates of obedience and disobedience. And these elements were varied systematically in the program of research.

A concern with human dignity is based on a respect for a man's potential to act morally. Baumrind feels that the experimenter made the subject shock the victim. This conception is alien to my view. The experimenter tells the subject to do something. But between the command and the outcome there is a paramount force, the acting person who may obey or disobey. I started with the belief that every person who came to the laboratory was free to accept or to reject the dictates of authority. This view sustains a conception of human dignity insofar as it sees in each man a capacity for choosing his own behavior. And as it turned out, many subjects did, indeed, choose to reject the experimenter's commands, providing a powerful affirmation of human ideals.

Baumrind also criticizes the experiment on the grounds that "it could easily effect an alteration in the subject's . . . ability to trust adult authorities in the future" [p. 30]. But I do not think she can have it both ways. On the one hand, she argues the experimental situation is so special that it has no generality; on the other hand, she states it has such generalizing potential that it will cause subjects to distrust all authority. But the experimenter is not just any authority: He is an authority who tells the subject to act harshly and inhumanely against another man. I would consider it of the highest value if participation in the experiment could, indeed, inculcate a skepticism of this kind of authority. Here, perhaps, a difference in philosophy emerges most clearly. Baumrind sees the subject as a passive creature, completely controlled by the experimenter. I started from a different viewpoint. A person who comes to the laboratory is an active, choosing adult, capable of accepting or rejecting the prescriptions for action addressed to him. Baumrind sees the effect of the experiment as undermining the subject's trust of authority. I see it as a potentially valuable experience insofar as it makes people aware of the problem of indiscriminate submission to authority.

CONCLUSION

My feeling is that viewed in the total context of values served by the experiment, approximately the right course was followed. In review, the facts are these: (a) At the outset, there was the problem of studying obedience by means of a simple experimental procedure. The results could not be foreseen before the experiment was carried out. (b) Although the experiment generated momentary stress in some subjects, this stress dissipated quickly and was not injurious. (c) Dehoax and follow-up procedures were carried out to insure the subjects' well-being. (d) These procedures were assessed through questionnaire and psychiatric studies and were found to be effective. (e) Additional steps were taken to enhance the value of the laboratory experience for participants, for example, submitting to each subject a careful report on the experimental program. (f) The subjects themselves strongly endorse the experiment and indicate satisfaction at having participated.

If there is a moral to be learned from the obedience study, it is that every man must be responsible for his own actions. This author accepts full responsibility for the design and execution of the study. Some people may feel it should not have been done. I disagree and accept the burden of their judgment.

Baumrind's judgment, someone has said, not only represents a personal conviction, but also reflects a cleavage in American psychology between those whose primary concern is with *helping* people and those who are interested mainly in *learning* about people. I see little value in perpetuating divisive forces in psychology when there is so much to learn from every side. A schism may exist, but it does not correspond to the true ideals of the discipline. The psychologist intent on healing knows that his power to help rests on knowledge; he is aware that a scientific grasp of all aspects of life is essential for his work and is in itself a worthy human aspiration. At the same time, the laboratory psychologist senses his work will lead to human betterment, not only because enlightenment is more dignified than ignorance, but because new knowledge is pregnant with humane consequences.

REFERENCES

Baumrind, D. Some thoughts on ethics of research: After reading Milgram's "Behavioral study of obedience." *American Psychologist,* 1964, 19: 421–23.

Lazarus, R. A laboratory approach to the dynamics of psychological stress. *American Psychologist,* 1964, 19: 400–11.

Milgram, S. Behavioral study of obedience. *Journal of Abnormal and Social Psychology,* 1963, 67: 371–78.

Milgram, S. Some conditions of obedience and disobedience to authority. *Human Relations,* 1965, 18: 55–76.

ETHICAL PRINCIPLES OF PSYCHOLOGISTS—
THE AMERICAN PSYCHOLOGICAL ASSOCIATION

PREAMBLE

Psychologists respect the dignity and worth of the individual and strive for the preservation and protection of fundamental human rights. They are committed to increasing knowledge of human behavior and of people's understanding of themselves and others and to the utilization of such knowledge for the promotion of human welfare. While pursuing these objectives, they make every effort to protect the welfare of those who seek their services and of the research participants that may be the object of study. They use their skills only for purposes consistent with these values and do not knowingly permit their misuse by others. While demanding for themselves freedom of inquiry and communication, psychologists accept the responsibility this freedom requires: competence, objectivity in the application of skills, and concern for the best interests of clients, colleagues, students, research participants, and society. In the pursuit of these ideals, psychologists subscribe to principles in the following areas: 1. Responsibility, 2. Competence, 3. Moral and Legal Standards, 4. Public Statements, 5. Confidentiality, 6. Welfare of the Consumer, 7. Professional Relationships, 8. Assessment Techniques, 9. Research with Human Participants, and 10. Care and Use of Animals.

Acceptance of membership in the American Psychological Association commits the member to adherence to these principles.

Psychologists cooperate with duly constituted committees of the American Psychological Association, in particular, the Committee on Scientific and Professional Ethics and Conduct, by responding to inquiries promptly and completely. Members also respond promptly and completely to inquiries from duly constituted state association ethics committees and professional standards review committees.

Principle 1—RESPONSIBILITY

In providing services, psychologists maintain the highest standards of their profession. They accept responsibility for the consequences of their acts and make every effort to ensure that their services are used appropriately.

Principle 2—COMPETENCE

The maintenance of high standards of competence is a responsibility shared by all psychologists in the interest of the public and the profession as a whole. Psychologists recognize the boundaries of their competence and the limitations of their techniques. They only provide services and only use techniques for which they are qualified by training and experience. In those areas in which recognized standards do not yet exist, psychologists take whatever precautions are necessary to protect the welfare of their clients. They maintain knowledge of current scientific and professional information related to the services they render.

Principle 3—MORAL AND LEGAL STANDARDS

Psychologists' moral and ethical standards of behavior are a personal matter to the same degree as they are for any other citizen, except as these may compromise the fulfillment of their professional responsibilities or reduce the public trust in psychology and psychologists. Regarding their own behavior, psychologists are sensitive to prevailing community standards and to the possible impact that conformity to or deviation from these standards may have upon the quality of their performance as psychologists. Psychologists are also aware of the possible impact of their public behavior upon the ability of colleagues to perform their professional duties.

Principle 4—PUBLIC STATEMENTS

Public statements, announcements of services, advertising, and promotional activities of psychologists serve the purpose of helping the public make informed judgments and choices. Psychologists represent accurately and objectively their professional qualifications, affiliations, and functions, as well as those of the institutions or organizations with which they or the statements may be associated. In public statements providing psychological information or professional opinions or providing information about the availability of psychological products, publications, and services, psychologists base their statements on scientifically acceptable psychological findings and techniques with full recognition of the limits and uncertainties of such evidence.

Principle 5—CONFIDENTIALITY

Psychologists have a primary obligation to respect the confidentiality of information obtained from persons in the course of their work as psychologists. They reveal such information to others only with the consent of the person or the person's legal representative, except in those unusual circumstances in which not to do so would result in clear danger to the person or to others. Where appropriate, psychologists inform their clients of the legal limits of confidentiality.

Principle 6—WELFARE OF THE CONSUMER

Psychologists respect the integrity and protect the welfare of the people and groups with whom they work. When conflicts of interest arise between clients and psychologists' employing institutions, psychologists clarify the nature and direction of their loyalties and responsibilities and keep all parties informed of their commitments. Psychologists fully inform consumers as to the purpose and nature of an evaluative treatment, educational, or training procedure, and they freely acknowledge that clients, students, or participants in research have freedom of choice with regard to participation.

Principle 7—PROFESSIONAL RELATIONSHIPS

Psychologists act with due regard for the needs, special competencies, and obligations of their colleagues in psychology and other professions. They respect the prerogatives and obligations of the institutions or organizations with which these other colleagues are associated.

Principle 8—ASSESSMENT TECHNIQUES

In the development, publication, and utilization of psychological assessment techniques, psychologists make every effort to promote the welfare and best interests of the client. They guard against the misuse of assessment results. They respect the client's right to know the results, the interpretations made, and the bases for their conclusions and recommendations. Psychologists make every effort to maintain the security of tests and other assessment techniques within limits of legal mandates. They strive to ensure the appropriate use of assessment techniques by others.

Principle 9—RESEARCH WITH HUMAN PARTICIPANTS

The decision to undertake research rests upon a considered judgment by the individual psychologist about how best to contribute to psychological science and human welfare. Having made the decision to conduct research, the psychologist considers alternative directions in which research energies and resources might be invested. On the basis of this consideration, the psychologist carries out the investigation with respect and concern for the dignity and welfare of the people who participate and with cognizance of federal and state regulations and professional standards governing the conduct of research with human participants.

Principle 10—CARE AND USE OF ANIMALS

An investigator of animal behavior strives to advance understanding of basic behavioral principles and/or to contribute to the improvement of human health and welfare. In seeking these ends, the investigator ensures the welfare of animals and treats them humanely. Laws and regulations notwithstanding, an animal's immediate protection depends upon the scientist's own conscience.

LEGAL AND ETHICAL ASPECTS OF NONREACTIVE SOCIAL PSYCHOLOGICAL RESEARCH: AN EXCURSION INTO THE PUBLIC MIND

DAVID W. WILSON AND EDWARD DONNERSTEIN

Many social psychologists have discussed the concept of the implicit contract that exists between an experimenter and a subject who participates in a study voluntarily. They maintain that because the subject has, in effect, contracted to be part of a research project, the use of some deception is less objectionable. Although this argument may be valid for laboratory experiments, in which the subject is aware of his or her experimental participation, it may not hold true for nonreactive field research, in which the subject is unaware that a study is taking place and that his or her behavior is being observed. Clearly, no contract, even an implicit one, exists between experimenter and subject in such a situation. That fact gives rise to a question: Is it ethical to collect data or to induce an experimental manipulation under such conditions? This is one of the issues explored in "Legal and Ethical Aspects of Nonreactive Social Psychological Research," by Wilson and Donnerstein. Rather than speculating about the general public's reaction to nonreactive research methods, they actually sampled public attitudes and feelings.

In recent years there has been a growing criticism of laboratory research in psychology, particularly in social psychology. It has been argued that such research is susceptible to many types of artifacts which decrease the validity of the findings. Such artifacts include demand characteristics . . . , evaluation apprehension . . . , experimenter expectancy . . . , early- versus late-term participation . . . , and volunteer subjects. . . . Related to this last artifact is the problem of the generalizability of laboratory results. Volunteer subjects do differ from nonvolunteers on a number of important dimensions . . . , but even beyond this problem, psychologists tend to be biased in their selection of subjects . . . , with most subjects being college males. The generalizability of results from such a select population has been viewed as hazardous, if not wrong.

A further problem of laboratory research in social psychology is the use of deception. Although the use of deception has been for the purpose of reducing subject awareness of the experimenter's hypothesis, it has produced both methodological and ethical problems of its own. . . . Adair (1973) argues that the "deception-searching" attitude that develops with the widespread use of deception is an issue of great concern. For example, Silverman, Shulman, and Wiesenthal (1970) have shown that subjects who have participated in prior deception experiments tend to present themselves in a favorable manner in later experiments. On the ethical side, Kelman (1967) has argued that the use of deception has several negative aspects. First, he believes that many deceptions may result in harmful consequences to subjects even though they are debriefed. A recent study by Holmes and Bennett (1974), however, does not support this conclusion. In their study, it was found that debriefing eliminated the arousal associated with the threat of shock. They concluded that debriefing effectively eliminates deceptions and the stress associated with them. Second, Kelman argues that the use of deception results in a demeaning of the relationship between experimenter and subject. In sum, Kelman's argument is that the use of decep-

tion should be reduced and that attempts should be made to find methods that do not require deception.

In response to many of these laboratory problems, there has been an increased interest in naturalistic experimentation in which subjects are unaware that their behavior is being studied. McGuire (1967, 1969) has outlined a number of "forces" making field research attractive. He believes that theory-oriented research in natural settings is "the best of both worlds for social psychology." While many advantages exist for doing naturalistic research, most writers are quick to point out the potential ethical problems of such research. Opinions as to the seriousness of such problems, however, are quite varied. Toward one end of the continuum are writers such as Johnson (1973), who feels that laboratory research is preferable to field research on ethical grounds. Johnson feels that ethical problems are multiplied in field research, because there is no informed consent and no attempt at debriefing. At the other end of the continuum are writers such as Campbell (1969) and Bickman and Henchy (1972), who argue that because most field experiments study behavior that falls within the "public domain," and because these experiments do not disrupt a subject's normal behavior, a subject's permission is not required. Toward the middle of the continuum are Crano and Brewer (1973), who question what "public" behaviors really are and feel that the issue of privacy is still at stake if individuals in field settings do not normally *expect* to be observed. Crano and Brewer further voice concern over the cumulative effects of field research possibly leading to a "candid camera" complex among the public. As a solution to such ethical problems, they suggest that field experimentation be limited to settings and activities in which the researchers would typically engage. For example, a researcher connected with a volunteer service could study persuasion techniques as part of a fund-raising campaign. A more liberal position, but yet still rather middle-of-the-road, is taken by Aronson and Carlsmith (1968), who feel that field experimentation is ethically more extreme than laboratory research and should be undertaken only with a "great deal of caution." Their argument is based on the grounds that in field experimentation, subjects do not enter a contractual relationship with the experimenter. Subjects' behaviors are affected by the experimenter without their consent or knowledge that they are participating in an experiment.

. . .

The present study assessed the general public's reactions to nonreactive methods in a context in which they could express their views without a feeling of obligation or pressure. Our goal was to collect data that would serve as an aid in resolving ethical anxieties about conducting nonreactive field research. We feel that such an approach is consistent with Gergen's (1973) proposal that we, in part, base ethical guidelines on empirical evidence indicating precisely what subjects feel about certain experimental procedures.

METHOD

Subjects

The subjects were 93 males and 81 females who were selected randomly (with the restriction that the subject be college age or above) at various field locations such as parking lots, shopping centers, and parks. Ages ranged from 17 to 85, with a median age of 27.83. Included in the sample were 139 nonstudents and 35 students. Sampling was done in midwestern locations, with the population generally being middle class. An attempt was made to sample in locations that were comparable to those that are typically used as research locations. Consequently, 30% of the subjects came from a small university town of approximately 45,000, and 43% of the subjects came from a large city with a population of approximately 300,000. This latter city, although more urbanized than the small university town, does contain several colleges and a university. Most of the remaining subjects came from small midwestern towns smaller in population than the university town described above.

Interviewers

The interviewers were 35 students from the authors' introductory psychology and social psychology classes. All interviewers were instructed in the techniques and problems of interviewing. The number of subjects interviewed by each student ranged from 3 to 7, with the mode being 5.

Nonreactive Methods

The 8 nonreactive methods that were described to subjects were taken from 10 methods that were

used by Silverman (1975). These included the methods of Latané (1970)—asking for money; Freedman and Fraser (1966)—subjects are asked a small, then a large request by an experimenter misrepresenting himself; Piliavan and Piliavin (1972)—subjects witness a staged emergency on a subway; Milgram (1969)—letters are dropped in various locations; Milgram (1970)—asking to enter home and use telephone; Zimbardo (1969)—filming of subjects who have contact with abandoned automobiles; Schaps (1972)—experimenter's accomplice rejecting whatever the shoe salesman shows her during busy store hours; and Abelson and Miller (1967)—subjects are personally insulted. The summaries that appeared in Silverman (1975, p. 765) were used verbatim to describe the methods to the subjects. These summaries are reproduced in the following section.

Summaries of Nonreactive Methods—
Taken from Silverman (1975)

1. Experimenters, walking singly or in pairs, ask politely for either 10¢ or 20¢ from passerby, sometimes offering an explanation for why they need the money (Latané, 1970).

2. The experimenter comes to a home, says that he has misplaced the address of a friend who lives nearby, and asks to use the phone. If the party admits him, he pretends to make the call (Milgram, 1970).

3. Automobiles, parked on streets, look as if they were abandoned. (License plates are removed and hoods are raised.) Experimenters hide in nearby buildings and film people who have any contact with the cars (Zimbardo, 1969).

4. A female and a confederate experimenter visit shoe stores at times when there are more customers than salesmen. One of them is wearing a shoe with a broken heel. She rejects whatever the salesman shows her. The confederate, posing as a friend of the customer, surreptitiously takes notes on the salesman's behavior (Schaps, 1972).

5. Housewives are phoned. The caller names a fictitious consumer's group that he claims to represent and interviews them about the soap products they use for a report in a "public service publication," which is also given a fictitious name. Several days later the experimenter calls again and asks if the housewives would allow five or six men into their homes to "enu-

merate and classify" all of their household products for another report in the same publication. If the party agrees, the caller says he is just collecting names of willing people at present and that she will be contacted if it is decided to use her in the survey. No one is contacted again (Freedman & Fraser, 1966).

6. People sitting alone on park benches are asked to be interviewed by an experimenter who gives the name of a fictitious survey research organization that he claims to represent. At the beginning of the interview, the experimenter asks a person sitting nearby, who is actually a confederate, if he would mind answering the questions at the same time. The confederate responds with opinions that are clearly opposite those of the subject and makes demeaning remarks about the subject's answers; for example, "that's ridiculous"; "that's just the sort of thing you'd expect to hear in this park" (Abelson & Miller, 1967).

7. A person walking with cane pretends to collapse in a subway car. "Stage blood" trickles from his mouth. If someone approaches the victim, he allows the party to help him to his feet. If no one approaches before the trains slows to a stop, another experimenter, posing as a passenger, pretends to do so and both leave the train (Piliavin & Piliavin, 1972).

8. Letters, stamped and addressed to fictitious organizations at the same post office box number, are dropped in various locations, as if they were lost on the way to being mailed. Some are placed under automobile windshield wipers with a penciled note saying "found near car" (Milgram, 1969).

Four of the eight summaries were described to each subject. Half of the subjects heard descriptions of the first four experiments described above, and the other half heard the second four.

Procedure

Upon randomly choosing a subject, the interviewer approached the subject, introduced him/herself, and asked if the subject would be willing to take 10 minutes to answer some questions for a psychology class project. Subjects were told that the interview would be totally anonymous. If the subject agreed or at least tentatively agreed to be

interviewed, the interviewer went on to explain by stating:

> What we would like to do is simply find out how people like yourself feel about certain procedures that are sometimes used in research in social psychology, particularly that research which is conducted in natural settings using people like yourself as subjects. As I describe these various procedures to you, try to put yourself in the position of a subject in one of these experiments and judge as best and honestly as you can how you would feel about being a subject in such an experiment. Keep in mind as you hear each description that the purpose in each of these experiments is simply to observe the reactions of the subject. For each question I ask you, answer "no," "not sure," or "yes."

The interviewer then read the descriptions of four nonreactive methods to the subject. After reading each description, the interviewer asked a series of questions regarding legal and ethical aspects of the method. These questions included: (1) If you discovered that you had been a subject in this experiment, would you feel that you had been harassed or annoyed? (2) If you discovered that you had been a subject in this experiment, would you feel that your privacy had been invaded? (3) Do you feel that such an experiment is unethical or immoral? (4) Would you mind being a subject in such an experiment? (5) Do you feel that psychologists should be doing such an experiment? (6) Is doing such an experiment justified by its contribution to our scientific knowledge of behavior? (7) Does such an experiment lower your trust in social scientists and their work? (8) Do you feel that the psychologist's actions in this experiment are against the law? (9) If you discovered that the psychologist's actions were illegal, would you attempt to see a lawyer, and press charges? (10) If you discovered that you had been a subject in this experiment, would you feel that trespassing had been committed?

After all four descriptions had been read and responded to, five more general questions were asked. These were: (1) Should psychologists stop deceiving the public as they do in these experiments? (2) Should the public protest against the actions that were described in these examples? (3) Is it all right for social scientists to deceive the public? (4) Is it all right for politicians to deceive the public? (5) Is it all right for the military to deceive the public?

Following the completion of these questions, the subject was thanked for participating in the study and the interview was completed.

RESULTS

The results of the interviews are presented in Tables 1 and 2. No systematic sex, age, or locale differences were found, so, consequently, the data were collapsed over these variables for all other analyses. Table 1 shows the percentages of subjects responding "no," "not sure," or "yes" to each question for each nonreactive method. Table 2 shows the results of the subjects' responses to the five general questions. As can be seen in Table 1, the largest percentage of subjects who expressed feelings of harassment responded to the Schaps (1972) study (72%). Subjects felt least harassed by the Zimbardo (1969) study (24%). For four of the eight studies, a majority of the subjects expressed feelings of harassment. For the other four studies, the minority expressing such feelings was quite sizable, being as high as 44% in one case. With regard to feelings of invasion of privacy, none of the studies elicited such feelings from the majority of the subjects, with the largest percentage (47%) being in the case of Freedman and Fraser (1966), followed closely by 46% for the Milgram (1970) study. The lowest percentage (11%) was in the case of Milgram (1969). Clearly these are noteworthy minorities, however. Also, the majority of subjects did not see the studies as being unethical, although the percentages in several cases were considerable, with the highest being 47% for Piliavin and Piliavin (1972) followed by 43% for Latané (1970). The lowest such percentage was 18% for Zimbardo (1969). When asked if they would mind being subjects in the experiments, a majority said they would mind in five of the experiments, the highest percentage being 65% for Schaps (1972), the lowest 28% for Zimbardo (1969).

When the subjects were asked if psychologists should be doing such an experiment, the responses were much more varied than on the questions thus far. For two of the studies, half or more of the subjects said that psychologists should not be doing the experiment. These two studies were Latané (1970) (54%) and Piliavin and Piliavin (1972) (50%). For the remaining studies, rather large minorities felt that the experiments should not be done. Responses were again quite varied with regard to whether the experiment was justified by its contribution to our scientific knowledge of behavior. For none of the studies did a majority of the subjects say it was not justified. However, neither did a majority in any case feel the experiment was justified. In general, rather substantial minorities saw the experiments as not being justified. A large majority of the subjects felt that the experi-

ments did not lower their trust in social scientists and their work. Still, a respectable number of people in many cases felt the experiments did lower their trust, with the highest percentage being 37% for Piliavin and Piliavin (1972). When asked if the methods were against the law, very few subjects in general perceived them as such, with the highest percentage being 26% for Milgram (1970). Given that the methods were known to be illegal, a majority of the subjects in each case said they would not see a lawyer, with the largest percentage (73%) being in the case of Schaps (1972). Nevertheless, sizable minorities of subjects, as high as 32% for Piliavin and Piliavin (1972), said they would see a lawyer. For three of the methods, subjects were asked if they felt the experimenter committed trespassing. Rather large minorities of subjects felt this to be the case, with 40% indicating this for Milgram (1970), 33% for Freedman and Fraser (1966), and 14% for Schaps (1972).

It is also possible to get some indication of which particular methods were most or least acceptable overall. To do this, the methods were ranked from the most to the least objectionable for each interview question. Each method's mean ranking was then computed. The methods as listed in Table 1 are in precisely this order, from most to least objectionable. As can be seen, Latané's (1970) method was the least acceptable while Zimbardo's (1969) method was the most acceptable.

As can be seen in Table 2, responses to whether psychologists should stop deceiving the public were consistent with the responses presented thus far. Thirty-eight percent of the subjects felt that such deception should be stopped. A rather sizable minority (21%) were uncertain on the issue. As to whether the public should protest against the methods, again 38% felt that they should. A rather interesting comparison can be made for the final three questions. While 91% and 81% said it was not all right for politicians and the military, respectively, to deceive the public, 61% believed that it was not all right for social scientists to do so.

. . .

DISCUSSION

The results of the present study pose somewhat of a dilemma. That is, one can make several opposing conclusions from the data. We will point out these possible interpretations and let debate take its course.

It seems reasonable that one possible interpre-

TABLE 1. SUBJECTS' RESPONSES TO QUESTIONS ASKED ABOUT EACH NONREACTIVE METHOD

						QUESTION				
ANSWER	FEEL HA-RASSED?	PRIVACY IN-VADED?	UNETHI-CAL?	MIND BEING SUBJECT?	DO SUCH EXPERI-MENT?	JUSTIFIED BY SCIEN-TIFIC CON-TRIBU-TION?	LOWER TRUST?	AGAINST LAW	SEE LAW-YER?	TRESPASS-ING COM-MITTED?
				Latané (1970)—Asking for Money						
No	40	56	46	38	54	48	62	57	64	—
Not sure	3	1	1	8	27	23	9	23	10	—
Yes	57	43	43	54	19	29	29	20	26	—
				Piliavin & Piliavin (1972)—Blood Study						
No	55	81	43	42	50	38	59	60	58	—
Not sure	2	1	10	5	18	36	4	19	11	—
Yes	43	18	47	53	32	27	37	20	32	—
				Milgram (1970)—Ask to Enter Home and Use Telephone						
No	51	46	48	46	46	41	64	55	60	48
Not sure	5	8	15	10	22	24	5	19	21	12
Yes	44	46	38	44	31	35	31	26	19	40
				Freedman & Fraser (1966)—Foot-in-the-Door Technique						
No	45	50	53	41	36	38	69	59	58	63
Not sure	1	3	12	6	30	30	10	24	13	4
Yes	54	47	35	53	34	32	22	17	29	33
				Abelson & Miller (1967)—Personal Insult Study						
No	28	48	42	40	35	30	68	73	68	—
Not sure	9	7	16	9	28	27	7	12	19	—
Yes	63	44	42	52	37	43	25	15	14	—
				Schaps (1972)—Shoe Store Study						
No	20	60	52	28	49	42	68	75	73	72
Not sure	8	14	16	8	20	16	11	18	16	14
Yes	72	26	31	65	31	41	21	8	10	14
				Milgram (1969)—Lost Letter Technique						
No	70	87	68	54	34	37	70	75	69	—
Not sure	3	2	8	8	33	31	10	15	10	—
Yes	26	11	24	38	32	32	20	10	22	—
				Zimbardo (1969)—Abandoned Automobiles Study						
No	72	74	65	65	22	18	78	75	72	—
Not sure	5	5	16	6	28	32	5	18	18	—
Yes	24	21	18	28	49	49	17	6	10	—

Note: All data are given as percentages. Number of subjects on which percentages are based ranges from 79 to 93 . . .

TABLE 2. SUBJECTS' RESPONSES TO GENERAL QUESTIONS

	QUESTION				
RESPONSE	STOP DECEIVING PUBLIC?	PUBLIC PROTEST?	ALL RIGHT FOR SOCIAL SCIENTISTS TO DECEIVE PUBLIC?	ALL RIGHT FOR POLITICIANS TO DECEIVE PUBLIC?	ALL RIGHT FOR MILITARY TO DECEIVE PUBLIC?
No	41	45	61	91	81
Not sure	21	17	13	6	10
Yes	38	38	26	2	9

Note: All data are given as percentages. Percentages based on $N = 172$ . . .

tation of the present data is that the public generally does not negatively view the use of nonreactive methods. Such an interpretation, of course, must be based on the premise that one's concern is with what the "majority" of the public feels. That is, this view dictates that if the majority of the public views a particular technique as acceptable, then we will consider that technique to be as such. The implicit assumption here is that no technique will be acceptable to all potential subjects and that we must therefore use a "majority rule" criterion for deciding the acceptability of a particular procedure.

The data do in fact indicate that in many cases the majority of subjects did not react negatively to the unobtrusive measures. Four of the eight studies were seen as harassing by a majority of the subjects, but in no case did a majority see the procedures as invading their privacy or as unethical. In only one case did a strong majority indicate that they would mind being a subject in the experiment, while in four other cases a little more than half of the subjects indicated that they would mind being a subject. In only two cases did half or more of the subjects say the experiment should not be done. In no case did a majority feel that an experiment was unjustified by its scientific contribution, and usually strong majorities indicated that the experiments did not lower their trust in social scientists. For experiments in which it is conceivable that trespassing may have been committed, less than a majority felt this to be the case. Interestingly, a majority of the subjects did not perceive any of the methods as illegal, and more interesting, they indicated that they would not see a lawyer even if such illegality existed.

Furthermore, less than a majority felt that deception in nonreactive research should be stopped or that a protest should be mounted against such research. Also, while most subjects felt that it was not all right for social scientists, politicians, and the military to deceive the public, more leeway was given to social scientists.

If one does indeed interpret the results in terms of "public acceptance" of nonreactive techniques, then these results are obviously contrary to what some believe to be the case. It is probably true that one reason for having ethical guidelines in the first place is that if we did not, subjects would react negatively. It is interesting, then, that the picture painted thus far is much different than that presented by Warwick (1975), who feels that nonreactive research is highly frowned upon by the public and is contributing to a growing feeling of mistrust in America. Apparently, there is still some feeling among the public that anything done for the sake of science is legitimate. Furthermore, the present findings could be viewed as being consistent with many findings cited earlier which show that subjects are not as concerned about ethical issues as we might think.

A totally different interpretation of the present results is perhaps more appealing to many readers. This interpretation puts less of an emphasis on the majority and instead emphasizes the substantial minorities in many cases who view the procedures negatively. Such an approach has as its basic premise the belief that if *any* number of subjects find a particular technique unacceptable, then such a technique will indeed be classified as such. The extreme case, of course, with such an interpretation is when only one individual objects to a given technique. This may in fact be rare, but nevertheless this approach assumes that only one negative response is enough to cause concern. It takes only one person to publicly protest the use of nonreactive methods or only one person to take us to court to convince us that a negative response can be devastating. With this attitude in mind, the data of the present study are indeed quite alarming. Obviously, many subjects were quite distressed with the techniques. More than one in three of our subjects felt that social scientists should stop deceiving the public and that a public protest should be mounted. It is interesting to speculate as to why such protests have not occurred. Presumably, public awareness of the extent of usage of nonreactive techniques is not great. As public awareness does increase, however, 38% of the potential subject population is more than enough to lay to rest any ambitions social scientists may once have had regarding the use of nonreactive methods. In general, one might take the following attitude. Can we justify using a nonreactive measure when we know that maybe one third or more of our subjects would be distressed if they were aware of what we were doing and probably would not want to be in the experiment? After all, we must remember that they have not entered a contractual relationship with us. Subjects may also view our laboratory procedures as unacceptable, but at least there they would be aware that they were being studied. If the researcher chooses to proceed with the knowledge that one third of the subjects would object, the risks involved are unlikely to be precisely known but can be potentially very costly, especially in terms of legal repercussions to the researcher.

The data of the present study were intentionally collected in such a way as to minimize feelings of obligation or pressure to respond in certain ways. There is always the possibility, however, that subjects would react differently toward these nonreactive methods if they were actually subjects in one of the described experiments. Such a possibility could be investigated by debriefing subjects in a nonreactive experiment and asking them their reactions to the experiment. It might be that in such a case, subjects would react even more positively than they did in the present study if they were told the rationale for the experiment. Or on the other hand, the immediacy of the situation and the knowledge that they had been deceived might result in more negative reactions. Data on this issue are clearly needed.

The implied theme of this article is that in the future, investigators using nonreactive methods should take into consideration the public's attitudes toward that method. . . . Presently, most researchers are likely to consider only their own views or those of their peers without considering the views of their potential subjects. By finding out from the subject pool the aspects of the method that are objectionable, the researcher can explore other viable alternatives, possibly even with the aid of members of the subject pool. Not only would

such a procedure keep the researcher from using an objectionable technique but it also would allow him or her to use a particular method without feelings of guilt or the burden of having to justify the use of the method to others. The APA Committee on Ethical Standards in Psychological Research (1973) has noted that disguised field experimentation "can be considered only with misgivings, for which the help of ethical consultants will be needed to resolve" (p. 33). We simply feel that potential subjects should have the opportunity to participate in this consulting process.

The use of potential subjects as consultants raises several issues. One issue is how much weight should be given to the public view. For instance, it might be that the investigator and his or her peers feel that the use of a particular method is justified by the scientific contribution made by the study. Potential subjects, on the other hand, may object to the technique. What, then, does the experimenter do? We have suggested that the public view be taken into account, but how much weight it should be given is a matter for debate.

A second issue that has already been dealt with is the problem of what percentage of the public must object to a particular method before we conclude that the general public attitude toward that technique is "negative." That is, assuming that the public opinion is weighted heavily in the investigator's decision, what percentage of subjects expressing a negative attitude is enough to veto use of the method? Must it be a majority? 5%? Is one negative response enough? Again, this is not an issue with an easy solution and we do not pretend to have the answer.

. . .

In summary, an experimenter, in deciding whether to use a particular nonreactive technique, has recourse to several bodies of ethical consultants. We have suggested that the general public be considered as one such consultant by gauging the public attitude toward the method. The results of the present study can be used as a gauge for investigators wanting to use methods similar to those described to our subjects. If a method different from the ones described here is desired, the experimenter should conduct his or her own survey to determine its viability. Given that ethical guidelines are constructed to protect the rights of subjects, we feel that the most ethical study is one in which subjects themselves have had a voice in determining its methods.

REFERENCES

Abelson, R. P., & Miller, J. C. Negative persuasion via personal insult. *Journal of Experimental Social Psychology*, 1967, *3*, 321–33.

Adair, J. G. *The human subject: The social psychology of the psychological experiment*. Boston, Mass.: Little, Brown, 1973.

APA Committee on Ethical Standards in Psychological Research. *Ethical principles in the conduct of research with human participants*. Washington, D.C.: American Psychological Association, 1973.

Aronson, E., & Carlsmith, J. M. Experimentation in social psychology. In G. Lindzey & E. Aronson (Eds.), *The handbook of social psychology* (Vol. 2). Reading, Mass.: Addison-Wesley, 1968.

Bickman, L., & Henchy, T. (Eds.). *Beyond the laboratory: Field research in social psychology*. New York: McGraw-Hill, 1972.

Campbell, D. T. Prospective: Artifact and control. In R. Rosenthal & R. L. Rosnow (Eds.), *Artifact in behavioral research*. New York: Academic Press, 1969.

Crano, W. D., & Brewer, M. B. *Principles of research in social psychology*. New York: McGraw-Hill, 1973.

Freedman, J. L., & Fraser, S. C. Compliance without pressure: The foot-in-the-door technique. *Journal of Personality and Social Psychology*, 1966, *4*, 195–202.

Gergen, K. J. The codification of research ethics: Views of a doubting Thomas. *American Psychologist*, 1973, *28*, 907–12.

Holmes, D. S., & Bennett, D. H. Experiments to answer questions raised by the use of deception in psychological research: I. Role playing as an alternative to deception; II. Effectiveness of debriefing after a deception; III. Effect of informed consent on deception. *Journal of Personality and Social Psychology*, 1974, *29*, 358–67.

Johnson, D. W. (Ed.). *Contemporary social psychology*. Philadelphia, Pa.: Lippincott, 1973.

Kelman, H. C. Human use of human subjects: The problem of deception in social psychological experiments. *Psychological Bulletin*, 1967, *67*, 1–11.

Latané, B. Field studies of altruistic compliance. *Representative Research in Social Psychology*, 1970, *1*, 49–60.

McGuire, W. J. Some impending reorientations in social psychology. *Journal of Experimental Social Psychology*, 1967, *3*, 124–39.

McGuire, W. J. Theory-oriented research in natural settings: The best of both worlds for social psychology. In M. Sherif & C. W. Sherif (Eds.), *Interdisciplinary relationships in the social sciences*. Chicago, Ill.: Aldine, 1969.

Milgram, S. The lost-letter technique. *Psychology Today*, June 1969, pp. 30–33, 66, 68.

Milgram, S. The experience of living in cities. *Science*, 1970, *167*, 1461–68.

Piliavin, J. A. & Piliavin, I. M. Effect of blood on reactions to a victim. *Journal of Personality and Social Psychology*, 1972, *23*, 353–61.

Schaps, E. Cost, dependency and helping. *Journal of Personality and Social Psychology*, 1972, *21*, 74–78.

Silverman, I. Nonreactive methods and the law. *American Psychologist*, 1975, *30*, 764–69.

Silverman, I., Shulman, A. D., & Wiesenthal, D. L. Effects of deceiving and debriefing psychological subjects on performance in later experiments. *Journal of Personality and Social Psychology*, 1970, *14*, 203–12.

Warwick, D. P. Social scientists ought to stop lying. *Psychology Today*, February 1975, pp. 38, 40, 105–6.

Zimbardo, P. The human choice: Individuation, reason and order versus deindividuation, impulse and chaos. In W. J. Arnold & D. Levine (Eds.), *Nebraska Symposium on Motivation* (Vol. 17). Lincoln: University of Nebraska Press, 1969.

ETHICAL ISSUES IN FIELD EXPERIMENTS

Ethical problems of a rather obvious nature arise in the experiments in which deception has potentially harmful consequences for the subject. Take, for example, the brilliant experiment by Mulder and Stemerding on the effects of threat on attraction to the group and need for strong leadership.[1] In this study—one of the very rare examples of an ex-

From Kelman, Herbert. Human use of human subjects: The problem of deception in social psychological experiments. *Psychological Bulletin*, 1967, 67, 2. Copyright © 1963 by The American Psychological Association and reprinted with permission of author and The American Psychological Association.

[1]M. Mulder and A. Stemerding, "Threat, Attraction to Group, and Need for Strong Leadership," *Human Relations*, 1963, *16*, 317–334.

periment conducted in a natural setting—independent food merchants in a number of Dutch towns were brought together for group meetings, in the course of which they were informed that a large organization was planning to open up a series of supermarkets in the Netherlands. In the High Threat condition, subjects were told that there was a high probability that their town would be selected as a site for such markets, and that the advent of these markets would cause a considerable drop in their business. On the advice of the executives of the shopkeepers' organizations, who had helped to arrange the group meetings, the investigators did not reveal the experimental manipulations to their subjects. I have been worried about these Dutch merchants ever since I heard about this study for the first time. Did some of them go out of business in anticipation of the heavy competition? Do some of them have an anxiety reaction every time they see a bulldozer? Chances are that they soon forgot about this threat (unless, of course, supermarkets actually did move into town) and that it became just one of the many little moments of anxiety that must occur in every shopkeeper's life. Do we have a right, however, to add to life's little anxieties and to risk the possibility of more extensive anxiety purely for the purposes of our experiments, particularly since deception deprives the subject of the opportunity to choose whether or not he wishes to expose himself to the risks that might be entailed?

PROJECTS

Name _____

Date _____

2.1: WHAT IS THE ETHICAL PROBLEM?

This exercise presents various ethical problems raised by research in social psychology. As you evaluate each of the studies summarized below, consider whether the potential findings were important enough (either theoretically or practically) to justify the procedure that was used. In a class discussion, compare your responses with those of your fellow students.

A. After the subjects had performed an experimental task, the investigator made it clear, through words and gestures, that the experiment was over and that he would now "like to explain what this has been all about so you'll have some idea of why you were doing this." The explanation was false and was designed to serve as a basis for the true experimental manipulation, which involved asking subjects to serve as the experimenter's accomplices. The task of the accomplice was to tell the next subject that the experiment in which he had just participated had been interesting and enjoyable. (It was, in fact, a rather boring experience.) He or she was also asked to be on call on unspecified future occasions when his or her services as accomplice might be needed because "the regular fellow couldn't make it, and we had a subject scheduled." These newly recruited accomplices were, of course, the true subjects, and the subjects were the experimenter's true accomplices. For their services as accomplices, the true subjects were paid in advance. Half of them received $1; the other half, $20. However, when they completed their tasks, the investigators asked them to return the money. (Festinger, L., and Carlsmith, J. M. Cognitive consequences of forced compliance. *Journal of Abnormal and Social Psychology*, 1959, *58*, 203–10.)

1. What are the ethical problems raised by the study?

2. Was the dignity or privacy of the subjects endangered? If so, how?

B. Bramel led male undergraduates to believe that they were homosexually aroused by photographs of men. Bergin gave subjects of both sexes discrepant information about their level of masculinity or feminity. In one experimental condition, that information was presumably based on an elaborate series of psychological tests in which the subjects had participated. In all three studies, the deception was explained to the subject at the end of the experiment. (Bramel, D. A Dissonance theory approach to defensive projection. *Journal of Abnormal and Social Psychology*, 1962, 64, 121–29. Selection of a target for defensive projection. *Journal of Abnormal and Social Psychology*, 1963, 66, 318–24. Bergin, A. E. The effect of dissonant persuasive communications on changes in a self-referring attitude. *Journal of Personality*, 1962, 30, 423–38.)

1. What ethical problems do you see in these studies?

2. Was there a danger to the subjects' physical or psychological well-being? If so, what was it?

Name _____

Date _____

C. The subject was led to believe that he was participating in a learning study and was instructed to administer increasingly severe shocks to another person, who, after a while, began to protest vehemently. In fact, the victim was the experimenter's accomplice and did not receive any shocks. Depending on the conditions, sizable proportions of the subjects obeyed the experimenter's instructions and continued to shock the other person up to the maximum level, which they believed to be extremely painful. (Milgram, S. Behavioral study of obedience. *Journal of Abnormal and Social Psychology,* 1963, *67,* 371–78. Some conditions of obedience and disobedience to authority. *Human Relations,* 1965, *18,* 57–76.)

1. What are some of the ethical problems posed by this research?

2. How stressful do you think the experience was for the subject? How would you assess the level of stress?

D. In an experiment designed to study the establishment of a conditioned response in a situation that is traumatic but not painful, the experimenters used a drug to induce a temporary interruption of respiration in their subjects. "This has no permanently harmful physical consequences but is nonetheless a severe stress which is not in itself painful. . . . The subjects' reports confirmed that this was a "horrific" experience for them. All the subjects . . . said that they thought they were dying." Of course, the subjects, "male alcoholic patients who volunteered for the experiment when they were told that it was connected with a possible therapy for alcoholism," were not warned in advance about the effect of the drug, because that information would have reduced the traumatic impact of the experience. (Campbell, D., Sanderson, R. E., & Laverty, S. Characteristics of a conditioned response in human subjects during extinction trials following a single traumatic conditioning trial. *Journal of Abnormal and Social Psychology*, 1964, *68*, 627–39.)

1. What ethical problems does this study raise?

2. What difficulties would be introduced if the experimenter first obtained the subjects' informed consent?

2.2: EVALUATING ETHICAL ISSUES

This project presents you with a complex task in order to help you understand the spirit in which social scientists approach their research. It involves a rather detailed description of a research program carried out in military settings by Berkum, Bialek, Kern, and Yagi ("Experimental Studies of Psychological Stress in Man," *Psychological Monographs*, 1962, *76*, 15). This program investigated cognitive stress in general and the effect of battle stress on performance in particular. The specific question addressed was: Is there a deterioration of performance during combat?

A. Sixty-six men who were passengers aboard an airplane served (without their prior knowledge) as subjects in the study. (All were in their first eight weeks of army basic training.) When the plane had reached an altitude of 5,000 feet, subjects saw that one propeller had stopped turning and heard about other malfunctions over the intercom; they were then informed directly that there was an emergency. A simulated pilot-to-tower conversation was provided to the subjects over their earphones to support the deception. As the aircraft passed within sight of the airfield, subjects could see firetrucks and ambulances on the airstrip in apparent expectation of a crash-landing. After several minutes, the pilot ordered the plane steward to prepare the passengers for ditching in the nearby ocean because the landing gear would not function properly. This was a signal for the steward to administer the questionnaires (which was the test of impaired performance). The subjects were asked to fill out two forms: one, an emergency form, involving deliberately complicated directions for twenty-three categories of items, that included a description of, and instructions for, disposition of the individual's personal possessions in case of death; the other, emergency instructions that had twelve multiple-choice items testing retention of airborne emergency instructions that all subjects had been required to read as a standard operating procedure before the flight. These papers were supposed to be put in a waterproof container and jettisoned before the aircraft came down on the ocean. After a specific time had elapsed, the aircraft made a safe landing at the airport. Blood and urine samples were then collected from all subjects. A postexperimental inquiry indicated that subjects suffered various degrees of anxiety about the possibility of death or injury. (See next page.)

What ethical problems does the study raise? That is, do you think that the study involved undue or unnecessary risks, invasion of privacy, disrespect for human dignity, and/or physical, physiological, or social harm? Was the requirement of informed consent fulfilled? Do you think that the beneficial outcomes of the research outweigh the risks to which the participants were subjected? Did the use of deception involve a particular ethical problem?

B. In this study, there was no threat of injury to the subject himself. Rather, he was made to feel responsible for an injury to someone he knew or with whom he had been working. (This, by the way, proved to be the most stressful situation for the subjects.) Army trainees were brought individually to an isolated area on the edge of a military post. They were told that a crew was wiring some explosives in the canyon below but needed a remote control circuit to blow up a charge of TNT. The subjects were then told how to build the circuit and to throw the switch. Each was also told that his radio was the only communication he and the crew in the canyon had with the army base. After the subject threw the switch and set off a five-pound charge of TNT, he heard over the intercom that someone was hurt by the explosion and that it was his responsibility to get help. But when he tried to transmit his call for help, he discovered that his radio did not work. Impaired performance was measured by how long it took subjects to repair the radio. Blood and urine samples were collected from the subjects after the termination of the experimental situation. (See next page.)

Name _____

Date _____

C. Put yourself in the place of the scientist who wants to find out whether stress really impairs performance. This is a very important issue. For example, it is vital to understand and thus be able to anticipate the responses of people who work in highly stressful jobs (e.g., police, hospital emergency room staff, firemen). How would you study the general issue of the effect of stress on performance and yet avoid the ethical issues you have raised in your answers in the previous questions?

ATTITUDE AND BEHAVIOR CHANGE

3

Throughout our lives, we influence other people and are influenced by them. Sometimes, we attempt to change a person's attitude. For example, we may try to change someone's opinion about the trustworthiness of a particular politician, the value of a proposed law, or the usefulness of a new product. At other times, we may seek to influence a person's behavior. For example, we may try to persuade someone to vote for one candidate rather than another, to buy a certain gift, or to join us for a cup of coffee. However, whether we focus our efforts on changing attitudes or behavior, we usually assume that the two go together. Thus, if we succeed in changing someone's attitude toward a political candidate, we expect corresponding changes in his or her behavior toward that candidate (votes, campaign contributions, endorsements, and so on). The link between attitudes and behavior is presumed to be a causal one. Furthermore, in most cases, it is believed that internal attitudes cause and direct external behavior.

Social psychologists have done a vast amount of research into the nature of attitudes, their development, and the ways in which they change. Various definitions of *attitude* have been proposed, all of which assume a consistency between attitudes and behavior. Indeed, some definitions include behavior as one of the components of attitude. Several models of attitude formation and change have been developed, some of which also support the common-sense view that changes in attitudes cause corresponding changes in behavior. However, other theories (most notably, cognitive dissonance and self-perception) argue the reverse: that changes in behavior cause corresponding changes in attitudes. The practical implications of these theories are obviously quite different because they suggest opposite approaches to bringing about change in others.

ON THE CONSISTENCY BETWEEN ATTITUDES AND BEHAVIOR: LOOK TO THE METHOD OF ATTITUDE FORMATION

DENNIS T. REGAN AND RUSSELL FAZIO

It has been a longstanding assumption that the behavior of people is consistent with their attitudes. If attitudes cause and direct behavior, then it follows that the two should be highly correlated; however, such high correlations have not been readily found. This inconsistency has led some researchers to challenge the concept of attitude and argue for its abandonment altogether. Other researchers have looked for alternative explanations for the low level of attitude–behavior consistency: For example, there may be problems in measuring attitudes accurately, or it may be that one attitude is linked to many different behaviors, rather than just a single action (and vice versa). In this article, Regan and Fazio develop another argument, namely, that there are certain attitudes that are strongly linked to behavior, while certain others are not. The critical difference, they say, lies in how the attitudes were initially formed: If they are based on direct experience, then there should be greater attitude–behavior consistency. To test this idea, the authors conducted studies in both the field and the laboratory.

Throughout the history of social psychology, the study of the nature, determinants, and consequences of people's attitudes has occupied a central, often dominant position. Indeed, Thomas and Znaniecki (1918) defined social psychology as the study of attitudes, and in the half-century since, a tremendous quantity of research on attitudes has been published. . . . There were, of course, many reasons for this fierce concentration of activity, including the early development of sophisticated measuring tools, and the emergence of provocative and competing theoretical positions. But a key factor underlying this activity also seems to have been the widely shared assumption that attitudes occupy a crucial position in the mental makeup of the individual, and that, in particular, they serve as a powerful energizer and director of overt behavior. It was assumed, at least implicitly, that to understand a person's attitudes is often to understand and be able to predict accurately his behavior. This notion that an individual's overt behavior springs reliably from his attitudes is nicely reflected in the influential definition of attitudes proposed by Allport (1935): "An attitude is a mental and neural state of readiness, organized through experience, *exerting a directive or dynamic influence upon the individual's response to all objects and situations with which it is related*" (emphasis ours).

Although there were early skeptics who challenged the notion that there exists a simple predictive relationship between attitudes and behavior, it was not until the last decade that this assumption came under careful conceptual and empirical scrutiny. It is safe to say that this attention has resulted in the refutation of the notion that there invariably exists a strong, simple, cross-situational relationship between a person's measured attitudes and his subsequent overt behavior. For example, Wicker (1969) did an exten-

sive review of the empirical literature on attitude–behavior consistency, citing studies in a wide variety of settings, with many different types of attitude, overt behavior, empirical methodology, and subject population, and concluded that "taken as a whole, these studies suggest that it is considerably more likely that attitudes will be unrelated or only slightly related to overt behaviors than that attitudes will be closely related to actions" (p. 65). He found "little evidence to support the postulated existence of stable, underlying attitudes within the individual which influence both his verbal expressions and his actions" (p. 75).

Five years earlier, Festinger (1964) had been unable to uncover any evidence whatever that attitude *change* produced consistent behavior change. This contrasts sharply with the wealth of evidence produced by both dissonance theorists and self-perception theorists that an individual's attitudes are very easily changed by inducing him to engage in attitude-discrepant behavior under specifiable conditions. All of this negative evidence led some to a "valley of theoretical despond," wherein attitudes are seen as mere epiphenomena—after-the-fact interpretations or justifications for behavior which have little or no implication for future behavior. Attitudes toward an object did not seem to have any consistent effect on subsequent behavior toward that object; whatever minimal relationship might exist between attitudes and behavior seemed instead to result from behavior change causing attitude change.

Nevertheless, it would be premature to banish the concept of attitude from social psychology on these grounds. As Kelman (1974) has recently pointed out, there is other empirical evidence, largely deriving from survey studies, that does demonstrate a strong relationship between attitudes and behavior. For example, high consistency has been documented between political attitudes and political participation of various sorts, and between attitudes toward racial and national groups and association with members of those groups. . . .

Thus, while the predictive relationship between attitudes and behavior does not appear to be as simple or as general as traditionally thought, impressive attitude–behavior consistency is sometimes observed. The question facing researchers is, therefore, no longer *whether* an individual's attitudes can be used to predict his overt behavior, but *when*. The task is to specify those variables which determine whether an observed attitude-behavior relationship will be relatively strong or weak. Already, evidence has been produced that the relationship is responsive to certain aspects of the situation in which the behavior is observed, a good example being the work on the presence or absence of situational constraints and social distance. In addition, qualities of the individual have been suggested which might make him relatively likely or unlikely to act consistently with his attitudes, such as self-image as a "doer," the existence of other attitudes, the individual's competence to engage in a particular behavior, and others.

The research reported below was conducted to test the hypothesis that a crucial determinant of attitude–behavior consistency is the method by which the individual formed his attitude. As operationalized in most empirical research, an individual's attitude is inferred solely from the response he makes to a set of verbal questions. Attitude measures seldom if ever tap the experience on which the individual bases his responses; they are instead usually designed merely to assign him a score indicating relative favorability or unfavorability toward the attitude object in question. Thus, the very same attitude, as measured by most attitude scales, may have developed in a variety of ways. For example, a person's attitude may derive from direct behavioral experience with the object; it may have been produced by a persuasive communication from others; it may be an inference from information which the individual knows to be incomplete.

The basic notion tested here is that attitudes which have been formed and developed through direct personal interaction with the attitude object are maximally likely to influence, and therefore be good predictors of, subsequent behavior toward the attitude object. Attitudes formed on the basis of direct personal experience have a stronger dynamic relationship to subsequent behavior than those deriving from external sources. Like Kelman (1974), we view attitudes as linked with action both in their formation and in their consequences. Attitudes which have not yet been tested in the behavioral arena lack the stability and clarity which make them sometimes a determinant of action. This

implies that two individuals having the same attitude, as determined by conventional measures, may differ considerably in the degree to which they will act consistently with the attitude. The person whose attitude is a product of direct interaction with the attitude object will be more likely, in general, to behave consistently with that attitude than someone whose attitude was formed in a less direct manner.

A field study and a laboratory experiment are described below in support of this hypothesis. These investigations were conducted under very different circumstances, utilizing different attitudes, measurement techniques, and types of behavior. After describing both investigations, a more concrete explication of the rationale for the hypothesis will be presented, along with further suggestions about the precise mechanisms involved.

EXPERIMENT I

A housing crisis among incoming freshman at Cornell University in the Fall of 1973 provided the opportunity for the field study to be described. At Cornell, dormitory rooms on campus are allocated to students on a first-come, first-served basis. Applications by incoming freshman for dormitory facilities for the Fall of 1973 considerably outstripped both expectation and the number of rooms available. As a consequence, a large group of freshmen—those who had applied after the rooms ran out—arrived on campus with no place to stay. The University made serious attempts to arrange housing for these students, but many of them (thereafter referred to as the Temporary group) were forced to stay in temporary quarters, sometimes for as long as 2 months. Typically, these "quarters" consisted of a cot in the lounge of a dormitory. These students clearly suffered directly from the housing crisis and had direct interactional experience with the crisis.

In order to investigate attitude–behavior consistency among these students, a form (described below) was sent to them which included both a crude measure of their attitudes and an opportunity to engage in a variety of behaviors related to the crisis. The responses on these measures were compared with a group of freshmen (hereafter called the Permanent group) who knew about the crisis but had not experienced it because they had been assigned to permanent housing. The hypothesis was that the consistency between measured attitudes and overt behavior would be greater in the Temporary group than in the Permanent group.

METHOD

The form which was mailed to all students surveyed in this study ostensibly came from the "Research Group on Campus Housing," and purported to be an attempt to assess student reaction to the housing crisis; anonymity was assured (and maintained), and students were told that a copy of the results would be forwarded to the University Housing Office (it was). The form basically consisted of two parts. In the first part students expressed their attitudes toward the housing crisis and provided a bit of background information. In the second part, they were given an opportunity to take a variety of actions related to the crisis.

After indicating whether or not he had been provided with permanent housing upon arrival on campus, the subject indicated his attitude toward the crisis by responding to a set of seven questions constructed on an intuitive basis, each question being answered on a 5-point scale with all points labeled. In order, the subject indicated how tolerable or intolerable he found the crisis, how much he thought students had suffered because of it, how adequate he found the administration's efforts to alleviate the crisis, what priority he thought the administration should assign to solving the housing shortage, how concerned the administration was about the scarcity of on-campus housing for incoming students, and also responded to two items designed to assess the perceived effectiveness of taking action to move the administration on the issue. These two items asked to what degree the administration would consider student opinion in deciding how to handle the housing shortage and to what degree pressure is capable of changing the administration's housing policies.

Three 5-point items were appended to check on expected differences in knowledge and prior behavior between the Permanent and Temporary groups. The first asked the student how much contact he had with any administration official about the crisis, the second asked whether he had attempted to place any pressure on any administration official, and the final item asked the subject how informed he felt about the housing crisis.

The measure of overt behavior was taken from several subsequent pages which provided the opportunity for "a number of actions which you might want to take," any and all of which would also be forwarded to the housing office. "If any of the items appeal to you, please complete them (as many of them as you want) and return them along with your questionnaire. . . . Mail the questionnaire and only completed items." There were six behavioral opportunities provided. In order, the subject could sign a petition, including his address, asking the administration to take several concrete actions to alleviate the housing crisis, he could get other students to sign this petition, indicate interest in attending a meeting of the research group in the near future to discuss various proposals with dorm residents, indicate interest in joining a committee of dorm residents to investigate the housing situation and make recommendations, list in writing recommendations or suggestions for solving the housing crisis, and write a letter expressing opinions which the research group would forward to the housing office.

Subjects

The housing office provided the complete list of freshmen who had been assigned to temporary housing at the beginning of the Fall session, and forms were sent to all 111 students for whom a mailing address was provided. In addition, a list of 125 freshmen who had been assigned to permanent housing from the beginning, and whose experience of the housing crisis was thus indirect, was randomly drawn from the class list. Questionnaires were thus mailed out to a total of 236 freshmen. Five questionnaires in the Permanent group and three in the Temporary group were returned because students had moved to different dorms or left Cornell entirely. Questionnaires were returned by 64 of the 120 permanently housed subjects (53 percent), and by 61 of the 108 subjects in temporary housing (56 percent). Results from three subjects in the Temporary group and two from the Permanent group were not included in the analysis because of failure to complete all the attitudinal items. Thus, the total N for the study was 120, with 58 subjects (40 males and 18 females) in the Temporary group and 62 subjects (34 males and 28 females) in the Permanent group. All subjects in the Temporary group had originally been assigned to temporary housing: at the time of the study, which was run approximately 1 month after the beginning of school, 64 percent of the subjects in this group had found permanent housing.

RESULTS

Because there were no differences approaching significance between male and female subjects in means or standard deviations on any of the atti-

TABLE 1. ATTITUDE–BEHAVIOR CORRELATIONS IN EXPERIMENT I

DEPENDENT VARIABLE	GROUP	CRISIS ITEMS	PRESSURE ITEMS
Guttman scale score	Temporary	+.421	−.501
	Permanent	+.037	−.049

tudinal or behavioral items, and also no differences in the attitude–behavior relationship, the results for the two sexes have been combined in the analyses presented below. It will be recalled that three items were included in the questionnaire sent to all subjects in order to check on differences between the Temporary and Permanent groups in prior behavioral experience with and knowledge about the housing crisis. The results show clearly that the two groups differed as expected regarding their direct experience with the crisis. Subjects in the Temporary group reported having had more contact with administration officials about the crisis (Temporary $\bar{X}$ = 3.21. Permanent $\bar{X}$ = 1.18). Temporary subjects also reported significantly more attempts to pressure the administration to change housing policy ($\bar{X}$ = 1.59) than did Permanent subjects ($\bar{X}$ = 1.10). Finally, Temporary subjects said they felt more informed about the crisis ($\bar{X}$ = 3.16) than Permanent subjects ($\bar{X}$ = 2.81). In short, as expected, Temporary subjects reported more direct experience with the crisis than Permanent subjects, and indicated that they felt better informed about it.

There were seven items designed to assess individuals' attitudes toward the housing crisis. On all seven items, the scores of the Temporary and Permanent groups were very similar. On the other hand, there was a difference in the number of behavioral items engaged in. . . . On the average, subjects in the Temporary group completed 1.48 behavioral items, while Permanent group subjects completed 0.66 items.

We may now turn to the major results on the *consistency* between attitudes and behavior demonstrated by subjects in the two groups. In the Temporary group the seven attitudinal measures

together accounted for a statistically significant 31 percent of the behavioral variance. In the Permanent group, a nonsignificant 7 percent of the behavioral variance was accounted for by the attitude measures.

The results indicate that the slope of the attitude–behavior relationship in the two groups differed reliably; the consistency between expressed attitude and overt behavior was significantly greater in the Temporary group than in the Permanent group, as predicted. This finding is particularly encouraging in light of the admittedly crude and untested attitude and behavior scales utilized to take rapid advantage of a crisis over which the experimenters had no control.

Nevertheless, a correlational analysis was conducted in order to gain clearer insight into the predicted difference between the two groups in attitude–behavior consistency (see Table 1). There were two clusters of attitudinal items, which will be hereafter treated separately as Pressure items (the two items assessing the perceived effectiveness of pressure on the administration) and Crisis items (the first five items assessing evaluation of the crisis itself).

The behavioral measure so far computed—the simple number of items completed—is somewhat crude as it counts "easy" items such as signing the petition equally with more "difficult" items, such as writing a letter or agreeing to attend a committee meeting. Accordingly, a four-step Guttman scale (scored from 0 to 3) was constructed, and is defined in Table 2. . . . If we compute the correlations between the two types of attitude items and behavioral score on the Guttman scale, the difference between the Temporary and Permanent groups emerges more clearly. As Table 1 indi-

TABLE 2. THE GUTTMAN BEHAVIORAL SCALE

SCORE	BEHAVIOR
0	Perform no behavior
1	Sign petition and/or write one suggestion
2	Get others to sign petition and/or express interest in attending meeting
3	Express interest in joining committee and/or write two or more suggestions and/or write letter

cates, the correlation between attitudes and behavior is significantly stronger in the Temporary group on both the Crisis and the Pressure items.

The results of this study are impressively consistent. Despite the crudeness of the attitudinal and behavioral measures utilized, the relationship between attitudes and behavior was significantly stronger among subjects in the Temporary than in the Permanent group. We have suggested that this is because subjects in the Temporary group had a greater amount of prior direct personal experience with the attitude object (the housing crisis). The manipulation checks reported above indicated that, as expected, Temporary subjects did report more prior direct experience, in the form of contact with administration officials and attempts to pressure the administration to change housing policy. We find it difficult to provide a compelling alternative explanation for the difference in attitude–behavior consistency between the two groups.

Nevertheless, the laboratory experiment reported below was conducted for two reasons. First, it seemed desirable to examine the consistency and generality of the effect under different conditions. Thus, the consistency between measured attitudes and overt behavior was assessed using different materials and in a setting very different from that described above. Secondly, it was possible in this conceptual replication to assign subjects to conditions perfectly randomly, and to maintain all differences in procedure between experimental groups under specifiable control. The hypothesis remained exactly the same: Subjects who have had direct behavioral experience with an attitude object will demonstrate greater consistency between measured attitudes and subsequent overt behavior than subjects who have not had such experience.

EXPERIMENT II

In this experiment, all subjects were introduced to five different types of intellectual puzzle. Some subjects were introduced to the materials through direct behavioral interaction with them, by attempting to solve sample puzzles; others had similar information presented indirectly, through the experimenter's descriptions. Attitudes indicating interest in the five types of puzzle were then measured, and all subjects were given an opportunity in a free play situation to solve whatever types they chose, in whatever order. The dependent variable was the consistency between the subjects' expressed attitudes toward the puzzles

and their actual choice of puzzles in the free play situation. The prediction was that this consistency would be higher among subjects in the direct experience group than in the indirect experience group.

METHOD

Subjects

The subjects were 28 Cornell freshman volunteers who participated in individual sessions. They were randomly assigned to the two conditions, with eight males and six females in each condition. No subject indicated suspicion of the cover story or anticipated the hypothesis.

Procedure

Upon arrival at the laboratory, the experimenter told the subject that the purpose of the experiment was to obtain feedback on various types of problems that had been devised for an aptitude test on "observational skill and strategy development." A test was supposedly being devised by the psychology department in concert with the vocational guidance and testing center, which would be useful in predicting success at various academic majors and later careers. An instructional page reinforced this cover story, and indicated that the test was in its early stages and feedback was needed from students regarding whether the test possessed "face validity" . . . and interest value. Accordingly, the student would be exposed to several types of problems, different from those usually encountered on academic aptitude tests, and then provide ratings on these dimensions.

All subjects were then showed samples of five types of problems supposedly being considered for inclusion in the test. These were (1) Letter Series, in which a series of letters which form a pattern are presented, and the series must be completed by the subjects; (2) Spatial Perspective, in which the subject must decide which of four figures is a different view of a target figure; (3) Reasoning, in which the validity of a conclusion given certain premises must be assessed; (4) Figures, in which the subject must decide which of five choices accurately depicts how various target figures would appear if they were fit together to form a single figure; (5) Mazes, in which the subject must discover the path from a starting point to a finishing point. The puzzles were always presented in this order.

Manipulation

Subjects in the Direct Experience condition were given five pages of problems. Each page presented one type of problem, and consisted of instructions about how to do the problem and one or two unanswered examples of the type of problem. The subjects were simply told to "get acquainted" with each type by working the examples provided. Subjects in the Indirect Experience condition examined the same five pages in the same order, but they were never given an opportunity actually to work the problems. The problems had already been worked out, and the answers were clearly visible on the sheet. The experimenter showed the subject each page, explained the instructions for completing the problem, and went through the examples with the subject. An attempt was made to provide equivalent information and exposure time in the two conditions. Subjects in the Direct Experience condition were told to take "about five minutes" to solve the examples, and the experimenter monitored them such that they did take approximately five minutes on average. In the Indirect Experience condition, the experimenter spent five minutes demonstrating the example to the subject.

Dependent Measures

After exposure to the problem types and sample problems, all subjects were asked to rate each type of problem on two dimensions—face validity and interest value. The latter ratings provided the measure of the subject's attitude toward the problem types, and were indicated on an 11-point scale labeled at the extremes "extremely boring" (-5) and "extremely interesting" ($+5$). Instructions told the subjects to remember that "you are rating the type of item, not the specific example that was given of each type," and they wrote the integer describing their interest level next to the name of each type of problem. Following this, subjects also indicated on a single 11-point scale "how informed do you feel you are about the types of problems you just rated?"

Subjects were then told that the first phase of the experiment was over, and that they would now be given a chance actually to do some of the problems devised so far. Three separate pages of each type of problem were placed on the subject's desk, and he was told that he would have 15 minutes to work any of them he chose. He was told that this was a totally free situation, that he could work as many or as few problems as he chose in any order, and that this was not a test and he would not be assigned a test-ranking. These instructions were included to minimize the likelihood that subjects would choose only those problems which they thought they could easily solve, rather than those toward which they had a favorable attitude. The experimenter told the subject to number each particular problem as he did it, and then left the subject alone for 15 minutes. Thus, two behavioral measures were employed: the order in which the problems were worked, and the proportion of each type which was attempted. Following this "free play" session, the experiment was terminated and subjects were thoroughly debriefed.

RESULTS

Because there were no differences in means or correlations attributable to sex, the data from male and female subjects were combined. Two measures of attitude–behavior consistency were computed for each subject. A Spearman rank-order correlation was computed between the interest ratings (the attitude) and the order in which the types of problems were attempted (behavior). In addition, a rank-order correlation was also computed for each subject between the interest ratings and the proportion of each type attempted. These mean correlations for the two conditions are presented in Table 3. The prediction that attitude–behavior consistency would be greater in the Direct Experience group than in the Indirect Experience group was confirmed for both measures. Subjects who had formed their attitude on the basis of direct behavioral interaction with the attitude object showed significantly greater attitude–behavior

TABLE 3. AVERAGE ATTITUDE–BEHAVIOR CORRELATIONS IN EXPERIMENT II

CORRELATION	DIRECT CONDITION	INDIRECT CONDITION
r attitude, order	.514	.224
r attitude, proportion	.544	.199

consistency than did subjects whose attitude was formed indirectly, on the basis of information presented by the experimenter.

A number of subsidiary analyses were conducted to ascertain that the two groups did not differ in aspects which might have artifactually produced the difference in average attitude–behavior correlations. There was no difference between groups in the average amount of interest indicated across all five problem types. Nor were there differences in the amount of interest expressed in any of the five types of problems considered separately. Nevertheless, the attitude–behavior correlation in the Indirect Experience group could have been artifactually attenuated if the range of interest scores was particularly small and/or the number of tied interest rankings was particularly large. This might have occurred if the experimenter's demonstration of the problem types for this group was so unclear or undifferentiated that subjects thought they could not distinguish among the problems in terms of interest value. However, the two groups did not differ significantly either in the range of interest scores indicated, or in the number of interest score ties. Furthermore, there was no difference between groups in how informed subjects felt about the types of problems. . . .

GENERAL DISCUSSION

The two studies reported above share several features. In both, attitude–behavior consistency was investigated in two groups of subjects. One group had prior direct behavioral experience with the attitude object in question. The other group of subjects indicated similar attitudes, but had not had the same direct experience. In both studies, greater attitude–behavior consistency was demonstrated by the subjects who had direct prior action experience with the attitude object. This occurred despite considerable differences between the studies in the attitudes and behaviors investigated, measuring instruments, and procedure. Even though a person without prior behavioral experience with the attitude object may indicate an attitude in response to scale items, his attitude appears to be different in fundamental ways from that of a person who has had such experience. In what follows we shall try briefly to indicate what some of these differences may be.

We suggest that, when a person has had direct prior interactional experience with the attitude object, this results in an attitude which is more

clearly and confidently held. Such an attitude is likely to be more closely tied to an individual's self image than one formed through more indirect means. Faced with a situation providing a variety of action alternatives, the individual is likely to be both more highly motivated to act consistently with the attitude, and more confident of the likely consequences of his action.

There already exists considerable evidence, largely gathered by dissonance and self-perception theorists, that under certain conditions a person's overt behavior has powerful effects on his attitudes. These theorists have indicated a strong functional relationship between behavior and attitudes; we suggest a similar relationship between attitudes and behavior, and a parallel between some of the earlier literature and the results described above.

When a person engages in behavior discrepant with an earlier attitude, particularly under the self-revealing conditions of experienced responsibility for the consequences of the action, his attitude is likely to change so as to become more consistent with the behavior. In self-perception terms, the individual has clear grounds for an inference as to what his attitude actually is following such behavior. It is but one more step to the conclusion that such an attitude, being more confidently held, is likely to be more accurately predictive of *subsequent* behavior than an attitude formed through more indirect means.

This conclusion is consistent with the results of the "forced compliance" research which employed a behavioral dependent variable. For example, children who abstain from playing with an attractive toy under mild threat conditions (conditions designed to maximize attitude change toward derogation of the toy) have been subsequently found in free play situations actually to play less with the toy than children whose original abstention occurred under conditions less likely to produce attitude change. Similarly, children who engage in an attractive activity in order to achieve an external reward (a condition designed to produce attitude change toward devaluing the activity) have been found subsequently less likely to engage in the activity in a free play situation. In these cases, subsequent behavioral differences were observed which are parallel to the attitudinal effects produced by the individual's overt behavior. Unlike the present experiment, these studies varied the *conditions* under which prior behavioral experience occurred, rather than the *amount* of such experience. Nevertheless, the results are consistent with the basic notion offered here, that if one develops an attitude on the basis of direct behavioral experience, such an attitude is likely to be predictive of and consistent with subsequent behavior.

The research clearly indicates that the method of attitude formation is an important variable affecting attitude–behavior consistency. . . . But much future research will be required to isolate more precisely the mechanisms underlying the observed relationship. The very notion of "direct behavioral experience" itself demands refinement. Exactly which kinds of experience, under what conditions, will produce an attitude maximally likely to be predictive of subsequent behavior? Does direct behavioral experience produce information about the attitude object which is different from or greater than that which can be obtained by other means? Although in Experiment II subjects in the Direct Experience condition did not report feeling more informed about the types of problems, it would be premature to argue against a qualitative difference in the information provided by the two types of experience.

Whatever the precise mechanisms involved, these results strongly suggest that, in atempting to predict subsequent behavior from an attitudinal measure, it would be helpful to know whether the individual has based his attitude on direct personal experience with the attitude object. Furthermore, the results are encouraging with respect to the viability of the concept of attitude itself. In a recent experiment, Wicker (1971) found that attitudes ranked only third among four verbal predictors of church-related behavior, correlating on the average only .22 with overt behavior. Among the possible implications of this weak relationship cited by Wicker was that "it may be desirable to abandon the attitude concept and other verbal predictors in favor of direct study of the overt behavior of interest and the variables which affect that behavior" (Wicker, 1971, p. 29). We have argued, to the contrary, against premature abandonment of the attitude concept, on the grounds that *sometimes* attitudes can be relatively good predictors of subsequent behavior. We view the present results as more consistent with Kelman's optimistic thesis that "not only is attitude an integral part of action, but action is an integral part of the development, testing, and crystallization of attitudes" (1974, p. 324).

REFERENCES

Allport, G. W. Attitudes. In C. Murchison (Ed.), *Handbook of social psychology.* Worcester, Mass.: Clark University Press, 1935.

Festinger, L. Behavioral support for opinion change. *Public Opinion Quarterly,* 1964, *28,* 404–17.

Kelman, H. C. Attitudes are alive and well and gainfully employed in the sphere of action. *American Psychologist,* 1974, *29,* 310–24.

Thomas, W. I., & Znaniecki, F. *The Polish peasant in Europe and America.* Boston: Badger, 1918.

Wicker, A. W. Attitudes versus actions: The relationship of verbal and overt behavioral responses to attitude objects. *Journal of Social Issues,* 1969, *25,* No. 4, 41–78.

Wicker, A. W. An examination of the "other variables" explanation of attitude–behavior inconsistency. *Journal of Personality and Social Psychology,* 1971, *19,* 18–30.

FOCUSING ON PRACTICAL APPLICATIONS OF PRINCIPLES OF ATTITUDE AND BEHAVIOR CHANGE

PHILIP G. ZIMBARDO, EBBE B. EBBESEN, AND CHRISTINA MASLACH

Much of the research on attitude and behavior change has been carried out in controlled laboratory settings. The laboratory approach has numerous advantages for the development of theory because it allows the researcher to specify critical variables in order to study the pattern of causal relationships. But what happens when we move from the laboratory to events in the real world? How well do the research models predict and explain the effects of the many influences to which we are all subjected, all the time? According to Zimbardo, Ebbesen, and Maslach, there is still a large gap between the questions posed by practical problems and the answers provided by theory and research. However, they demonstrate that an analysis of actual attempts to influence attitudes and behavior can also provide some answers to these questions by showing us what does and does not work in various situations.

We ask you to consider with us the following range of problems, from which will be drawn practical, concrete illustrations of attitude and behavior change programs in action. Is "creating an image" a *new* Madison Avenue approach? In what sense is our educational system a propaganda mill? . . . How can the prejudiced attitudes of a given woman toward a minority group be changed? . . . How can a person's need for freedom and self-assertion be incorporated into a persuasion program? . . .

CREATING AN IMAGE, OR "PACKAGING" THE COMMUNICATOR

Television has made us aware of the extensive use of public relations firms to promote the campaigns of political candidates. Hair style, clothes style, and speech style are modified to fit an image fashioned by opinion polls, advisers, and media experts. Thus former President Ford was trained to use hand gestures, albeit woodenly, when making key points during TV speeches. This image management strategy was first used many years ago. An enterprising public relations man (whose pseudonym was Ivy Lee) was hired to change the prevailing stereotype of John D. Rockefeller. Mr. Rockefeller was generally considered a self-aggrandizing robber baron. A complete image reversal was called for, one in which the public would view him as a philanthropic, kindly gentleman. The strategy was deceptively simple: One of the most effective techniques was to publicize pictures and stories of Rockefeller giving shiny new dimes to every child he met in the streets. It is tougher on the tummy these days with urban politicians having to appeal to diverse ethnic constituencies. The TV image comes to mind of suave John Lindsay, New York's former mayor, making

the rounds eating knishes, pizza, Polish sausage, ribs, fried bananas, and egg rolls, topped off with an all-American hot dog from Nathan's delicatessen.

EDUCATION: HIDDEN PROPAGANDA FOR THE ESTABLISHMENT

Traditionally, *propaganda* is defined as an attempt to influence public opinion and public behavior through specialized techniques. It is contrasted with *education*, in which there is also an attempt to change attitudes and behavior, but through information, evidence, facts, and logical reasoning. In an ideal sense, educators teach students not *what* to think, but only *how* to think. In this way, propagandists differ from educators because they intentionally try to bias what people see, think, and feel in the hope that they will adopt their viewpoint.

But are there concealed, subtle forms of indoctrination in education that cloud these neat distinctions? Think back to the examples used in your textbooks to teach you the purely objective, academic discipline of mathematics. Most of the work problems dealt with buying, selling, renting, working for wages, and computing interest. These examples not only reflect the system of economic capitalism in which the education takes place, but are also an endorsement or subconscious legitimization of it. To illustrate, take an example that might be used to make concrete the arithmetic operations involved in dividing 90 by 60. "John wants to borrow $90, but Joe can only lend him $60. What percentage of the amount he wanted does John obtain?" The same conceptual operations could be equally well learned with a different illustration, perhaps less likely in our country: "John earns $60 a week from Company X. Medical and health authorities are agreed that the weekly cost of living for a family of four is $90. What percentage of a decent, acceptable minimal wage does Company X pay John?"

While such an example may seem farfetched,

Reprinted by special permission from Philip G. Zimbardo, Ebbe B. Ebbesen, Christina Maslach, *Influencing Attitudes and Changing Behavior*, 2nd Edition, 1977, Addison-Wesley, Reading, Mass.

consider the complaints of the black community that textbooks in all areas omit reference in word or picture to the reality of black history, black culture, or even black existence—except as related to slavery and primitive native customs. Such an omission fosters the majority attitude among black and other minority children that their race and they, as members of it, are insignificant. If this is not an intentional goal of our educational process, then its impact should be assessed, and correctives considered.

. . .

WHO'S PREJUDICED? YOUR MOTHER!

Racial, ethnic, and religious prejudice may be viewed as a negative evaluation, and as a rejection of an individual solely because of his or her membership in a particular group. If those discriminated against (as well as those who are prejudiced) suffer because of this prejudice, then why do we not eliminate it? Dedicated social scientists and humanitarians have been concerned with this problem for a number of years. The United Nations and the United States have spent millions of dollars on *information* campaigns to correct stereotypes about minority groups, to present the facts, and to help people to get to know one another. They assumed that prejudice was based on ignorance and that every person's desire to know the truth would dispel false beliefs. From every indication we have, these campaigns have been very limited in their effectiveness.

A second approach used to combat prejudiced attitudes has assumed that *contact*, or physical proximity between members of the groups in question, would make attitudes more favorable. For example, you take a class of white students on a tour of Harlem, or you mix races in a public housing project, a summer camp, an infantry outfit, or the classroom.

There is some equivocal evidence that as long as the contact continues, the prejudiced attitudes may weaken. However, once the person returns to a situation where the norms do not support tolerant attitudes, the newfound tolerance slips back into old prejudiced habits of thought, speech, and action. This raises the key issue not only of whether the techniques used produce a big immediate change, but also of whether the change generalizes to the social environment or group that supports the old behavior. Criminal recidivism and the return to drugs by "cured" drug addicts may be traced to "changed" individuals being sent back

to an unchanged social setting in which their new attitudes and behavior are not socially supported. A newly emerging philosophy of change in therapeutic communities such as Synanon and San Francisco's Delancey Street Foundation (for former prisoners, prostitutes, and drug addicts) is to *not* send the members back if they want to stay on. You cannot go home to old stimuli and expect old responses not to be evoked. You cannot put cucumbers in a vinegar barrel and expect them not to emerge as pickles.

Judge for yourself whether information and contact alone are sufficient conditions for changing prejudice. Here is a case study of a college freshman trying to persuade a middle-aged housewife that she holds untenable attitudes toward Puerto Ricans who were then (1954) just beginning to move into "her" Southeast Bronx neighborhood. The woman has already had a great deal of contact with Puerto Ricans who live in her building, shop at the same stores, own some of these stores, and are friends of her daughters. The boy provides sensible, rational arguments in favor of a general attitude of tolerance and understanding of the problems of this new group of migrants to the American melting pot. In reading this account of the transcript,[1] note not only the student's efforts to change the woman's attitude, but also the techniques the woman uses to bolster her position. Also, try to see beyond her rational manifest concern to the nature and the variety of topics she raises, especially those that emerge when the student has trapped her in an inconsistency. There seems to be something lurking below the surface of her conscious rationality.

INTERVIEWER (P. ZIMBARDO):   You've been living in this neighborhood quite a number of years. Do you think there's been any change in the composition of the neighborhood?

WOMAN: There certainly has. I've been living in this house now for twenty-one years, and I daresay I'm ashamed to tell people that I live in the neighborhood, I do.

STUDENT: Why is that?

WOMAN: Because of what the Puerto Ricans have done to it.

STUDENT: What do you mean, specifically?

---

[1]A transcript of a tape recording made by Zimbardo in a community center in New York City. The participants agreed to talk about conditions in their neighborhood and were aware they were being recorded. Comments by other participants were deleted from this presentation for purposes of space.

WOMAN: Well, to start with, their filth. Second, the language they use, and third, because the teachers waste eight hours a day with them in school and find that they get nowhere the minute the children are released.

STUDENT: You mean you never heard that language from anyone else but a Puerto Rican?

WOMAN: I certainly have, but not as much as I hear it from them.

STUDENT: Maybe you listen to it from them more often than you listen to it from others.

WOMAN: I can't help it, because the streets are overcrowded with them.

STUDENT: Well, why are they overcrowded with them?

WOMAN: It doesn't have to be overcrowded, they can live somewhere else, or gather somewhere else. But I find that this is the biggest dope center, because there's nothing done about it. We pay police the salaries that we do, we pay taxes, and yet what has been done?

STUDENT: What do you know about dope centers? You say this is the *biggest* dope center. Do you know of other dope centers . . . ?

WOMAN: I think they're the filthiest race, they're devoid of brains, and it's a disgrace with what goes on.

STUDENT: Why do you say they're the filthiest race?

WOMAN: They are, because I've worked with colored people, and I find that they're 50 percent more immaculate than the Puerto Ricans.

STUDENT: Well why are they dirty? Isn't there a reason why they're dirty?

WOMAN: They don't know any better, unfortunately.

STUDENT: So then, how can you condemn them because they don't know better? If you find a person that's ignorant, are you gonna condemn him?

WOMAN: You can condemn people for being poor, but you can't condemn them for being filthy. [She means the opposite, or does she?] Soap and water doesn't cost much. If a person is ignorant, he knows nothing about cleanliness. And if he's devoid of brains, he certainly doesn't know.

STUDENT: All right, look, you say they're filthy and all that. But look at the sanitation problems in Puerto Rico.

WOMAN: I've never been to Puerto Rico, so I can't speak about Puerto Rico. I live in the Bronx and I can only tell you what happens here.

STUDENT (overlaps): In New York here or even in the United States we have the highest standard of living. They don't have that in other places; if a person just comes over from a low standard of living into a high standard of living . . .

WOMAN (interrupts): Why is it that most of the Puerto Ricans own the most beautiful cars, and yet 90 percent of them are on relief [social welfare]?

STUDENT: A lot of people own cars and don't have a lot of money.

WOMAN: Not a lot. Puerto Ricans more than any other race.

STUDENT: Why Puerto Ricans more than any other race?

WOMAN: 'Cause I happen to know someone that works on the Home Relief Bureau [Welfare Service]; and more Puerto Ricans than any other race. . . . But they know how to make babies every nine months.

STUDENT: So are you going to condemn them for having *kids*?

WOMAN: Why do they have so many of them? *You could condemn them for having kids.* They should go out and look for jobs! The hospitals are flooded with them today. Do they know about going to pediatricians? No! Do they know how to raise children? No! What do they bring them up on? When the child's seven months old, it learns to drink beer from a can!

STUDENT (interrupts): My God, the people . . . the people just came over here, how long have they been in the United States? What chance have they had?

WOMAN: They've been here much too long to suit me. [Discussion of Puerto Rican girls going behind the school yard at night with boys.].

STUDENT: So you blame them for being *obvious* instead of hiding it . . . right? Instead of being sneaks about it?

WOMAN: Yes, because their parents don't know enough to take care of them

STUDENT: How do you know their parents don't know?

WOMAN: Because if you go to dance halls, who do you find there? More Puerto Ricans.

STUDENT: You find anybody at dance halls. You mean before the Puerto Ricans came there were no dance halls.

WOMAN: Refined, but not like now. I lived in a building that was the most upstanding house on the block. Today it's disgraceful, because it's surrounded with Puerto Ricans.

STUDENT: Surrounded with . . . Why? Do you think just because a person's Puerto Rican, right away he's filthy and he's dirty and he's dumb? You think just because a person's a Puerto Rican or something like that, that you call him dumb and ignorant because he's born Puerto Rican? A few years ago there was prejudice against the Jewish people. They weren't allowed in certain jobs, they're not allowed in colleges, they're not allowed in, uh. . . .

WOMAN (not listening): Then they shouldn't come here. They should stay in Puerto Rico.

STUDENT: Is it so easy to find apartments now that you can go out and get all the apartments you want? So then why are you condemning?

WOMAN: It isn't easy, because I'm a little fussy. I want to stay away from them. I want to go to a neighborhood that *restricts them.*

STUDENT: But you still didn't answer a question I asked before. Just because the . . . they're Puerto Ricans or something like that, they're . . . that they're filthy, they're dirty. How many years ago was it before the Jewish people were, uh, discriminated against?

WOMAN: Not that I know of.

STUDENT: Not that you know of! How . . . the Jewish people . . . A Jewish person couldn't get into law school or anything like that then, you couldn't get into the Bell Telephone Company, you couldn't get into . . . to millions of jobs.

WOMAN: That's only hearsay. But can you prove it?

STUDENT: It isn't, yes, I can prove it. I have relatives that tried out for the Bell Telephone Company and they couldn't get in because they were Jewish. I had a . . . one of my relatives graduated from law school. He was one of the first people who graduated like that.

DAUGHTER: So tell us why has the Bronx come down so much?

STUDENT: Because it's overpopulated?

DAUGHER: With dirty Spics!

STUDENT: So what reason do you have to call them dirty Spics?

DAUGHTER: What reason!

WOMAN: One, because they don't know how to bring up children. Second, because their morale [morals?] is so low. Third, because they're known to consume more alcohol than any other race in this world. And fourth, they're the biggest marijuana smokers.

STUDENT: Who drinks more beer than Irish people?

WOMAN: Who wanted to shoot the President, if not the Puerto Ricans [reference to assassination attempt on President Truman by Puerto Rican Nationalists]?

STUDENT: What about John Wilkes Booth, who tried to shoot Abraham Lincoln, what was he?

WOMAN: You're going back so many years! You pick up the paper and read about prostitutes. Who's involved? Puerto Ricans.

INTERVIEWER: We seem to be going off on a tangent, so let's wind up the discussion with your views on how the problem could be solved.

WOMAN: It could be solved by dropping a token in the subway and sending them all back where they came from!

The student clearly had good intentions and worked hard to dissuade the woman from her anti-Puerto Rican position. He gave some sound arguments, refuted some of the opposing arguments, gave personal examples of prejudice toward him, and made a sincere appeal to view prejudice as ignorance that can be overcome by simply getting to know your disliked neighbors regardless of their race, religion, or ethnic background. And to what effect? The woman exhibited a "boomerang" effect, reacting with more overt hostility and prejudice than she showed initially.

Good intentions unsupported by sound psy-chological knowledge may get the student into heaven, but they will never change this woman's attitude. Where he failed was in not assessing the function her attitude serves in her total psychological makeup, and by accepting her rationalizations as rational statements. The major consequence of his puncturing one of her arguments, or directly confronting her with contrary evidence, was for her to become both emotionally upset (at points, both she and daughter were near hysteria) and more openly hostile over the course of the interview. Her tactical weapon was a non sequitur flank attack. She changed topics and regained her composure, while her adversary was shifting gears in order to make sense of and reply to a non sequitur that she had tossed off. Then she would counter-attack again.

. . .

SELLING FREEDOM: AGREEING TO DISAGREE

The approaches we have outlined so far have been based on experience, trial and error, clinical intuition, psychoanalytic theory, ingenuity, many implicit assumptions, and a smattering of low-level psychological principles. Although some of them have been successful, their success depended more on the particular person who was employing the techniques, or "practicing his or her art," than on a sound social science base. When there is such a base, however, the control of behavior is predicated upon an understanding of the causal relations and, because it is explicitly spelled out, can be implemented by anyone. The approach adopted by Jacobo Varela (1971) tries to achieve this goal through the practical, systematic application of principles derived from psychological theories, and especially from the results of social psychological experiments.

This approach begins by rejecting two of the criticisms often leveled at the possible utility of laboratory-experimental findings: (1) that you cannot extrapolate from the laboratory to the real world when laboratory subjects are a captive audience in a novel environment that is under a high degree of control by the experimenter, and (2) that the time interval used in laboratory studies is rarely more than one hour, while in real life there is no such time constraint.

Instead of insisting on bringing more of real life into the laboratory, this approach says that since laboratory studies are shown to be effective in changing attitudes, then bring the laboratory into real life. If an hour is enough to persuade an intelligent, often critical undergraduate subject, it should be enough to change the behavior of the average businessperson or others—if a planned, concentrated, and powerful manipulation is used and tailored to the target audience.

Varela combines several basic techniques suggested from attitude-change research into a systematic persuasion program. This planned program is then brought to bear on particular individuals identified as decision-makers or as holding attitudes or acting in ways that call for change. They might be people who control resources and do not want to buy your product, or who will not give you, or certain minorities, jobs or improved work/living conditions. They might be people who engage in antisocial behavior that may also be injurious to their health (such as crime, violence, and drug addiction). Or they can be individuals who need help to break phobias (of flying, for example), to control compulsions, or to handle personal family conflicts.

The basic approach is to tailor an individualized program of change to each specific person. This consists of first diagnosing exactly what are the person's relevant attitudes, beliefs, and current behaviors. Then a systematic attempt is made to confront each of these components of the person's overall attitude on the issue.

Attitude Change by Successive Approximations

To change a strongly held set of attitudes and beliefs, Varela proposes a strategy of successive approximations. In this strategy, the most weakly held attitude elements are changed first. Then, one by one, each of the more staunchly endorsed elements is subjected to change tactics. To begin with, it is determined how strongly the person feels about various aspects of the issue. This is done by devising a series of statements that range from those that would be accepted by the person to those that would be rejected. These statements may come from one's knowledge of what the person has said previously or from an analysis of possible statements the person would be likely to endorse.

Next, each of these statements is subtly presented to the person during a conversation in order to discover how strongly he or she feels about each one. On the basis of that evaluative information, a scale of statements graded by intensity of affect is constructed. The scale items range from those the person accepts most strongly, to accepts,

rejects, and rejects most strongly. Those that are accepted constitute the *latitude of acceptance*, while the rejected statements comprise the *latitude of rejection*. . . .

Armed with this knowledge of where the person stands on the issue and how much feeling and psychological energy are invested in various aspects of the general issue, a person other than the one who collected the initial latitude information proceeds with Part 2 of the change program. The unique feature of this phase is to create *reactance* in the target person.

According to Jack Brehm's theory of reactance, "the perception that a communication is attempting to influence will tend to be seen as a threat to one's freedom to decide for oneself" (1966, p. 94). This is a reverse use of manipulative intent, and is also the "Marc Antony effect." Reactance can be used in an ingenious way to get the person to disagree with statements that he or she would ordinarily agree with, and to agree with statements that were previously disagreed with. The attitude change agent merely implies that there is some limit on the freedom of the person to decide for himself or herself. Reactance is generated by asserting what the person already agrees with in terms such as "There is no question but . . . ," "You would have to say that . . . ," "It is always the case that . . . ," and so on. The induced reactance leads the person to mildly disagree with these unqualified assertions, and thus weakens support for his or her original position. Then the change agent proceeds in the same way to strongly disagree with statements in the person's latitude of rejection ("There's no way anyone could support the view that . . ."). The target person continues to disagree with the change agent's persuasive assertion, in order to maintain his or her perceived freedom of opinion, and in so doing agrees with the attitude item that had previously been most strongly rejected.

When this is done, the entire attitude structure has shifted its direction and resistance to change has been substantially weakened. The change agent ultimately reinforces each of the person's disagreements and is seen as "coming around" to agree with him or her. It is almost as if the person being changed perceives the change agent as the one he or she has influenced. Where the goal is to have the target person be more optimistic and positive about the topic (or problem), the latitude of acceptance is expanded. Where the goal is to develop a more negative attitude toward the topic (such as taking drugs), the method used is to expand the latitude of rejection.

Let's look at this approach in actual practice. The salesperson's goal here is to get a retail store owner to stop buying from a competitor and thus to be open to new accounts from—guess who.

The customer has often bought from Company A, which is a very reputable firm that has high-quality goods at reasonable prices with excellent payment terms. However, it makes few model changes and does not give exclusive lines. This last point is a source of irritation to many retailers, who do not wish to see the same goods that they are selling available at the lowest quality stores in lower-class sections of town.

The customer's initial attitudes toward the rival company are systematically manipulated by a combination of the reactance approach and the reinforcement approach. An example of how this technique can be employed follows.

(−3) *Company A gives exclusive lines*
SALESPERSON: [Saying he liked a style in the customer's store and wonders whether Company A made it] Yes? Well, you are lucky to have that made *exclusively* for you!
RETAILER: No, they don't give exclusives.

(−2) *Company A makes frequent style changes*
SALESPERSON: [In an apparent defense of Company A] You're right, that's too bad, but at least they make frequent style changes.
RETAILER: Sorry, I must disagree, they rarely do.

(−1) *Company A is very regular in deliveries*
SALESPERSON: Even if it is true that they don't (and I do believe you), you must admit that they make up for it by being regular and prompt in their deliveries.
RETAILER: Here you're just wrong, they aren't so prompt, and their deliveries are often irregular.

(+1) *Company A offers good promotional assistance*
SALESPERSON: That's surprising to hear, but judging from what I know of other companies, Company A is certainly good in things like promotional assistance.
RETAILER: [Now disagreeing mildly with a statement he previously would have agreed with] Well, sometimes they do, but you're not right if you mean they always do.

(+2) *Company A offers very favorable terms*
SALESPERSON: Of course, *you* know better than I do about that, but I've heard that there's *no question* about the very favorable terms Company A offers.
RETAILER: I don't know where you get your information but there *is* some question about that issue; their terms are favorable to them, but not necessarily for the small shopowner.

(+3) *Company A is a very responsible firm*
[This is the "most accepted" statement that is to be modified.]
SALESPERSON: You may be right, I never thought of it like that, but I am sure that you would *have to say* that Company A is a very responsible firm.
RETAILER: [As actually happened in one case] Not at all! They *used* to be a very responsible firm, but they aren't any longer!

In this way, the customer is not only guided to buy now, and to reject old loyalties to the opposition, but the general approach used is likely to engender a long-term commitment on the part of the client, because he or she has not been forced to buy anything. Rather, the sales people have been attentive, approving, reinforcing, concerned with his opinions, altruistic in saying nice things about their rivals—and they have allowed most of the work of persuasion to be done by the retailer.

WHEN PROPHECY FAILS

LEON FESTINGER, HENRY W. RIECKEN, AND STANLEY SCHACHTER

Festinger's theory of cognitive dissonance is one of the most influential theoretical models of attitude and behavior change. When it was first published (1957), it evoked great controversy among social psychologists because it challenged much of the research being done on attitudes. Its motivational basis contrasted with the traditional learning approach then in vogue, and some of its nonobvious predictions were directly opposed to those based on concepts of reinforcement. Furthermore, Festinger argued that discrepancies between attitudes and behavior could be reduced by changing the attitude to fit the behavior. He thus reversed the traditional idea that attitudes are always the cause and therefore the forerunners of behavior.

Although many of the hypotheses derived from cognitive dissonance theory have been tested in elaborately staged experiments, one of the classic studies involved an unusual real-life situation. A woman had announced that a city would be destroyed by flood on a specific date. The basis for this prophecy, she maintained, was a series of messages from beings on another planet. What interested the dissonance researchers about this situation was that the woman and her followers had publicly stated their belief in a forthcoming event that had been pinpointed in time. When, as the researchers assumed, the prophesied event did not occur, what would happen to these people's belief systems? How would they resolve the dissonance between their commitment to the belief and the evidence that that belief was in error? In order to study these issues, the researchers became members of the group of believers. In this way, they were able to take notes on everything that happened both before and after the failure of the predicted flood. This research method is known as participant observation. In their article, "When Prophecy Fails," Festinger, Riecken, and Schachter describe the response of the believers to the events that disconfirmed their prophecy and analyze these behavioral changes in terms of cognitive dissonance theory.

A man with a conviction is a hard man to change. Tell him you disagree and he turns away. Show him facts or figures and he questions your sources. Appeal to logic and he fails to see your point. We are familiar with the variety of ingenious defenses with which people protect their convictions, managing to keep them unscathed through the most devastating attacks.

But man's resourcefulness goes beyond simply protecting a belief. Suppose an individual believes something with his whole heart; suppose further that he has a commitment to this belief and that he has taken irrevocable actions because of it; finally, suppose that he is presented with evidence, unequivocal and undeniable evidence, that his belief is wrong: what will happen? The individual will frequently emerge, not only unshaken, but even more convinced of the truth of his beliefs than ever before. Indeed, he may even show a new fervor for convincing and converting other people to his view.

How and why does such a response to contradictory evidence come about? Let us begin by stating the conditions under which we would expect to observe increased fervor following the disconfirmation of a belief. There are five such conditions.

1. A belief must be held with deep conviction and it must have some relevance to action, that is, to what the believer does or how he behaves.

2. The person holding the belief must have committed himself to it; that is, for the sake of his belief, he must have taken some important action that is difficult to undo. In general, the more important such actions and the more difficult they are to undo, the greater is the individual's commitment to the belief.

3. The belief must be sufficiently specific and sufficiently concerned with the real world so that events may unequivocally refute the belief.

4. Such undeniable disconfirmatory evidence must occur and must be recognized by the individual holding the belief.

The first two of these conditions specify the circumstances that will make the belief resistant to change. The third and fourth conditions, on the other hand, point to factors that would exert powerful pressure on a believer to discard his belief. It is, of course, possible that an individual, even though deeply convinced of a belief, may discard it in the face of unequivocal disconfirmation. We must, therefore, state a fifth condition specifying the circumstances under which it will be maintained with new fervor.

5. The individual believer must have social support. It is unlikely that one isolated believer could withstand the kind of disconfirming evi-

Leon Festinger, Henry W. Riecken, and Stanley Schachter, *When Prophecy Fails* (Minneapolis, Minn.: University of Minnesota Press, 1956). Copyright © 1956 by the University of Minnesota, University of Minnesota Press, Minneapolis.

dence we have specified. If, however, the believer is a member of a group of convinced persons who can support one another, we would expect the belief to be maintained and the believers to attempt to proselytize or to persuade nonmembers that the belief is correct.

These five conditions specify the circumstances under which increased proselytizing would be expected to follow disconfirmation. Given this set of hypotheses, our immediate concern is to locate data that will allow a test of the prediction of increased proselytizing. Fortunately, throughout history there have been recurring instances of social movements which satisfy the conditions adequately. These are the millennial or messianic movements, a contemporary instance of which forms the basis for the present study. Let us see just how such movements do satisfy the five conditions we have specified.

Typically, millennial or messianic movements are organized around the prediction of some future events. Our conditions are satisfied, however, only by those movements that specify a date or an interval of time within which the predicted events will occur as well as detailing exactly what is to happen. Sometimes the predicted event is the second coming of Christ and the beginning of Christ's reign on earth; sometimes it is the destruction of the world through a cataclysm (usually with some select group slated for rescue from the disaster); or sometimes the prediction is concerned with particular occurrences that the messiah or a miracle worker will bring about. Whatever the event predicted, the fact that its nature and the time of its happening are specified satisfies the third point on our list of conditions.

The second condition specifies strong behavioral commitment to the belief. This usually follows almost as a consequence of the situation. If one really believes a prediction (the first condition), for example, that on a given date the world will be destroyed by fire, that the sinners will die and the good be saved, he does things about it and makes certain preparations as a matter of course. These actions may range all the way from simple public declarations to the neglect of worldy things and the disposal of earthly possessions. Through such actions and through the mocking and scoffing of nonbelievers, the believers usually establish a heavy commitment. What they do by way of preparation is difficult to undo, and the jeering of nonbelievers simply makes it far more difficult for the adherents to withdraw from the movement and admit that they were wrong.

Our fourth specification has invariably been

provided. The predicted events have not occurred. There is usually no mistaking the fact that they did not occur and the believers know that. In other words, the unequivocal disconfirmation does materialize and makes its impact on the believers.

Finally, our fifth condition is ordinarily satisfied—such movements do attract adherents and disciples, sometimes only a handful, occasionally hundreds of thousands. The reasons why people join such movements are outside the scope of our present discussion, but the fact remains that there are usually one or more groups of believers who can support one another.

History has recorded many such movements. Ever since the crucifixion of Jesus, many Christians have hoped for the second coming of Christ and movements predicting specific dates for this event have not been rare. However, most of the very early ones were not recorded in such a fashion that we can be sure of the reactions of believers to the disconfirmations they may have experienced. Occasionally historians make passing reference to such reactions as does Hughes in his description of the Montanists:

> Montanus, who appeared in the second half of the second century, does not appear as an innovator in matters of belief. His one personal contribution to the life of the time was the fixed conviction that the second coming of Our Lord was at hand. The event was to take place at Pepuza—near the modern Angora—and thither all true followers of Our Lord should make their way. His authority for the statement was an alleged private inspiration, and the new prophet's personality and eloquence won him a host of disciples, who flocked in such numbers to the appointed spot that a new town sprang up to house them. *Nor did the delay of the second advent put an end to the movement. On the contrary, it gave new life and form as a kind of Christianity of the elite, whom no other authority guided in their new life but the Holy Spirit working directly upon them.* . . . [Italics ours.][1]

In this brief statement are all the essential elements of the typical messianic movement. There are convinced followers; they commit themselves by uprooting their lives and going to a new place where they build a new town; the Second Advent does not occur. And, we note, far from halting the movement, this disconfirmation gives it new life.

Why does increased proselytizing follow the

[1]P. Hughes, *A Popular History of the Catholic Church* (Garden City, N.Y.: Doubleday), 1954, p. 10.

disconfirmation of a prediction? How can we explain it, and what are the factors that will determine whether or not it will occur? For our explanation, we shall introduce the concepts of consonance and dissonance.

Dissonance and consonance are relations among cognitions—that is, among opinions, beliefs, knowledge of the environment, and knowledge of one's own actions and feelings. Two opinions, or beliefs, or items of knowledge are dissonant with each other if they do not fit together—that is, if they are inconsistent, or if, considering only the particular two items, one does not follow from the other. For example, a cigarette smoker who believes that smoking is bad for his health has an opinion that is dissonant with the knowledge that he is continuing to smoke.

Dissonance produces discomfort and, correspondingly, there will arise attempts to reduce dissonance. Such attempts may take any or all of three forms. The person may try to change one or more of the beliefs, opinions, or behaviors involved in the dissonance; to acquire new information or beliefs that will increase the existing consonance and thus cause the total dissonance to be reduced; or to forget or reduce the importance of those cognitions that are in a dissonant relationship.

If any of these attempts is to be successful, it must be met with support from either the physical or the social environment. In the absence of such support, the most determined efforts to reduce dissonance may be unsuccessful.

Theoretically, then, what is the situation of the individual believer at the predisconfirmation stage of a messianic movement? He has a strongly held belief in a prediction—for example, that Christ will return—a belief that is supported by the other members of the movement. By way of preparation for the predicted event, he has engaged in many activities that are entirely consistent with his belief. In other words, most of the relations among relevant cognitions are, at this point, consonant.

Now what is the effect of the disconfirmation, of the unequivocal fact that the prediction was wrong, upon the believer? The disconfirmation introduces an important and painful dissonance. The fact that the predicted events did not occur is dissonant with continuing to believe both the prediction and the remainder of the ideology of which the prediction was the central item. The failure of the prediction is also dissonant with all the actions that the believer took in preparation for its fulfillment. The magnitude of the dissonance will, of course, depend on the importance of the belief

to the individual and on the magnitude of his preparatory activity.

In the type of movement we have discussed, the central belief and its accompanying ideology are usually of crucial importance in the believers' lives and hence the dissonance is very strong—and very painful to tolerate. Accordingly, we should expect to observe believers making determined efforts to eliminate the dissonance or, at least, to reduce its magnitude. How may they accomplish this end? The dissonance would be largely eliminated if they discarded the belief that had been disconfirmed, ceased the behavior which had been initiated in preparation for the fulfillment of the prediction, and returned to a more usual existence. Indeed, this pattern sometimes occurs. But frequently the behavioral commitment to the belief system is so strong that almost any other course of action is preferable. It may even be less painful to tolerate the dissonance than to discard the belief and admit one had been wrong. When that is the case, dissonance cannot be eliminated by abandoning the belief.

Alternatively, the dissonance would be reduced or eliminated if the members of a movement effectively blind themselves to the fact that the prediction has not been fulfilled. But most people, including members of such movements, are in touch with reality and simply cannot blot out of their cognition such an unequivocal and undeniable fact. They can try to ignore it, however, and they usually do try. They may convince themselves that the date was wrong but that the prediction will, after all, be shortly confirmed; or they may even set another date. Believers may try to find reasonable explanations, very often ingenious ones, for the failure of their prediction. Rationalization can reduce dissonance somewhat, but for rationalization to be fully effective, support from others is needed to make the explanation or the revision seem correct. Fortunately, the disappointed believer can usually turn to others in the same movement, who have the same dissonance and the same pressures to reduce it. Support for the new explanation is, hence, forthcoming and the members of the movement can recover somewhat from the shock of the disconfirmation.

Whatever the explanation, it is still by itself not sufficient. The dissonance is too important and though they may try to hide it, even from themselves, the believers still know that the prediction was false and all their preparations were in vain. The dissonance cannot be eliminated completely by denying or rationalizing the disconfirmation. There is, however, a way in which the remaining dissonance can be reduced. *If more and more people can be persuaded that the system of belief is correct, then clearly it must, after all, be correct.* It is for this reason that we observe the increase in proselytizing following disconfirmation. If the proselytizing proves successful, then by gathering more adherents and effectively surrounding himself with supporters the believer reduces dissonance to the point where he can live with it.

In the light of this explanation of the phenomenon that proselytizing increases as a result of a disconfirmation, we sought a modern instance of disconfirmation, an instance which could be observed closely enough so that our explanation could be put to an empirical test.

One day at the end of September the Lake City *Herald* carried a two-column story, on a back page, headlined: PROPHECY FROM PLANET. CLARION CALL TO CITY: FLEE THAT FLOOD. IT'LL SWAMP US ON DEC. 21, OUTER SPACE TELLS SUBURBANITE. The body of the story expanded somewhat on these bare facts:

> Lake City will be destroyed by a flood from Great Lake just before dawn, Dec. 21, according to a suburban housewife. Mrs. Marian Keech, of 847 West School Street, says the prophecy is not her own. It is the purport of many messages she has received by automatic writing, she says. . . . The messages, according to Mrs. Keech, are sent to her by superior beings from a planet called "Clarion." These beings have been visiting the earth, she says, in what we call flying saucers. During their visits, she says, they have observed fault lines in the earth's crust that foretoken the deluge. Mrs. Keech reports she was told the flood will spread to form an inland sea stretching from the Arctic Circle to the Gulf of Mexico. At the same time, she says, a cataclysm will submerge the West Coast from Seattle, Wash., to Chile in South America.

Since Mrs. Keech's pronouncement made a specific prediction of a specific event; since she, at least, was publicly committed to belief in it; and since she was apparently interested to some extent in informing a wider public about it, this seemed to be an opportunity to conduct a "field" test of the theoretical ideas to which the reader has been introduced. Therefore, the authors joined Mrs. Keech's group in early October and remained in constant touch with it throughout the events to be narrated here.

About nine months before the newspaper story appeared, Marian Keech had begun to receive messages in "automatic writing" from beings who said they existed in outer space and were instructing her to act as their representative to warn the people of earth of the coming cataclysm. Mrs. Keech told many of her friends and acquaintances of her messages, and by September had attracted a small following of believers. Among them was Dr. Thomas Armstrong, a physician who lived in a college town in a nearby state. Dr. Armstrong spread the word among a group of students ("The Seekers") who met at his home regularly to discuss spiritual problems and cosmology. Dr. Armstrong and his wife also visited Lake City frequently to attend meetings of Mrs. Keech's group there.

Throughout the fall months the groups in Lake City and Collegeville held a series of meetings to discuss the lessons from outer space and to prepare themselves for salvation from cataclysm. As December 21 drew near some members gave up their jobs, others gave away their possessions, and nearly all made public declarations of their conviction. In September, Dr. Armstrong had prepared two "news releases" about the prediction of flood, although Mrs. Keech had not sought any publicity herself and had given only the one interview to the Lake City reporter who called on her after he had seen one of Dr. Armstrong's news releases. Except for that interview, Mrs. Keech had confined her proselytizing to friends and acquaintances, and Dr. Armstrong had virtually limited his activities to "The Seekers." During October and November, a policy of increasingly strict secrecy about the beliefs and activities of the believers had been developing in both Collegeville and Lake City.

In December, Dr. Armstrong was dismissed from his hospital post, and the action brought him nationwide publicity. Had the group been interested in carrying their message to the world and securing new converts, they would have been presented with a priceless opportunity on December 16 when representatives of the nation's major news reporting services converged on the Keech home, hungry for a story to follow up the news break on Dr. Armstrong's dismissal from the college. But the press received a cold, almost hostile reception, and their most persistent efforts were resisted. In two days of constant vigil, the newspapermen succeeded in winning only one brief broadcast tape and one interview with Dr. Armstrong and Mrs. Keech—and that only after a reporter had virtually threatened to print his own version of their beliefs. A cameraman who surreptitiously violated the believers' prohibition against taking photographs was threatened with a lawsuit. Between December 16 and the early morning of December 21, the Keech home was the object of a barrage of telephone calls and a steady stream of visitors who came seeking enlightenment or even offering themselves for conversion. The telephone calls from reporters were answered by a flat, unqualified "No comment." The visitors, mostly potential converts, were paid the most casual attention and the believers made only sporadic attempts to explain their views to these inquirers.

By the late afternoon of December 20—the eve of the predicted cataclysm—the hullaballoo in the house had died down somewhat, and the believers began making their final preparations for salvation. Late that morning, Mrs. Keech had received a message instructing the group to be ready to receive a visitor who would arrive at midnight and escort them to a parked flying saucer that would whisk them away from the flood to a place of safety, presumably in outer space. Early in the evening, the ten believers from Lake City and Collegeville had begun rehearsing for their departure. First, they went through the ritual to be followed when their escort arrived at midnight. Dr. Armstrong was to act as sentry and, having made sure of the caller's identity, admit him. The group drilled carefully on the ritual responses they would make to the specific challenges of their unearthly visitor, and the passwords they would have to give in boarding the saucer. Next, the believers removed all metal from their persons. The messages from outer space left no doubt in anyone's mind that it would be extremely dangerous to travel in a saucer while wearing or carrying anything metallic, and all of the group complied painstakingly with this order—excepting only the fillings in their teeth.

The last ten minutes before midnight were tense ones for the group assembled in Mrs. Keech's living room. They had nothing to do but sit and wait, their coats in their laps. In the silence two clocks ticked loudly, one about ten minutes faster than the other. When the faster clock pointed to 12:05, someone remarked about the time aloud. A chorus of people replied that midnight had not yet come. One member affirmed that the slower clock was correct; he had set it himself only that afternoon. It showed only four minutes before midnight.

Those four minutes passed in complete silence except for a single utterance. When the (slower) clock on the mantel showed only one minute remaining before the guide to the saucer was due, Mrs. Keech exclaimed in a strained, high-pitched voice: "And not a plan has gone astray!" The clock chimed twelve, each stroke painfully clear in the expectant hush. The believers sat motionless.

One might have expected some visible reac-

tion, as the minutes passed. Midnight had come and gone, and nothing had happened. The cataclysm itself was less than seven hours away. But there was little to see in the reactions of the people in that room. There was no talking, nor sound of any sort. People sat stock still, their faces seemingly frozen and expressionless.

Gradually, painfully, an atmosphere of despair and confusion settled over the group. They re-examined the prediction and the accompanying messages. Dr. Armstrong and Mrs. Keech reiterated their faith. The believers mulled over their predicament and discarded explanation after explanation as unsatisfactory. At one point, toward 4 A.M., Mrs. Keech broke down and cried bitterly. She knew, she sobbed, that there were some who were beginning to doubt but that the group must beam light to those who needed it most, and that the group must hold together. The rest of the believers were losing their composure, too. They were all visibly shaken and many were close to tears. It was now almost 4:30 A.M. and still no way of handling the disconfirmation had been found. By now, too, most of the group were talking openly about the failure of the escort to come at midnight. The group seemed near dissolution.

But this atmosphere did not continue long. At about 4:45 A.M. Mrs. Keech summoned everyone to attention, announcing that she had just received a message. She then read aloud these momentous words: "For this day it is established that there is but one God of Earth and He is in thy midst, and from his hand thou hast written these words. And mighty is the word of God—and by his word have ye been saved—for from the mouth of death have ye been delivered and at no time has there been such a force loosed upon the Earth. Not since the beginning of time upon this Earth has there been such a force of Good and light as now floods this room and that which has been loosed within this room now floods the entire Earth. As thy God has spoken through the two who sit within these walls as he manifested that which he has given thee to do."

This message was received with enthusiasm. It was an adequate, even an elegant, explanation of the disconfirmation. The cataclysm had been called off. The little group, sitting all night long, had spread so much light that God had saved the world from destruction.

The atmosphere in the group changed abruptly and so did their behavior. Within minutes after she had read the message explaining the disconfirmation, Mrs. Keech received another message instructing her to publicize the explanation. She reached for the telephone and began dialing the number of a newspaper. While she was waiting to be connected, someone asked: "Marian, is this the first time you have called the newspaper yourself?" Her reply was immediate: "Oh, yes, this is the first time I have ever called them. I have never had anything to tell them before, but now I feel it is urgent." The whole group could have echoed her feelings, for they all felt a sense of urgency. As soon as Marian had finished her call, the other members took turns telephoning newspapers, wire services, radio stations, and national magazines to spread the explanation of the failure of the flood. In their desire to spread the word quickly and resoundingly, the believers now opened for public attention matters that had been thus far utterly secret. Where only hours earlier they had shunned newspaper reporters and felt that the attention they were getting in the press was painful, they now became avid seekers of publicity. During the rest of December 21, the believers thrust themselves willingly before microphones, talked freely to reporters, and enthusiastically proselytized the visitors and inquirers who called at the house. In the ensuing days they made new bids for attention. Mrs. Keech made further predictions of visits by spacemen and invited newspapermen to witness the event. Like the millennial groups of history, this one, too, reacted to disconfirmation by standing firm in their beliefs and doubling their efforts to win converts. The believers in Lake City clearly displayed the reaction to disconfirmation that our theory predicted.

Among the members of the Collegeville group who had not gone to Lake City for the flood, matters took quite a different turn. Most of them were students who had gone to their homes for Christmas vacation. All but two of them spent December 20 and 21 in isolation from each other, surrounded by unbelievers. These isolates reacted to the disconfirmation in a very different fashion from their fellows in Lake City. Instead of recovering from the initial shock of disconfirmation, they either gave up their beliefs completely or found their conviction seriously weakened. There was no upsurge of proselytizing among the stay-at-homes in "The Seekers" even after they had been informed of the message rationalizing the disconfirmation. Indeed, the reverse seems to have occurred in two cases where the individuals attempted to conceal their membership in "The Seekers." Thus, most of the Collegeville group reduced the dissonance created by disconfirmation by giving up all their beliefs, whereas in Lake City the members held fast and tried to create a supportive circle of believers.

The comparison of the two situations—Lake City and Collegeville—permits at least a crude test of the importance of one element of the theory proposed to explain the proselytizing reaction to disconfirmation: namely, the element of social support. In Lake City, most of the members were in the constant presence of fellow believers during the period immediately following disconfirmation. They had social support; they were able to accept the rationalization; and they regained confidence in their beliefs. On the other hand, all of the members of the Collegeville group, with the exception of one pair, faced the morning of December 21 and the following days either with people who neither agreed nor disagreed or with people who were openly opposed to the views of "The Seekers." It would seem that the presence of supporting cobelievers is an indispensable requirement for recovery from disconfirmation.

At the beginning of this article, we specified the conditions under which disconfirmation would lead to increased proselytizing and, for most of the members of the Lake City group, these specifications were satisfied. Most of them believed in Mrs. Keech's prediction and were heavily committed to this belief. Disconfirmation was unequivocal, and the attempted rationalization by itself was never completely successful in dispelling dissonance. Finally, the members of the group faced disconfirmation and its aftermath together. The members responded with strong, persistent attempts at proselytizing. Among "The Seekers," all the conditions were the same except that the supportive group of cobelievers was missing. Among these isolates there was no increase in proselytizing, no attempt to seek publicity, but rather their characteristic response was to give up their belief and even to conceal their earlier membership.

WHAT YOU NEED IS A GOOD LAWYER

Editors' Note: *Lawyers are, by definition, practitioners of behavior change. As such, claims Israeli humorist Ephraim Kishon, they know what methods of communication are most effective in producing results.*

Tel Aviv—Ten years ago Billitzer borrowed 20 pounds off me for two hours. He promised to return the money within a day. As he didn't I gave him a call and he asked for a week's grace. After a week I went to see him to demand my money back. He promised he'd fix it by Monday noon. Thursday evening I consulted a solicitor and he sent Billitzer a notice that "due steps will be taken in default of claim being met within a period of 72 hours after receipt of this communication."

No reply came from Billitzer within a period of two months, following which the solicitor stated that there was nothing more he could do, as Billitzer refused to pay.

I took the case out of his hands and placed it in those of a better solicitor. We sued Billitzer. The hear-

ing took place after five months, but Billitzer didn't show up because of illness. The hearing was therefore adjourned to a later date next year.

Then it didn't take place either, because Billitzer had meanwhile gone abroad. I waited for a year and a half, but as he didn't come back I applied to another quite well-known lawyer who tried to reopen the proceedings, but the judge refused to conduct the case in the absence of the defendant.

We appealed to a higher court, which rejected the case in accordance with the regulation that a court of that level does not handle civil claims involving less than 50 pounds.

We waited a year or two for Billitzer to come back from abroad, and when he did, I sent him another 30 pounds' loan by notary to raise his debt to a round fifty. Now the higher court did accept our case and ordered the lower court to conduct the hearing in defendant's absentia.

Since, however, defendant wasn't in absentia because Billitzer had meanwhile returned from abroad, as mentioned, the hearing was adjourned pending clarification.

I hired an even better-known lawyer and we petitioned the Supreme Court for an order nisi calling upon the Minister of Justice to show cause why I shouldn't have my money back from Billitzer. The Minister of Justice said I should apply to the courts. Thereupon we renewed the proceedings but they were adjourned because Billitzer asked for an adjournment.

I went to the biggest lawyer in Israel and told him my story. He listened attentively and suggested I go to Billitzer and beat him up.

I went to Billitzer and beat him up. He gave me my 50 pounds in cash right away. It pays to consult a really good lawyer.

Reprinted by permission of E. Kishon.

PROJECTS

Name _____

Date _____

3.1: INFLUENCING ATTITUDES

This project is designed to help you analyze the effects of a group discussion on the formation and change of a particular attitude. Your analysis will be based on the point of view either of someone actively involved in the discussion or of someone who is listening to it. Your instructor will divide the class into two groups, discussants and observers, and will assign a particular topic to be discussed. After the discussion has taken place, answer the following questions.

1. What topic was discussed? _____

2. Were you a discussant or an observer? _____

3. On the form below, rate the attitudes of the discussants. Begin by listing each discussant by name in the left-hand column. Then indicate what position each argued (circle either "pro" or "anti"). Finally, rate each discussant according to how much you think he or she *actually* believed the position being argued. The rating scale ranges from 1 (did not believe at all) to 7 (believed very strongly). Circle the appropriate rating number.

Discussants	Position Argued	Actual Belief in Position Argued						
		Did Not Believe at All						Believed Very Strongly
1. _____	pro anti	1	2	3	4	5	6	7
2. _____	pro anti	1	2	3	4	5	6	7
3. _____	pro anti	1	2	3	4	5	6	7
4. _____	pro anti	1	2	3	4	5	6	7
5. _____	pro anti	1	2	3	4	5	6	7
6. _____	pro anti	1	2	3	4	5	6	7
7. _____	pro anti	1	2	3	4	5	6	7
8. _____	pro anti	1	2	3	4	5	6	7
9. _____	pro anti	1	2	3	4	5	6	7
10. _____	pro anti	1	2	3	4	5	6	7

4. What was the basis for your ratings? That is, what led you to the conclusion that discussants actually did or did not believe what they were arguing?

5. How would you rate *your* attitude on this issue? (Circle the appropriate number.)

$$1 \qquad 2 \qquad 3 \qquad 4 \qquad 5 \qquad 6 \qquad 7$$

agree strongly   agree strongly
with "pro" position   with "anti" position

6. Was you own attitude affected by the group discussion?   *Yes*   *No*

7. If you answered yes, describe the way in which your attitude was affected.

8. Do you have any additional comments about the project as a whole or any particular aspect of it?

Name _____

Date _____

3.2: BECOMING AN AGENT OF SOCIAL CHANGE

Imagine that you are a professional specializing in persuasive communications and that you have been hired to bring about change in one of the following areas:

a. Get people to stop discriminating against a particular minority group (e.g., by hiring more people from his group or by changing their attitude toward it).

b. Get people to adopt one or more conservation behaviors (e.g., reducing gasoline consumption or using biodegradable products).

c. Get people to vote for a political candidate who is currently running far behind in the polls.

d. [Some other problem devised by you or your instructor.]

In answering the following questions, assume that you have access to sufficient money, and resources to mount the ideal campaign for change. On the work sheet, list what your *specific* goals would be and then outline the steps that you would take to achieve them. Wherever appropriate, cite the theoretical principles (modeling, reinforcement, dissonance, reactance, and so on) that you are using in developing your change techniques.

1. Which of the problem areas have you chosen to work on?

2. List the *specific* goal(s) that you have set in this change program. In other words, what actual behavior(s) should show a change as a result of your efforts (e.g., more positive scores on an attitude scale, reduced automobile driving)?

3. What techniques would you use to produce the changes you listed in question 2? Give concrete examples: for instance, what the ad would look like, what you would say to people as you conducted your door-to-door campaign, or what incentives or rewards you would give.

4. What are the theoretical principles on which your techniques are based? For example, giving everyone a dime if they buy a new biodegradable product is a technique based on reinforcement principles.

5. How will you know if your behavior change program has been successful? That is, how will you actually assess the amount of change in the behavior(s) that you listed in question 2?

Name _____

Date _____

3.3: THE PERSUASIVE POWER OF ADVERTISING

In this project, you will be collecting data on persuasive appeals—specifically, television ads. Watch several hours of television programs and record the content of the ads on the following data sheet. First, note the product being sold (soap, beer, car, and so forth). Next, describe the primary person(s) making the advertising pitch (sex, age, status, and so forth). Then analyze the type of persuasive appeal(s) being used in the ad. For example, some ads appeal to one's desire to be popular and well liked, others capitalize on guilt feelings, and so forth. Keep in mind that the persuasive appeal is not limited to the words that are actually spoken, but includes the way in which the product is visually displayed. After you have analyzed the different persuasive techniques that are being used, you can discuss and compare your findings with the rest of the class.

Ads	Product Being Sold	Primary Person(s) Making the Advertising Pitch	Type(s) of Persuasive Appeal
1.			
2.			
3.			
4.			
5.			
6.			
7.			
8.			
9.			
10.			
11.			
12.			
13.			
14.			
15.			
16.			

17. _____

18. _____

19. _____

20. _____

1. What, if any, were the predominant types of persuasive appeals?

2. Did you notice any patterns in these appeals, such as whether the appeals were different: if the persuader was a man rather than a woman; if the target audience was made up of children rather than adults, and so forth.

3. In your own opinion, what persuasive appeals are most effective, and why?

PREJUDICE AND DISCRIMINATION

4

Suppose you were asked to rate yourself on a scale designed to measure racial prejudice, and the choices ranged from "very racially prejudiced" at one end of the scale to "very racially tolerant" at the other. You would probably place yourself at the tolerant end of the scale. If you were asked to rate yourself on a sexual prejudice scale, your self-evaluation would probably be the same. In fact, few of today's college students would willingly admit to considering racial groups, ethnic minorities, or women inferior. But what about other forms of prejudice? In our youth-oriented society, many people deride old age; "dirty old man" jokes are just one way that our society uses ridicule to censure and ostracize the elderly. Many people, especially those who regard themselves as intellectuals, will openly acknowledge that they cannot tolerate "stupid" people. Somehow, stupidity or lack of education is considered sufficient justification for otherwise liberal and humanistic individuals to treat certain human beings in a rude, derisive manner.

What is it about the way we live that tends to foster prejudicial attitudes? The world around us bombards our senses with an infinite number of stimuli. No one person can perceive and understand them all. Therefore, each individual perceives only a selected number of stimuli, organizes them, and encodes their meaning. Social psychologists believe that this process of selective perception of, and response to, our environment may contribute to the formation of prejudice. Such perceptual shortcuts are necessary if the individual is to bring some order to the surrounding chaos, but they inevitably involve a loss of information and consequently produce perceptual distortions. Because these distortions may lead to the formation of negative attitudes that can be used to justify discrimination, they are especially dangerous.

A CASE OF PREJUDICE

The ease with which people adopt prejudices and, even worse, the ease with which the subjects of prejudice accept their unjust fate are illustrated by an incident that occurred in Israel in 1967, just before the outbreak of the Six Day War. Egyptian President Gámal Abdel Nasser had closed the Tiran Sea Gates to Africa to Israeli ships, and all diplomatic negotiations had proved futile. Tensions were rising rapidly, and the inevitability of war was becoming increasingly clear to everyone. The only question on people's minds was: When will the war start?

The 5:30 P.M. bus to Hertseliya from Tel Aviv was crowded with rush-hour commuters. All the passengers seemed tired, worried, and sweaty, weary from their long workday and looking forward to getting home and unwinding. Shortly after the bus left Tel Aviv, a confrontation developed in the last two rows of the bus. A young man was listening to his transistor radio. The man sitting behind him told him rather rudely to turn the radio down. The youth's response was predictable: He turned the volume up. With that, the man demanded even more firmly that he turn it down; again, his response was to turn it up even higher.

The incident might have ended with the two arguing it out if the older man had not then abruptly accused the boy of being an Arab spy. He shouted, "Arab! . . . You are an Arab . . . an Arab spy!" Within seconds, everyone on the still moving bus was involved in the fight. "I am not an Arab spy, I swear. Let me show you my identification card," the youth protested pitifully. No one examined the card. No one listened to him. Suddenly, all the strained, withdrawn faces grew flushed. Eyes shone with excitement at the prospect of capturing an Arab spy.

Although in a great hurry to get home from work, the passengers unanimously decided to make a wide detour and drop the "spy" at the Hertseliya police station. The youth seemed quiet, subdued, totally resigned to his fate as he was taken into the station house by an escort of six enthusiastic volunteers who had been his fellow passengers on the bus.

83

PREJUDICE AND FOLKLORE

. . . Ever since the coining of the term "stereotype" by journalist Walter Lippmann in his book *Public Opinion* in 1922, social psychologists among others have actively sought to refine the concept and to document its existence and influence. Attention has been given both to stereotypes of self and to stereotypes of others. In addition, there have been special studies concerned with the relationship between stereotypes and prejudice. It seems clear that stereotypes do contribute materially to the formation and perpetuation of deep-seated prejudices.

Yet, in examining the extensive national character and stereotype scholarship, one finds surprisingly little reference to the materials of folklore. Stereotypes are described almost solely on the basis of questionnaires or interviews in which an a priori set of adjectives, such as "honest" or "stingy," are assigned by informants to national or ethnic groups. One wonders, methodologically speaking, just how the researcher selects the initial list of adjectives and whether or not his personal bias in making up the list does not partially invalidate the results. What psychologists and others fail to realize is that folklore represents an important and virtually untapped source of information for students of national character, stereotypes, and prejudice. The folk have been making national character studies (that is, folk national character studies) for centuries. People A have numerous traditions about the character of People B as do People B about People A. And it is precisely these traditions that transmit stereotypes from one generation to another. The stereotypes are thus already "recorded" and would presumably be free from the inevitable investigator bias found in the unduly leading questionnaires.

. . .

The inadequacy of the term "ethnic slur" concerns essentially the definition of "folk" itself. Some folk groups are ethnic groups, and in such cases, the label "ethnic slur" seems to be very appropriate; however, there are many folk groups which are not ethnic, and in such cases, the term seems inappropriate. This is clear if one accepts the modern, flexible definition of "folk" as meaning not a peasant society but any group whatsoever sharing at least one common factor.[1] The linking factor could be ethnicity, but it could just as well be political or religious affiliation, geographical location, or occupation. Any group is potentially both producer and victim of slurs. Some slurs are very much in-group traditions; some are strictly out-group traditions; some are used as often by the in-group as by the out-group. One reasonably empirical and eminently practical way of determining whether a given group does have a folk identity separate from the general culture surrounding it is to determine if that group has, or is the subject of, slurs. In medicine, general practitioners have jokes about proctologists, such as calling them "rear admirals." In academic life, university professors have jokes about deans, "Old deans never die, they just lose their faculties." Within Catholicism, one finds jokes about Jesuits, often commenting upon their intellectual rather than mystical approach to life and religion, for example, "There was a meeting of three clergymen, and the three were in a room. There was a Dominican, a Franciscan, and a Jesuit. In the middle of the meeting, the lights went out. Undeterred by the darkness, the Dominican stands up and says, 'Let us consider the nature of light and of darkness, and their meaning.' The Franciscan begins to sing a hymn in honor of our Little Sister Darkness. The Jesuit goes out and replaces the

[1] Dundes, *The Study of Folklore*, 2.

fuse." It is sometimes difficult to collect such in-group traditions inasmuch as the subgroups may close ranks when confronted by what they take to be a threatening outsider who is only posing as a harmless folklorist–collector.

In using the term "ethnic" or "national slur," then, one needs to keep in mind that it is a functional rather than generic category, and also that there are slurs having nothing to do with ethnicity. The ethnic slur depends upon an alleged national or ethnic trait. More often than not, the trait or traits are mocked and demeaned. What is of primary interest here is determining precisely the trait or set of traits the folk has singled out for emphasis.

. . .

No doubt some will argue that the study of ethnic slurs may serve no other purpose than to increase the circulation of such slurs and by so doing unwittingly assist the rise of further ethnic and racial prejudice. However, a more realistic view would be that the slurs are used by the folk whether the folklorist studies them or not. Most children in the United States hear these slurs fairly early in their public school careers. I would maintain therefore that an open discussion of the slurs and an objective analysis of the stereotypes contained therein could do no harm and might possibly do a great deal of good in fighting bigotry and prejudice. Only by knowing and recognizing folk stereotypes can children be taught to guard against them so that they may have a better chance of succeeding in judging individuals on an individual basis.

Reproduced by permission of American Folklore Society and the author Alan Dundes, from "A Study of Ethnic Slurs: The Jew and the Polack in the United States," *Journal of American Folklore*, 84 (332):186–87, 190, and 203, 1971.

JIGSAW GROUPS AND THE DESEGREGATED CLASSROOM: IN PURSUIT OF COMMON GOALS

ELLIOT ARONSON AND DIANE BRIDGEMAN

When we hear about the hurt, pain, and other negative consequences of prejudice, some part in us is probably thinking, "If we could only talk to the people who carry these prejudices, if we could educate them, and explain things to them. . . . " We are convinced we can make them understand. What Aronson and Bridgeman show us in the following article is that explanations, even good explanations, are not enough. Nor is it enough to put prejudiced people together with the objects of their prejudices, as there tends to be a self-fulfilling prophecy—both for the ones holding the prejudice and the ones who are subject to it. Thus, busing and forcing students to spend time with minority students is not enough. In order to change people's attitudes, the whole pattern of prejudiced behavior needs to be changed, and what is needed is a change in the environment that will encourage such behavioral change. The change that Aronson and Bridgeman introduced and investigated is the structured interdependence they termed jigsaw.

There were high hopes when the Supreme Court outlawed school segregation a quarter of a century ago. If black and white children could share classrooms and become friends, it was thought that perhaps they could develop relatively free of racial prejudice and some of the problems which accompany prejudice. The case that brought about the court's landmark decision was that of *Oliver Brown* v. *Board of Education of Topeka, Kansas;* the decision reversed the 1896 ruling (*Plessy v. Ferguson*) which held that it was permissible to segregate racially, as long as equal facilities were provided for both races. In the *Brown* case, the court held that psychologically there could be no such thing as "separate but equal." The mere fact of separation implied to the minority group in question that its members were inferior to those of the majority.

The *Brown* decision was not only a humane interpretation of the Constitution, it was also the beginning of a profound and exciting social ex-

periment. The testimony of social psychologists in the *Brown* case, as well as in previous similar cases in state supreme courts, suggested strongly that desegregation would not only reduce prejudice but also increase the self-esteem of minority groups and improve their academic performance. Of course the social psychologists who testified never meant to imply that such benefits would accrue automatically. Certain preconditions must be met. These preconditions were most articulately stated by Gordon Allport in his classic *The Nature of Prejudice,* published the same year as the Supreme Court decision:

> Prejudice . . . may be reduced by equal status contact between majority and minority groups in the pursuit of common goals. The effect is greatly enhanced if this contact is sanctioned by institutional supports (i.e., by law, custom or local atmosphere), and provided it is of a sort that leads to the perception of common interests and common humanity between members of the two groups. (Allport, 1954, p. 281)

THE EFFECTS OF DESEGREGATION

A quarter of a century after desegregation was begun, an assessment of its effectiveness is not encouraging. One of the most careful and thorough-going longitudinal studies of desegregation was

Reprinted from Elliot Aronson and Diane Bridgeman, "Jigsaw Groups and the Desegregated Classroom: In Pursuit of Common Goals," *Personality and Social Psychology Bulletin*, Vol. 5, No. 4 (October 1979), 438–46. Copyright © 1979 by the Society for Personality and Social Psychology, with permission of Sage Publications, Inc.

the Riverside project conducted by Harold Gerard and Norman Miller (1975). They found that long after the schools were desegregated, black, white, and Mexican-American children tended not to integrate but to hang together in their own ethnic clusters. Moreover, anxiety increased and remained high long after desegregation occurred. These trends are echoed in several other studies. Indeed, the most careful, scholarly reviews of the research show few, if any, benefits. For example, according to Stephan's 1978 review, there is no single study that shows a significant increase in the self-esteem of minority children following desegregation; in fact, in fully 25 percent of the studies desegregation is followed by a significant decrease in the self-esteem of young minority children. Moreover, Stephan reports that desegregation reduced the prejudice of whites toward blacks in only 13 percent of the school systems studied. The prejudice of blacks toward whites increased in about as many cases as it decreased. Similarly, studies of the effects of desegregation on the academic performance of minority children present a mixed and highly variable picture.

What went wrong? Let us return to Allport's prediction. Equal status contact in pursuit of common goals, sanctioned by authority will produce beneficial effects. We will look at each of these three factors separately.

Sanction by Authority

In some school districts there was clear acceptance and enforcement of the ruling by responsible authority. In others the acceptance was not as clear. In still others, especially in the early years, local authorities were in open defiance of the law. Pettigrew (1961) has shown that desegregation proceeded more smoothly and with less violence in those localities where local authorities sanctioned integration. But such variables as self-esteem and the reduction of prejudice do not necessarily change for the better even where authority clearly sanctions desegregation. While sanction by authority may be necessary, it is clearly not a sufficient condition.

Equal Status Contact

The definition of equal status is a trifle slippery. In the case of school desegregation, we could claim that there is equal status on the grounds that all children in the fifth grade, for example, have the same "occupational" status—that is, they are all

fifth grade students. On the other hand, if the teacher is prejudiced against blacks, she or he may treat them less fairly than she or he treats whites, thus lowering their perceived status in the classroom. Moreover, if, because of an inferior education (prior to desegregation) or because of language difficulties, black or Mexican-American students perform poorly in the classroom, this could also lower their status among their peers. An interesting complication was introduced by Elizabeth Cohen (1972). While Allport (1954) predicted that positive interactions will result if cooperative equal status is achieved, expectation theory, as developed by Cohen, holds that even in such an environment biased expectations by both whites and blacks may lead to sustained white dominance. Cohen reasoned that both of these groups accept the premise that the majority group's competence results in dominance and superior achievement. She suggested that alternatives be created to reverse these often unconscious expectations. According to Cohen, at least a temporary exchange of majority and minority roles is therefore required as a prelude to equal status. In one study, for example, black children were instructed in building radios and in how to teach this skill to others. Then a group of white children and the newly trained black children viewed a film of themselves building the radios. This was followed by some of the black children teaching the whites how to construct radios while others taught a black administrator. Then all the children came together in small groups. Equal status interactions were found in the groups where black children had taught whites how to construct the radios. The other group, however, demonstrated the usual white dominance. We will return to this point in a moment.

In Pursuit of Common Goals

In the typical American classroom, children are almost never engaged in the pursuit of common goals. During the past several years, we and our colleagues have systematically observed scores of elementary school classrooms and have found that, in the vast majority of these cases, the process of education is highly competitive. Children vie with one another for good grades, the respect of the teacher, and so on. This occurs not only during the quizzes and exams but in the informal give-and-take of the classroom where, typically, children learn to raise their hands (often frantically) in response to questions from the teacher, groan when someone else is called upon, and revel in the failure of their classmates. This pervasive competitive atmosphere unwittingly leads the children to view one another as foes to be heckled and vanquished. In a newly desegregated school, all other things being equal, this atmosphere could exacerbate whatever prejudice existed prior to desegregation.

A dramatic example of dysfunctional competition was demonstrated by Sherif et al. (1961) in their classic "Robber's Cave" experiment. In this field experiment, the investigators encouraged intergroup competition between two teams of boys at a summer camp; this created fertile ground for anger and hostility even in previously benign, noncompetitive circumstances—like watching a movie. Positive relations between the groups were ultimately achieved only after both groups were required to work cooperatively to solve a common problem.

It is our contention that the competitive process interacts with equal status contact. That is to say, whatever differences in ability existed between minority children and white children prior to desegregation are emphasized by the competitive structure of the learning environment, and since segregated school facilities are rarely equal, minority children frequently enter the newly desegregated school at a distinct disadvantage, which is made more salient by the competitive atmosphere.

It was this reasoning that led Aronson and his colleagues to develop the hypothesis that interdependent learning environments would establish the conditions necessary for the increase in self-esteem and performance and the decrease in prejudice that were expected to occur as a function of desegregation. Toward this end they developed a highly structured method of interdependent learning and systematically tested its effects in a number of elementary school classrooms. The aim of this research program was not merely to compare the effects of cooperation and competition in a classroom setting. This has been ably demonstrated by other investigators. Rather, the intent was to devise a cooperative classroom structure that could be utilized easily by classroom teachers on a long-term, sustained basis and to evaluate the effects of this intervention via a well-controlled series of field experiments. In short, this project is an action research program aimed at developing and evaluating a classroom atmosphere that can be sustained by the classroom teachers long after the researchers have packed up their questionnaires and returned to the more cozy environment of the social psychological laboratory.

Briefly, students are placed in six-person learning groups. The day's lesson is divided into six paragraphs such that each student has one and only one segment of the written material. Each student has a unique and vital part of the information which, like the pieces of a jigsaw puzzle, must be put together for any of the students to learn the whole picture. The individual must learn his or her own section and teach it to the other members of the group. The reader will note that in this method each child spends part of the time in the role of expert. Thus, the method incorporates Cohen's findings (previously discussed) within the context of an equal-status-contact situation.

Working with this "jigsaw" technique, children gradually learn that the old competitive behaviors are no longer appropriate. Rather, in order to learn all the material (and thus perform well on a quiz), each child must begin to listen to the others, ask appropriate questions, and so on. The process opens the possibility for children to pay attention to one another and begin to appreciate one another as potentially valuable resources. It is important to emphasize that the motivation of the students is not necessarily altruistic; rather, it is primarily self-interest which, in this case, happens also to produce outcomes which are beneficial to others.

EXPERIMENTS IN THE CLASSROOM

Systematic research in the classroom has produced consistently positive results. The first experiment to investigate the effects of the jigsaw technique was conducted by Blaney, Stephan, Rosenfield, Aronson, and Sikes (1977). The schools in Austin, Texas, had recently been desegregated, producing a great deal of tension and even some interracial skirmishes throughout the school system. In this tense atmosphere, the jigsaw technique was introduced in ten fifth-grade classrooms in seven elementary schools. Three classes from among the same schools were also used as controls. The control classes were taught by teachers who, while using traditional techniques, were rated very highly by their peers. The experimental classes met in jigsaw groups for about 45 minutes a day, three days a week, for six weeks. The curriculum was basically the same for the experimental and control classes. Students in the jigsaw groups showed significant increases in their liking for their groupmates both within and across ethnic boundaries. Moreover, children in jigsaw groups showed a significantly greater increase in self-esteem than children in the control classrooms. This was true for Anglo children as well as ethnic minorities. Anglos and blacks showed greater liking for schools in the jigsaw classrooms than in traditional classrooms. (The Mexican-American students showed a tendency to like school *less* in the jigsaw classes; this will be discussed in a moment.)

These results were essentially replicated in a Ph.D. dissertation by Geffner (1978) in Watsonville, California—a community consisting of approximately 50 percent Anglos and 50 percent Mexican-Americans. As a control for the possibility of a Hawthorne effect, Geffner compared the behavior of children in classrooms using the jigsaw and other cooperative learning techniques with that of children in highly innovative (but not interdependent) classroom environments, as well as with those in traditional classrooms. Geffner found consistent and significant gains within classrooms using jigsaw and other cooperative learning techniques. Specifically, children in these classes showed increases in self-esteem as well as increases in liking for school. Negative ethnic stereotypes were also diminished—that is, these children increased their positive general attitudes toward their own ethnic group, as well as toward members of other ethnic groups, to a far greater extent than did children in traditional and innovative classrooms.

Changes in academic performance were assessed in an experiment by Lucker, Rosenfield, Sikes, and Aronson (1977). The subjects were 303 fifth- and sixth-grade students from five elementary schools in Austin, Texas. Six classrooms were taught in the jigsaw manner, while five classrooms were taught traditionally by highly competent teachers. For two weeks children were taught a unit on colonial America taken from a fifth-grade textbook. All children were then given the same standardized test. The results showed that Anglo students performed just as well in jigsaw classes as they did in traditional classes ($\bar{x} = 66.6$ and 67.3 respectively), and minority children performed significantly better in jigsaw classes than in traditional classes ($\bar{x} = 56.6$ and 49.7 respectively). The difference for minority students was highly significant. Only two weeks of jigsaw activity succeeded in narrowing the performance gap between Anglos and minorities from more than 17 percentage points to about 10 percentage points. Interestingly enough, the jigsaw method apparently does *not* work a special hardship on high-ability students: Students in the highest quartile in reading ability benefited just as much as students in the lowest quartile.

UNDERLYING MECHANISMS

Increased Participation

We have seen that learning in a small interdependent group leads to greater interpersonal attraction, self-esteem, liking for school, more positive interethnic and intra-ethnic perceptions, and, for ethnic minorities, an improvement in academic performance. We think that some of our findings are due to more active involvement in the learning process under conditions of reduced anxiety. In jigsaw groups, children are required to participate. This increase in participation should enhance interest, which would result in an improvement in performance, as well as an increased liking for school, all other things being equal. But all other things are sometimes not equal. For example, in the study by Blaney et al. (1977) there was some indication from our observation of the groups that many of the Mexican-American children were experiencing some anxiety as a result of being required to participate more actively. This seemed to be due to the fact that these children had difficulty with the English language which produced some embarrassment in working with a group dominated by Anglos. In a traditional classroom, it is relatively easy to "become invisible" by remaining quiet, refusing to volunteer, and so forth. . . . Not so in jigsaw. This observation was confirmed by the data on liking for school. Blaney et al. found that Anglos and blacks in the jigsaw classrooms liked school better than those in the traditional classrooms, while for Mexican-Americans the reverse was true. This anxiety could be reduced if Mexican-American children were in a situation where it was not embarrassing to be more articulate in Spanish than in English. Thus, Geffner (1978), working in a situation where both the residential and school population was approximately 50 percent Spanish-speaking, found that Mexican-American children (like Anglos and blacks) increased their liking for school to a greater extent in the cooperative groups than in traditional classrooms.

Increases in Empathic Role-Taking

Only a small subset of our results is attributable to increases in active participation in and of itself. We believe that people working together in an interdependent fashion increase their ability to take one another's perspective. For example, suppose that Jane and Carlos are in a jigsaw group. Carlos is reporting, and Jane is having difficulty following him. She doesn't quite understand because his style of presentation is different from what she is accustomed to. Not only must she pay close attention, but in addition, she must find a way to ask questions which Carlos will understand and which will elicit the additional information that she needs. In order to accomplish this, she must get to know Carlos, "put herself in his shoes"— empathize.

Bridgeman (1977) tested this notion. She reasoned that taking one another's perspective is required and practiced in jigsaw learning. Accordingly, the more experience students have with the jigsaw process, the greater will their role-taking abilities become. In her experiment, Bridgeman administered a revised version of Chandler's (1973) role-taking cartoon series to 120 fifth-grade students. Roughly half the students spent eight weeks in a jigsaw learning environment while the others were taught in either traditional or innovative small-group classrooms. Each of the cartoons in the Chandler test depicts a central character caught up in a chain of psychological cause-and-effect, such that the character's subsequent behavior was shaped by and fully comprehensible only in terms of the events preceding them. In one of the sequences, for example, a boy who had been saddened by seeing his father off at the airport began to cry when he later received a gift of a toy airplane similar to the one which had carried his father away. Midway into each sequence, a second character is introduced in the role of a late-arriving bystander who witnessed the resultant behaviors of the principal character, but was not privy to the causal events. Thus, the subject is in a privileged position relative to the story character whose role the subject is later asked to assume. The cartoon series measures the degree to which the subject is able to set aside facts known only to him- or herself and adopt a perspective measurably different from his or her own. For example, while the subject knows why the child in the above sequence cried when he received the toy airplane, the mailman who delivered the toy is not privy to this knowledge. What happens when the subject is asked to take the mailman's perspective?

After eight weeks, students in the jigsaw classrooms were better able to put themselves in the bystander's place than students in the control classrooms. For example, when the mailman delivered the toy airplane to the little boy, students in the control classrooms tended to assume that the mailman knew the boy would cry—that is, they behaved as if they believed that the mailman knew that the boy's father had recently left town on an airplane—simply because they (the subjects) had this information. On the other hand, students who had participated in a jigsaw group were much more successful at taking the mailman's role, realizing that the mailman could not possibly understand why the boy would cry upon receiving a toy airplane.

Attributions for Success and Failure

Working together in the pursuit of common goals changes the "observer's" attributional patterns. There is some evidence to support the notion that cooperation increases the tendency for individuals to make the same kind of attributions for success and failure to their partners as they do for themselves. In an experiment by Stephan, Presser, Kennedy, and Aronson (1978), it was found (as it has been in several experiments by others) that when an individual succeeds at a task, he tends to attribute his success dispositionally (to skill, for example), but when he fails he tends to make a situational attribution (to luck, for example). Stephan et al. went on to demonstrate that individuals engaged in an *interdependent* task make the same kinds of attributions to their partner's performance as they do to their own. This was not the case in competitive interactions.

Effects of Dependent Variables on One Another

It is reasonable to assume that the various consequences of interdependent learning become antecedents for one another. Just as low self-esteem can work to inhibit a child from performing well, anything that increases self-esteem is likely to produce an increase in performance among those underachievers. Conversely, increases in performance should bring about increases in self-esteem. Similarly, being treated with increased attention and respect by one's peers (as almost inevitably happens in jigsaw groups) is another important antecedent of self-esteem. There is ample evidence for a two-way causal connection between performance and self-esteem.

OTHER COOPERATIVE TECHNIQUES

In recent years a few research teams utilizing rather different techniques for structuring cooperative behavior have produced an array of data consistent with those resulting from the jigsaw technique study. For example, Stuart Cook and his colleagues at the University of Colorado (1978) have shown that interracial cooperative groups in the laboratory underwent a significant improvement in attitudes about people of other races. In subsequent field experiments, Cook and his colleagues found that interdependent groups produced more improved attitudes to members of previously disliked racial groups than was present in noninterdependent groups. It should be noted, however, that no evidence for generalization was found—that is, the positive change was limited to the specific members of the interdependent group and did not extend to the racial group as a whole. . . .

In a different vein, Slavin (1978), DeVries (1978), and their colleagues at Johns Hopkins University have developed two highly structured techniques that combine within-group cooperation with across-group competition. These techniques, "Teams, Games, and Tournaments" (TGT) and "Student Teams Achievement Divisions" (STAD) have consistently produced beneficial results in lower class, multiracial classrooms. Basically, in TGT and STAD, children from heterogeneous five-person teams; each member of a team is given a reasonably good opportunity to do well by dint of the fact that she competes against a member of a different team with similar skills to her own. Her individual performance contributes to her team's score. The results are similar to those in the jigsaw study: Children participating in TGT and STAD groups show a greater increase in sociometric, cross-racial friendship choices and more observed cross-racial interactions than children in control conditions. They also show more satisfaction with school than the controls do. Similarly, TGT and STAD produce greater learning effectiveness among racial minorities than the control groups.

It is interesting to note that the basic results of TGT and STAD are similar to those of the jigsaw technique, in spite of one major difference in procedure: While the jigsaw technique makes an overt attempt to minimize competition, TGT and STAD actually promote competitiveness and utilize it across teams—within the context of intrateam cooperation. We believe that this difference is more apparent than real. In most classrooms where jigsaw has been utilized, the students are in the jigsaw group for less than two hours per day. The rest of the class time is spent in a myriad of process activities, many of which are competitive in nature. Thus, what seems important in both techniques is that *some* specific time is structured around cooperativeness. Whether the beneficial results are produced in spite of a surrounding atmosphere of competitiveness or because of it is the task of future research to determine.

CONCLUSIONS

We are not suggesting that jigsaw learning or any other cooperative method constitutes the solution to our interethnic problems. What we have shown is that beneficial effects occur as a result of structuring the social-psychological aspects of classroom learning so that children spend at least a portion of their time in pursuit of common goals. These effects are in accordance with predictions made by social scientists in their testimony favoring desegregating schools some 25 years ago. It is important to emphasize the fact that the jigsaw method has proved effective even if it is employed for as little as 20 percent of a child's time in the classroom. Moreover, other techniques have produced beneficial results even when interdependent learning was purposely accompanied by competitive activities. Thus, the data do not indicate the placing of a serious limit on classroom competition, or interfering with individually guided education. Interdependent learning can and does coexist easily with almost any other method used by teachers in the classroom.

REFERENCES

Blaney, N.T., Stephan, C., Rosenfield, D., Aronson, E., and Sikes, J. Interdependence in the classroom: A field study, *Journal of Educational Psychology*, 1977, 69, 139–46.

Bridgeman, D.L. The influence of cooperative, interdependent learning on role-taking and moral reasoning: A theoretical and empirical field study with fifth-grade students. Doctoral dissertation, University of California, Santa Cruz, 1977.

Chandler, M.J. Egocentrism and antisocial behavior: The assessment and training of social perspective-taking skills, *Developmental Psychology*, 1973, 9, 326–32.

Cohen, E. Interracial interaction disability, *Human Relations*, 1972, 25(1), 9–24.

Cook, S.W. Interpersonal and attitudinal outcomes in co-operating interracial groups, *Journal of Research and Development in Education*, 1978.

DeVries, D.L., Edwards, K.J., and Slavin, R.E. Bi-racial learning teams and race relations in the classroom: Four field experiments on Teams-Games-Tournament, *Journal of Educational Psychology*.

Geffner, R.A. The effects of interdependent learning on self-esteem, inter-ethnic relations, and intra-ethnic attitudes of elementary school children: A field experiment. Doctoral dissertation, University of California, Santa Cruz, 1978.

Lucker, G.W., Rosenfield, D., Sikes, J., and Aronson, E. Performance in the interdependent classroom: A field study, *American Educational Research Journal*, 1977, 13, 115–23.

Pettigrew, T. Social psychology and desegregation research, *American Psychologist*, 1961, 15, 61–71.

Purkey, W.W. *Self-Concept and School Achievement*. Englewood Cliffs, New Jersey: Prentice-Hall, 1970.

Sherif, M., Harvey, O.J., White, J., Hood, W., and Sherif, C. *Intergroup Conflict and Cooperation: The Robber's Cave Experiment*. Norman, Oklahoma: University of Oklahoma Institute of Intergroup Relations, 1961.

Slavin, R.E. Student teams and achievement divisions, *Journal of Research and Development in Education*, in press.

Stephan, C., Presser, N.R., Kennedy, J.C., and Aronson, E. Attributions to success and failure in cooperative, competitive and interdependent interactions, *European Journal of Social Psychology*, 1978.

Stephan, W.G. School desegregation: An evaluation of predictions made in Brown vs. The Board of Education, *Psychological Bulletin*, 1978, 85, 217–38.

RESEARCH HIGHLIGHT

COGNITIVE BASES OF STEREOTYPING

Shelley Taylor, a UCLA psychologist interested in social cognition, has recently suggested that "categorical processes are sufficient to understand much of importance about stereotyping" (Taylor and Falcone, 1982, p. 426). Taylor argues that stereotypes are attributes that are tagged to category labels (such as race, age, sex) and imputed to individuals. The usefulness of Taylor's categorization approach to stereotyping was illustrated in two of her recent studies—one examining the effect of race as a category label, the other, the effect of sex.

In the first study, subjects saw a slide and tape presentation of a group discussion involving six men—three blacks and three whites. After the discussion was over, subjects were given a list of the suggestions made during the discussion and were asked to match up which speaker had made which suggestion. It was found that those subjects who categorize others on the basis of their race were able to remember whether a black or a white made a particular comment, but not necessarily which black or which white made it. This, in turn, produced much higher within-race errors than between-race errors. The second study replicated the effect with a six-person group of three men and three women. Together the two studies provided evidence that people organize their social environment into social categories to organize the flow of social interaction.

S.E. Taylor and H.T. Falcone, "Cognitive bases of stereotyping: the relationship between categorization and prejudice." *Personality and Social Psychology Bulletin*, 1982, 8(3), 426–32.

AGING LABELS

JUDITH RODIN AND ELLEN LANGER

In the introduction to this chapter, we mentioned the fact that our youth oriented society often derogates old age. Agism, which is prejudice against old people, is tolerated nowadays more than prejudice toward racial minorities. Even on network comedy shows, old people are often the target of jokes and ridicule.

The problem with prejudices in general is that they tend to develop a life of their own and thus perpetuate the existence of negative stereotypes. In this article, Rodin and Langer show how negative labeling and stigmatization of the elderly cause old people to behave in ways that confirm the stereotypes against them, and what is even worse, to lower their self-esteem and sense of control over their environment. In other words, it causes them to internalize the negative label and behave in ways that make it come true.

The crucial question, of course, is how can the consequences of these negative labels and overattribution to age-related deficits be reversed? One answer has to do with social change, and it is advanced by the authors. Another answer has to do with environmental interventions aimed at increasing the elderly's self-esteem and sense of control. In this latter realm Rodin and Langer report some very exciting findings.

By the year 2000, it is estimated that over 15 percent of the population, 30 million people, will be 65 or over. Although aging affords status to people in some countries, in the United States and other industrialized nations, the elderly often suffer a loss of status, reduction in personal contacts and income, and a social climate that views aging with fearfulness and distaste. Even in some earlier civilizations, aging was viewed as a negative process. For example, the Nambikwara Indians have a single word that means "young and beautiful" and another that means "old and ugly." Since in the United States less than 5 percent of all people over 65 actually require custodial care, it may be asserted that at least 95 percent of the aged do not conform to the stereotype of the helpless and sick old person. Nevertheless, such stereotypes exist. Indeed, a number of studies examining such diverse cultural influences as children's and adolescent's literature, contemporary fiction and poetry, and popular jokes all found at least some negative stereotypes of the elderly.

In this paper, we describe several studies that investigated the social-psycholgical correlates of aging. Our goal was to understand how negative labeling and stigmatization of the elderly might contribute to behavior that actually confirmed prevalent stereotypes of old age and led to lowered self-esteem and diminished feelings of control. Given that stereotypes and social labels are in a sense simply summaries of cultural expectations, such expectations might be assumed to affect all members of the culture, including those about whom the labels are held. If one's self-image and behavior come to portray these negative stereotypes, self-esteem should decline. As self-esteem decreases, belief in one's ability to exercise control over the environment also declines.

Aging individuals may therefore overestimate decrements in their capacities that may be experienced as discrepant with their evaluative standards for competent behavior, and the effects of this awareness may be more debilitating than the change itself. When, in addition, there actually is a reduction of the number and kinds of potential options for control of the environment, as is the case for the elderly, this self-view is reconfirmed.

If these deleterious causal relationships can in fact be demonstrated, the underlying mechanisms determined, and the effects reversed, we expect that there would follow a restoration of both a more positive self-concept and a greater sense of control for the aged, as well as less age-stereotyped behavior. A simplified diagrammatic illustration of this process appears on page 93.

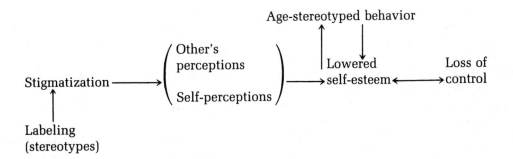

The next section examines some of the research bearing on these questions.

NEGATIVE STEREOTYPES TOWARD OLD AGE

If our society has developed labels that create certain sets of negative expectations with regard to aging, it is likely that people will act in a manner that is consistent with these labels. To the extent that a particular stereotype is actually believed, elderly persons may also begin to act in a manner that is consistent with that stereotype. Expectations based on the label senility, for example, may have a great impact on the way old people and those approaching old age view themselves.

Every time a mistake is made or a thought is forgotten, older people may question whether their mental capacities are diminishing. If people are worrying about their failing memory while in a situation where new learning could take place (e.g., learning the name of a new acquaintance), they might indeed "forget" what they had just learned. However, the problem would have been in the conditions surrounding the learning (distraction) and not a problem of memory at all. But how could the elderly come to this more benign conclusion in the face of the salient stereotypes that exist with respect to their cognitive capacities? Any such fears the elderly have about themselves are exacerbated by the dearth of appropriate role models who could serve as counter examples of what life after seventy might be like. Thus, it is critical to determine what negative stereotypes exist about the elderly, what behaviors they produce, and the extent to which older people also accept these views.

Langer and Mulvey[1] conducted a study to determine what specific behaviors are most commonly cited as characteristic of older people. Since

they expected senility to be prominent among them, they also asked whether there is a single conception of senility of whether these views change as a result of age? And most important, they questioned whether being old is seen as akin to being senile.

In this study, questionnaires were used to assess beliefs about the behavior of old age, and to determine whether information and attitudes about senile behavior vary as a function of age and familiarity with the elderly. Subjects were seventy-five adults between the ages of 25 and 40, twenty-five between the ages of 45 and 60, and twenty-five over the age of 70.

Following an introduction describing the purpose of the interview, several social demographic factors (e.g., size of family, education, and income) were assessed. None of these factors significantly affected the results. As part of the interview, respondents were then asked to list those behaviors they believed to be characteristic of people in three different age groups: 35–45, 65–75, and 75 and older. They were asked to go back over all the behaviors they had listed and indicate which, if any, they believed to be indications of senility. Next, they read descriptions of various events and were asked to describe what a senile person was likely to do in each situation. For example, "A senile person walks into a store and picks up a loaf of bread. He or she then _____." Finally, respondents were asked to indicate the likelihood that they themselves will become senile.

Responses were rated by judges who were unaware of both the population that the respondent represented and the experimental hypotheses. Categories of behaviors were tallied, and the descriptive passages were rated along the dimensions of negative–positive and active–passive, as well as on intelligence-related, memory-related, social-related, and personality-related dimensions.

The young and middle-age samples perceived old people as involved primarily in nonsocial be-

[1]Langer, E., and Mulvey, A. Unpublished data.

haviors and passive activities, and as possessing negative psychological characteristics to a much greater extent than positive ones. The old sample perceived just the opposite, placing significantly greater emphasis on social activities and positive psychological characteristics. Similarly, the younger population was more likely than their older counterparts to view the elderly as sickly. While the reactions of the elderly to general behavior seem more positive, we will see in the next study that when age-stereotyped behaviors are involved, their reactions become even more negative than those of younger adults.

For elderly, middle-aged and young respondents alike, there appeared to be a stereotype of the elderly adult that included a fairly well defined conception of senility. All age group samples viewed senility in very negative terms and labeled it as a condition of physical deterioration evidenced by memory loss, mental incompetence, loss of contact with reality, and helplessness. In addition, and most interesting, was the finding that over 65 percent of the younger group felt certain that they would not become senile, while only 10 percent of the elderly group expressed this sentiment. Thus, it appears that the fear of senility is very real for elderly people, even though according to medical criteria only 4 percent of persons over 65 years old suffer from a severe form of senility, and only another 10 percent of this population suffer from a milder version.

The approach used in this study was also intended to develop a list of behaviors associated with senility and to assess attitudes towards these behaviors. One factor limiting the validity of its results, however, is that responses to questions with value-laden content are always difficult to interpret. In an attempt to give what is felt to be the socially desirable answer, people very often respond as they think they should respond, even if the response is at odds with the way they actually think or feel. This is especially true when people are asked to express negative attitudes.

Consequently, we designed a second study to determine the extent to which different subject populations spontaneously apply the label "senility" to those behaviors most frequently listed by subjects in the first experiment, and to assess the consequences of those labels for other attitudes.

Forty female high school students, 40 middle-age women, and 40 older women were recruited for a study on person perception. To reduce differences among the age groups due to socioeconomic status and religion, the adults were the mothers and grandmothers of the students, who were randomly selected from a local high school. Each of the three groups of subjects was randomly assigned to one of two experimental conditions described below.

The three members of each family, tested individually, were shown three videotaped scenes involving dyadic interactions that they were asked to rate. Two of the scenes were the same for all subjects: one was of a young child and mother pleasantly interacting, and one was of two friends quarreling. These served as filler items. The experimental question was tested in the third scene, which for half the subjects in each age group depicted an interview where the target person, the interviewee, appeared forgetful by asking the interviewer to repeat something he said earlier on three separate occasions. This was the behavior most frequently cited in Study 1 as indicative of senility. The third scene for the remaining subjects also depicted an interview, but here the target person responded to the interviewer's questions without engaging in forgetful behavior.

Each group was further subdivided so that for half of the subjects in each group above, the person engaging in the senility-related or nonrelated behavior appeared to be about 35 years old, and for the other half, about 75 years old. These manipulations also provided an opportunity to assess the generality of the negative labeling process. Specifically, we were interested in learning whether even non-age-related behaviors of the elderly were likely to be labeled as evidence of senility and whether any of these behaviors, regardless of the label, were seen as more negative in older than younger persons.

To summarize, the study was a $3 \times 2 \times 2$ design where age of subject (approximately 18 years old, 40 years old, and 65 years old), behavior of target (senility-related or nonrelated), and age of target (young or old) were the independent variables. The relevant measures were responses to a questionnaire that followed each scene. The items were designed to determine whether the behavior of elderly persons was spontaneously labeled as senile and/or whether their behavior was generally evaluated more negatively. Subjects were asked to rate, for example, how much they liked the target person, how alert they thought she was, and how stable she appeared to be, on a series of 10-point scales. Open-ended questions asked for description of the people and interactions in the videotaped sequences.

We found a main effect for age of the target person for both measures. Regardless of the subjects' age, they were more likely to label the older target as senile than the young target person, which is hardly surprising. However, subjects also evaluated the same behaviors more negatively in the older target person than in the younger. We also found that the older, not the younger, respondents tended to evaluate the forgetful, elderly target most negatively, suggesting that the older one gets, the more frightened one is of being or becoming senile or showing other presumably age-related negative traits. This fear is likely to motivate older people to distance themselves, psychologically, from old people with difficulties such as forgetfulness, by evaluating them as negatively as possible, and thereby making them seem different from themselves. Taking this finding together with the data from the Langer and Mulvey study, it appears that older people are more positive towards the elderly overall than are younger people, but are also more negative than young people about the negative features of old age.

In general, this study also suggests that old age per se carries with it enough negative expectations so that a behavior that is seen as normal in a young person may be seized upon when engaged in by an elderly person as confirmation of the stereotype, and cloud the perception of the rest of the (target) individual's behavior.

EFFECTS OF AGE-RELEVANT LABELS ON BEHAVIOR

In the next study, we considered the extent to which professionals who may deal with the elderly use age as a cue for interpreting behavior, and whether the labels they assign then affect their behavior. Miller, Lowenstein, and Winston (1976) have reported very negative attitudes among physicians working with the aged ill. In this study, Caplovitz and Rodin[2] provided psychotherapists with information describing the pathological behavior of seven different individuals, randomly ordered in a questionnaire. These questionnaires were given to psychologists and psychiatrists asking them to provide a DSM-II diagnosis, describe briefly the course of treatment plan, and describe the site of treatment (e.g., hospital, community mental health center, or outpatient facility). Identical behaviors were described to all therapists, the only difference being that for half the subjects, six of the cases gave a young age as part of the case history. For the other half of the subjects, the target person was described as in his or her sixties or seventies. As a control, the seventh case described a middle-aged person and was identical for all subjects.

The experiment showed a greater propensity to diagnose the same psychotic behavior as organically based when the individual was old rather than young. When the pathology was less serious, both older and younger target persons received the diagnosis of depression about equally often, but the treatment prescribed for the two age groups varied in many cases. Not surprisingly, more long-term therapy was prescribed for younger than older targets. However, in addition, less use of drug therapy and more community-based and group treatments were suggested for the young individuals. The same case history for an older individual elicited treatment diagnoses that were often drug-related and more demanding of acute institutionalization. Thus, it is apparent that age does influence both diagnosis and recommendations for treatment of elderly persons. We are not implying that age does not provide some useful diagnostic or treatment information, but simply that it may be accounting for too much of the variance in these decisions.

Having demonstrated some features of the nature and extent of labeling processes regarding the elderly, we next wished to consider how these labels and negative stereotypes might affect actual interactions involving older people. In the following study, we investigated the effects of expectations regarding the elderly on the demands that a younger person was willing to make on an older person.

Subjects were asked to participate in a study on interviewing methods and were told that our goal was to determine the effectiveness of open-ended questions in learning about personality. Subjects were drawn from a population of middle-aged adults and were randomly assigned to one of two conditions. They were given biographical information leading them to expect to interact with, and interview, either a person 42 years old or a person 71 years old. Each group was further subdivided and given additional expectations regarding the interviewee's competence: They were told that the person was either typical for her age, below average for her age, or above average for her age in mental alertness. All subjects were given a questionnaire, which presumably was to guide their subsequent interview, and were asked to look it over and check off those questions they intended to ask. The questions covered several areas and were of varying difficulty.

---

[2]Caplovitz, L., and Rodin, J. Unpublished data.

Older targets were given, on the average, easier questions than younger targets, regardless of their competence level. Furthermore, preliminary analyses also suggest that the interviewee's competence was a more important determinant of question selection for the younger target than for the older. The questions were more difficult for the young respondent presumed to be competent; this was less true for the older target.

The studies described thus far have tried to determine whether or not some negative stereotypes regarding aging exist. They do indeed appear to be salient and prevalent. For example, while only a small proportion of elderly people actually are senile, attributions of senility were extensive. While 95 percent of elderly adults are not in need of custodial care, younger people assume that the typical elderly adult is sick. The studies discussed thus far also were designed to assess deleterious effects of negative labels. The results point to the kind (or lack) of treatment older people might get from health practitioners, and to the kind (or lack) of demands that society-at-large might make on them, which may work to lower self-esteem and actually bring about performance decrements. It should be kept in mind that negative stereotyping is detrimental for all people. However, we believe that it is particularly harmful for the aged because they are a highly vulnerable population due to increased incidence of significant life changes and environmental strains. The following studies were designed to begin to specify why these stereotypes, reflecting an overestimate of the population frequency or intensity of the characteristics being rated, exist.

Reasons for the Occurrence of Negative Labels

One might first want to consider why certain negative stereotypes of the elderly persist in the absence of large numbers of helpless elderly people. One explanation lies in the work on the use of the availability and representativeness heuristics in judging frequency. This work suggests that the more easily instances come to mind, the more frequent they are judged to be. Consider this in conjunction with the likehood that older people who are physically fit are often mistaken for younger adults, leaving the extremes of the aged population as the most salient members of the class. (Of course, the error of mistaking old-looking young people for older adults would lead to the same conclusion.) Images of these elderly people would then be called to mind most readily when one

thinks of old age, resulting in inappropriate conclusions about late adulthood.

Factors other than availability-based errors also contribute to the maintenance of negative stereotypes. Langer, Taylor, Fiske, and Chanowitz (1976) have shown that persons from relatively unfamiliar groups make others uncomfortable and are often avoided, and that such negative reactions are the result of a conflict that these persons arouse in others. On the one hand, people are motivated to stare at unfamiliar or novel stimuli in an attempt to understand them; while on the other hand, there are strong proscriptive norms that prohibit engaging in that very behavior when the novel stimulus is another person. The conflict is resolved by avoiding that person. This has been demonstrated to be true when the novel stimuli are people with physical handicaps or pregnant women. Specifically, the hypothesis tested was that sanctioned visual access to a novel stimulus person, prior to an interaction with that person, would result in subject behavior similar to that which follows sanctioned visual access to a "normal" adult. This hypothesis received strong support in the Langer et al. (1976) studies.

Most of the settings where younger adults and children spend their time are not places likely to have a great number of older persons present, for example, sports activities and work sites. This may make older persons relatively novel stimuli when they are present, for example, at restaurants. We could deduce, therefore, that negative feelings and avoidance would be likely on those occasions. By removing the conflict that novel-stimulus persons create, avoidance should be reduced. Thus, we reasoned that at least some of the bias against the elderly may be decreased by making them less novel.

If the old are avoided, and this avoidance has in other contexts been shown to be reduced by allowing someone simply to watch the person, it seems worthwhile to broaden the scope of our inquiry in two ways:

1. by studying the impact of avoidance on the elderly's self-concept and behavior;
2. by studying the effects of increased exposure to effective elderly persons on the behavior of both elderly and nonelderly populations.

We have already begun a study to determine how avoidance by others affects one's self-concept and behavior. It has been suggested in the literature on aging that dissociation is produced by a nonaccepting culture. Strauss (1963), for example, maintains that those elderly persons who perceive the environment as one that devalues them tend, as a result, to withdraw from involvement in their surroundings and instead engage in more solitary activities. While this argument is compelling, virtually all data reported in this area are correlational, making it difficult to separate cause from effect. Do people retreat because they are rejected, or do they appear to be rejected merely because they have voluntarily retreated, as disengagement theory suggests?

In a study on avoidance and self-concept, we have been developing an experimental model of the rejection process using a nonelderly population to determine whether rejection can produce the social withdrawal and disengagement-like behavior frequently seen in the aged. Clearly, persons who are already old do not provide the appropriate sample with which to test the causal factors of this process, because it is assumed that they are currently displaying the effects. We therefore are testing younger subjects who are either avoided or not avoided. It is expected that being avoided will lead to negative feelings and withdrawal. To reverse these effects, in half the cases subjects are encouraged to attribute this result to some aspect of the situation. It is expected that attribution to the situation, rather than to oneself, will lessen the impact of social avoidance.

Attribution About Aging

We have observed that chronological age per se is not sufficient to provide a person with the self-definition of "old," although obviously there is some relationship between chronological age and self-perception. Rather, a series of events or experiences forces acceptance, although reluctantly, of the fact that one is old, and often these events have avoidance and/or the loss of control at their core. Once this occurs, it may be that older people then evaluate themselves on the basis of feelings and behaviors that they attribute to aging rather than to the environment and circumstance.

Negative attributional processes deriving from feeling avoided and from reduced feelings of control can create at least two different types of problems for older people that may lower their number of coping attempts and thus detrimentally affect their health. First, there is a tendency to overattribute most of their negative physical symptoms to aging per se, especially to the presumed physical decline with which aging is associated. Bio-

logical attributions may incorrectly focus the person away from situational and social factors, such as the loss of a loved one or feeling unsafe; these are stress-inducing in part because they are associated with a loss of control. Recent work has shown that even among healthy college students, loss of control is related to increased experience of symptoms. Second, when events are attributed to the aging process, they are seen as inevitable; and remedial steps that could be extremely beneficial may not be undertaken.

The negative self-concept of elderly persons would further increase the likelihood that they will make damaging self, rather than situational, attributions when they perceive, whether veridically or not, that they are being avoided, or when they experience reduced feelings of control. Interventions might then be developed to redirect these attributions. We have already conducted some work on this question, looking more generally at the consequences of attributional processes and the possibility of changing them.

We interviewed people in the week that followed their entering a nursing home, and selected the 80 percent who made explicit negative attributions to physical decline associated with aging as either causing or contributing greatly to some of their problems. We took a variety of premeasures including interviews, health measures, and observations of level of participation. There were three randomly assigned groups: one group was untreated; one group was simply given information trying to argue against physical decline in aging as being the real source of their problems (using material taken from doctors' reports and journal articles); and the third group was given environmental explanations (or at least age–environment interactional attributions) as being the source of their problems.

As an example of some environmental attributions that were used, subjects in the latter group were told that the floors in the nursing home are very slippery because they are tiled in order to keep them clean. Even young people slip on them. By this means, we tried to reduce the attribution that slipping was due to weak knees or poor movement that resulted from their age. As another example, they were reminded that they were awakened at 5:30 in the morning, which would make most people tired by evening. Again, we tried to minimize the likelihood that they would attribute their weariness to aging per se. Thus, we simply attempted to refocus their explanations for their own feelings and behavior onto plausible factors in the environment that could have been producing some of the physical symptoms they were likely to be experiencing.

As a result of the reattribution intervention, patients showed greatly improved behavior, including an increase in active participation and sociability relative to groups simply given information or to untreated controls. There were also benefits in the area of general health and indices of stress. Thus, debilitating and often excessive attribution to physical states associated with aging and decline can be refocused, with beneficial effects, onto more easily changed aspects of the environment.

In another study, we demonstrated that attributions about whether the same task was a memory test, or was a new activity being introduced into the nursing home, dramatically influenced subjects' subsequent performance. Those expecting to be tested performed significantly less well than those expecting to try out a new "activity."

Reversing Memory "Loss"

Overattribution to aging rather than to environmental sources, coupled with the negative labeling process described above, work together to decrease self-esteem and diminish performance. Often this results in a lack of motivation to engage in a variety of behaviors, rather than an inability to do so. Over time, and with disuse, the abilities themselves may also decline.

Taking loss of memory as an example, we speculated that some component of memory loss may be due to the operation of these social-psychological factors, which produce symptoms of forgetfulness and confusion that have nothing to do with aging per se. We reasoned that, in some older individuals, apparently diminished memory could be reversed by increasing motivation for thinking and remembering.

In two studies, we attempted to motivate elderly nursing home residents to adhere to a recommended course of action over time that asked them to think about and remember a variety of events. In the first study, we tried to increase motivation to remember by providing the opportunity for reciprocal self-disclosure between the subject and an interviewer who recommended the particular course of cognitive activity. Janis and Rodin (1979) have hypothesized that establishing referent power is an important way to increase motivation and promote commitment. Persons have referent power for those who perceive them as benevolent and accepting. Eliciting and some-

times reciprocating self-disclosure is one factor that is critical in helping a person to establish referent power. In the second study we tried to increase motivation to use one's memory by setting up a contingency in which greater cognitive effort resulted in greater tangible reward (chips that could be traded for gifts). In both studies, the recommended course of action involved remembering a series of questions and probing the environment and one's long-term memory for information relevant to their answers. Both studies had "no treatment" controls as well as a control group treated in all ways identical to experimental subjects except that, in the first study, *low* reciprocal self-disclosure was elicited and, in the second study, the rewards were *not contingent* upon performance.

In both studies, experimental subjects showed a significant improvement on standard short-term memory tests including probe and pattern recall, as well as improvement on nurses' ratings of alertness, mental activity, and social adjustment, relative to controls. Thus, we found that restructuring the environment to make it more demanding, and then motivating elderly people to increase their cognitive activity, leads to improvements in memory that are generalizable. It is critical to note that the experimental treatments provided no explicit training for the memory tests that constituted the dependent variables of greatest interest. While we did not measure self-esteem directly, we found that experimental subjects were rated as happier and more involved following the intervention, and we may infer that they were feeling better about themselves.

Thus, it appears that the consequences of major changes associated with aging, overattribution to physical decline associated with aging, and the effects of negative stereotypes regarding aging can be reversed by appropriate environmental manipulations. We predict that this will be true for many factors other than apparent memory loss, which have been adduced to be inevitable consequences of aging for most persons. Our earliest work in this area showed that when even relatively debilitated nursing home residents were given the opportunity to make decisions and to feel increased responsibility, thus potentially reducing their negative self-labeling, they became more involved, active and self-initiating, as well as considerably happier, and they showed dramatic health-related benefits. Thus, reversals are even possible in nursing home environments, which foster a sense of dependency and loss of control.

CONCLUSIONS

Although there have been papers suggesting that aging is correlated with negative labels, for the most part these notions have not been examined under controlled experimental conditions, nor have the antecedent variables been elucidated. In this paper, we described our studies examining the relationship between aging and cognitive social psychological factors with specific references to labeling, control and self-concept. In this research, we investigated if and how the aged are negatively stereotyped, and the consequences of negative labels associated with aging. We demonstrated how such labels and attributions may, in turn, affect the self-concept and behavior of the elderly, and lead to decrements in perceived control. We then investigated how changing labels, and giving control experiences, can serve to reinstate motivation in some elderly individuals, thereby promoting more self-benefiting behavior. However, we also believe that making these changes at the individual level is only a short-term solution.

Social change is a complex process that does not lend itself to easy analysis. Nevertheless, it seems that every successful movement has at least included the following elements: (1) There is a public protest when media or important professional groups are intentionally or unintentionally (usually the latter) insulting. (2) The social stereotype of the affected group becomes so well known that it becomes a public joke and an emblem of bigotry. Comic villains like Archie Bunker bring home the message. (3) There is exposure of the person for whom acceptance is sought. The first black was seen on a television commercial in New York City in the late sixties. Now it is routine. The exposure seems to shift first from merely including the person in situations from which they were previously omitted—for example, an office setting—to gradually presenting them in a positive light, and then making them the focal heroes or heroines.

The elderly have not yet been this fortunate. In the mid-1970s, one of the three major networks pilot-tested a situation comedy in which two elderly people lived together, rather than marrying, in order to keep earning maximal Social Security benefits. Their relationship to their shocked, conservative children and to the outside world formed the basis for the satire. It was funny, endearing, and very human. But the project was abandoned; neither commercial sponsors nor the test market were ready. Perhaps the turn of the decade will prove a more opportune time to reverse cultural biases against this population.

However, we must end with two important caveats. First, the solicitousness and increased care that this type of consciousness-raising may bring could result in even greater debilitation for the elderly. What is needed is not simply attention or pampering, which foster dependency, but rather increased opportunities for esteem-building and self-control. Second, this line of reasoning argues strongly for social change that provides opportunities for real control, not simply strategies that increase perceived control while options for actual control remain unavailable. If older persons are led to expect more control over their destinies, which they then find themselves unable to exercise, they are most likely to blame themselves. Once again, this could produce great debilitation and even death, given the strong association between chronic stress induced by a lack of control and ill health among the elderly.

REFERENCES

Janis, I., & Rodin, J. Attitude, control, and decision-making: Social psychology and health care. In G. Stone, N. Adler, & F. Cohen (eds.), *Health Psychology.* San Francisco: Jossey-Bass, 1979.

Langer, E., Taylor, S., Fiske, S., & Chanowitz, B. Stigma, staring and discomfort. *Journal of Experimental Social Psychology,* 1976, *12,* 451–63.

Miller, D. B., Lowenstein, R., & Winston, R. Physicians' attitudes toward the ill aged and nursing homes. *Journal of the American Geriatrics Society,* 1976, *24,* 498–505.

Strauss, D. The relationship between perception of the environment and the retrenchment syndrome in a geriatric population. *Dissertation Abstracts,* 1963, *24,* 1975–76.

PROJECTS

Name _____

Date _____

4.1: IMPRESSION FORMATION AND AGE

The purpose of this project is to investigate the way we form first impressions about people and how these impressions are affected by the person's age.

You will notice that the two patient profiles presented on the next two pages are identical with only one exception, namely, the patient's age: In one, the patient is 69 years old, in the other 29. In order to discover the difference that age makes, choose two people as subjects. Show each subject one of the profiles. It is important that the two subjects you choose are of the same sex, race, cultural background, and approximate age, so that the differences you find in their impressions of the patient cannot be attributed to these critical differences. Since the instructions are printed on the questionnaire, have the subjects read them and indicate whether they are clear. Once the subjects have responded to the questionnaires, you can explain to them the exact nature of the study and offer to share with them the results, once they are analyzed in the class. (When you promise to share the results, it is essential that you keep your promise.)

Once questionnaires have been collected from all the students in the class, they can be tabulated on the blackboard in two columns, representing the two ages. A *t*-test will indicate whether the differences between the impressions of the subject when she was thought to be 29 are significantly different from the impressions of her when she was thought to be 69.

What do the results tell you about aging labels?

Sex _____

Age _____

Impression Formation Study

This is a study in what is called "impression formation": the factors that enter into the judgments a person makes about what another person is like. In this particular investigation, we are concerned about the impressions that are formed from quite limited information about another person.

What you will be reading is a portion of a clinical interview.

After you read it, you will be asked to respond to a series of questions about the person, in the form of a multiple-choice questionnaire. There are no "correct" or "true" answers. What we are interested in finding out is how the person strikes you—your guesses and impressions.

Patient Profile

The patient is a 69-year-old married female who has had one child. She is a historian of science with a Ph.D. degree. Although she has no physical abnormalities and an extensive battery of medical tests gave all indications of a normal, healthy woman, the patient complains of a recent and drastic change in mood and affect and is suffering from outwardly visible tension and anxiety. From self-report, she is currently given to fits of rage, both verbal and physical, in the home environment, though she is able to handle the work situation fairly well with only momentary lapses in concentration. In family life she is unable to deal with her family responsibilities and finds it impossible to be a loving companion to her spouse. She is anxious about the utter lack of affection and warmth she exhibits in interacting with her family and especially about what she describes as periods of extreme alienation from her spouse. She also complains of great difficulty in sleeping since she is often awakened by disturbingly vivid nightmares. Patient also suffers from periods of hopelessness and despair, in which she constantly questions the value of life and her own adequacy as a woman.

In the following items, you are to rate the person on each attribute by circling the number which best matches your judgment.

1. Independent	1	2	3	4	5	6	Dependent
2. Insincere	1	2	3	3	5	6	Sincere
3. Not at all success-oriented	1	2	3	4	5	6	Success-oriented
4. Unintelligent	1	2	3	4	5	6	Intelligent
5. Active	1	2	3	4	5	6	Passive
6. Competent	1	2	3	4	5	6	Incompetent
7. Opinionated	1	2	3	4	5	6	Open-minded
8. Unambitious	1	2	3	4	5	6	Ambitious
9. Not at all kind	1	2	3	4	5	6	Kind
10. Well adjusted	1	2	3	4	5	6	Maladjusted
11. Unaggressive	1	2	3	4	5	6	Aggressive
12. Insensitive	1	2	3	4	5	6	Sensitive
13. Dominant	1	2	3	4	5	6	Submissive
14. Warm	1	2	3	4	5	6	Cold
15. Not at all determined	1	2	3	4	5	6	Determined
16. Stands up well under pressure	1	2	3	4	5	6	Goes to pieces under pressure
17. Forgetful	1	2	3	4	5	6	Excellent memory

Sex _____

Age _____

Impression Formation Study

This is a study in what is called "impression formation": the factors that enter into the judgments a person makes about what another person is like. In this particular investigation, we are concerned about the impressions that are formed from quite limited information about another person.

What you will be reading is a portion of a clinical interview.

After you read it, you will be asked to respond to a series of questions about the person, in the form of a multiple-choice questionnaire. There are no "correct" or "true" answers. What we are interested in finding out is how the person strikes you—your guesses and impressions.

Patient Profile

The patient is a 29-year-old married female who has one child. She is a historian of science with a Ph.D. degree. Although she has no physical abnormalities and an extensive battery of medical tests gave all indications of a normal, healthy woman, the patient complains of a recent and drastic change in mood and affect and is suffering from outwardly visible tension and anxiety. From self-report, she is currently given to fits of rage, both verbal and physical, in the home environment, though she is able to handle the work situation fairly well with only momentary lapses in concentration. In family life she is unable to deal with her family responsibilities and finds it impossible to be a loving companion to her spouse. She is anxious about the utter lack of affection and warmth she exhibits in interacting with her family and especially about what she describes as periods of extreme alienation from her spouse. She also complains of great difficulty in sleeping since she is often awakened by disturbingly vivid nightmares. Patient also suffers from periods of hopelessness and despair, in which she constantly questions the value of life and her own adequacy as a woman.

In the following items, you are to rate the person on each attribute by circling the number which best matches your judgment.

1.	Independent	1	2	3	4	5	6	Dependent
2.	Insincere	1	2	3	4	5	6	Sincere
3.	Not at all success-oriented	1	2	3	4	5	6	Success-oriented
4.	Unintelligent	1	2	3	4	5	6	Intelligent
5.	Active	1	2	3	4	5	6	Passive
6.	Competent	1	2	3	4	5	6	Incompetent
7.	Opinionated	1	2	3	4	5	6	Open-minded
8.	Unambitious	1	2	3	4	5	6	Ambitious
9.	Not at all kind	1	2	3	4	5	6	Kind
10.	Well adjusted	1	2	3	4	5	6	Maladjusted
11.	Unaggressive	1	2	3	4	5	6	Aggressive
12.	Insensitive	1	2	3	4	5	6	Sensitive
13.	Dominant	1	2	3	4	5	6	Submissive
14.	Warm	1	2	3	4	5	6	Cold
15.	Not at all determined	1	2	3	4	5	6	Determined
16.	Stands up well under pressure	1	2	3	4	5	6	Goes to pieces under pressure
17.	Forgetful	1	2	3	4	5	6	Excellent memory

4.2: PERCEPTIONS INFLUENCED BY AWARENESS OF A PERSON'S ETHNICITY

What are Jews like? Poles? Italians? Chinese? Blacks? Do people hold generalized perceptions of other people because of their ethnicity? This project will help you discover that for yourself. First you have to decide what ethnic group you would like to study (as a class or as an individual project). Each student should approach at least two people and ask them to take part in an impression formation study. Those who agree to participate should be asked to conjure up an image of a particular ethnic group and then describe it on the rating scales that follow. Half the subjects should be asked to describe a white Anglo-Saxon Protestant, and the other half a member of the ethnic group chosen for study. The data collected from all the students will enable a comparison of the subject's perceptions as influenced by awareness of a person's ethnicity.

The person you have in mind is: _____

dominant	1	2	3	4	5	6	submissive
warm	1	2	3	4	5	6	cold
unambitious	1	2	3	4	5	6	ambitious
stupid	1	2	3	4	5	6	smart
clean	1	2	3	4	5	6	dirty
disliked	1	2	3	4	5	6	liked
poised	1	2	3	4	5	6	unpoised
unaggressive	1	2	3	4	5	6	aggressive
insensitive	1	2	3	4	5	6	sensitive
active	1	2	3	4	5	6	passive

The person you have in mind is: _____

dominant	1	2	3	4	5	6	submissive
warm	1	2	3	4	5	6	cold
unambitious	1	2	3	4	5	6	ambitious
stupid	1	2	3	4	5	6	smart
clean	1	2	3	4	5	6	dirty
disliked	1	2	3	4	5	6	liked
poised	1	2	3	4	5	6	unpoised
unaggressive	1	2	3	4	5	6	aggressive
insensitive	1	2	3	4	5	6	sensitive
active	1	2	3	4	5	6	passive

The person you have in mind is: _____

dominant	1	2	3	4	5	6	submissive
warm	1	2	3	4	5	6	cold
unambitious	1	2	3	4	5	6	ambitious
stupid	1	2	3	4	5	6	smart
clean	1	2	3	4	5	6	dirty
disliked	1	2	3	4	5	6	liked
poised	1	2	3	4	5	6	unpoised
unaggressive	1	2	3	4	5	6	aggressive
insensitive	1	2	3	4	5	6	sensitive
active	1	2	3	4	5	6	passive

Name _____

Date _____

4.3: BEING DEVIANT FOR A DAY

In many instances, the kinds of behavior that people view as strange, bizarre, or even pathological are those that deviate from the normative standards in a particular situation. These standards are often unwritten and implicit, but their influence is quite strong, as we can see by people's reactions when someone violates them. The use of such situational norms to define what is deviant is an example of the social basis of prejudice.

This project is designed to help you gain an increased awareness of the power of normative standards through engaging in one of the norm-violating behaviors listed below.

a. Dress in a fashion that is very atypical of you, such as wearing a dress or suit if you usually wear jeans, and note your friends' reactions. Or dress in a fashion that is considered out of place or inappropriate for a particular situation (e.g., wear a sweat shirt and jeans to a formal dance).

b. Whenever someone asks you how you are or how you are feeling, respond with a detailed answer describing your feelings, recent activities, state of health, and so on.

c. When talking to someone, stand either too close (within one foot) or too far away (about three feet). Try to maintain this distance, even if the other person moves to change it.

1. How did people react to you when you violated a norm? List both their verbal and their nonverbal responses.

2. How did you feel while you were behaving in a deviant way?

AFFILIATION, ATTRACTION, AND LOVE

5

One of the basic assumptions of social psychology is that people are "social animals." That is, they live with other people, interact with others, influence others, and are affected by others. John Donne eloquently stated this principle: "No man is an island, entire of itself; every man is a piece of the continent. . . ."

Clearly, all of us are social beings. But why is this so? What do we get from other people that we could not get from ourselves? Why do we seem to need others so much? To begin with, other people are necessary for our basic survival. As infants or young children, we cannot care for ourselves. Furthermore, we need people to teach us language, as well as intellectual and motor skills. We turn to other people for information about the world and for help and guidance in dealing with it. We achieve self-knowledge through other people's reactions to us—that is, how we see ourselves is to a large extent determined by whether we are loved or neglected, approved of or disapproved of, encouraged or discouraged by others. Although we may feel that we could do without particular people, we cannot do without them all. Everyone in the world needs people, and the most fortunate may be those who recognize those needs and satisfy them successfully.

MEASUREMENT OF ROMANTIC LOVE

ZICK RUBIN

It is likely that more has been written about love than about any other human experience. Given this overwhelming preoccupation, it is somewhat surprising to discover that love has not been a major topic of study by social psychologists. Indeed, it is only within the last fifteen years that they have taken a systematic look at love, and the article that follows, "Measurement of Romantic Love," reports one of the first of these research projects.

Why have psychologists paid so little attention to love? There are several possible answers. The behaviorist tradition in psychology has led researchers to focus on observable external behavior. Because love is considered an internal emotion, it may have been regarded as not particularly susceptible to scientific study. Furthermore, the popular view of love is that it is a mystical, ineffable state that cannot be precisely defined or described, only experienced. To the extent that psychologists agreed with this viewpoint, they may not have considered studying love, at least not until the recent development of research on various states of consciousness. Another explanation is that there is a general bias in psychology toward studying pathologies. In other words, more attention is focused on such things as mental illness, prejudice, and aggres-

sion, all of which cause some form of personal and social suffering and demand immediate solutions. Because love is not considered to be a problem in the same sense, there has been no comparable sense of an urgent need to study it. Finally, there is the popular belief that the scientific study of something as mysterious as love will only destroy it in some way, and thus there is the recurring admonition to scientists to leave well enough alone. Some of these attitudes were reflected in Senator William Proxmire's recent criticism of federally funded research on love and attraction, to which he gave a "Golden Fleece Award" for apparently absurd expenditures of taxpayers' money. These attitudes also occur with some regularity in springtime newspaper editorials decrying any attempt to objectify love (see the boxed excerpt "Psychologists and Love").

The research described by Rubin has itself been criticized on these grounds. Some people have felt that it is absurd to use a scale to measure love. Others have taken a "So, what else is new?" attitude about his findings. Nevertheless, this research is important for breaking new theoretical ground and for helping to open the doors to a new area of scientific concern. And in view of the enormous problems in and failures of love relationships (as reflected in divorce statistics, the numbers of people who seek outside help for their love problems, articles in print about such problems, and so on), it would serve the cause of greater human happiness and well-being to give serious study to the subject.

Love is generally regarded to be the deepest and most meaningful of sentiments. It has occupied a preeminent position in the art and literature of every age, and it is presumably experienced, at least occasionally, by the vast majority of people. In Western culture, moreover, the association between love and marriage gives it a unique status as a link between the individual and the structure of society.

In view of these considerations, it is surprising to discover that social psychologists have devoted virtually no attention to love. Although interpersonal attraction has been a major focus of social-psychological theory and research, workers in this area have not attempted to conceptualize love as an independent entity. For Heider (1958), for example, "loving" is merely intense liking—there is no discussion of possible qualitative differences between the two. Newcomb (1960) does not include love on his list of the "varieties of interpersonal attraction." Even in experiments directed specifically at "romantic" attraction . . ., the dependent measure is simply a verbal report of "liking."

The present research was predicated on the assumption that love may be independently con-

ceptualized and measured. In keeping with a strategy of construct validation, the attempts to define love, to measure it, and to assess its relationships to other variables are all seen as parts of a single endeavor. An initial assumption in this enterprise is that love is an *attitude* held by a person toward a particular other person, involving predispositions to think, feel, and behave in certain ways toward that other person. This assumption places love in the mainstream of social-psychological approaches to interpersonal attraction, alongside such other varieties of attraction as liking, admiration, and respect.

The view of love as a multifaceted attitude implies a broader perspective than that held by those theorists who view love as an "emotion," a "need," or a set of behaviors. On the other hand, its linkage to a particular target implies a more restricted view than that held by those who regard love as an aspect of the individual's personality or experience which transcends particular persons and situations. As Orlinsky (1972) has suggested, there may well be important common elements among different varieties of "love" (e.g., filial love, marital love, love of God). The focus of the present research, however, was restricted to *romantic love*, which may be defined simply as love between unmarried opposite-sex peers, of the sort which could possibly lead to marriage.

The research had three major phases. First, a paper-and-pencil love scale was developed. Second, the love scale was employed in a questionnaire study of student dating couples. Third, the predictive validity of the love scale was assessed in a laboratory experiment.

DEVELOPING A LOVE SCALE

The development of a love scale was guided by several considerations:

1. Inasmuch as the content of the scale would constitute the initial conceptual definition of romantic love, its items must be grounded in existing theoretical and popular conceptions of love.

2. Responses to these items, if they are tapping a single underlying attitude, must be highly intercorrelated.

3. In order to establish the discriminant validity of the love scale, it was constructed in conjunction with a parallel scale of liking. The goal was to develop internally consistent scales of love and of liking which would be conceptually distinct from one another and which would, in practice, be only moderately intercorrelated.

The first step in this procedure was the assembling of a large pool of questionnaire items referring to a respondent's attitude toward a particular other person (the "target person"). Half of these items were suggested by a wide range of speculations about the nature of love. These items referred to physical attraction, idealization, a predisposition to help, the desire to share emotions and experiences, feelings of exclusiveness and absorption, felt affiliative and dependent needs, the holding of ambivalent feelings, and the relative unimportance of universalistic norms in the relationship. The other half of the items were suggested by the existing theoretical and empirical literature on interpersonal attraction (or liking). They included references to the desire to affiliate with the target in various settings, evaluation of the target on several dimensions, the salience of norms of responsibility and equity, feelings of respect and trust, and the perception that the target is similar to oneself. . . .

To provide some degree of consensual validation for this initial categorization of items, two successive panels of student and faculty judges sorted the items into love and liking categories, relying simply on their personal understanding of the connotations of the two labels. Following this screening procedure, a revised set of 70 items was administered to 198 introductory psychology students during their regular class sessions. Each respondent completed the items with reference to his or her girlfriend or boyfriend (if he had one), and also with reference to a nonromantically viewed platonic friend of the opposite sex. The scales of love and of liking which were employed in the subsequent phases of the research were arrived at through factor analyses of these responses. . . . There was a general factor accounting for a large proportion of the total variance. The items loading highest on this general factor, particularly for lovers, were almost exclusively those which had previously been categorized as love items. These high-loading items defined the more circumscribed conception of love adopted. The items forming the liking scale were based on those which loaded highly on the second factor with respect to platonic friends. . . .

Components of Romantic Love

1. *Affiliative and dependent need*—for example, "If I could never be with _____, I would feel miserable"; "It would be hard for me to get along without _____."

2. *Predisposition to help*—for example, "If _____ were feeling badly, my first duty would be to cheer him (her) up"; "I would do almost anything for _____."

3. *Exclusiveness and absorption*—for example, "I feel very possessive toward _____"; "I feel that I can confide in _____ about virtually everything."

The emerging conception of romantic love, as defined by the content of the scale, has an eclectic flavor. The affiliative and dependent need component evokes both Freud's (1955) view of love as sublimated sexuality and Harlow's (1958) equation of love with attachment behavior. The predisposition to help is congruent with Fromm's (1956) analysis of the components of love, which he identifies as care, responsibility, respect, and knowledge. Absorption in a single other person is the aspect of love which is pointed to most directly by Slater's (1963) analysis of the social-structural implications of dyadic intimacy. The conception of liking, as defined by the liking-scale items, includes components of favorable evaluation and respect for the target person, as well as the perception that the target is similar to oneself. It is in reasonably close accord with measures of attraction employed in previous research.

QUESTIONNAIRE STUDY

The 13-item love and liking scales, with their component items interspersed, were included in a questionnaire administered in October 1968 to 158 dating (but nonengaged) couples at the University of Michigan, recruited by means of posters and newspaper ads. In addition to the love and liking scales, completed first with respect to one's dating partner and later with respect to a close, same-sex friend, the questionnaire contained several personality scales and requests for background information about the dating relationship. Each partner completed the questionnaire individually and was paid $1 for taking part. The modal couple consisted of a junior man and a sophomore or junior woman who had been dating for about 1 year. . . .

The love scale had high internal consistency and, as desired, was only moderately correlated with the liking scale. The finding that love and liking were more highly correlated among men than among women was unexpected. It provides at least suggestive support for the notion that women discriminate more sharply between the two sentiments than men do. . . .

The love scores of men (for their girlfriends) and women (for their boyfriends) were almost identical. Women *liked* their boyfriends somewhat more than they were liked in return, however. Inspection of the item means in Table 1 indicates that this sex difference may be attributed to the higher ratings given by women to their boyfriends on such "task-related" dimensions as intelligence, good judgment, and leadership potential. To the extent that these items accurately represent the construct of liking, men may indeed tend to be more "likable" (but not more "lovable") than women. There was no such sex difference with respect to the respondents' liking for their same-sex friends. The mean liking-for-friend scores for the two sexes were virtually identical. Thus, the data do not support the conclusion that men are generally more likable than women, but only that they are liked more in the context of the dating relationship.

Women tended to *love* their same-sex friends more than men did. This result is in accord with cultural stereotypes concerning male and female friendships. It is more socially acceptable for female than for male friends to speak of themselves as "loving" one another, and it has been reported that women tend to confide in same-sex friends more than men do (Jourard & Lasakow, 1958). Finally, . . . whereas both women and men *liked* their

dating partners only slightly more than they liked their same-sex friends, they *loved* their dating partners much more than their friends. . . .

TABLE 1. MUTUAL GAZING (IN SECONDS)

GROUP	$\bar{x}$
Strong together	56.2
Weak together	44.7
Strong apart	46.7
Weak apart	40.0

Although love scores were highly related to perceived marriage probability, these variables may be distinguished from one another on empirical as well as conceptual grounds. The length of time that the couple had been dating was unrelated to love scores among men, and only slightly related among women. In contrast, the respondents' perceptions of their closeness to marriage were significantly correlated with length of dating among both men and women. These results are in keeping with the common observations that although love may develop rather quickly, progress toward marriage typically occurs only over a longer period of time. . . .

LABORATORY EXPERIMENT: LOVE AND GAZING

Although the questionnaire results provided evidence for the construct validity of the emerging conception of romantic love, it remained to be determined whether love-scale scores could be used to predict behavior outside the realm of questionnaire responses. The notion that romantic love includes a component of exclusiveness and absorption led to the prediction that in an unstructured laboratory situation, dating partners who loved each other a great deal would gaze into one another's eyes more than would partners who loved each other to a lesser degree.

The test of the prediction involved a comparison between "strong-love" and "weak-love" couples, as categorized by their scores on the love scale. To control for the possibility that "strong" and "weak" lovers differ from one another in their more general interpersonal orientations, additional groups were included in which subjects were paired with opposite-sex strangers. The love scores of subjects in these "apart" groups were equated with those of the subjects who were paired with their own dating partners (the "together" groups). In contrast to the prediction for the together groups, no difference in the amount of eye contact engaged in by the strong-apart and weak-apart groups was expected.

METHOD

Subjects

Two pools of subjects were established from among the couples who completed the questionnaire. Those couples in which both partners scored above the median on the love scale (92 or higher) were designated strong-love couples, and those in which both partners scored below the median were designated weak-love couples. Couples in which one partner scored above and the other below the median were not included in the experiment. Within each of the two pools, the couples were divided into two subgroups with approximately equal love scores. One subgroup in each pool was randomly designated as a together group, the other as an apart group. Subjects in the together groups were invited to take part in the experiment together with their boyfriends or girlfriends. Subjects in the apart groups were requested to appear at the experimental session individually, where they would be paired with other people's boyfriends or girlfriends. Pairings in the apart conditions were made on the basis of scheduling convenience, with the additional guideline that women should not be paired with men who were younger than themselves. In this way, four experimental groups were created: strong together (19 pairs), weak together (19 pairs), strong apart (21 pairs), and weak apart (20 pairs). Only 5 of the couples contacted (not included in the above cell sizes) refused to participate—2 who had been preassigned to the strong together group, 2 to the weak together group, and 1 to the strong apart group. No changes in the preassignment of subjects to groups were requested or permitted. As desired, none of the pairs of subjects created in the apart groups were previously acquainted. Each subject was paid $1.25 for his participation.

Sessions

When both members of a scheduled pair had arrived at the laboratory, they were seated across a 52-inch table from one another in an observation room. The experimenter, a male graduate student, explained that the experiment was part of a study of communication among dating and unacquainted couples. The subjects were then asked to read a paragraph about "a couple contemplating marriage." They were told that they would subsequently discuss the case, and that their discussion would be tape recorded. The experimenter told the pair that it would take a few minutes for him to set up the tape recorder, and that meanwhile they could talk about anything except the case to be discussed. He then left the room. After 1 minute had elapsed (to allow the subjects to adapt themselves to the situation), their visual behavior was observed for a 3-minute period.

Measurement

The subjects' visual behavior was recorded by two observers stationed behind a one-way mirror, one facing each subject. Each observer pressed a button, which was connected to a cumulative clock, whenever the subject he was watching was looking across the table at his partner's face. The readings on these clocks provided measures of *individual gazing*. In addition, a third clock was activated whenever the two observers were pressing their buttons simultaneously. The reading on this clock provided a measure of *mutal gazing*. The mean percentage of agreement between pairs of observers in 12 reliability trials, interspersed among the experimental sessions, was 92.8. The observers never knew whether a pair of subjects was in a strong-love or weak-love group. They were sometimes able to infer whether the pair was in the together or the apart condition, however. Each observer's assignment alternated between watching the woman and watching the man in successive sessions.

RESULTS

Table 1 reveals that as predicted, there was a tendency for strong-together couples to engage in more mutual gazing (or "eye contact") than weak-together couples. Although there was also a tendency for strong-apart couples to make more eye contact than weak-apart couples, it was not a reliable one.

Another approach toward assessing the couples' visual behavior is to consider the percentage of "total gazing" time (that is, the amount of time during which at least one of the partners was looking at the other) which was occupied by mutual gazing. This measure, to be referred to as *mutual focus*, differs from mutual gazing in that it specifically takes into account the individual gazing tendencies of the two partners. It is possible, for example, that neither member of a particular pair gazed very much at his partner, but that when they did gaze, they did so simultaneously. Such a pair would have a low mutual gazing score, but a high mutual focus score. Within certain limits, the converse of this situation is also possible. Using this measure (see Table 2), the difference between the strong-together and the weak-together groups was more striking than it was in the case of mutual gazing. The difference between the strong-apart and weak-apart groups was clearly not significant.

TABLE 2. MUTUAL FOCUS

GROUP	$\bar{x}$
Strong together	44.0
Weak together	34.7
Strong apart	35.3
Weak apart	32.5

Finally, the individual gazing scores of subjects in the four experimental groups are presented in Table 3. The only significant finding was that in all groups, the women spent much more time looking at the men than the men spent looking at the women. Although there was a tendency for strong-together subjects of both sexes to look at their partners more than weak-together subjects, these comparisons did not approach significance.

DISCUSSION

The main prediction of the experiment was confirmed. Couples who were strongly in love, as categorized by their scores on the love scale, spent more time gazing into one another's eyes than did couples who were only weakly in love. With respect to the measure of individual gazing, however, the tendency for strong-together subjects to devote more time than the weak-together subjects to looking at their partners was not substantial for either women or men. This finding suggests that the obtained difference in mutual gazing between these two groups must be attributed to differences in the *simultaneousness*, rather than in the sheer

quantity, of gazing. This conclusion is bolstered by the fact that the clearest difference between the strong-together and weak-together groups emerged on the percentage measure of mutual focus.

This pattern of results is in accord with the assumption that gazing is a manifestation of the exclusive and absorptive component of romantic

TABLE 3. INDIVIDUAL GAZING (IN SECONDS)

GROUP	WOMEN $\bar{x}$	MEN $\bar{x}$
Strong together	98.7	83.7
Weak together	87.4	77.7
Strong apart	94.5	75.0
Weak apart	96.8	64.0

love. Freud (1955) maintained that "The more [two people] are in love, the more completely they suffice for each other (p. 140)." More recently, Slater (1963) has linked Freud's theory of love to the popular concept of "the oblivious lovers, who are 'all wrapped up in each other,' and somewhat careless of their social obligations (p. 349)." One way in which this oblivious absorption may be manifested is through eye contact. As the popular song has it, "Millions of people go by, but they all disappear from view—'cause I only have eyes for you."

Another possible explanation for the findings is that people who are in love (or who complete attitude scales in such a way as to indicate that they are in love) are also the sort of people who are most predisposed to make eye contact with others, regardless of whether or not those others are the people they are in love with. The inclusion of the apart groups helped to rule out this possibility, however. Although there was a slight tendency for strong-apart couples to engage in more eye contact than weak-apart couples (see Table 2), it fell far short of significance. Moreover, when the percentage measure of mutual focus was employed (see Table 3), this difference virtually disappeared. It should be noted that no predictions were made concerning the comparisons between strong-together and strong-apart couples or between weak-together and weak-apart couples. It seemed plausible that unacquainted couples might make use of a relatively large amount of eye contact as a means of getting acquainted. The results indicate, in fact, that subjects in the apart groups typically engaged in as much eye contact as those in the weak-together group, with strong-together subjects outgazing the other three groups. Future studies which systematically vary the extent to which partners are acquainted would be useful in specifying the acquaintance-seeking functions of eye contact.

The finding that in all experimental groups, women spent more time looking at men that vice versa may reflect the frequently reported tendency of women to specialize in the "social-emotional" aspect of interaction. Gazing may serve as a vehicle of emotional expression for women and, in addition, may allow women to obtain cues from their male partners concerning the appropriateness of their behavior. The present result is in accord with earlier findings that women tend to make more eye contact than men in same-sex groups and in an interview situation, regardless of the sex of the interviewer.

CONCLUSION

"So far as love or affection is concerned," Harlow wrote in 1958, "psychologists have failed in their mission. The little we know about love does not transcend simple observation, and the little we write about it has been written better by poets and novelists (p. 673)." The research reported in this paper represents an attempt to improve this situation by introducing and validating a preliminary social-psychological conception of romantic love. A distinction was drawn between love and liking, and its reasonableness was attested to by the results of the questionnaire study. It was found, for example, that respondents' estimates of the likelihood that they would marry their partners were more highly related to their love than to their liking for their partners. In light of the culturally prescribed association between love and marriage (but not necessarily between liking and marriage), this pattern of correlations seems appropriate. Other findings of the questionnaire study . . . point to the value of a measurable construct of romantic love as a link between the individual and social-structural levels of analysis of social behavior.

Although the present investigation was aimed at developing a unitary conception of romantic love, a promising direction for future research is the attempt to distinguish among patterns of romantic love relationships. One theoretical basis for such distinctions is the nature of the interpersonal rewards exchanged between partners. The attitudes and behaviors of romantic love may differ, for example, depending on whether the most salient rewards exchanged are those of security or those of stimulation. Some of the behavioral variables which might be focused on in the attempt to distinguish among such patterns are in the areas of sexual behavior, helping, and self-disclosure.

REFERENCES

Freud, S. Group psychology and the analysis of the ego. In *The Standard Edition of the Complete Psychological Works of Sigmund Freud*, Vol. 18. London: Hogarth, 1955.

Fromm, E. *The Art of Loving*. New York: Harper, 1956.

Harlow, H. F. The nature of love. *American Psychologist*, 1958, *13*, 673–85.

Heider, F. *The Psychology of Interpersonal Relations*. New York: Wiley, 1958.

Jourard, S. M., & Lasakov, P. Some factors in self-disclosure. *Journal of Abnormal and Social Psychology*, 1958, *56*, 91–98.

Newcomb, T. M. The varieties of interpersonal attraction. In D. Cartwright & A. Zander (eds.), *Group Dynamics*. (2nd ed.) Evanston, Ill.: Row, Peterson, 1960.

Orlinsky, D. E. Love relationships in the life cycle: A developmental interpersonal perspective. In H. A. Otto (ed.), *Love Today: A New Exploration*. New York: Association Press, 1972.

Slater, P. E. On social regression. *American Sociological Review*, 1963, *28*, 339–64.

PSYCHOLOGISTS AND LOVE

Let's take a one-item test. February's most popular date will be Feb. 2 (Groundhog day), Feb. 12 (Lincoln's Birthday), Feb. 18 (start of the Chinese New Year), Feb. 22 (Washington's Birthday), or None of the above.

The answer is as plain as the nose on Cyrano de Bergerac's face, at least to those who know that *love is sweeping the country* because *what the world needs now is love. Love makes the world go round,* both for the teenager who's *younger than springtime* and the octogenarian who claims that even though *my heart stood still . . . it's never too late to love.* Make no mistake about it, it is love love love, and it is neither chance nor high camp that has kept alive for *sweethearts forever* that cloyingly sentimental ballad, *Indian love call* ("When I'm calling you-oo-oo-oo-oo-oo-oo, will you answer too-oo-oo-oo-oo-oo-oo?").

Give yourself a perfect score if you selected (E), none of the above, because far and away the most beloved date in February, and possibly in the entire year as well, is Feb. 14, St. Valentine's Day. No more proof of this is needed than the torrent of long distance calls lovers make on that day, not to mention lovers' trysts over candlelight dinners seasoned *tenderly* with soft music while *dancing cheek to cheek.* And don't forget the tons of candy, truckloads of flowers and bales of valentine cards whose sales gorge February's cash registers from coast to coast.

The paradox of all this is that so few psychologists are into love, with the notable exceptions (1) of Harry Harlow's celebrated studies probing the nature of love in monkeys and (2) of scientific voyeurs like Ellen Ber-scheid, Donn Byrne, Zick Rubin and Elaine Walster, who muse whether *I love you truly* loads more on the *I can't stop loving you* factor than on the factor tentatively identified as *I got it bad and that ain't good.* Although *they say that falling in love is wonderful,* Zick and Donn and Elaine and Ellen constitute a chillingly bare minority of psychologists willing to observe love in the field, or manipulate it in the laboratory.

The power of love to generate seminal hypotheses and to impact upon society is enormous. Freud, for example, realized early on that for most people it is a base canard that *it doesn't cost you anything to dream.* Scientific concepts of love and its correlates have inspired popular songs. A case in point is Freud's Electra complex, which sparked the hit tune, *My heart belongs to daddy,* while research by developmental psychologists analyzing infant behavior triggered such money-makers as *I'll be your baby tonight* and *I can't give you anything but love, baby.*

Although a handful of psychologists—exemplified by trailblazers Zick and Donn and Elaine and Ellen—are *lucky in love* because they have been *doin' what comes naturally,* psychologists have generally avoided love like *the devil and the deep blue sea.* This is documented in Fred McKinney's "Fifty Years of Psychology" (*American Psychologist,* December 1976), where terms like learning, set, temperament, cognition, meaning and symbolism are in abundance; but, oh, Fred, I ask you, Fred, *where is love? Where is love?* When I discovered that psychology has been bereft of love lo these past fifty years, *zing! went the strings of my heart.* I wondered *what kind of fool am I* to identify with a learned discipline which tells love *I hate you, darling.* As *bewitched, bothered and bewildered am I* by a loveless psychology as by thoughts of a rockless geology, a numberless mathematics or a matterless physics.

Psychologists who study love use impotent terms like "affiliation," "dependency," "mate selection," "penetration (social)," "romance," "relationships (meaningful)" and "self-esteem." Yet, in *Bartlett's Familiar Quotations* the foregoing words average less than one inch of space, whereas to "love" a whopping 139 inches is allocated! While lovers adjure one another in plain and endearing language to *light my fire, love me tender* and *love me tonight,* all that we psychologists can prattle about is—ugh!—attraction, courtship, involvement, popularity and romantic choices. But *where is love?* Poets, lyricists, balladeers, troubadors, and copywriters caress us with streams and dreams, lips and trips, thrills and chills, charms and arms, trees and bees, and June and moon and spoon. No offense, Zick and Donn and Elaine and Ellen, but better you should deluge us with more of your streams and dreams and lips and trips, and skip all that jazz about body image, satisfaction, personality, likableness and assertiveness. Let us not pooh-pooh the fact that lovers are turned on by the words and music of Irving Berlin (to whom President Ford awarded the Medal of Freedom . . .), Bob Dylan, the Jefferson Airplane, Jerome Kern, Cole Porter, and The Who.

METAPHORS OF LOVE

GEORGE LAKOFF AND MARK JOHNSON

What is love? We are sure you can formulate an answer to this question and probably use a nice metaphor as an illustration. On love, everyone is an expert—so much so, in fact, that Henry Finck concluded in his book, Romantic Love and Personal Beauty, published at the turn of the century, that "love is such a tissue of paradoxes, and exists in such an endless variety of forms and shades, that you may say almost anything about it that you please, and it is likely to be correct." Finck was probably right to some extent, and yet some beliefs about love we do share. One way to find out about such common conceptualizations, according to Lakoff and Johnson, is by looking at language, and more specifically, by looking at metaphors. The metaphors we use not only reflect our conceptual system, they play an active role in determining what it is we perceive, and this determines our life's reality. In their book, Lakoff and Johnson examine all the metaphors we live by; however, we will focus only on their discussion of metaphors of love.

Metaphor is for most people a device of the poetic imagination and the rhetorical flourish—a matter of extraordinary rather than ordinary language. Moreover, metaphor is typically viewed as characteristic of language alone, a matter of words rather than thought or action. For this reason, most people think they can get along perfectly well without metaphor. We have found, on the contrary, that metaphor is pervasive in everyday life, not just in language but in thought and action. Our ordinary conceptual system, in terms of which we both think and act, is fundamentally metaphorical in nature.

The concepts that govern our thought are not just matters of the intellect. They also govern our everyday functioning, down to the most mundane details. Our concepts structure what we perceive, how we get around in the world, and how we relate to other people. Our conceptual system thus plays a central role in defining our everyday realities. If we are right in suggesting that our conceptual system is largely metaphorical, then the way we think, what we experience, and what we do every day is very much a matter of metaphor.

But our conceptual system is not something we are normally aware of. In most of the little things we do every day, we simply think and act more or less automatically along certain lines. Just what these lines are is by no means obvious. One way to find out is by looking at language. Since communication is based on the same conceptual system that we use in thinking and acting, language is an important source of evidence for what that system is like.

Metaphors and metonymies are not random but instead form coherent systems in terms of which we conceptualize our experience. But it is easy to find apparent incoherences in everyday metaphorical expressions. We have not made a complete study of these, but those that we have looked at in detail have turned out not to be incoherent at all, though they appeared that way at first. Let us consider . . .

Love Is a Journey

Look *how far we've come.*

We're *at a crossroads.*

We'll just have to *go our separate ways.*

We can't *turn back now.*

I don't think this relationship is *going anywhere.*

Where are we?

We're *stuck.*

It's been a *long, bumpy road.*

This relationship is a *dead-end street.*

We're just *spinning our wheels.*

Our marriage is *on the rocks.*

We've gotten *off the track.*

This relationship is *foundering.*

George Lakoff and Mark Johnson, *Metaphors We Live By* (Chicago: University of Chicago Press, 1980), pp. 3, 41, 45, 49. Reprinted by permission of the University of Chicago Press.

Here the basic metaphor is that of a journey, and there are various types of journeys that one can make: a car trip, a train trip, or a sea voyage.

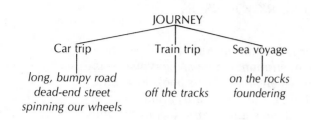

There is no single, consistent image that the journey metaphors all fit. What make them coherent is that they are all journey metaphors, though they specify different means of travel. The same sort of thing occurs with the time-is-a-moving-object metaphor, where there are various ways in which something can move. Thus, *time flies, time creeps along, time speeds by.* In general, metaphorical concepts are defined not in terms of concrete images (flying, creeping, going down the road, etc.), but in terms of more general categories, like passing. . . .

Some Further Examples
[of the Metaphors of Love]

Love Is a Physical Force (Electromagnetic, Gravitational, etc.). I could feel the *electricity* between us. There were *sparks.* I was *magnetically drawn* to her. They are uncontrollably *attracted* to each other. They *gravitated* to each other immediately. His whole life *revolves* around her. The *atmosphere* around them is always *charged.* There is incredible *energy* in their relationship. They lost their *momentum.*

Love Is a Patient. This is a *sick* relationship. They have a *strong, healthy* marriage. The marriage is *dead*—it can't be *revived.* Their marriage is *on the mend.* We're getting *back on our feet.* Their relationship is *in really good shape.* They've got a *listless* marriage. Their marriage is *on its last legs.* It's a *tired* affair.

Love Is Madness. I'm *crazy* about her. She *drives me out of my mind.* He constantly *raves* about her. He's gone *mad* over her. I'm just *wild* about Harry. I'm *insane* about her.

Love Is Magic. She *cast her spell* over me. The *magic* is gone. I was *spellbound.* She had me *hypnotized.* He has me *in a trance.* I was *entranced* by him. I'm *charmed* by her. She is *bewitching.*

Love Is War. He is known for his many rapid *conquests.* She *fought for* him, but his mistress *won out.* He *fled from* her *advances.* She pursued him *relentlessly.* He is slowly *gaining ground* with her. He *won* her *hand* in marriage. He *overpowered* her. She is *besieged* by suitors. He has to *fend* them *off.* He *enlisted the aid* of her friends. He *made an ally* of her mother. Theirs is a *misalliance* if I've ever seen one.

ANTECEDENTS, CORRELATES, AND CONSEQUENCES OF SEXUAL JEALOUSY— THE SHADOW OF LOVE

AYALA PINES AND ELLIOT ARONSON

"Love is strong as death, jealousy cruel as hell. It blazes up like blazing fire, fiercer than any flame," says the poet in the Song of Songs, and similarly Orage in his writing, A Love, says, "Jealousy is the dragon in paradise, the hell of heaven; and the most bitter of emotions because it is associated with the sweetest." Both these poets, as well as many others who have written on the subject, noted the close connection between love and jealousy.

"Jealousy is the shadow of love," claim Pines and Aronson in this article. Whatever the shape of love, so is the shape of the jealousy shadow it will cast. In the following article, they propose an alternative to the clinical approach that has dominated the study and treatment of jealousy, with its emphasis on pathological jealousy that is dispositional and innate. Pines and Aronson propose, instead, a social-psychological approach that emphasizes the role of the situation, both in understanding the causes of jealousy and in the proposed treatment of its casualties.

Sexual jealousy has produced pathology, drama, and tragedy from time immemorial. A wide range of hostile, bitter, and painful events has been attributed to jealousy: family murder followed by suicide, murder, suicide attempts, wife battering, marital problems and divorce, problems of cohabiting couples, destruction of romantic relationships, depression, aggression, criminal behavior, hatred, and violence.

Sexual jealousy is the shadow of love. Whatever the shape of the love relationship, so is the shape of the shadow it casts, and sexual jealousy seems universal; it is experienced whenever a valued romantic relationship is threatened. As a protective reaction to such perceived threats, jealousy is different from envy, in which one desires something one does not have (in jealousy, one protects what one has). As a reaction that occurs whenever a valued *romantic* relationship is threatened, sexual jealousy is different from reactions that occur when other valued relationships are threatened, such as sibling relationships and graduate student–mentor relationships. Poets,

playwrights, and novelists have produced rich descriptions of the experience of sexual jealousy, its causes, and consequences. Some of the best known descriptions of jealousy appear in Shakespeare's *Othello* and *A Winter's Tale*, Tolstoy's *The Kreutzer Sonata*, De Maupassant's *One Evening*, Cervantes' *The Jealous Estremaduran*, Burton's *Anatomy of Melancholy*, Robbe-Grillet's *Jealousy*, and Boccaccio's *The Decameron*.

Scientists in various fields of the humanities and the social sciences have tried to gain a better understanding of sexual jealousy. Philosophical, sociological, anthropological, and psychoanalytic writings constitute a rich and interesting vein of speculations, hypotheses, and ideas, but they do not provide us with systematic data. When we think of a jealousy-producing situation, the obvious image that comes to mind is that of an interpersonal event involving at least three people (and thus different from rivalry, which involves only two). Traditionally, the behavioral science that has been best equipped to perform empirical research on interpersonal dynamics under well controlled and often dramatically intense situations is social psychology. And yet, until the mid-1970s, social psychologists remained at the periphery of the study of jealousy.

One of the major contributors to the dramatic

Adapted and reprinted with permission from *Journal of Personality*, 54, 1 (1983), 108–135. Copyright © 1983, Duke University Press, Durham, North Carolina.

change in the research picture has been Greg White. White (1977, 1980) began a systematic empirical investigation using questionnaires as research tools. His subjects consisted of 150 romantically involved heterosexual couples, predominantly white (84 percent), and students in college (91 percent). His research investigates the correlates of jealousy among these 150 couples. For example, White found that for both sexes, jealousy is positively related to exclusivity, feelings of inadequacy as a partner, and the degree of dependence of self-esteem upon partner's evaluations. For males, jealousy was also negatively related to chronic low self-esteem and positively related to sex-role traditionalism. In an earlier paper, White reported that people who are relatively more involved in their relationship than their partners are more likely to be jealous. White also suggested that females' self-perception of inadequacy as a partner leads to jealousy, while for males it is jealousy that leads to self-perception of inadequacy. Females were also more likely to report that they had induced sexual jealousy than were males.

Other correlational studies of jealousy focus on dispositional correlates of jealousy and indicate that highly jealous people tend to be self-deprecating, unhappy, externally controlled, arousable, anxious, and dogmatic. Corzin (1979) found that nonjealous people possess more integrative personality characteristics than jealous people. Jaremko and Lindsey (1979) found that jealousy was positively correlated with anxiety and negatively correlated with social desirability and self-esteem. Tipton et al. (1978) factor-analyzed responses to a jealousy scale and found that "need for loyalty" accounted for 36 percent of the variance; "moodiness," "self-confidence," and "envy" accounted for 9 percent, 8 percent and 7 percent respectively.

The closest attempts to study jealousy experimentally were two quasi-experiments by Shettel-Neuber, Bryson, and Young (1978) and Teismann and Mosher (1978). Shettel-Neuber et al. showed subjects videotapes of jealousy-evoking situations and asked how likely they were to respond to the situations in certain ways. Results revealed that males were more likely to report that they would react with anger; females were more likely to react with depression and attempts to improve the relationship. Teismann and Mosher (1978), using role-playing situations, discovered that in a jealousy condition, subjects used significantly more rejecting and coercive acts and significantly fewer cognitive, resolving, reconciling, and appealing acts than did persons in the nonjealous condition. Persons experiencing jealousy also used significantly more guilt-inducing acts.

After reviewing the scientific writing of philosophers, sociologists, humanistic psychologists, psychoanalysts, and anthropologists, it becomes clear that personality and social psychologists are the only ones attempting to answer questions about jealousy experimentally and in a systematic manner. Unfortunately, most often there is a selective sample of subjects used in the studies, namely, undergraduate college students primarily involved in short-term dating relationships. And there are many problems with the primary research tool of personality and social psychologists—the questionnaire. For example, it is not clear how aware people are of their own feelings or how willing they are to be truthful if a disclosure might put them in what they consider to be an undesirable light.

For the past few years, we have been studying the dynamics of sexual jealousy, using a wide range of methods. We have conducted workshops for people having special problems with jealousy; we have collected extensive questionnaire data; we have observed people living in an alternative lifestyle who claim that they have managed to eliminate jealousy (Pines and Aronson, 1981); we have conducted personal interviews, lectures, and seminars; and we have read the scientific writings of philosophers, sociologists, humanistic psychologists, psychoanalysts, and anthropologists. Thus, even though our major research tool in the present study is still the questionnaire, we feel that corroborating evidence from the literature (scientific, as well as nonscientific), from discussions with people at workshops, and from many hours of personal in-depth interviews enables us to trust the information we gather via our questionnaire more than we otherwise could or would. Based on our research and group work, we came to appreciate the importance of a social-psychological approach to understanding jealousy.

A SOCIAL-PSYCHOLOGICAL PERSPECTIVE ON JEALOUSY

People often explain their own and other people's behavior in dispositional terms. For example, when they experience certain feelings and physical symptoms in response to a jealousy-triggering situation, they say, "The reason I am experiencing a jealous reaction is because I am a jealous person." Social psychology introduces a new and exciting perspective to the study and understanding of such complex emotions as jealousy by emphasizing situational attributions—that is to say, it focuses attention on environmental factors that cause people to act in a jealous manner. For example, when people experience jealous reactions, they could say, "The reason I am experiencing this jealous reaction is because of the situation that triggered it." The social-psychological approach does not deny the importance of individual traits, characteristics, and dispositions; rather, it suggests that human emotions such as jealousy also have a social basis or component.

The difference between self-attributions that are situational and self-attributions that are dispositional is not a semantic difference. It has many far-reaching implications for the individual making the attributions. Individuals who are making dispositional self-attributions of jealousy are saying, "The reason why I reacted with jealousy is that I am that kind of person; I simply am a jealous person." That explanation puts them in what Philip Zimbardo called "a prison of their own mind," a mental prison from which there is no way out. Individuals who are making situational self-attributions, on the other hand, are saying, "The reason why I am reacting with jealousy is because of the person or the situation that triggered it," which means that "with another person or in another situation, I may react very differently." Such people are more likely to get out of relationships where they are feeling unhappy or insecure and actively look for a relationship in which they are less likely to experience jealousy.

METHOD

Subjects

One hundred and three subjects participated in the study; 35 were males and 68 were females. Subjects' ages ranged from 21 to 64 years ($\bar{x}$ = 34). The education range was from less than 12 years to graduate degrees (Ph.D. and M.A.). . . . Nineteen percent were single and never married, 41 percent were married, 21 percent were partnered or cohabiting, 9 percent were divorced, 4 percent were separated, 3 percent were widowed, and 3 percent were in some other situation. The length of the intimate relationship discussed ranged from several days to 40 years (the average was 72 months). . . . Each subject was asked to take part in a questionnaire study investigating sexual jealousy. Total anonymity was assured. All subjects approached agreed to participate in the study.

Instrument

A specially designed "Sexual Jealousy Inventory" was used. Items in the questionnaire are based on a thorough review of the literature concerning sexual jealousy, as well as on many in-depth interviews. Earlier versions of the questionnaire were pretested to assure the relevance of the items to a wide range of people, to eliminate any language ambiguities, and to provide evidence of psychometric adequacy. The questionnaire in its final form includes: background information, questions about jealousy prevalence, attitudes and feelings that are jealousy correlates, jealousy elicitors, physical and emotional reactions to jealousy, effects of jealousy, modes of coping with it, and reasons for it. Most responses were based on a 7-point scale. Background information included, for example: sex, age, siblings, education, and occupation, and a series of questions about the intimate relationship in which the respondent is involved. Questions about the relationship included: length of the relationship, how long one expected it to last, how it could be described, who held the control in it, security in it, and so on. . . . Attitudes and feelings that are jealousy correlates included: self-concept, feelings about one's looks, sexual desirability, physical and emotional attraction to partner, and partner's jealousy.

Questions about jealousy prevalence included such questions as: Do you consider yourself a jealous person? Have any of your relationships ended because of jealousy? Do other people consider you jealous? Jealousy elicitors included people and situations presented in two Guttman scales. Examples of people eliciting jealousy are: someone you don't know personally and have a low opinion of, someone you know personally and distrust, your very best friend and confidante. Examples of situations eliciting jealousy are: your mate is having an affair, but is extremely discreet about it and a scandal erupts in the middle of a party; your mate is very discreet, no one else knows about it, and she or he doesn't know that you know. Other jealousy triggers included such short scenarios as: your phone rings and the person on the other end of the line either says, "Sorry, wrong number," or simply hangs up; you are at a party and your mate disappears for a long period of time; your mate is being very flirtatious and spends a great deal of time during a party intimately dancing and behaving provocatively with another.

Reactions to jealousy included physical (e.g., hot, cold, dizzy, nauseous) and emotional (e.g., inferior, humiliated, angry, anxious) reactions.

Coping with jealousy included such items as: rational discussion, sarcasm, denial, crying, physical violence, and humor. Jealousy variables included such questions as: Do you consider your jealousy a problem? Do you like being jealous? Would you like to get rid of your jealousy if you could? Do you like your partner to be jealous? Do you consider jealousy an appropriate reaction in extreme situations? Do you believe someone who tells you he or she is not jealous in such a situation? How desirable is jealousy as a personal characteristic? Can you stop yourself from being jealous?

Positive effects included such items as: jealousy is a sign of love; brings excitement to a listless relationship; teaches people not to take each other for granted. Negative effects included such items as: jealousy causes physical distress, may result in violence, and puts strain on relationships. Reasons for jealousy included such things as: jealousy is a normal reaction accompanying love; a result of personal insecurity; and, the result of feeling excluded and left out.

Total anonymity and confidentiality were assured in an effort to maximize honesty of responses. The universality of the experience of jealousy was stressed in order to reduce social undesirability. It is important to note that in no place in the questionnaire were subjects presented with a definition of jealousy. When asked to evaluate their own degree of jealousy, the assumption was that they were using their own definition of the experiences—that is to say, even if two subjects were, in fact, very different in terms of their jealousy, if they reported equal degrees of jealousy, we accepted this report as data and tried to find correlations between this self-reported jealousy and a variety of antecedents, correlates, and consequences. This seemed simpler and more meaningful than introducing to subjects the very many different definitions of jealousy found in the literature, or trying to differentiate the many complex facets of the experience. And indeed, subjects' overwhelming response to the questionnaire was very positive, with the most frequent response being, "It made me get in touch and explore my feelings of jealousy in a meaningful way."

Antecedents

Sexual jealousy appears to be experienced whenever there is a perceived threat to a valued romantic relationship. All the subjects in the present study reported experiencing some sexual jealousy at some point in their lives, and the experience itself appeared rather similar in all the cases. Differences among people were more a result of the frequency and the intensity of the experience than its emotional and physical components. It may very well be true, as Freud (1922) suggested, that jealousy is universal and inevitable because it originates very early in life in relation to rivalry for the exclusive love of the mother. It is felt again whenever the fear of losing the object of our love is aroused. The childhood experiences do not cause the later ones, but they are evoked and help shape the form and intensity of our response to jealousy-provoking situations in adult life. Indeed, the data of the present study show that subjects reported being most jealous during adolescence, a period when youngsters are most likely to experience the fear of losing their love object, given the intensity of feelings experienced and the lack of mutual commitment characterizing most relationships at that age.

Subjects reported decreasing levels of jealousy with age—less during young adulthood than during adolescence, and less during advanced adulthood than during young adulthood. There are several ways to interpret these findings: It is possible that people develop better coping strategies for dealing with jealousy over time. It is possible that with growing experience, people avoid getting involved in, and get out of, relationships in which their jealousy is likely to be triggered often. It is possible that with age most people develop a relatively stable self-concept, and thus are less likely to be threatened by jealousy triggers. It is possible that with time most couples develop a sense of trust in their relationship and thus are less likely to view jealousy-triggering incidents as threats to the relationship.

The fact that all the increasing correlations between jealousy during different stages of life and current jealousy were statistically significant lends support to such personality psychologists as Robert Bringle who claim that differences between people in the propensity to behave emotionally in a jealous situation (defined as dispositional jealousy) are valid and reliable over time. And as noted earlier, it also provides evidence in favor of the measure used in the study.

Family constellations can be viewed as another antecedent of jealousy. In the present study, the number of older brothers was positively correlated with jealousy (the more older brothers, the more jealousy), while the number of younger brothers was negatively correlated with jealousy (the more younger brothers, the less jealousy). Developmental psychologists show the roots of adult jealousy in sibling rivalry. The psychological pattern of reacting to jealousy in later life, they argue, is usually determined by the child's first experiences of jealousy when his desire for exclusivity is threatened by a sibling.

In the present study, adult jealousy was only correlated with the number of brothers. There was an almost zero correlation between number of either older or younger sisters and jealousy. Thus, it appears that it is not the presence of a sibling in and of itself which triggers jealousy; it has to be a sibling who is in a position of power (that is, an older sibling, and a male). A power perspective on sexual jealousy was offered by Greg White. White (1977) suggested that sexual jealousy is one consequence of an imbalance of power in the romantic relationship. As noted by Gillispie (1971), males may have relatively greater power because of their status in society.

Sex differences can be, and have been, viewed as antecedents of jealousy. For example, some research has identified different patterns of jealous reactions for males and females. Males, it was found, are more likely to respond with self-esteem-maintaining behavior, while females will make a greater effort to maintain the relationship. Because of the lack of power relative to men, and their greater degree of involvement in the relationship, females are more likely to induce jealousy.

The present study supported some of the notions about sex differences reported in previous research. For example, females believed in monogamy significantly more than men and reported higher levels of jealousy in response to partner's involvement with another person. In terms of the experience of jealousy itself and its general effects, however, there were no sex differences, and yet, when asked directly who is more jealous, men or women, the response was "equally jealous." These results corroborated previous research that failed to find sex differences in self-reports of jealousy. The few sex differences found in the study (women were more likely than men to feel "close to a nervous breakdown," "inferior" and "humiliated," and to experience "fear of loss," "grief," and "vulnerability") could be explained again by White's conceptualization as resulting from the woman's lack of power in the relationship or in society at large.

Earlier in this paper it was noted that it is not clear how willing people are to be truthful if what they report might put them in an undesirable light. The results of the study suggest that they may be as motivated to present themselves favorably in other social encounters as they are when responding to a questionnaire. The average response given by subjects when asked whether most people who know them well will consider them jealous was 2.5. When asked whether people they have been intimate with would consider them jealous, the average response was 3.3. Evidently, people are less likely to express jealous behavior in public or in casual relationships and more likely to express jealousy in intimate relationships. This can be a result of the fact that sexual jealousy is a socially undesirable feature, or that in intimate relationships, by definition, there are likely to be more triggers for jealousy. The study identified numerous jealousy triggers, both in terms of the interloper and the situation involved.

Every person with whom one found out one's intimate partner had been having a sexual relationship caused some degree of jealousy. Yet, the five highest triggers were all people whom one knew personally, while the least jealousy provoking were people unknown to the subject. Thus, it appears that not knowing the third person helped subjects deal with the jealousy that was triggered. When the third person was known, it made very little difference whether it was someone one distrusted or someone one trusted and considered a friend. It may be that the pain, hurt, and sense of betrayal triggered when one discovers the affair are so intense as to overshadow the differences in the identity of the third person involved.

Similar findings were obtained from the analysis of jealousy-triggering situations. The average response to discovering that one's sexual partner was having an illicit affair was rather strong jealousy, independent of the special circumstances of the affair. The strongest jealousy was triggered by situations in which many other people knew about the affair. This result seems to tie to the finding reported earlier concerning the difference between people in general and people one was intimately involved with, in terms of perceiving one as jealous. The reader will recall that people one was involved with intimately were more likely to perceive one's jealousy accurately than people in general. Thus it appears that in public, people are more likely to minimize their jealous responses. The public performance may then, in fact, help them manage their jealousy.

The more jealous individuals are, the more people and situations are likely to elicit their jealousy. People who describe themselves as less jealous are likely to be more discriminating. Yet, an interesting finding concerning all the jealousy-triggering people and situations studied in the present study is the fact that there was a high level of agreement among people in terms of their rank ordering. Thus, for example, most subjects do not get jealous when they call their mate and the phone is busy, but may have a pang of jealousy when the person (of the same sex) calling their home says "Sorry, wrong number." Similarly, most subjects are more likely to respond with jealousy when their mate spends a great deal of time during a party talking to another person of the opposite sex than they do when they are at a party and their mate disappears for a long period of time. Both these situations, in turn, elicit more jealousy than the previous two telephone scenarios.

When all the antecedents of jealousy are examined together, it appears that even though people differ in their dispositional jealousy (resulting from different experiences with mother and siblings, different sexual identity, and physical condition), the situational antecedents of jealousy (the sexual involvement of a partner with another person) overshadow the dispositional ones.

Correlates

In addition to studying antecedents of jealousy, the study investigated a variety of jealousy correlates [Table 1]. Physical and mental conditions were both negatively correlated with jealousy. Like other emotionally stressful conditions, it appears that jealousy is more likely to be experienced by people who are in poor mental and physical shape. However, a word of caution is needed: Since a correlation does not imply causality, we do not know whether it is the poor physical and mental condition that makes some individuals more likely to experience jealousy, or whether it is frequent experiences of jealousy which make them become run-down, physically and mentally. It is also possible that it is the same people who are willing to admit to experiencing jealousy who also admit to being in poor physical and mental shape, and thus the correlation reflects differences in degree of openness rather than true individual differences in jealousy.

Belief in monogamy was found to be another significant correlate of sexual jealousy. People who believe in monogamous relationships were less likely to be jealous. An interesting exception to this finding was described in a paper entitled, "Polyfidelity: Alternative Life Style Without Sexual Jealousy?" (Pines and Aronson, 1981). *Polyfidelity* is a coined word describing nine women and six men who were living as a family unit with

sexual intimacy occurring equally between all members of the opposite sex, yet no sexual involvement occurring outside the group. The experiences of the polyfidelitous family suggest that the key factor is not monogamy, but rather the fidelity bond and the security within the relationship. Indeed, the present data suggest that people whose partners had been unfaithful to them, either sexually or in some other way, reported being more jealous than individuals who had not experienced such unfaithfulness. This reality-based jealousy contradicts post-Freudian psychoanalytical interpretations of jealousy in which the tendency is "to bypass consideration of the reality factors which may have prompted the immediate jealousy and to assume that *all* jealousy is to some degree *delusional* jealousy. Little attention is paid to the factor of literal infidelity, except sometimes to show how I provoked, in some sense desired, the very betrayal that arouses my anger and anxiety" (Downing, 1977).

The data of the study may be interpreted as supporting Freud's notion about the operation of projection in the experience of jealousy. Projective jealousy, according to Freud (1922), is derived either from one's own actual unfaithfulness in real life, or from impulses toward it which have succumbed to repression. In the present study, individuals who were more jealous were likely to think that more other people were jealous. And individuals who have themselves been unfaithful to their partners, who frequently fantasize sexual involvement with others, and who saw themselves as more sexually desirable, also reported being more jealous. Since the data are correlational, however, and do not imply causality, it is also possible to argue that people in unstable, insecure relationships are more likely to be jealous, more likely to see threats to the relationship, and probably have partners who are, in fact, likely to be unfaithful. And indeed, it was found that the more satisfied people reported being with the sexual partner, the less jealousy they reported experiencing.

The more jealousy individuals reported "at present," the more relationships they had which ended as a result of their jealousy; and the younger the respondent, the more relationships ended because of jealousy. If one is not to accept the idea that older people simply forget about the many relationships they had in their youth which ended as a result of jealousy, one is left with the possible conclusion that the new morality with its open sexuality is increasing the potential for jealousy in younger couples.

TABLE 1. JEALOUSY VARIABLES

BACKGROUND	CORRELATIONS*
Age	−.19
Number of older brothers	.25
Number of younger brothers	−.15
Physical condition	−.23
Mental condition	−.31
How long have you been with partner?	−.00
How long do you expect the relationship to last?	−.24
How secure do you feel about the relationship?	−.29
If you found someone else, would you leave?	−.23
Do you believe in monogamy?	−.16
Has your partner ever been unfaithful sexually?	.17
Has your partner ever been unfaithful in any other way?	.32
Have you ever been unfaithful?	.22
Have you fantasized sexual involvement?	.22
Your general desirability as a sexual partner	.17
General feeling about sexual partner	−.22

PREVALENCE	
How jealous were you during childhood?	.18
adolescence?	.23
young adulthood?	.50
advanced adulthood?	.72
Have any intimate relationships ended because of jealousy?	.15
Do most people consider you a jealous person?	.50
Do people in intimate relationships with you consider you jealous?	.59
Percentage of people answering the questionnaire who will admit to being jealous	.14
Who are more jealous, men or women?	.18
How often do you experience jealousy?	.54
When you experience jealousy, how long does it last?	.19

JEALOUSY ELICITORS	
Average response to people eliciting jealousy	.33
Average response to incidents eliciting jealousy	.43
Average response to partner's behaviors eliciting jealousy	.51
Average response to partner's affairs as a jealousy trigger	.31
Average response to discovering partner's affair	.36

REACTIONS TO JEALOUSY	
Average physical reactions to jealousy	.24
Average emotional reactions to jealousy	.37
Do you consider your jealousy a problem?	.48
Do you like your partner to be jealous?	.35
How desirable to you think jealousy is?	.23
Can you stop yourself from being jealous?	−.35

POSITIVE EFFECTS OF JEALOUSY	
Jealousy is a sign of love	.29
Indicates you love your partner	.35
Brings excitement to listless relationships	.33
Teaches people not to take each other for granted	.37
Makes life more interesting	.22
Makes partners look more desirable	.31
Makes one feel alive	.23
Makes relationships last longer	.36
Makes one examine one's relationship	.24

TABLE 1. JEALOUSY VARIABLES (CONTINUED)

REASONS FOR JEALOUSY	
Normal reaction accompanying love	.20
Instinctive reaction to threat	.25
Wards off infidelity impulses	.18
Immaturity and a defective self	− .17
Self-blame	.18

NOTE: Correlations with responses to the question: How jealous are you at this stage of your life? $n = 103$ (1 = not jealous at all; 7 = extremely jealous). All correlations are statistically significant.

Consequences

A variety of interesting consequences of sexual jealousy were explored in the study. The first ones were the physical and emotional reactions to jealousy. For most subjects, extreme jealousy was associated with feeling hot, nervous, and shaky, with a fast heartbeat and emptiness in the stomach. The emotional reactions felt most strongly were anxiety, fear of loss, pain, anger, vulnerability, and hopelessness.

People who described themselves as more jealous were likely to experience more reactions to jealousy, more intensely, more often, and for longer periods of time. They were also more likely to see their jealousy as a personal problem. Yet it is interesting that the more jealous people tended to see jealousy as a more positive personality characteristic, liked their partners to be more jealous, saw (more than less jealous people) all the positive effects of jealousy, and were likely to perceive it as a normal reaction accompanying love, or as an instinctive reaction to threat. They were less likely to perceive it as a sign of immaturity and a defect of self.

When the positive consequences of jealousy are compared to the negative ones, it appears that most subjects see more negative consequences (all the averages given for negative effects were higher than the averages given for the positive ones). Clearly, jealousy is a very negative physical, emotional, and mental state that had been experienced, at some point in their lives, by all subjects in the study. In addition, 54 percent of the subjects described themselves as jealous people. This percentage is very interesting, not only because it documents the extent of the problem of jealousy, but also because it indirectly validates the sexual jealousy inventory. When asked what percentage of the people answering the questionnaire will admit to being "a jealous person," the average response was 57 percent, which is surprisingly close to the 54 percent actually obtained. When asked

subsequently what percentage of the people answering the questionnaire "are actually jealous," the response was 75 percent. If the accuracy in predicting the number of people who will admit to being jealous is to be used as a criterion, one can rather safely assume that many more people are sexually jealous than care to admit it. And if the problem of sexual jealousy as it was documented in the present study is serious, one can only guess the extent of the pain and suffering actually caused by it.

The results of the study strongly suggest that persons tend to make dispositional rather than situational attributions for their jealousy. Over half the subjects described themselves as "a jealous person," even though there were numerous situational differences between those "jealous" people and those who claimed they were not jealous. For example, those who were not jealous felt more secure in their relationship, expected it to last longer, and were more sure that their partner had never been unfaithful to them than those who described themselves as jealous. Thus it appears that even when people had very good situational reasons to feel less secure in their relationships and to experience jealousy, they still explained their jealousy in dispositional terms.

CONCLUSION

In the present study, the social psychological approach was applied to the study of the antecedents, correlates, and consequences of sexual jealousy. Even though people who described themselves as "a jealous person" reported significantly higher jealousy responses to the various people and situations that triggered their jealousy, their rank ordering of the various triggers was almost identical to that of those people who described themselves as "not jealous": For example, both reacted more strongly when the third person having an affair with their mate was known to them than when unknown. In terms of the physical and emotional reactions to jealousy, again there was a great similarity in the rank ordering of the symptoms, with feelings of nervousness being experienced far more intensely than, for example, blacking out, and the most intense emotional reactions to jealousy being anxiety, fear of loss, and pain.

Given the great agreement among people about jealousy triggers and jealousy responses, it is rather amazing that some chose to explain it as a personality characteristic about which there is nothing they can do, while others explained it as a characteristic unique to the situation about which there is quite a lot that they can do. It is possible, of course, that some people make dispositional self-attributions because they easily explain their otherwise unacceptable jealous actions. As Jon Wagner noted, "Sexual jealousy functions as an integrative experience, and is one of the few widely accepted grounds for moral indignation. In this respect, feeling jealous 'explains' to others a whole range of hostile, bitter, and violent actions. These same actions, without the legitimizing context of jealousy, are usually taken to be symptoms of personal disorganization or derangement" (Wagner, 1976, p. 269).

Even though dispositional self-attributions can be effective in excusing certain unacceptable behaviors, in the long run they are very much to be avoided because they greatly reduce one's freedom to act and ability to cope actively and directly with jealousy triggers. This conclusion applies to therapists and counselors working with individuals and couples presenting jealousy as a problematic issue; it also applies to people experiencing jealousy as a personal problem. In all cases, situational variables should be examined as possible antecedents of jealousy, and the manipulation of those variables should be considered a prerequisite for improved coping. Future research could and should investigate the relative merits of person-oriented versus situation-oriented research and clinical work concerning sexual jealousy.

REFERENCES

Corzine, L.W. The phenomenon of jealousy: A theoretic and empirical analysis. Ph.D. dissertation, United States International University (Chairperson, Dorothy L. Harris), 1974.

Downing, C. Jealousy: A psychological perspective. In G. Clanton and L. Smith (eds.), *Jealousy*. Englewood Cliffs, N.J.: Prentice-Hall, 1977, 72–80.

Freud, S. Certain neurotic mechanisms in jealousy, paranoia and homosexuality. *Collected Papers Vol. 2*. New York: Basic Books, 1959

Gillispie, D.L. Who has the power? The marital struggle. *Journal of Marriage and Family Living, 33,* (1971) 445–58.

Jaremko, M., and Lindsey, R. Stress-coping abilities of individuals high and low in jealousy. *Psychological Reports, 44,* (1979) 547–53.

Pines, A., and Aronson, E. Polyfidelity: An alternative lifestyle without sexual jealousy? In G. Clanton (ed.), *Jealousy,* a special issue of *Alternative Lifestyles*. Beverly Hills, Cal.: Sage Publications, 1981.

Shettel-Neuber, J., Bryson, J.B., and Young, L.E. Physical attractiveness of the "other person" and jealousy. *Personality and Social Psychology Bulletin,* vol. 4, no. 4 (1978): 612–16.

Teismann, M.W., and Mosher, D.L. Jealous conflict in dating couples. *Psychological Reports, 42,* (1978) 1211–16.

Tipton, R.M., Benedictson, C.S., Mahoney, J., and Hartnett, J. Development of a scale for assessment of jealousy. *Psychological Reports, 42* (1978) 1217–18.

Wagner, J. Jealousy, extended intimacies and sexual affirmation. *E.T.C.* vol. 33, no. 13, (1976): 269–88.

White, G. Jealousy model. In G. Clanton and L. Smith (eds.), *Jealousy*. Englewood Cliffs, N.J.: Prentice-Hall, 1977.

White, G. Inducing jealousy: A power perspective. *Personality and Social Psychology Bulletin, 6* (1980) 222–27.

PROJECTS

Name _____

Date _____

5.1: HOW DID YOU KNOW IT WAS LOVE?

The goal of this project is to identify the different dimensions of the experience of love through an introspective look at your first "real" love. Try to recall as much as you can about that love, focusing on your own experience of love rather than on the unique characteristics of the loved person. How did you know it was love? Once you have described the variables that made up your love experience, compare your answers with those of the other people in your class. Is there any agreement among you about what constitutes love? If so, what is it?

FILL IN THE BLANKS IN THIRD COLUMN

Dimensions	*Possible Variables*	*Personal Experience*
Physical symptoms	What did you experience physically in the presence of your loved one (e.g., pounding heart, blushing, great excitement)?	_____ _____ _____ _____ _____
Changed perceptions	How did you perceive your loved one? What attributes made him or her worthy of your love (e.g., good looks, intelligence, poise, kindness, sexiness)?	_____ _____ _____ _____ _____
Behavioral symptoms	What unusual behaviors made you realize you were in love (e.g., thought about him or her all the time, started to stammer when talking to him or her)?	_____ _____ _____ _____ _____

Name _____

Date _____

5.2: NONVERBAL COMMUNICATION OF AFFILIATION

People approach what they like and avoid what they dislike. That principle allows us to infer feelings from observations of people's movements toward or away from people, things, and even ideas. Scientists who study nonverbal communication have found that greater liking is conveyed by standing close instead of far, leaning forward instead of back while seated, facing directly instead of turning to one side, touching, having mutual gaze or eye contact, extending bodily contact as during handshake, prolonging goodbyes, and using gestures during a greeting which imply a reaching out toward the other person who is at a distance. [Albert Mehrabian, *Silent Messages* (Belmont, Calif.: Wadsworth), 1971, p. 22.]

Through this project you will be studying nonverbal communication more systematically by doing two observational tasks in a social setting such as a restaurant, a classroom, or a park. The observations are to focus on two male–female dyads. One couple should be chosen because they appear to be close friends or lovers (high affiliation); the other dyad should involve two people who appear to be strangers and who have just met (low affiliation). Observe the nonverbal communication between the members of each dyad and record your observations on the data sheet. Then compare your ratings, and describe the similarities and/or differences in this form of communication that existed between the two couples.

Nonverbal Communication of Affiliation

Nonverbal Behavior	High-Affiliation Dyad	Low-Affiliation Dyad	Comments on Similarities and Differences
1. Mutual eye contact			
2. Distance between dyad members			
3. Touching			
4. Posture			
5. Body orientation (facing forward or sideways, leaning)			
6. Facial expressions			
7. Hand gestures			
8. (Other) _____			

Name _____

Date _____

5.3: SEXUAL JEALOUSY

Who do you think experiences more sexual jealousy—men or women? People in long-term relationships or people in short-term relationships? Young people or old people? This project will enable you to test your hypothesis, whatever that hypothesis may be.

First decide as a class what sample you are interested in (e.g., men versus women, people who have been with their partner over 20 years versus people who have been together less than one year). Then, each student should approach two people (e.g., a man and a woman), explain that you are doing a class project on sexual jealousy and ask whether they will be willing to help you by responding to a short questionnaire. To those who indicate an interest, present a copy of the Sexual Jealousy Inventory subscale, "Reaction to Jealousy," and ask them to respond to it with reference to their most intense experience of jealousy ever. After they complete the questionnaire, ask them whether they would be interested in the data once they are analyzed. (If they indicate an interest, make sure you give a report to them later.) In order to test your hypothesis, compare the means of the two samples, and then use a *t*-test to find if that difference is statistically significant. You can compare the means of the subjects' physical reactions, and the means of the emotional reactions in addition to the overall differences.

If you are interested in the subject for an individual project rather than a joint class project, you will need to interview at least 30 people, 15 in each group, in order to be relatively secure in your conclusions and generalizations for the sample.

Sex _____

Age _____

REACTIONS TO JEALOUSY

Try to recall the situation which produced your most extreme experience of jealousy. To what extent did you experience each one of the following physical and emotional reactions? (Please use the same scale for all items.)

1	2	3	4	5	6	7
very intensely			a moderate degree			not at all

Physical reactions

hot _____

cold _____

dizzy _____

headachy _____

fainting or
blacking out _____

blood rushing to head _____

feeling you are going to have
a nervous breakdown _____

feeling aroused and energized _____

sexually aroused _____

physically exhausted _____

other (please specify) _____

loss of appetite _____

nervous and shaky _____

nausea _____

hands sweaty or trembling _____

feeling of emptiness
in stomach _____

stomach cramps _____

fast heart beating _____

shortness of breath _____

nightmares _____

trouble falling or
staying asleep _____

Emotional reactions

rage _____

inferiority _____

anxiety _____

humiliation _____

frustration _____

depression _____

self-pity _____

fear of loss _____

guilt _____

confusion _____

envy _____

grief _____

pain _____

anger _____

helplessness _____

possessiveness _____

aggression _____

vulnerability _____

blame _____

passion _____

excitement _____

resentment _____

hopelessness _____

entrapment _____

self-righteousness _____

irritability and
annoyance _____

lowered self-esteem _____

exclusion _____

emotional exhaustion _____

self-knowledge _____

other (please specify)

_____

Adapted from Pines and Aronson (1982).

AGGRESSION AND VIOLENCE

6

It is commonly said that we are living in violent times. There are wars all around the world, and in the United States the incidence of such violent crimes as murder, rape, and assault is clearly on the rise. The statistics on battered wives and abused children are alarming testimony to the fact that the home is as violent as the street. Violence is an integral part of many sports, such as hockey and football, which are sometimes accompanied by spectator violence as well. Furthermore, violence is increasingly being depicted in the mass media, both as entertainment and as information. News reports routinely feature graphic representations and discussions of wars, terrorist events, and sensational crimes. Children's cartoons have long been known for the number and variety of aggressive acts they depict, and adult television programs and films are filled with every imaginable type of interpersonal violence. Meanwhile, more and more research has demonstrated that exposure to violence fosters aggressiveness in the viewers. Media executives often respond that violence sells and that they, after all, are only giving the public what it wants. Yet even these notions are being disputed by recent research and by some effective consumer boycotts of the products of advertisers who sponsor violent shows.

The long history of widespread aggression and the seriousness of its consequences have prompted extensive study, by psychologists and others, of the causes of violent behavior. (Paradoxically, such positive social behaviors as love and altruism have only recently become legitimate topics for study by psychologists.) Several different theories of aggression have emerged. Some, such as Freudian and ethological theories, maintain that the source of aggression is within the individual, either as an aggressive instinct or as particular physiological factors or personality characteristics. Other theories focus on causes of aggression found in the external environment. How a person reacts to frustration and certain stimuli associated with aggression is given special emphasis in frustration-aggression models of aggressive behavior. Social learning theory has pointed to the ways in which aggression is learned in our society, and researchers working within this framework have studied the impact of aggressive models, the importance of reinforcements for aggressive behavior, and the pervasiveness of social norms that sanction aggression (such as the norm for males to "be a man and use your fists"). The causes of aggressive behavior are clearly multiple and complex, and it is equally clear that any solutions proposed for the problems of violence must take all of these factors into account.

THE STORY OF CAIN AND ABEL, FROM GENESIS 4:1–12

And the man knew Eve his wife; and she conceived and bore Cain, and said: 'I have gotten a man with the help of the LORD.' And again she bore his brother Abel. And Abel was a keeper of sheep, but Cain was a tiller of the ground. And in process of time it came to pass, that Cain brought of the fruit of the ground an offering unto the LORD. And Abel, he also brought of the firstlings of his flock and of the fat thereof. And the LORD had respect unto Abel and to his offering; but unto Cain and to his offering He had not respect. And Cain was very wroth, and his countenance fell. And the Lord said unto Cain: 'Why art thou wroth? and why is thy countenance fallen? If thou doest well, shall it not be lifted up? and if thou doest not well, sin coucheth at the door; and unto thee is its desire, but thou mayest rule over it.' And Cain spoke unto Abel his brother. And it came to pass, when they were in the field, that Cain rose up against Abel his brother, and slew him.

And the LORD said unto Cain: 'Where is Abel thy brother?' And he said: 'I know not; am I my brother's keeper?' And He said: 'What hast thou done? the voice of thy brother's blood crieth unto Me from the ground. And now cursed art thou from the ground, which hath opened her mouth to receive thy brother's blood from thy hand. When thou tillest the ground, it shall not henceforth yield unto thee her strength; a fugitive and a wanderer shalt thou be in the earth.'

RESEARCH HIGHLIGHT

TELEVISION AND VIOLENCE

Reviewing all the available studies on the subject of television and violence, the Surgeon General's Scientific Advisory Committee on Television and Social Behavior concluded that viewing televised violence causes the viewer to become more aggressive, at least in the short run. Given the considerable amount of violence portrayed on television, and the considerable amount of time spent in front of the television set, this conclusion is an obvious cause of concern, especially with regard to children. The reason for the special concern for TV's impact on children is their impressionability, the amount of their exposure (on the average, preschoolers spend approximately half of an adult work week sitting in front of the television set), and the violent nature of their preferred programs (cartoons are among the most violent programs on television).

Paul Ekman and his associates at the Langley Porter Neuropsychiatric Institute were interested in studying the facial expression of children's emotions, as predictions of subsequent aggression, while watching televised violence. In their experiment, five- and six-year-old boys first viewed part of an actual television program depicting either violence or nonviolent sports; they were then given an opportunity to engage in aggressive behavior against a peer. Videotape records were taken of the children's facial expressions of emotion while they watched television. Results indicated that boys whose facial expressions during the shooting or fighting episodes showed happiness, pleasantness, and not sadness, tended to use the "hurt" button more than boys whose facial expressions showed unpleasantness, sadness, and not happiness. The hurt button was supposedly connected by wires to the handle of a game played by another child in the adjacent room. When the button was pushed it made the handle hot, hurting the other child, causing him to release it. Findings also showed that it was not simply the emotional reaction to television that predicted subsequent aggression, but more specifically, the emotional reaction to a violent program. Emotional reaction to sports programs or to a commercial did not relate to subsequent aggression.

P. Ekman et al., *"Facial expression of emotion while watching televised violence as predictors of subsequent aggression,"* a technical report to the Surgeon General's Scientific Advisory Committee on Television and Social Behavior (Washington, D.C.: U.S. Government Printing Office, 1972).

NATURALISTIC STUDIES OF AGGRESSIVE BEHAVIOR: AGGRESSIVE STIMULI, VICTIM VISIBILITY, AND HORN-HONKING

CHARLES W. TURNER, JOHN F. LAYTON, AND LYNN STANLEY SIMONS

When we think about aggression, the images we usually conjure up have to do with destruction, violence, and pain, such as gladiators in a ring. But aggression is not always that extreme and not always physical. Sometimes a cruel comment can be more aggressive and more painful than a slap in the face. Turner, Layton, and Simons seem to agree. These three studied a rather mild form of aggression, namely, horn-honking. They felt the need to get out of the laboratory and conduct naturalistic studies because, in an earlier laboratory study, Turner and Simons discovered that the subjects' awareness of the experimenter's purpose caused them to inhibit their aggressive behavior— that is, when they believed the experimenter was monitoring their response to a weapon, they were less likely to shock their partner with it. Turner, Layton, and Simons decided to use horn-honking as an aggressive behavior for a number of reasons explained in their article. They describe here three different studies in which they attempted to manipulate the horn-honking of unaware subjects by introducing aggressive stimuli and by varying the victim's visibility. It worked.

There has been considerable recent controversy about the validity of laboratory studies of aggression. For example, some researchers have suggested that the commonly used measures of aggression may not have external validity. Thus, variables which affect laboratory-based responses may not influence naturally occurring aggressive responses.

One possible limitation of the laboratory setting is that subjects may sharply modify their behavior if they believe that someone is carefully monitoring and evaluating their reactions. In order to reduce the subjects' inhibitions, researchers have introduced a variety of deceptions to minimize beliefs that the experiment was designed to evaluate aggressive behavior. However, many subjects today may be too sophisticated for the deceptions commonly used in the laboratory. Thus, some laboratory findings could be artifactual for two reasons. First, subjects may be responding primarily to awareness of deceptions rather than

the experimental treatments. Second, their primary motivation may often be to portray themselves in a favorable light to the experimenter.

Since some laboratory results may be produced by experimental artifacts such as evaluation apprehension, suspicion, negativism, and sophistication, it is important that attempts be made to investigate aggressive behavior in subjects who are not aware that they are being studied. The primary purpose of the present research was to assess whether naturalistic manipulations conceptually similar to laboratory procedures can affect human aggressive responses. Laboratory researchers have attempted to manipulate arousal, aggressive stimulation, and dehumanization. In an exploratory attempt to extend laboratory research to a naturalistic setting, a rifle in an aggressive context (aggressive stimuli) and victim visibility (dehumanization) were manipulated in the present study for obstructed (and possibly aroused) drivers at a signal light.

In order to develop an appropriate naturalistic setting to measure aggressive responses, guidelines were adapted from Webb, Campbell, Schwartz, and Sechrest's (1966) analysis of unobtrusive measures. The following criteria were

From *Journal of Personality and Social Psychology*, 1975, 31(6), 1098–1107. Copyright 1975 by American Psychological Association. Reprinted by permission.

adopted to reduce subjects' perceptions that they were being studied and to develop adequately sensitive and independent measures of aggression: (a) There should be relatively low inhibitions about the behavior so that the base level responding would be considerably above zero probability, (b) the response should not be likely to produce contagion effects on other's aggression, (c) the subjects' anonymity should be preserved, (d) the experimental setting should be reasonably naturalistic so that the procedures would not be an unusual imposition on the subjects or endanger them in any way, (e) the subjects should remain in the experimental setting for short periods of time such that they would not be exposed to more than one experimental treatment, and (f) the experimental treatments could be randomly assigned to subjects.

STUDY 1

Doob and Gross (1968) have offered one possible procedure for a naturalistic study of aggression. Their findings suggest that horn-honking might be an aggressive reaction toward low-status drivers who prevent the flow of traffic at a signal light. Anecdotal evidence suggests that many drivers become aggressive when "frustrated" by the behavior of other drivers. Parry (1968) surveyed English drivers concerning their aggressive reactions while driving. His findings suggest that hostile reactions while driving included facial expressions, verbalizations, such as swearing, hand gestures, tailgating, light flashing (high beams), and horn-honking. Some drivers also reported actual fist fights or attempts to chase other drivers off the road. Parry's findings suggest that many drivers may become angry and aggressive while driving. In order to determine whether similar hostile reactions occur in Salt Lake City, a survey was conducted based on Parry's questionnaire. Thus, Study 1 was designed to determine whether there was a sufficiently high base rate of anger and aggressive responses from drivers so that experimental treatments might be expected to produce reliable results.

METHOD

Subjects and Procedure

The subjects were sampled from the population of frequent drivers in Salt Lake City. One hundred homes were randomly selected from the city address directory. When an investigator located a residence, the most frequent male or the most fre-

quent female driver (randomly determined) was asked to complete Parry's (1968) driving survey. Acceptable subjects were located in 93 homes. The subjects were given a stamped envelope to return the questionnaire. If they did not respond within 2 weeks, they were again encouraged to complete the questionnaire. The subjects were assured of the complete confidentiality of their responses. Fifty-nine (63 percent) of the delivered questionnaires were returned.

RESULTS AND DISCUSSION

The findings suggest that a high proportion of "frequent" drivers sometimes become angry or are irritated by the driving behaviors of other drivers. For example, 77 percent of males and 56 percent of females reported "swearing under their breaths" at other drivers, while 50 percent of males and 15 percent of female drivers reported "flashing their lights in anger" at other drivers. While overt hostile responses were not reported by a majority of drivers on every question, there does appear to be evidence that hostile reactions to other drivers are a frequent occurrence. If the verbal reports are accurate reflections of actual driving situations, then a large number of drivers might be frequently irritated by the behavior of other drivers. This anger or irritation could sometimes lead to an overt aggressive response if such a response is readily available (such as horn-honking following an obstruction at a signal light).

STUDY 2

The present research was primarily designed to extend laboratory-based procedures for investigating possible determinants of aggressive reaction in a naturalistic setting. Hence, the procedure of Doob and Gross (1968) was adapted in order to manipulate exposure to aggressive stimuli and to attempt manipulations of inhibitions by dehumanizations of the subject's "victim." The alleged victim (an experimental confederate) would potentially frustrate all subjects by obstructing them at a signal light.

Berkowitz and LePage (1967) manipulated aggressive stimulation by exposing some subjects to a pistol and shotgun. One possible analogous field manipulation of aggressive stimuli would be to present a rifle in the gun rack of a pickup truck, especially since rifles are often carried that way in Utah. However, a high proportion (perhaps 50 percent) of Utah males have used rifles frequently in a "sporting" context. It is possible that weapons (a rifle or a pistol) are not always perceived as aggressive stimuli when they have been observed frequently in a nonaggressive context; for example, the rifles may be perceived as sporting equipment, somewhat like a fishing pole or skis. In the present experiment, an attempt was made to vary the salience of an aggressive meaning for a rifle by pairing it with an ostensible bumper sticker having an aggressive or a nonaggressive label. This manipulation is somewhat analogous to one employed by Berkowitz and Alioto (1973). They led some subjects to believe that a filmed football game was a "grudge" match, while other subjects were encouraged to think of the game simply as a sporting event. Subjects watching an apparent grudge match were more likely to see an aggressive meaning to the players' actions and were more likely to shock a partner who had previously angered them. Berkowitz and Alioto's (1973) findings suggest that the *context* of stimulus materials may play an important role in determining whether the material is viewed with an aggressive meaning.

In an attempt to vary the subjects' inhibitions about being aggressive, the mutual visibility of the victim and subject was varied. According to findings by Milgram (1965), subjects appeared to be more willing to administer shock to an ostensible fellow subject when they were both less likely to see and to be seen by the victim. In addition, Zimbardo (1969) has proposed that deindividuation of both the subject and victim (dehumanization) can increase the probability of aggressive behavior.

METHOD

Subjects

Experimental treatments were randomly assigned to 92 male drivers who served as subjects. Nine additional subjects were dropped from the sample, since they were females (n = 4) or male drivers of older vehicles (n = 5). These subjects were approximately evenly distributed across conditions. The subjects were an arbitrarily selected sample of drivers of late-model vehicles (less than six years of age) in a 20 × 20 block region of a mixed business–residential district of Salt Lake City. Only newer car drivers were employed because high-status victims seem to lead to inhibitions in honking (Doob and Gross, 1968). It is possible that older-car drivers would perceive themselves as having low status relative to the victim, which could lead to inhibitions masking the effects of independent variables. The experimental treatments were run

on Saturdays from 9 A.M. to 5 P.M. It was assumed that Saturdays would produce a broader based sample of drivers from the potential population of all drivers, since fewer would be working. Moreover, the influence of "rush hour" traffic conditions could be minimized by testing on Saturdays.

Experimental Design

A 3 × 2 between-subjects factorial design was employed to manipulate aggressive stimulation and victim visibility (dehumanization). The subject was obstructed at a signal light for 12 seconds by an older model (1964) pickup truck with a gun rack in the rear window. The aggressive stimulation variable had three levels: (a) The gun rack was left empty (control), (b) a .303-calibre military rifle was placed in the gun rack and a bumper sticker was attached to the truck in order to reduce the perceived aggressiveness of the rifle (Rifle & "Friend" bumper sticker), or (c) the rifle was paired with a bumper sticker designed to increase the perceived aggressiveness of the rifle (Rifle & "Vengeance" bumper sticker). The bumper stickers were attached to the tailgate of the truck directly in line with the subject's vision, and they could be easily removed and reattached after each trial. The bumper stickers measured approximately 4 × 15 inches (102 × 381 mm), and the words (3 inches, or 76 mm, high) were printed with broad lettering (⅜ inch, or 9.5 mm, thick), so that they could be easily read at 50 feet (15 m). The words *friend* and *vengeance* were selected from the aggressive or altruistic lists of Parke, Ewall, and Slaby (1972). Ratings by 30 college students indicated that the word *vengeance* was highest (without also being rated high in anxiety) and *friend* was lowest on an aggressive–nonaggressive dimension from the words in Parke et al.'s lists.

Victim visibility (dehumanization) was manipulated by closing a curtain across the rear window of the pickup (without obstructing the view of the gun rack) in half of the conditions (low visibility) and leaving the curtain open in the other conditions (high visibility). The experimental conditions were run in blocks of six such that each condition was completed before any condition was replicated.

Procedure

The procedure was modeled closely after Doob and Gross (1968). An experimental confederate driving a pickup truck timed his arrival at an intersection at approximately the same time that the light turned red. If a male driver of a late-model, apparently privately-owned vehicle came to a complete stop behind the confederate before the light changed to green, the driver-confederate started the trial (if the conditions were not satisfied, the trial was aborted). When the light turned green, the driver-confederate started a stopwatch, faced straight ahead, and kept his brake lights on to avoid any indication that he might be having trouble with the pickup. At the end of 12 seconds, the confederate moved forward with the traffic. Thus, the subjects were obstructed at the light for 12 seconds. The first driver in line behind the confederate was always considered to be the subject. An observer was placed in an inconspicuous spot at the intersection so that the subject would be unlikely to see him. The observer rated demographic characteristics of the subject before the trial began (such as age and sex of subject; age of car, make of car, number of occupants, and general traffic density). Based on the observer's ratings, nine subjects were dropped from the sample, since they were either females or male drivers of older vehicles. The deleted subjects were inadvertently exposed to treatments when the driver-confederate could not see them clearly in his mirror. The driver's side-view mirror was partly obstructed with tape so that his reflection would not be visible to the subjects behind him when the curtain was closed. The tape also prevented the confederate from clearly seeing the subject's vehicle, and he misjudged the sex or vehicle age of some subjects. The observer's judgments were employed to establish the vehicle age or sex of subjects. The observers started a stopwatch when the light turned green and recorded the latency and frequency of honks from the subject. The observers received at least 1 hour of pretraining in the rating procedures.

RESULTS AND DISCUSSION

Subjects' honking responses were dichotomized into those honking (scored as 1) and those not honking (scored as 0).

The rates of honking are reported in Table 1.

The results indicated that the closed curtain significantly increased the rate of honking compared with the open-curtain treatment. In addition, the honking rate for the rifle/vengeance condition ($\overline{X} = .765$) was significantly higher than the average ($\overline{X} = .400$) of the other two conditions when the curtain was closed, but the effect was not significant when the curtain was open.

TABLE 1. PERCENTAGE OF HORN-HONKING IN THE EXPERIMENTAL CONDITIONS OF STUDY 2

| VICTIM VISIBILITY | AGGRESSIVE STIMULATION | | | |
| | | RIFLE PRESENT | | |
	CONTROL [%]	FRIEND BUMPER STICKER [%]	VEN-GEANCE BUMPER STICKER [%]	MEAN %
Low visibility (curtain closed)	33.3	46.7	76.5	52.2
High visibility (curtain open)	21.4	29.4	42.9	31.2
Mean %	27.4	38.0	59.7	

Note. Cell entries refer to the percentages of subjects producing at least one honk.

The results of the present study are generally consistent with the reasoning that led to the procedures, since both victim visibility and the rifle/vengeance condition increased horn-honking. Thus, the present findings tentatively suggest that dehumanization and the presence of a rifle which is perceived as an aggressive stimulus can increase the probability of aggressive responding in a naturalistic setting. The rifle did not significantly influence the rate of honking when it was in a friendly or "prosocial" context, nor did the rifle/vengeance condition significantly influence honking when the victim was visible. The fact that the rifle/vengeance condition honking rate was significantly higher only when the victim was not visible may be consistent with laboratory procedures used to study aggressive behavior. That is, most researchers in the laboratory typically isolate the victim from the subject in order to lower inhibitions about giving shocks. Similarly, in the present study, reduced visibility of the victim (when the curtain was closed) might have increased the rate by reducing inhibitions.

STUDY 3

One limitation of the procedure in Study 2 was that the rifle and the vengeance bumper sticker were not independently manipulated. Thus, the findings for the rifle/vengeance condition might have been due to either object alone or to the interactive effects of both objects. In Study 3, the rifle and the vengeance bumper sticker were independently manipulated so that their hypothesized interactive effects on horn-honking could be tested.

The vengeance bumper sticker was designed to increase the likelihood that subjects would perceive an aggressive connotation to the rifle. Previous laboratory findings suggest that uninhibited subjects would be more aggressive when they viewed stimuli with an aggressive meaning. Since it was possible that inhibitions might mask any effects of the rifle and the vengeance bumper sticker, the dehumanization (curtain) manipulation of Study 2 was employed for all conditions in an attempt to lower inhibitions.

The work of Doob and Gross (1968) suggests that there may be strong individual differences (such as status and sex differences) in drivers' reactions to obstruction at a stoplight. Based, in part, on Doob and Gross's findings, male drivers of older vehicles and female drivers were not used as subjects in Study 2 because it was assumed that they would inhibit horn-honking. Doob and Gross found that male subjects honked less at higher-than lower-status victims, possibly because high-status victims produced inhibitions about honking. Presumably, the lower the subject's self-perceived status, the higher the victim's status (relatively) is likely to appear. Thus, self-perceived status relative to the victim may influence willingness to honk as an aggressive response.

In the present investigation, the subjects were divided into two groups based on the age of the vehicle they were driving. This procedure was employed in an attempt to derive an exploratory measure of subject's self-perceived status. It is possible that the older a person's car, the less likely he would be to perceive himself as higher in status than the confederate in the pickup truck. Since the vehicle age variable could reflect other differences than self-perceived status (such as differential likelihoods of being frustrated due to different experiences with stalled automobiles), the variable was included only as an exploratory assessment of possible status differences.[1]

Several researchers have found different patterns of male and female aggressive behavior. Further, Doob and Gross (1968) found different horn-honking reactions in men and women, since

women had longer latencies for their first honks. Based on these findings, it was assumed that males and females might not respond with horn-honking in the same way to the manipulations of the present study if horn-honking reactions to obstruction at a signal light reflect aggressive responses. Hence, the subject's sex was recorded to permit separate comparisons of the experimental manipulations for males and females. It is possible that the effects of the rifle or the vengeance bumper sticker would be significant only with male subjects driving new vehicles, since other subjects might inhibit horn-honking responses.

METHOD

Subjects

Male ($n = 137$) and female ($n = 63$) drivers of apparently privately owned vehicles served as subjects. Subjects were selected by the same procedures used in Study 2 except that no restrictions were placed on the age of drivers' vehicles or sex of subjects. Four additional subjects were dropped from the sample due to recording errors (that is, not recording age of vehicle or sex of subject).

Experimental Design

Each subject was exposed to one level of a weapon (rifle versus no rifle) manipulation and one level of the bumper sticker (vengeance bumper sticker versus no bumper sticker) manipulation in an attempt to independently manipulate perceived aggressiveness of the rifle. The status of the subjects was also classified according to a median split (approximately) on the age of the subjects' vehicles (new vehicle: less than or equal to four years old; old vehicle: more than four years old).

Procedure

The procedure was identical to Study 2 except for the independent manipulation of the bumper sticker and the rifle. In addition, both male and female drivers were exposed to the treatments. Two pickup trucks (1969 models) were used to introduce the experimental conditions. These trucks were five to six years newer than the truck used in Study 2. Hence, the victims' perceived status in Study 3 might have been higher than that of the victim in Study 2.

Hidden observers started a stopwatch when the

---

[1]Status was varied by vehicle age rather than model for several reasons. It was assumed that different models might not be consistently perceived as representing high or low status by all drivers (such as sports cars versus luxury sedans). Moreover, it was difficult to determine how subjects would judge older model, expensive vehicles relative to newer model, less expensive vehicles. There might be considerable inconsistency in perceptions of status for model-cost and model-age variations.

light turned green and recorded the latency and frequency of honks. The raters also recorded information about subjects' age, sex, and age of vehicle. The raters received at least one hour of pretraining in the rating procedures. In order to assess the reliability of observer ratings, two raters were employed for two separate samples of subjects (Sample A = 62 subjects from Study 3; Sample B = 46 subjects from an unpublished study testing other hypotheses about the effects of a rifle). The percentage agreement between the raters for presence or absence of a honk was 100 percent in Sample A and 96 percent in Sample B. The reliability for rated age of subject's auto was .83 for Sample A and .78 for Sample B; most of the disagreements occurred for older age autos. Reliabilities for frequency of honking were .94 in Sample A and .87 in Sample B; reliability for latency of honking was .90 for both Samples A and B. No attempt was made to record or rate duration of honks, since reliabilities of ratings would have been too low, and adequately sensitive, portable tape recorders were not available to record the honks.

RESULTS AND DISCUSSION

As in Study 2, subjects' horn-honking responses were dichotomized into those honking (scored as 1) and those not honking (scored as 0). According to the reasoning advanced above, it was assumed that the effects of the rifle would be most pronounced when it appeared in an aggressive context (that is, with the bumper sticker). The mean rates (proportions) of subject honking which are reported separately for new- and old-vehicle male drivers and for female drivers are presented in Table 2.

New-Vehicle Male Drivers

The results indicated that the rate of honking in the rifle/vengeance condition with new-vehicle male drivers was significantly higher than the average of the other three rifle/bumper sticker conditions. The other three conditions did not differ significantly from each other. Hence, the results tentatively support the predictions leading to the present procedures. Although the rifle/vengeance condition was significantly different from the average of the other three conditions, a careful inspection of the means reported in Table 2 indicates that it was not significantly different from the control condition. One possible explanation for the somewhat weaker results obtained in Study

TABLE 2. PERCENTAGE OF HORN-HONKING IN THE EXPERIMENTAL CONDITIONS OF STUDY 3

EXPERIMENTAL CONDITIONS			
NO RIFLE PRESENT		RIFLE PRESENT	
No bumper sticker [%]	Vengeance bumper sticker [%]	No bumper sticker [%]	Vengeance bumper sticker [%]
Male Drivers of New Vehicles			
50.0	33.3	30.4	65.0
Male Drivers of Old Vehicles			
56.2	38.1	46.2	14.3
Female Drivers			
80.0	50.0	50.0	50.0

Note. Cell entries refer to the percentages of subjects producing at least one honk.

3 is based on the fact that the confederate-victims drove newer vehicles (three to four years old) in Study 3 as compared to an eight to nine-year-old vehicle in Study 2. Perhaps some subjects inhibited honking to victims in the newer trucks in Study 3 because the victims were perceived to be of relatively high status. Since Doob and Gross (1968) found evidence of inhibitory reactions toward high-status victims, perhaps the weaker findings in the present study were partly accounted for by inhibitory processes.[2]

Old-Vehicle Male Drivers

The results indicated that the rifle/vengeance condition produced significantly lower rates of honking than the other three conditions. The other three conditions did not differ significantly. One possible explanation can be offered for these findings:

---

[2]In order to assess the robustness of the aggressive stimulation manipulation which was reflected in the comparison of the rifle/vengeance condition to the control (no rifle/no bumper sticker) condition, the results for Study 2 and Study 3 were reanalyzed. The results indicated that the aggressive stimulation factor was significant, while neither the other factor (study replication) nor the interaction was significant. The absence of a significant interaction suggests that the pattern of results was similar in the two studies for the effect of the rifle/vengeance condition versus the control condition.

When the old-vehicle drivers were exposed to the rifle in an aggressive context (the bumper sticker), they were more likely to perceive an aggressive meaning to the rifle and hence to their own honking responses. If they perceived their honks as potentially aggressive, they might have inhibited reactions in the presence of a higher status victim. These interpretations are somewhat similar to those offered by Ellis, Weinir, and Miller (1972), who found that subjects produced lower levels of shock giving in the presence of a rifle and a pistol. Apparently for their subjects, the weapons produced inhibitions about being aggressive. The present findings tentatively suggest that the presence of a rifle in an aggressive context (like the bumper sticker) for some male subjects may produce inhibitions rather than stimulate more aggression.

Female Drivers

The differences between conditions were not significant, even when female subjects were divided by the age of their vehicles (new and old). However, the results for the females must be interpreted cautiously, since there were fewer subjects in any condition; thus, the condition differences might be significant with sample sizes as large as those obtained for the male subjects. The lower frequency of female subjects resulted from the fact that most drivers were males, at least on Saturdays.

GENERAL DISCUSSION

The primary reason for employing a naturalistic paradigm in the present research was to explore the possibility that laboratory procedures could be extended to a setting where subjects were unaware that they were being studied. While there are many advantages to naturalistic studies, one disadvantage results from the fact that it is difficult to obtain validity or manipulation checks from subjects to determine their perceptions of the experimental treatments. For example, it was not possible in the present research to assess directly any effects of the vengeance bumper sticker on the subject's perception of the rifle or to measure independently possible differences in inhibitions produced by the victim visibility or vehicle age variables. As a consequence, any inferences about possible mediating principles can be offered only very tentatively, since alternative interpretations can be offered for the present results. Additional research is required before any firm conclusions

are warranted about the present manipulations and the dependent measures.

The results of a survey and two naturalistic experiments in the present research tentatively suggest that findings somewhat analogous to laboratory research on aggression can be produced in a naturalistic setting. For example, male subjects in Study 2 were more likely to honk at a victim when he was not visible. Similarly, Milgram (1965) found in a laboratory setting that subjects were more likely to harm a victim who was not visible. Zimbardo's (1969) construct of dehumanization provides one possible explanation for the effects of victim visibility. According to the construct, inhibitions against harming a victim are lowered in the absence of cues which "humanize" a victim. The present curtain manipulations might have "dehumanized" the victim by removing visual cues from him which might have reduced possible inhibitions against horn-honking as an aggressive response.

However, there is another interpretation possible for effects of the curtain manipulation. For example, the horn-honking subsequent to obstruction at the light might be interpreted better as a "signal" response rather than as aggression. Since the subjects could not see the driver-confederate when the curtain was closed, they might have thought that he was being inattentive at the light. Thus, they might have used their horns to signal that the light had changed. Anecdotal evidence suggests that drivers often honk at others to attract their attention or to warn them about some danger. This alternative interpretation of the horn-honking measure cannot be dismissed. Nevertheless, the pattern of findings (including the results of the survey in Study 1) suggests that drivers may become frustrated and angry at other drivers, and this anger or frustration can lead to various hostile reactions, such as light flashing, swearing, or hand gestures. Presumably, horn-honking might also be perceived as an aggressive response by subjects, especially in the presence of aggressive stimuli.

Male drivers of new vehicles in Study 2 gave more honks when they were exposed to the rifle/vengeance bumper sticker condition but only if they could not see the confederate. In one sense, the findings of Study 3 replicate the results for Study 2, since the honking rate in the rifle/vengeance condition was significantly higher (Contrast A) only for male drivers of new vehicles (the confederate was not visible for any subjects in Study 3).

One important finding in Study 3 was the strong individual differences in subjects' reactions. Although male drivers of new vehicles with nonvisible victims honked more when exposed to both the rifle and the vengeance bumper sticker, the higher rates did not occur for all subjects. When male drivers of new vehicles *could* see their victim, or when male drivers of old vehicles and female drivers were exposed to the rifle/vengeance condition, they did not honk more. One possible explanation for the lower honking rates is that these subjects might have inhibited horn-honking responses, especially in the presence of the rifle/vengeance condition. For example, if male drivers of old vehicles perceived themselves to be of lower status than the confederate, they might have inhibited horn-honking as an aggressive response due to fears of retaliation from the high-status driver in front of them. The results suggest the possibility that the presence of aggressive stimuli might lead to lower levels of aggression from many individuals due to inhibitions about engaging in aggressive behavior. Hence, there might be important limitations on the generalizability for the effects of aggressive stimuli on horn-honking responses and, possibly, on other aggressive and antisocial responses.

As with the victim visibility manipulations, there are several possible explanations for the present aggressive stimulus manipulations. For example, the rifle/bumper sticker combination might have served as a classically conditioned aggressive stimulus which elicited aggression; it might have served as a retrieval cue to remind subjects of previous experiences with aggressive stimuli (such as violent portrayals in the mass media), or it might have served as a cue which changed the subjects' perceptions of the aggressive meaning of their responses.

Since there are alternative explanations for the present findings which cannot be dismissed, no firm conclusions can be offered about which principles best explain the results until additional research is completed. Still, the present research provides procedures which might be used to extend laboratory research to naturalistic settings where subjects do not know that they are being studied.

REFERENCES

Berkowitz, L., & Alioto, J. T. The meaning of an observed event as a determinant of its aggressive consequences. *Journal of Personality and Social Psychology*, 1973, *28*, 206–217.

Berkowitz, L., & LePage, A. Weapons as aggression-eliciting stimuli. *Journal of Personality and Social Psychology*, 1967, *7*, 202–207.

Doob, A. N., & Gross, A. E. Status of frustrator as an inhibitor of horn-honking responses. *Journal of Social Psychology*, 1968, *76*, 213–218.

Ellis, D. P., Weinir, P., & Miller, L. Does the trigger pull the finger? An experimental test of weapons as aggression eliciting stimuli. *Sociometry*, 1971, *34*, 453–465.

Milgram, S. Some conditions of obedience and disobedience to authority. *Human Relations*, 1965, *18*, 57–76.

Parry, M. *Aggression on the road.* London: Tavistock, 1968.

Webb, E. J., Campbell, D. T., Schwartz, R. D., & Sechrest, L. *Unobtrusive measures: Nonreactive research in the social sciences.* Chicago: Rand McNally, 1966.

Zimbardo, P. G. The human choice: Individuation, reason, and order versus deindividuation, impulse and chaos. In W. J. Arnold & D. Levine (eds.). *Nebraska Symposium on Motivation* (Vol. 17). Lincoln: University of Nebraska Press, 1969.

VICTIM REACTIONS IN AGGRESSIVE EROTIC FILMS AS A FACTOR IN VIOLENCE AGAINST WOMEN

EDWARD DONNERSTEIN AND LEONARD BERKOWITZ

One of the most popular theories of pornography has been the catharsis model, which describes pornography as merely a device that allows men to safely get rid of impulses to such antisocial behavior as rape and aggression against women. The most often cited proof of that theory is the "Danish experiment," in which it was found that with the liberalization of pornography laws and the increased availability of pornographic materials, there was a marked decrease in the number of sex offenses. However, it should be noted that rape was not one of the sex offenses that decreased in Denmark following the liberalization of pornography laws, while voyeurism, which did decrease, was one of the sex offenses that were decriminalized in Denmark in the interim between the liberalization of pornography and the study of its effect.

The alternative to the catharsis model of pornography is the modeling theory, in which the assumption is that men who view pornography containing aggression toward women are more likely to model this aggression in antisocial acts toward women. In a study in which Ayala Pines was involved, 200 street prostitutes were interviewed in depth about incidents of sexual abuse in their background. In that study, the modeling theory provided a far better explanation of the experiences reported by the women than did the catharsis model. Many of the prostitutes, when describing juvenile sexual exploitation in their childhood or violent rape on the street, reported frequent references to pornography by their rapists and molesters, such as "I know you love it, all of you c—s love it, I know. I saw it in the movies."

Donnerstein and Berkowitz are among the leading researchers investigating the effects of pornography and, as you will see, their findings support the unsolicited information obtained from the street prostitutes.

There has been increased concern in recent years about rape and other forms of aggression against women. Although many explanations have been offered for this apparent increase in violence against women, a number of writers have indicated that the mass media, and especially pornography, are important contributors to these assaults. Others disagree. The Presidential Commission on Obscenity and Pornography (1971) concluded that

Edward Donnerstein and Leonard Berkowitz, "Victim reactions in aggressive erotic films as a factor in violence against women," *Journal of Personality and Social Psychology*, 1981, 41:4, 710–24. Copyright © 1981 by the American Psychological Association. Reprinted by permission of the publisher and authors.

there was no direct relationship between exposure to pornography and subsequent sexual crimes. However, recent criticisms of the commission's findings have led several investigators to reexamine the issue. This later research has indicated that exposure to certain types of erotic materials can increase aggressive behavior.

By and large, these investigations have been aimed primarily at the question of whether sexual scenes can influence aggressive behavior generally. The more specific issue of the effect of these media portrayals on aggression against women in particular has only recently been studied. The experiments reported here are a continuation of these latter investigations within the framework of research on the stimulus qualities of the filmed event and the possible targets for aggression. We basically ask whether the behavioral characteristics of the people in the erotic film and the nature of the targets available for aggression afterward can affect the intensity of the aggression that is subsequently displayed.

One behavioral quality that could be important pertains to the amount of violence in the erotic scene. Several writers tell us that the incidence of aggressively toned pornography has increased in the last few years. Can it be that the addition of aggression heightens the chances that the erotic material will have an adverse impact on the viewers? Indeed, the violence in an aggressive erotic film could conceivably have a greater aggression-enhancing effect than the purely sexual nature of the film alone. According to Berkowitz's (1971, 1974) analysis of movie violence, the stimuli on the screen tend to elicit reactions that are semantically associated with them. Observed aggression should therefore evoke aggression-facilitating responses, whereas purely sexual stimuli should elicit primarily sexual reactions (although the general excitement that also accompanies the latter reactions might energize whatever aggressive responses the observers are set to perform in the given situation). This increased aggression produced by the violent content obviously should be greatest for those viewers who are angry at the moment; since they are disposed to attack someone, the aggression-associated movie stimuli could readily evoke aggressive reactions from them. Donnerstein (1980) obtained supporting evidence. Male subjects were angered or treated in a neutral manner by a male or female confederate and then were shown one of three films. Two of these movies were highly sexually arousing, but one of them also had explicit aggressive content whereas the other did not. The third film was neither sexually nor aggressively evocative. Donnerstein found that the men exposed to the aggressive erotic movie were subsequently more aggressive toward the confederate than were those who had seen the purely sexual film, and more so if they had been angered by the confederate beforehand.

A nearby person's stimulus characteristics can also determine the extent to which aggression is directed against this individual. Berkowitz's research indicates that people with certain stimulus qualities tend to evoke the strongest aggression-facilitating reactions from those who are ready to be aggressive. What is most relevant to us here is the available target's association with the victim of the movie violence. Perhaps because this association connects the possible target with the

successful (or positively reinforced) aggression shown on the screen, a person bearing the same characteristics as the victim of the observed violence tends to receive stronger attacks than those who would be labeled differently. Another of Donnerstein's results can be interpreted in just this way. When his subjects had been angered by a man and then were given an opportunity to punish this male confederate, the aggressive erotic film did not lead to any more aggression than did the sexual movie. However, if the subjects were paired with a female confederate, the aggressive erotica led to substantially stronger attacks than did the purely sexual film; this happened, furthermore, even when the woman confederate had not provoked the subjects earlier. The female confederate's sex-linked connection with the victim of the witnessed violence could have strengthened her capacity to elicit aggressive responses from the men.

Yet another factor that might affect an audience's aggressive reactions pertains to the outcome of the observed sexual attack. Opponents of pornography have noted that women are typically portrayed in this material as enjoying the assault upon them. From the viewers' perspective, the woman victim's pleasure could mean that she heightens the aggressor's enjoyment even further. They might then come to think, at least for a short while, that their own sexual aggression also would be profitable, thus reducing their restraints. Malamuth and Check (in press) recently reported evidence consistent with our analysis. In their study, male subjects' self-reported likelihood of raping a woman was highly correlated with both (a) their belief that the women in the aggressive erotic material presented to them had enjoyed being attacked and (b) their notion that women generally derive pleasure from being raped. These views diminish the moral reprehensibility of any witnessed assaults on women and, more than this, suggest that the sexual attacks may have a highly desirable outcome—for the victim as well as for the aggressor. Men having such beliefs might therefore be more likely to attack a woman after they see a supposedly "pleasurable" rape. Furthermore, since there is a substantial aggressive component in the sexual assault, we suggest that the favorable outcome lowers the observers' restraints against aggression toward women, as well as against sexual behavior with them.

All this does not mean that the victim's suffering will necessarily be interpreted by the attacker as pleasant for the victim. Angry people want to inflict injury. Information that someone, and especially the person who had provoked them, has been hurt would be particularly rewarding for them. As a stimulus associated with reinforcements for aggression, this information could theoretically lead to heightened attacks by the provoked observers. Now suppose that the male viewers of aggressive erotica happen to be very angry with women as they watch the movie. Seeing the woman victim being hurt by the assault on her might be very stimulating for them; her "pain cues" could elicit stronger aggression-facilitating reactions within them, to the extent that they want to injure the women in their own lives.

EXPERIMENT 1

The present article reports two sets of experiments designed to investigate these and related notions. In the first experiment, male subjects were first angered by either a male or a female confederate and then shown one of four films. Three of the movies were highly erotic in nature but differed in their aggressive content. The first was a nonaggressive, erotic film. The other two erotic films had an aggressive component but differed in terms of the scene's outcome: One had a positive conclusion, whereas the other ended on a decidedly negative note. The fourth film was neutral with respect to both sex and aggression. Since any increase in aggression after the movies might be due to the physiological arousal engendered by the observed scene, all of the erotic films were chosen on the basis of the basically equal level of arousal they produced. Finally, immediately after the men saw their respective movies, each of them had an opportunity to punish the confederate in a socially sanctioned manner.

We formulated several specific predictions. First, we expected the purely sexual erotic movie to lead to stronger attacks on the male than on the female confederate. On the basis of other studies, we assumed that the sexual arousal produced by the erotic film would intensify the aggressive reactions the angry men were disposed to make. However, we also thought the men would be somewhat reluctant to punish a woman severely even though she had provoked them earlier. Unless these restraints could be overcome—by conditions that lowered the men's inhibitions and/or strengthened the woman's capacity to evoke aggression-facilitating responses from them—the men should be more aggressive toward another male than toward a woman.

Second, we predicted that exposure to an ag-

gressive, erotic movie with a positive outcome (the woman victim apparently enjoying the assault) would lead to a relatively high level of aggression against the female target. This aggression should be higher than that displayed in the pure erotica condition or in the same movie condition having a male target for aggression. In this case, we reasoned that (a) the aggressive content of the sex film would evoke strong aggressive reactions from the angry viewers, (b) the positive outcome would lower their inhibitions against attacking women, and (c) the female target's sex-linked association with the victim of the assault on the screen would facilitate attacks on her.

Third, we also thought that the negative outcome of the aggressive erotic film (in which the woman victim was shown to be suffering) would also cause the confederate to be punished relatively strongly when this target was a female but perhaps not as strongly as in the positive-outcome condition. Here, too, the female confederate should draw stronger attacks than the male confederate in the same film condition. As we had suggested earlier, our reasoning was that the assaulted woman's suffering would serve as pain cues for these angry men and thus stimulate fairly strong aggressive reactions within them. However, some restraints against aggression should also be present in the viewers, since the witnessed attack was not portrayed as "worthwhile" or "justified." As a result, the aggressive responses evoked by both the aggressive content and the depicted suffering should be somewhat inhibited. And finally, the female confederate's connection with the movie victim should lead to stronger punishment of her than of the male confederate.

METHOD

Subjects

The subjects were 80 male undergraduates enrolled in a course in introductory psychology. Subjects participated to receive extra credit toward their final grade in the course.

Apparatus and Selection of Films

Four films were prepared for the present study. All were five minutes in length and were in black and white. The neutral film was of a talk show interview and contained no aggressive or erotic content. The purely erotic movie depicted a young couple engaged in various stages of sexual intercourse. It did not contain any aggressive content. The final two films were of an aggressive, erotic nature. Both were the same except for the introductory narrative and the final 30 seconds. Each film depicted a young woman who comes to study with two men. Both men have been drinking, and when she sits between them she is shoved around and also forced to drink. She is then tied up, stripped, slapped, and sexually attacked. In the *positive-outcome aggressive erotic* movie the ending shows the woman smiling and in no way "resisting" the two men. The introduction to the film also told the subjects that by film's end, the woman becomes a willing participant in the sexual activity. In the *negative-outcome aggressive erotic* film the woman's actions in the last 30 seconds of the scene indicate that she is suffering. The introduction to this version of the film reports that she finds the experience humiliating and disgusting. Pretesting indicated that the woman in the latter film was seen as suffering more and as having enjoyed her experience less than the woman in the positive-ending movie.

Design and Procedure

The basic design was a 2 × 4 factorial, with sex of target (male, female) and films (neutral, erotic, positive aggressive, negative aggressive) treated as factors. Four undergraduate males were randomly assigned to the role of experimenter and confederate, and two females also served as confederates.

On arriving for the experiment, the subject was met by an experimental confederate (male or female) posing as another subject. The experimenter then arrived and conducted the confederate and subject into the first experimental room.

Prerecorded taped instructions to the subject explained that the experiment was concerned with the effects of stress on learning and physiological responses. The subject and the confederate were informed that the experiment involved both receiving and delivering mild electric shocks to the fingertips. The two people were told that they could refuse to participate and still receive full experimental credit. After this, an informed-consent form was provided, which the subject and confederate were to read and sign, thus acknowledging their agreement to participate in an experiment involving electric shock. The form also indicated that full information on the nature and purpose of the study would be given at the conclusion of the session. All subjects then completed a medical-health

survey questionnaire to confirm that they were physically able to take part in the study and that they were under no medication that could influence blood pressure readings.

The taped instructions were then turned on again and described the remainder of the procedure more fully. In these instructions the subjects were told that each of them would be asked to perform a task under a stressful situation. Besides being interested in their performance on the task, the experimenter was depicted as interested in their physiological responses to the task and the experimental situation. Consequently, readings of blood pressure would be taken from each subject at various specified times during the experiment.

At this point, the experimenter selected one subject (always the confederate) to come into a second room, ostensibly to begin studying for his or her task. After waiting about 1 minute, the experimenter returned to the subject and conducted him to a second room. The subject was informed that his task was to assist the experimenter in administering the learning test that "the other subject" (the confederate) was studying. Subjects were told that the experimenter needed to remain free to measure physiological reactions during the entire experiment.

It was explained to the subject that while the confederate studied, the subject would perform his task. But first, a base-level measure of blood pressure would be needed for both people. The experimenter then attached the arm cuff of the sphygmomanometer to the subject, returned to the adjoining room, and recorded the blood-pressure reading (BP1 or base level).

Anger Manipulation. After the first blood-pressure measure was taken, the experimenter returned to the subject's room and presented the next segment of prerecorded instructions. The subjects were told that their task involved writing a short essay on the issue of the legalization of marijuana. The subjects were instructed to state their opinion on this issue and to write a short essay (approximately five minutes) supporting their stand. Stress was induced by telling the men that their essay would be evaluated by their partner in the other room by the use of electric shock and a short written evaluation. Following a procedure used in previous studies, it was noted that the shock evaluation could range from no shocks for a good rating to ten shocks for a very poor rating. The experimenter then left the room for five minutes while the subjects wrote their essays.

After this time had elapsed, the experimenter

reentered the room and said that he would now give the essay to the other person (the confederate) for evaluation. Upon returning to the subject (and while the confederate supposedly was "reading" the essay), the experimenter attached two electrodes to the fingers of the subject in preparation for the evaluation. The experimenter then left, ostensibly to collect the partner's written evaluation of the subject's essay, and then returned to the subject's room. He then contacted the confederate by intercom and instructed him or her to deliver the shock "evaluation." All subjects received nine shocks of mild intensity, each five seconds in duration. Following the shock evaluation, the subject was presented with the written evaluation of his task performance. This consisted of ratings on four 5-point rating scales and showed that the subject's partner had a poor opinion of his essay. A second measure of the subject's blood pressure was then recorded (BP2).

When this was completed, the experimenter removed the electrodes and told the subjects that their partner (the confederate) would soon perform his or her task. It was explained that the subject would help in the administration of that task, but because enough time had not elapsed for the confederate to finish studying, there would be a few minutes' delay in beginning the new phase of the experiment.

Film Conditions. At this point the rationale for the different film conditions was introduced. A subject assigned to the *neutral* movie condition was informed that while the "learner" was studying, the experimenter was interested in having the subject view a movie which he (the experimenter) was hoping to use in future research. Since it was not part of the initial experiment, the experimenter asked whether the subject would be willing to view the film, rate it on a number of dimensions, and have his blood pressure taken immediately following the film.

For the purely *erotic* and *aggressive erotic* film conditions, in addition to being given the above rationale, the subject was informed that the movie to be shown was highly erotic and depicted a scene of explicit sexual behavior. It was made clear that the subject was free to choose not to see the film and that credit for participation in the experiment would not in any way be affected by his decision. If he chose to continue and view the film (all subjects did), he was given an appropriate informed-consent form to read and sign.

All the men complied with the experimenter's request and subsequently saw the film while the experimenter returned to the control room. Upon completion of the movie (five minutes later), the subject's blood pressure was taken (BP3) and he then completed a short questionnaire regarding the film content. The subject was then informed that he could now proceed with the "learning under stress" experiment.

Aggression Opportunity. For the second task of the experiment, the subject was asked to present a prepared list of nonsense syllables to the confederate, ostensibly freeing the experimenter to monitor the other person's task performance and physiological reactions. The subject was supplied with the correct answer for each trial of the task and was informed that if his partner responded correctly on a trial, he was to give his partner a number of points (between 1 and 8), with each point equal to 1 cent. At the completion of the task, the partner was to receive the amount of money he or she had earned for correct responses. If the partner was incorrect, however, the subject was to deliver some level of shock (again on a scale between 1 and 8). The subject was also told that he could administer any number of points or any level of shock he felt appropriate for any trial, since the particular number or level would have no effect on the partner's performance.

The task consisted of 24 trials, with the confederate making errors on 16 trials and correct responses on 8 trials. After the last trial, a final measure of blood pressure (BP4) was taken.

Questionnaire and Debriefing. Following the last blood-pressure measure, the subject completed a short questionnaire that asked him to rate, on a 5-point scale, how he felt his essay was evaluated, how angry/not angry he felt after the rating, and how good/bad he felt. After completion of the rating scales, the subject was completely debriefed on the nature of the experiment and any questions he had were answered. Those men exposed to the aggressive, erotic films were given an additional debriefing on the nature of the films. The subject was then thanked for his participation and dismissed.

Aggressive Behavior

For male targets there were no increases in aggression as a function of film exposure (see Figure 1). For those subjects paired with a female target, however, the movie condition did significantly affect the subsequent aggressive behavior. Whereas

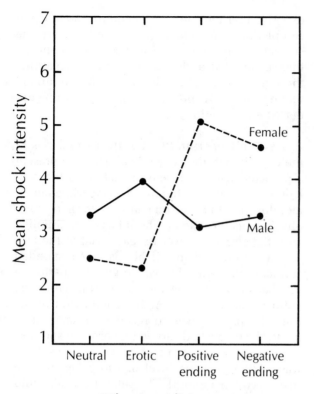

FIGURE 1. Mean shock intensity as a function of sex of target and film condition.

the purely erotic film did not heighten aggression, exposure to either aggressive, erotic film increased the level of aggression toward the female target significantly above that displayed by subjects viewing the neutral film or the purely erotic film. The positive and negative film versions did not differ from each other in their effects upon the subjects. This level of aggression toward the females in the two aggressive, erotic conditions was significantly higher than all other male target conditions, except for the men in the purely erotic film condition. . . .

DISCUSSION

Our first prediction was that aggression would be increased against a male, but not a female, target after exposure to the erotic film. However, although somewhat more aggression was directed against a male than a female in the erotic film group, the movie conditions did not differ reliably in the level of aggression against the male target, although the results were in the predicted direction.

The effects of exposure to the purely erotic film

on aggression toward females essentially replicates other studies using similar stimuli. These results tend to suggest, once again, that unless aggressive restraints are reduced and/or the stimulus value of the target is enhanced, exposure to highly arousing but nonaggressive erotica will not significantly increase violence toward women relative to men.

Our second prediction was that exposure to the positive-outcome aggressive, erotic film would heighten the angry viewers' attacks on a female target. Not only were there heightened attacks, but the level of aggression was greater than that received by male targets in the same condition. This latter difference points to the importance of the female target's association with the victim in the aggressive movie. Our final prediction was that the negative-outcome aggressive erotic film would also increase aggression against a female by angered male subjects, presumably because the filmed victim's suffering stimulated the angry observers. The results were highly supportive of our prediction.

The results of the present study once again suggest that aggressive erotica can increase aggression against women under certain conditions. Although the filmed assault did not seem to produce substantial differences in aggression, perhaps the intensified attacks occurred for different reasons in the two aggressive, erotic movies. As we conjectured earlier, in addition to the aggressive stimulation produced by the aggressive content, the positive ending might have lowered the men's inhibitions against attacking an available target. In a sense, the movie suggested that aggression can be justified.

On the other hand, the subjects exposed to the negative-outcome aggressive, erotic film could have been stimulated to intensified aggression by the sight of the victim's suffering. Since they were angry at the time and thus predisposed to hurt someone, the pain cues from the victim were associated with this predisposition and thus might have evoked a heightened aggressive inclination in them.

EXPERIMENT 2

The second experiment was designed to test this last-mentioned possibility. All the subjects in the initial study were angered by the available target, and this anger arousal presumably converted the movie victim's suffering into an aggression-eliciting cue for them. If our reasoning is correct, nonangry viewers should not be stimulated to increased attacks on a female target on seeing the film victim's pain and distress. We tested this expectation in the second investigation by promoting the belief in half the male subjects that their female partner had deliberately insulted them, whereas the remaining participants were treated in a neutral fashion by her so as not to promote anger. Thus, in keeping with our initial findings, we predicted that the negative-outcome aggressive erotic film would lead to increased aggression toward the female confederate when the men were angry with her but would have no such effect when the men had not been provoked. Indeed, other research suggests that the movie pain cues might actually produce a lowered level of overt aggression.

On the other hand, we made a second prediction that the positive-outcome aggressive, erotic movie would produce heightened attacks on the woman target (above that displayed in the neutral and purely erotic film groups), whether the subjects had been angered or not. In this case the film's aggressive content theoretically would stimulate intensified aggressive inclinations in both the angered and the nonangered men (although more strongly so in the former group), and the depicted positive outcome would lower their restraints against attacking the target.

METHOD

Subjects

The subjects were 80 male undergraduates enrolled in a course in introductory psychology. Subjects participated to receive extra credit toward their final grade in the course. None of the subjects had participated in Experiment 1.

Design and Procedure

The basic design was a 2 × 4 factorial, with anger (anger, no anger) and films (neutral, erotic, positive-outcome aggressive erotic, negative-outcome aggressive erotic) treated as factors. Two undergraduate males served as experimenters and four undergraduate females served as confederates so that the possible target was always a woman. All subjects were randomly assigned to conditions.

The experimental procedure was identical to that of Experiment 1 except for the inclusion of the nonangered condition. Subjects in the nonangered groups received one mild-intensity shock .5 second in duration, rather than the nine received by angered subjects. In addition, the writ-

ten evaluation judged the subject's essay positively on the four 5-point rating scales.

Aggressive Behavior

The interaction (presented in Figure 2) indicates that for the angered subjects both the positive and negative aggressive erotic films increased aggression above that displayed in the neutral and purely erotic film conditions. The reliable difference in provocation between the aggressive erotic subjects and the others confirms the results obtained when there was a female target in Experiment 1. Moreover, as we had expected, under nonangered conditions only the positive-outcome aggressive erotic film resulted in significantly higher aggression than that shown in the neutral and purely erotic movie groups. In sum, the viewers apparently had to be disposed to hurt someone before the movie victim's suffering could evoke heightened aggression from them.

From two weeks to four months after the subjects participated in the present study, they were again contacted in their introductory psychology classes

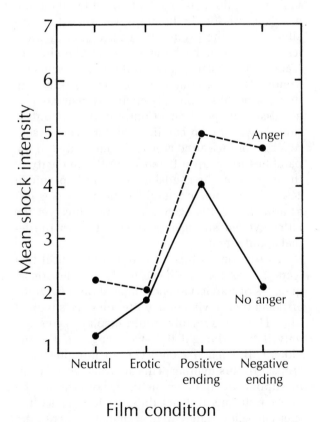

FIGURE 2. Mean shock intensity as a function of anger and film condition.

and asked to complete a questionnaire in order to determine what effects their participation in the study had on them. The questionnaire contained seven items from the Burt (1980) Rape Myth Acceptance and Acceptance of Interpersonal Violence scales. The return rate was 77 percent.

For each of the seven questions assessing subjects' attitudes toward rape and violence, a *t* test was conducted comparing the scores of the debriefed and control subjects (the latter were shown only the neutral film).

In all cases, the debriefed subjects indicated *less* acceptance of rape myths. For two questions there was no difference between the two groups, although the means were again in the less accepting direction for the debriefed subjects. All in all, then, the debriefing had evidently sensitized the subjects so that they were now less inclined to go along with the standard myths regarding rape and rape victims.

GENERAL DISCUSSION

The results of these two experiments have important theoretical as well as practical implications. For one thing, they can help us gain a greater understanding of the processes that cause scenes of violence in the mass media to heighten the audience's aggressive inclinations. Consider the possible role of the excitement engendered by movies. Some writers have suggested that film violence leads to increased aggression primarily because of a movie's exciting nature; the viewers' film-produced arousal supposedly energizes their existing aggressive dispositions. Contrary to this contention, however, the condition differences in self-reported or measured arousal in our study did not parallel the group differences in the intensity of the attacks on the available target. In Experiment 1, as an example, the purely erotic movie was just as arousing as the aggressive erotic films, yet the latter evoked stronger aggression toward the female confederate.

A variation on this "it is only the arousal that leads to aggression" theme holds that the consequences of movie violence depend on how viewers label their own feelings after they see a violent film. They presumably would display aggression only if they thought they were angry and if the violent film led the observers to interpret their arousal in this manner. This analysis received little support in our experiments. In both studies the film conditions did not differ in how angry the subjects believed they were even though there were group differences in attacks on the female target.

From some discussions of "misattribution" or "excitation transfer" effects, we might have expected a film-produced mislabeling of feelings in the provoked men shown the purely erotic movie. They could have attributed the arousal engendered by the film to their previous insult, so that they regarded themselves as highly angry and then behaved accordingly. But in actuality, this misattribution apparently did not occur. At any rate, there are no good indications that condition differences in overt aggression follow similar differences in reported anger.

All this is not to say, of course, that viewers' arousal level does not have any effect on the behavior they demonstrate after seeing a movie. Their general arousal probably interacts with the specific content of the film to influence their actions.

Yet another commonly held interpretation of movie violence emphasizes disinhibitory processes. According to this view, the filmed scene reduces observers' inhibitions against aggression so that they are more willing to attack an available target. In our estimation, the relatively high level of aggression exhibited by the subjects in the positive-outcome aggressive erotic condition in both experiments is probably due to this kind of disinhibition, as we suggested earlier. The indication that the woman had enjoyed being raped implied that the assault on her had been worthwhile from the attackers' perspective, and this implication could have given the observers the idea that their own aggression would also pay off.

However, while disinhibitory processes undoubtedly are important, they probably are not the only factors producing the media effects. In the realm of sexual behavior, Mann, Berkowitz, Sidman, Starr, and West (1974) demonstrated that married couples were more apt to make love after viewing erotic films than after seeing sexually neutral movies, apparently not because their restraints had been lowered but because they had been sexually stimulated. Berkowitz (1970) suggested that a conceptually analogous process occurs in the case of aggressive scenes. Just as sexual stimuli can evoke sexual reactions, the sight of aggression can elicit transient, aggression-facilitating responses. These responses are usually only fairly weak and short-lived, but at times they can be translated into open behavior.

Such an effect arose, we believe, in the subjects shown the aggressive erotic movies. The aggressive content in these films could have stimulated the viewers aggressively. Thus energized by their high level of arousal, these reactions could have led to heightened attacks on the female target.

Furthermore, as we discussed earlier, we also think that stimulus-response associations produced the greater level of aggression toward the female than the male target in Experiment 1. The woman confederate's sex-linked connection with the woman victim on the screen had apparently strengthened her aggressive cue value so that she drew stronger attacks from the angry men. Similarly, we also suggested that the woman victim's suffering in the negative-outcome movie stimulated the angry men to increased aggression because her pain was associated with prior reinforcements for aggression.

All in all, our findings point to the multiplicity of processes that can determine an audience's reactions to events in the mass media. Arousal level, lowered inhibitions, viewer's interpretations and understandings, and stimulus-response associations all play some part.

The findings reported here can also give us greater insight into the effects of pornography on people in an audience. Most obviously, they indicate that the addition of aggression to the sex in pornographic materials is probably more dangerous (in terms of possible aggressive consequences) than the display of pure erotica. As we noted earlier, this combination is appearing with increasing frequency in pornographic material, which could stimulate aggressively disposed men with weak inhibitions to assault available women.

Another important factor to consider is the reaction of the woman in the sexual scene to the attack on her. A common theme in pornography is that women enjoy being victimized. Both studies suggest that women depicted as enjoying assaults on them can serve to justify aggression and reduce general inhibitions against aggression.

Victim reactions in our study also tended to elicit responses other than overt displays of aggression. In both studies subjects exposed to the positive-outcome aggressive erotic film found the film less aggressive and the victim more responsible for her plight than those subjects who were exposed to the negative version. The finding regarding perceived aggression in the film seems to support the results obtained by researchers who have found that exposure to sexual violence reduces an audience's sensitivity to rape. The results for responsibility also have important implications. At least in the present study, a positive reaction on the part of the rape victim, independent of the events that occurred previously, seems to make the victim more responsible for her actions. This "shifting" of responsibility to the victim might be one factor that accounts for the increasingly callous attitudes toward rape and the self-reported willingness to commit rape observed in subjects who have been exposed to aggressive erotica. This shift in the focus of responsibility might also affect judicial decisions in rape cases. It would seem important, then, for future research to examine more closely the reasons and implications for this apparent change in attribution.

Another interesting aspect of the present research is the results obtained with the debriefing manipulation. Some critics have recently questioned the ethicality of research that exposes subjects to rape depictions. These concerns seem legitimate and were, in fact, the basis for the debriefing follow-up in Experiment 2. The results of this follow-up, however, strongly suggest that a proper debriefing can have quite beneficial effects. As we have seen, those subjects who viewed aggressive erotica and were debriefed revealed *less* acceptance of the standard rape myths.

REFERENCES

Berkowitz, L. The contagion of violence: An S-R mediational analysis of some effects of observed aggression. In W. J. Arnold & M. M. Page (eds.), *Nebraska Symposium on Motivation* (Vol. 18). Lincoln: University of Nebraska Press, 1970.

Berkowitz, L. Sex and violence: We can't have it both ways. *Psychology Today*, May 1971, pp. 14–23.

Berkowitz, L. Some determinants of impulsive aggression: The role of mediated associations with reinforcements for aggression. *Psychological Review*, 1974, *81*, 165–76.

Burt, M. R. Cultural myths and supports for rape. *Journal of Personality and Social Psychology*, 1980, *38*, 217–30.

Donnerstein, E. Aggressive erotica and violence against women. *Journal of Personality and Social Psychology*, 1980, *39*, 269–77.

Malamuth, N., & Check, J. Penile tumescence and perceptual responses to rape as a function of victim's perceived reactions. *Journal of Applied Social Psychology*, in press.

Mann, J., Berkowitz, L., Sidman, J., Starr, S., & West, S. Satiation of the transient stimulating effect of erotic films. *Journal of Personality and Social Psychology*, 1974, *30*, 729–35.

Presidential Commission on Obscenity and Pornography. *Report*. Washington, D.C.: U. S. Government Printing Office, 1971.

PROJECTS

Name _____

Date _____

6.1: AGGRESSION? SAYS WHO?

Psychologists have suggested a variety of definitions of aggression. For example: a response that delivers noxious stimuli to another organism; a response having for its goal the injury of a living organism; and behavior that results in personal injury and/or destruction of property (the injury may be psychological as well as physical). But the definitions do not always agree on what constitutes an aggressive behavior. The goal of this project is to stimulate you to examine your own definition of aggression more closely.

A. Listed below are a number of different actions that a person might engage in. Rate each act according to your opinion of its degree of aggressiveness. Circle the appropriate rating number.

Personal Ratings of Aggression

Action	Rating				
	Highly Aggressive				Not at All Aggressive
1. A baseball pitcher strikes a batter during a game.	5	4	3	2	1
2. A man slaps his wife during an argument.	5	4	3	2	1
3. A soldier shoots an enemy soldier during an attack in wartime.	5	4	3	2	1
4. A mother slaps a child who misbehaved.	5	4	3	2	1
5. A teacher disciplines a student who did not do his homework.	5	4	3	2	1
6. A woman kills her rapist.	5	4	3	2	1
7. A group of revolutionaries sets off a bomb at night in a bank as part of a political protest.	5	4	3	2	1
8. A disenchanted citizen decides not to vote.	5	4	3	2	1
9. Two young children fantasize about the horrible ways in which they will get back at their enemies.	5	4	3	2	1
10. A prison warden executes a convicted criminal.	5	4	3	2	1
11. During an argument a woman slaps her husband.	5	4	3	2	1
12. While watching a particularly bloody scene on television, a child bursts out laughing.	5	4	3	2	1
13. A person draws graffiti on the walls of a bathroom.	5	4	3	2	1
14. A person accidentally knocks a flowerpot off a ledge, which hits and injures a pedestrian.	5	4	3	2	1
15. Two people in a bar get upset and start yelling at each other.	5	4	3	2	1
16. Two policemen restrain and handcuff a demonstrator.	5	4	3	2	1

B. Ask another person to rate the same set of behaviors on the rating sheet on page 155. Try to select someone whose attitudes or political philosophy is different from your own. Compare your ratings with that person's and with the ratings of other people in your class.

C. Do your ratings of aggressiveness agree or disagree with the ratings of the person you selected to fill out the second rating sheet?

D. If there is disagreement, for what rated behaviors does it occur?

E. What is the reason for the disagreement? That is, how does your basic definition of aggression seem to differ from the other person's?

Name _____

Date _____

F. Rate the same actions according to each of the three definitions of aggression. Circle either "yes" or "no."

Rating Aggression by Definition

Action	Definition 1 "A response that delivers noxious stimuli to another organism"		Definition 2 "A response having for its goal the injury of a living organism"		Definition 3 "Behavior that results in personal injury and/or destruction of property; the injury may be psychological as well as physical"	
1. A baseball pitcher strikes a batter during a game.	yes	no	yes	no	yes	no
2. A man slaps his wife during an argument.	yes	no	yes	no	yes	no
3. A soldier shoots an enemy soldier during an attack in wartime.	yes	no	yes	no	yes	no
4. A mother slaps a child who misbehaved.	yes	no	yes	no	yes	no
5. A teacher disciplines a student who did not do his homework.	yes	no	yes	no	yes	no
6. A woman kills her rapist.	yes	no	yes	no	yes	no
7. A group of revolutionaries sets off a bomb at night in a bank as part of a political protest.	yes	no	yes	no	yes	no
8. A disenchanted citizen decides not to vote.	yes	no	yes	no	yes	no
9. Two young children fantasize about the horrible ways in which they will get back at their enemies.	yes	no	yes	no	yes	no
10. A prison warden executes a convicted criminal.	yes	no	yes	no	yes	no
11. During an argument, a woman slaps her husband.	yes	no	yes	no	yes	no
12. While watching a particularly bloody scene on television, a child bursts out laughing.	yes	no	yes	no	yes	no
13. A person draws graffiti on the walls of a bathroom.	yes	no	yes	no	yes	no
14. A person accidentally knocks a flowerpot off a ledge, which hits and injures a pedestrian.	yes	no	yes	no	yes	no
15. Two people in a bar get upset and start yelling at each other.	yes	no	yes	no	yes	no
16. Two policemen restrain and handcuff a demonstrator.	yes	no	yes	no	yes	no

Name _____

Date _____

6.2: A CASE OF VIOLENCE IN SEARCH OF A THEORY

THE LEEVILLE LYNCHING

This is the story of one of the twenty-one lynchings that occurred in 1930. The Southern Commission on the Study of Lynching (1931) investigated all twenty-one and the Leeville lynching is one of only eight in which the Southern Commission thought it fairly likely that the lynching victim had been actually guilty of the crime of which he was accused. The description that follows is based on an account by Cantril (1941).

One Saturday morning in the spring of 1930 a Negro laborer on a white man's farm near Leeville, Texas, dropped by the farmer's house to pick up the week's wages due him. The farmer's wife told him that her husband was away from the house and had not left the money. The Negro, feeling disgruntled, left the house but came back a short time later with a shotgun and demanded his money. The farmer's wife ordered him out of the house but he backed her into the bedroom and assaulted her sexually several times. Then he fled the house. The woman ran to a neighbor who phoned the sheriff. The Negro was soon captured; he confessed, agreed to plead guilty, and for safekeeping was taken to jail some miles from Leeville.

The above is the version that was commonly accepted by the white population of Leeville, but investigators listening to gossip heard other versions. Negroes in the area, for the most part, believed that the whole story was a frame-up to permit cheating the Negro laborer of his wages. Some of the white farmers said, in private, that they suspected the farmer's wife had invited the Negro to have intercourse with her and then had been frightened into a lie, possibly because her five-year-old child had interrupted the pair. A medical record showed only that intercourse had occurred; it was possible that the Negro was guilty of rape and possible that he was not. In others of the twenty-one lynchings of 1930 it was much less likely that the victim had been guilty.

In spite of the threatening mood of the Leeville community the judge insisted on holding the trial in that town, but he had four Texas Rangers detailed to preserve order. The Rangers brought the Negro into the courtroom early in the morning before any crowd had gathered. That day a large number of people came into Leeville from the farms outside of town. During the morning a crowd gathered in the courtyard and the crowd grew increasingly belligerent. At this critical juncture a rumor developed that the governor of the state had ordered the Rangers not to fire on the crowd in their efforts to protect the accused. The rumor was not true, but it was believed and it lifted the major restraint on the crowd.

About one o'clock the farmer's wife, the presumed rapist's victim, was brought from the hospital by ambulance to give testimony at the trial. When the presumably assaulted woman was carried in on a stretcher the crowd went wild. At first the Rangers kept them back with tear gas and the Negro was taken from the courtroom to a fireproof vault room. Later in the afternoon the mob burned down the court-house and that night they used an acetylene torch to make a hole in the vault. They inserted dynamite and blew a large enough hole to permit one man to crawl into the vault. A few minutes after disappearing he tossed out the dead body of the Negro.

The corpse was raised with a rope to an elm tree in the courthouse yard so that every one might see it. Then it was tied to a Ford car and dragged through the town; five thousand howling people paraded behind. Finally the body was chained to a tree in the Negro section of Leeville and burned. The Leeville lynching turned into prolonged terrorization of the Negro population and it took several hundred members of the National Guard to restore order. [From Roger Brown, Social Psychology (New York: Free Press), 1965. Copyright © 1965 by The Free Press. Reprinted by permission.]

After reading the preceding description of the Leeville lynching, answer the following questions, which relate various theories of aggression to the incidents that took place in Leeville.

1. How would a Freudian theory of aggression explain this case?

2. How would frustration–aggression theory explain the Leeville lynching?

3. How would social learning theory explain it?

4. What aspects of the Leeville case (if any) cannot be adequately explained by these three theories?

Name _____

Date _____

6.3: TV VIOLENCE A.M./P.M.

"The magnitude of television's involvement in our daily lives is rather impressive," noted John P. Murray of the National Institute of Mental Health when discussing the implications of the Surgeon General's Research Program investigating television and violence. Recent census figures estimate that 96 percent of the households in the U. S. contain a television set. The percentage is even higher for families with young children—99 percent. Data also indicate that these sets are turned on for an average of six hours a day, and that young children are among the heaviest watchers. What are children's programs like? That is the question we would like to propose for this project. Is it true, as some scholars claim, that they are among the most violent programs on television?

In order to find the answer to this question, we would like you to sample an hour of prime time programming for adults and a comparable hour of prime time programming for children. The former can be around 8:00 to 9:00 P.M., while the latter is around 8:00 to 9:00 A.M. While watching, note the number and nature of the aggressive acts portrayed.

		A.M.	P.M.
1.	Number of violent acts in which victims indicate pain		
2.	Number of violent acts in which there is a negative outcome		
3.	Number of violent acts in which violence has no consequences		
4.	Number of violent acts in which there is a positive outcome or happy ending		
5.	Violent acts made by the "good guy"		
6.	Total number of violent acts		

General comments and observations

ALTRUISM AND PROSOCIAL BEHAVIOR

7

The rates of crime and violence are rising in American society, and there is increased concern for personal safety and protection. One answer to this intensifying problem is greater individual and community involvement through helping people who are in danger. Surely you would want someone to help you if you were in need. Why not extend help to others? The solution seems clear-cut.

But in recent years, people have shown considerable reluctance to become involved and to help others. This has stimulated many expressions of shock and concern in the media and from ordinary citizens. The most celebrated case of bystander apathy was the murder of Kitty Genovese, who was stalked and killed by her assailant near an apartment building where over thirty-eight residents heard her cries but did nothing to help. In the aftermath of the Genovese incident, social psychologists conducted a series of experiments on helping behavior in an effort to determine the circumstances under which someone will assume the role of the Good Samaritan and come to the aid of a fellow human being in distress.

"FROM JERUSALEM TO JERICHO": A STUDY OF SITUATIONAL AND DISPOSITIONAL VARIABLES IN HELPING BEHAVIOR

JOHN M. DARLEY AND C. DANIEL BATSON

In the parable of the Good Samaritan, a priest and a Levite fail to help a robbery victim. In contrast, the Samaritan stops to take care of the injured man. What is responsible for this difference in behavior? Was the Samaritan an inherently more moral and responsible individual? Or was there some situational constraint that might explain the lack of altruism displayed by the men of religion?

In "From Jerusalem to Jericho," Darley and Batson recount an experiment designed to analyze the parable. They conclude that helping behavior may be affected by time—more precisely, by too little of it. Their study suggests that the pressures of daily life that are so important to each of us may prevent us from paying attention to the needs of others. The person who asks for help is perceived as an obstacle in our path, hindering the successful completion of our tasks.

Helping other people in distress is, among other things, an ethical act. That is, it is an act governed by ethical norms and precepts taught to children at home, in school, and in church. From Freudian and other personality theories, one would expect individual differences in internalization of these standards that would lead to differences between individuals in the likelihood with which they would help others. But recent research on bystander intervention in emergency situations has had bad luck in finding personality determinants of helping behavior. Although personality variables that one might expect to correlate with helping behavior have been measured (Machiavellianism, authoritarianism, social desirability, alienation, and social responsibility), these were not predictive of helping. Nor was this due to a generalized lack of predictability in the helping situation examined, since variations in the experimental situation, such as the availability of other people who might also help, produced marked changes in rates of helping behavior. These findings are reminiscent of Hartshorne and May's (1928) discovery that resistance to temptation, another ethically relevant act, did not seem to be a fixed characteristic of an individual. That is, a person who was likely to be honest in one situation was not particularly likely to be honest in the next (see also Burton, 1963).

The rather disappointing correlation between the social psychologist's traditional set of personality variables and helping behavior in emergency situations suggests the need for a fresh perspective on possible predictors of helping and possible situations in which to test them. Therefore, for inspiration we turned to the Bible, to what is perhaps the classical helping story in the Judeo-Christian tradition, the parable of the Good Samaritan. The parable proved of value in suggesting both personality and situational variables relevant to helping.

"And who is my neighbor?" Jesus replied. "A man was going down from Jerusalem to Jericho, and he fell among robbers, who stripped him and beat him, and departed, leaving him half dead. Now by chance a priest was going down the road; and when he saw him he passed by on the other side. So likewise a Levite, when he came to the place and saw him,

---

From *Journal of Personality and Social Psychology*, 1973, 27, 100–8. Copyright © 1973 by The American Psychological Association. Reprinted by permission of the authors and The American Psychological Association.

passed by on the other side. But a Samaritan, as he journeyed, came to where he was; and when he saw him, he had compassion, and went to him and bound his wounds, pouring on oil and wine; then he set him on his own beast and brought him to an inn, and took care of him. And the next day he took out two dennarii and gave them to the innkeeper, saying, "Take care of him; and whatever more you spend, I will repay you when I come back." Which of these three, do you think, proved neighbor to him who fell among the robbers? He said, "The one who showed mercy on him." And Jesus said to him, "Go and do likewise." [Luke 10:29–37 RSV]

To psychologists who reflect on the parable, it seems to suggest situational and personality differences between the nonhelpful priest and Levite and the helpful Samaritan. What might each have been thinking and doing when he came upon the robbery victim on that desolate road? What sort of persons were they?

One can speculate on differences in thought. Both the priest and the Levite were religious functionaries who could be expected to have their minds occupied with religious matters. The priest's role in religious activities is obvious. The Levite's role, although less obvious, is equally important: The Levites were necessary participants in temple ceremonies. Much less can be said with any confidence about what the Samaritan might have been thinking, but, in contrast to the others, it was most likely not of a religious nature, for Samaritans were religious outcasts.

Not only was the Samaritan most likely thinking about more mundane matters than the priest and Levite, but, because he was socially less important, it seems likely that he was operating on a quite different time schedule. One can imagine the priest and Levite, prominent public figures, hurrying along with little black books full of meetings and appointments, glancing furtively at their sundials. In contrast, the Samaritan would likely have far fewer and less important people counting on him to be at a particular place at a particular time, and therefore might be expected to be in less of a hurry than the prominent priest or Levite.

In addition to these situational variables, one finds personality factors suggested as well. Central among these, and apparently basic to the point that Jesus was trying to make, is a distinction between types of religiosity. Both the priest and Levite are extremely "religious." But it seems to be precisely their type of religiosity that the parable challenges. At issue is the motivation for one's religion and ethical behavior. Jesus seems to feel that the religious leaders of his time, though certainly respected and upstanding citizens, may be "virtuous" for what it will get them, both in terms of the admiration of their fellowmen and in the eyes of God. New Testament scholar R. W. Funk (1966) noted that the Samaritan is at the other end of the spectrum:

The Samaritan does not love with side glances at God. The need of neighbor alone is made self-evident, and the Samaritan responds without other motivation [pp. 218–219].

That is, the Samaritan is interpreted as responding spontaneously to the situation, not as being preoccupied with the abstract ethical or organizational do's and don'ts of religion as the priest and Levite would seem to be. This is not to say that the Samaritan is portrayed as irreligious. A major intent of the parable would seem to be to present the Samaritan as a religious and ethical example, but at the same time to contrast his type of religiosity with the more common conception of religiosity that the priest and Levite represent.

To summarize the variables suggested as affecting helping behavior by the parable, the situational variables include the content of one's thinking and the amount of hurry in one's journey. The major dispositional variable seems to be differing types of religiosity. Certainly these variables do not exhaust the list that could be elicited from the parable, but they do suggest several research hypotheses.

Hypothesis 1. The parable implies that people who encounter a situation possibly calling for a helping response while thinking religious and ethical thoughts will be no more likely to offer aid than persons thinking about something else. Such a hypothesis seems to run counter to a theory that focuses on norms as determining helping behavior because a normative account would predict that the increased salience of helping norms produced by thinking about religious and ethical examples would increase helping behavior.

Hypothesis 2. Persons encountering a possible helping situation when they are in a hurry will be less likely to offer aid than persons not in a hurry.

Hypothesis 3. Concerning types of religiosity, persons who are religious in a Samaritanlike fashion will help more frequently than those religious in a priest or Levite fashion.

Obviously, this last hypothesis is hardly operationalized as stated. Prior research by one of the investigators on types of religiosity, however, led us to differentiate three distinct ways of being religious: (a) for what it will gain one, (b) for its own intrinsic value, and (c) as a response to and quest for meaning in one's everyday life. Both of the latter conceptions would be proposed by their exponents as related to the more Samaritanlike "true" religiosity. Therefore, depending on the theorist one follows, the third hypothesis may be stated like this: People (a) who are religious for intrinsic reasons or (b) whose religion emerges out of questioning the meaning of their everyday lives will be more likely to stop to offer help to the victim.

The parable of the Good Samaritan also suggested how we would measure people's helping behavior—their response to a stranger slumped by the side of one's path. The victim should appear somewhat ambiguous—ill-dressed, possibly in need of help, but also possibly drunk or even potentially dangerous.

Further, the parable suggests a means by which the incident could be perceived as a real one rather than part of a psychological experiment in which one's behavior was under surveillance and might be shaped by demand characteristics, evaluation apprehension, or other potentially artifactual determinants of helping behavior. The victim should be encountered not in the experimental context but on the road between various tasks.

METHOD

In order to examine the influence of these variables on helping behavior, seminary students were asked to participate in a study on religious education and vocations. In the first testing session, personality questionnaires concerning types of religiosity were administered. In a second individual session, the subject began experimental procedures in one building and was asked to report to another building for later procedures. While in transit, the subject passed a slumped "victim" planted in an alleyway. The dependent variable was whether and how the subject helped the victim. The independent variables were the degree to which the subject was told to hurry in reaching the other building and the talk he was to give when he arrived there. Some subjects were to give a talk on the jobs in which seminary students would be most effective, others, on the parable of the Good Samaritan.

Subjects

The subjects for the questionnaire administration were 67 students at Princeton Theological Seminary. Forty-seven of them, those who could be reached by telephone, were scheduled for the experiment. Of the 47, 7 subjects' data were not included in the analyses—3 because of contamination of the experimental procedures during their testing and 4 due to suspicion of the experimental situation. Each subject was paid $1 for the questionnaire session and $1.50 for the experimental session.

Personality Measures

Detailed discussion of the personality scales used may be found elsewhere (Batson, 1971), so the present discussion will be brief. The general personality construct under examination was religiosity. Various conceptions of religiosity have been offered in recent years based on different psychometric scales. The conception seeming to generate the most interest is the Allport and Ross (1967) distinction between "intrinsic" versus "extrinsic" religiosity. . . . This bipolar conception of religiosity has been questioned by Brown (1964) and Batson (1971), who suggested three-dimensional analyses instead. Therefore, in the present research, types of religiosity were measured with three instruments which together provided six separate scales: (a) a doctrinal orthodoxy (D-O) scale patterned after that used by Glock and Stark (1966), scaling agreement with classic doctrines of Protestant theology; (b) the Allport-Ross extrinsic (AR-E) scale, measuring the use of religion as a means to an end rather than as an end in itself; (c) the Allport-Ross intrinsic (AR-I) scale, measuring the use of religion as an end in itself; (d) the extrinsic external scale of Batson's Religious Life Inventory (RELI-EE), designed to measure the influence of significant others and situations in generating one's religiosity; (e) the extrinsic internal scale of the Religious Life Inventory (RELI-EI), designed to measure the degree of "driveness" in one's religiosity; and (f) the intrinsic scale of the Religious Life Inventory (RELI-I), designed to measure the degree to which one's religiosity involves a questioning of the meaning of life arising out of one's interactions with his social environment. The order of presentation of the scales in the questionnaire was RELI, AR, D-O.

Scheduling of Experimental Study

Since the incident requiring a helping response was staged outdoors, the entire experimental study was run in 3 days, December 14–16, 1970, between 10 A.M. and 4 P.M. A tight schedule was used in an attempt to maintain reasonably consistent weather and light conditions. Temperature fluctuation according to the New York Times for the 3 days during these hours was not more than 5 degrees Fahrenheit. No rain or snow fell, although the third day was cloudy, whereas the first two were sunny. Within days the subjects were randomly assigned to experimental conditions.

Procedure

When a subject appeared for the experiment, an assistant (who was blind with respect to the personality scores) asked him to read a brief statement which explained that he was participating in a study of the vocational careers of seminary students. After developing the rationale for the study, the statement read:

What we have called you in for today is to provide us with some additional material which will give us a clearer picture of how you think than does the questionnaire material we have gathered thus far. Questionnaires are helpful, but tend to be somewhat oversimplified. Therefore, we would like to record a 3–5 minute talk you give based on the following passage. . . .

Variable 1: Message. In the task-relevant condition the passage read,

With increasing frequency the question is being asked: What jobs or professions do seminary students subsequently enjoy most, and in what jobs are they most effective? The answer to this question used to be so obvious that the question was not even asked. Seminary students were being trained for the ministry, and since both society at large and the seminary student himself had a relatively clear understanding of what made a "good" minister, there was no need even to raise the question of for what other jobs seminary experience seems to be an asset. Today, however, neither society nor many seminaries have a very clearly defined conception of what a "good" minister is or of what sorts of jobs and professions are the best context in which to minister. Many seminary students, apparently genuinely concerned with "ministering," seem to feel that it is impossible to minister in the professional clergy. Other students, no less concerned, find the clergy the most viable profession for ministry. But are there other jobs and/or professions for which seminary experience is an asset? And, indeed, how much of an asset is it for the professional ministry? Or, even more broadly, can one minister through an "establishment" job at all?

In the helping-relevant condition, the subject was given the parable of the Good Samaritan exactly as printed earlier in this article. Next, regardless of condition, all subjects were told.

You can say whatever you wish based on the passage. Because we are interested in how you think on your feet, you will not be allowed to use notes in giving the talk. Do you understand what you are to do? If not, the assistant will be glad to answer questions.

After a few minutes the assistant returned, asked if there were any questions, and then said:

Since they're rather tight on space in this building, we're using a free office in the building next door for recording the talks. Let me show you how to get there [draws and explains map on 3 × 5 card]. This is where Professor Steiner's laboratory is. If you go in this door [points at map], there's a secretary right here, and she'll direct you to the office we're using for recording. Another of Professor Steiner's assistants will set you up for recording your talk. Is the map clear?

Variable 2: Hurry. In the high-hurry condition the assistant then looked at his watch and said, "Oh, you're late. They were expecting you a few minutes ago. We'd better get moving. The assistant should be waiting for you so you'd better hurry. It shouldn't take but just a minute." In the intermediate-hurry condition he said, "The assistant is ready for you, so please go right over." In the low-hurry condition he said, "It'll be a few minutes before they're ready for you, but you might as well head on over. If you have to wait over there, it shouldn't be long."

The Incident. When the subject passed through the alley, the victim was sitting slumped in a doorway, head down, eyes closed, not moving. As the subject went by, the victim coughed twice and groaned, keeping his head down. If the subject

stopped and asked if something was wrong or offered to help, the victim, startled and somewhat groggy, said, "Oh, thank you [cough]. . . . No, it's all right. [Pause] I've got this respiratory condition [cough]. . . . The doctor's given me these pills to take, and I just took one. . . . If I just sit and rest for a few minutes I'll be O.K. . . . Thanks very much for stopping though [smiles weakly]." If the subject persisted, insisting on taking the victim inside the building, the victim allowed him to do so and thanked him.

Helping Ratings. The victim rated each subject on a scale of helping behavior as follows:

0 = failed to notice the victim as possibly in need at all; 1 = perceived the victim as possibly in need but did not offer aid; 2 = did not stop but helped indirectly (e.g., by telling Steiner's assistant about the victim); 3 = stopped and asked if victim needed help; 4 = after stopping, insisted on taking the victim inside and then left him.

The victim was blind to the personality scale scores and experimental conditions of all subjects. At the suggestion of the victim, another category was added to the rating scales, based on his observations of pilot subjects' behavior.

5 = after stopping, refused to leave the victim (after 3–5 minutes) and/or insisted on taking him somewhere outside experimental context (e.g., for coffee or to the infirmary).

(In some cases it was necessary to distinguish Category 0 from Category 1 by the postexperimental questionnaire and Category 2 from Category 1 on the report of the experimental assistant.)

This 6-point scale of helping behavior and a description of the victim were given to a panel of 10 judges (unacquainted with the research) who were asked to rank order the (unnumbered) categories in terms of "the amount of helping behavior displayed toward the person in the doorway." Of the 10, 1 judge reversed the order of Categories 0 and 1. Otherwise there was complete agreement with the ranking implied in the presentation of the scale above.

The Speech. After passing through the alley and entering the door marked on the map, the subject entered a secretary's office. She introduced him to the assistant who gave the subject time to prepare and privately record his talk.

Helping Behavior Questionnaire. After recording the talk, the subject was sent to another experimenter, who administered "an exploratory questionnaire on personal and social ethics." The questionnaire contained several initial questions about the interrelationship between social and personal ethics, and then asked three key questions: (a) "When was the last time you saw a person who seemed to be in need of help?" (b) "When was the last time you stopped to help someone in need?" (c) "Have you had experience helping persons in need? If so, outline briefly." These data were collected as a check on the victim's ratings of whether subjects who did not stop perceived the situation in the alley as one possibly involving need or not.

When he returned, the experimenter reviewed the subject's questionnaire, and, if no mention was made of the situation in the alley, probed for reactions to it and then phased into an elaborate debriefing and discussion session.

Debriefing

In the debriefing, the subject was told the exact nature of the study, including the deception involved, and the reasons for the deception were explained. The subject's reactions to the victim and to the study in general were discussed. The role of situational determinants of helping behavior was explained in relation to this particular incident and to other experiences of the subject. All subjects seemed readily to understand the necessity for the deception, and none indicated any resentment of it. After debriefing, the subject was thanked for his time and paid, then he left.

RESULTS AND DISCUSSION

Overall Helping Behavior

The average amount of help that a subject offered the victim, by condition, is shown in Table 1. Subjects in a hurry were likely to offer less help than were subjects not in a hurry. Whether the subject was going to give a speech on the parable of the

TABLE 1. MEANS OF GRADED HELPING RESPONSES

	M			
	HURRY			
MESSAGE	LOW	MEDIUM	HIGH	SUMMARY
Helping relevant	3.800	2.000	1.000	2.263
Task relevant	1.667	1.667	.500	1.333
Summary	3.000	1.818	.700	

Good Samaritan or not did not significantly affect his helping behavior on this analysis.

Other studies have focused on the question of whether a person initiates helping action or not, rather than on scaled kinds of helping. The data from the present study can also be analyzed on the following terms: Of the 40 subjects, 16 (40%) offered some form of direct or indirect aid to the victim (Coding Categories 2–5), 24 (60%) did not (Coding Categories 0 and 1). The percentages of subjects who offered aid by situational variable were, for low hurry, 63% offered help, intermediate hurry 45%, and high hurry 10%; for helping-relevant message 53%, task-relevant message 29%.

Reviewing the predictions in the light of these results, the second hypothesis, that the degree of hurry a person is in determines his helping behavior, was supported. The prediction involved in the first hypothesis concerning the message content was based on the parable. The parable itself seemed to suggest that thinking pious thoughts would not increase helping. Another and conflicting prediction might be produced by a norm salience theory. Thinking about the parable should make norms for helping salient and therefore produce more helping. The data, as hypothesized, are more congruent with the prediction drawn from the parable. A person going to speak on the parable of the Good Samaritan is not significantly more likely to stop to help a person by the side of the road than is a person going to talk about possible occupations for seminary graduates.

. . .

Notice also that neither form of the third hypothesis, that types of religiosity will predict helping, received support from these data. No correlation between the various measures of religiosity and any form of the dependent measure ever came near statistical significance.

CONCLUSION AND IMPLICATIONS

A person not in a hurry may stop and offer help to a person in distress. A person in a hurry is likely to keep going. Ironically, he is likely to keep going even if he is hurrying to speak on the parable of the Good Samaritan, thus inadvertently confirming the point of the parable. (Indeed, on several occasions, a seminary student going to give his talk on the parable of the Good Samaritan literally stepped over the victim as he hurried on his way!).

Although the degree to which a person was in a hurry had a clearly significant effect on his likelihood of offering the victim help, whether he was going to give a sermon on the parable or on possible vocational roles of ministers did not. This lack of effect of sermon topic raises certain difficulties for an explanation of helping behavior involving helping norms and their salience. It is hard to think of a context in which norms concerning helping those in distress are more salient than for a person thinking about the Good Samaritan, and yet it did not significantly increase helping behavior. The results were in the direction suggested by the norm salience hypothesis, but they were not significant. The most accurate conclusion seems to be that salience of helping norms is a less strong determinant of behavior in the present situation than many, including the present authors, would expect.

Thinking about the Good Samaritan did not increase helping behavior, but being in a hurry decreased it. It is difficult not to conclude from this that the frequently cited explanation that ethics becomes a luxury as the speed of our daily lives increases is at least an accurate description. The picture that this explanation conveys is of a person seeing another, consciously noting his distress, and consciously choosing to leave him in distress. But perhaps this is not entirely accurate, for, when a person is in a hurry, something seems to happen that is akin to Tolman's (1948) concept of the "narrowing of the cognitive map." Our seminarians in a hurry noticed the victim in that in the postexperiment interview almost all mentioned him as, on reflection, possibly in need of help. But it seems that they often had not worked this out when they were near the victim. Either the interpretation of the visual picture as a person in distress or the empathic reactions usually associated with that interpretation had been deferred because they were hurrying. According to the reflections of some of the subjects, it would be inaccurate to say that they realized the victim's possible distress, then chose to ignore it; instead, because of the time pressures, they did not perceive the scene in the alley as an occasion for an ethical decision.

For other subjects it seems more accurate to conclude that they decided not to stop. They appeared aroused and anxious after the encounter in the alley. For these subjects, what were the elements of the choice that they were making? Why were the seminarians hurrying? Because the experimenter, *whom the subject was helping,* was depending on him to get to a particular place quickly. In other words, he was in conflict between stopping to help the victim and continuing on his way to help the experimenter. And this is often true of people in a hurry; they hurry because somebody depends on their being somewhere. Conflict, rather than callousness, can explain their failure to stop.

. . .

REFERENCES

Allport, G. W., & Ross, J. M. Personal religious orientation and prejudice. *Journal of Personality and Social Psychology,* 1967, *5,* 432–43.

Batson, C. D. Creativity and religious development: Toward a structural–functional psychology of religion. Doctoral dissertation, Princeton Theological Seminary, 1971.

Brown, L. B. Classifications of religious orientation. *Journal for the Scientific Study of Religion,* 1964, *4,* 91–99.

Burton, R. V. The generality of honesty reconsidered. *Psychological Review,* 1963, *70,* 481–99.

Funk, R. W. *Language, hermeneutic, and word of God.* New York: Harper & Row, 1966.

Glock, C. Y., & Stark, R. *Christian beliefs and anti-Semitism.* New York: Harper & Row, 1966.

Hartshorne, H., & May, M. A. *Studies in the nature of character.* Vol. 1. *Studies in deceit.* New York: Macmillan, 1928.

Tolamn, E. C. Cognitive maps in rats and men. *Psychological Review,* 1948, *55,* 189–208.

WHY DO WE CALL THE GOOD SAMARITAN GOOD?

1. The Good Samaritan was traveling. We assume that there was a place to which he had to go. Nevertheless, he stopped and gave of his time to help the victim.
2. He gave his own money. When someone gives his own money freely, we tend to attribute a pure motive to that person.
3. Besides actually giving his own money, he offered to pay more if it was needed.
4. He took upon himself some personal responsibility for the victim's health. He said that he would stop at the inn on his return trip

so that he could assess the victim's condition as well as pay any extra costs.
5. He helped voluntarily, without coercion or social pressure.
6. He did something that exceeded social mores; that is, his actions exceeded what was expected of a despised Samaritan. The Samaritans were the outgroup of the first century. Nobody would expect one of them to do a good deed.
7. The Good Samaritan's helping behavior is vividly contrasted with that of the priest and Levite, two people who, according to the

standards of the society, ought to have helped.

The Good Samaritan performed a prosocial act without external justification, contrary to social mores, and at personal cost. Because of this cluster of factors, we attribute to him a pure altruistic motive. The attribution of goodness is to the person rather than to the context.

Adapted from Raymond F. Paloutzian, Note on the attribution and reinforcement analyses of altruism. *Journal of Psychology and Theology*, 1979, *7*, 114–17.

EFFECT OF FEELING GOOD ON HELPING: COOKIES AND KINDNESS

ALICE M. ISEN AND PAULA F. LEVIN

Social psychologists have devoted a lot of study to the question of when people will help during emergencies. Although helping behavior can be of critical importance in such situations, it can occur in other circumstances as well. Doing a favor or paying a compliment are examples of the small acts of kindness that most of us do every day without external pressure. But if the situation is not one that demands helpfulness, then why do we do good unto others? One answer, according to Isen and Levin, is that we do good when we feel good. Anything that induces a positive mood state in us will increase the likelihood that we will do something nice for someone else.

Recent investigations of determinants of helping have begun to focus on the role of mood state in producing differences in helpfulness. The first studies that indicated the relevance of a potential helper's internal affective state used reports of success and failure at a task as their independent variable. A study by Berkowitz and Connor (1966) indicated a relationship between success and

helping, when the beneficiary was dependent on the subject. A later study (Isen, 1970) also indicated a link between success and helping, where there was no relationship between the people involved and where helping was a low-cost, naturalistic, behavioral measure. It was postulated that in just such a situation (i.e., nonsolicited, low-cost helping), an important determinant of helpfulness may be the potential helper's positive affective state or "warm glow of success." In addition, even though their success/failure manipulation was not aimed specifically at affecting internal mood state, Berkowitz and Connor also made reference to a "glow of goodwill" in their discussion. In both of

A.M. Isen and P.F. Levin. Effect of feeling good on helping: cookies and kindness. *Journal of Personality and Social Psychology*, 1972, *21*:3, 384–88. Copyright © 1972 by the American Psychological Association. Reprinted by permission of the publisher and authors.

these studies, which suggested that "feeling good" may be a determinant of helping, positive affective state was induced via a report of success. However, report of success may not be an entirely satisfactory way of manipulating mood, since induced affective state may be confounded with estimates of competence.

Several recent studies have indicated that manipulation of affective state in ways other than via success/failure also results in differential helping, thus lending credibility to the hypothesis that a relationship between feeling good and helpfulness does exist. Two naturalistic experiments seem to indicate that good feeling aroused through positive verbal contact results in increased aid, both solicited and nonsolicited.

Studies by Aderman (1971) and Aderman and Berkowitz (1970), while conducted in an experimental setting, manipulated mood state in several novel ways. In the Aderman and Berkowitz study, the subject's mood state was varied by having him observe one of several interactions between two male college students, one who needed aid and one who was a potential helper. The experimental condition varied according to the person with whom the subject was instructed to empathize, the helping response of the second person (helped or did not help), and the reaction of the helped person (thanked the helper or did not). The subject then filled out a mood questionnaire and finally was given an opportunity to comply with the experimenter's request for help. The results of the experiment, though complex, tended to support the idea that feeling good can be related to increased helping under some circumstances (empathy with the thanked helper), while feeling bad can be associated with increased helping under other circumstances (empathy with the non-helped person in need).

In the study by Aderman (1971), elation or depression was induced in subjects by having them read sets of mood statements. Aderman found that following the reading of the cards, subjects in the elation condition wrote more numbers for the experimenter, when this task was presented as a favor rather than a requirement of the experiment. In addition, elation subjects volunteered more often for a future experiment. Such findings do lend credence to the "glow" hypothesis, yet one complexity of the findings is that the "help" was solicited.

A further question remaining is whether success, or good mood, leads specifically to helping or, more generally, to increased activity and/or productivity. In other words, does the good feeling lead to an increased desire to do something nice for someone else, or would subjects who have been made to feel good, as opposed to those who have not, engage in more or any subsequent activity?

Using a 2 × 2 design, we performed an experiment that attempted to answer the two questions posed above: first, whether feeling good leads to increased helping; second, whether, following the induction of good feeling, the response to an opportunity to help differs from the response to an opportunity to engage in some other activity. We predicted an interaction between the two independent variables such that those subjects who were feeling good would subsequently be more willing to help but less willing to hinder (distract) than those not made to feel good.

STUDY 1

METHOD

Subjects

The study, which spanned five sessions, was conducted in the libraries of a university and two colleges in the Philadelphia area. Fifty-two male college students who were studying in individual carrels served as subjects.

Procedure

At the beginning of the session, a coordinator randomly assigned rows of carrels to the feeling good or to the neutral condition. The assignment to condition was based on rows, rather than on individuals, in order to insure that subjects would be unaware that two conditions existed.

To induce good mood, confederates distributed cookies along the rows that had been assigned to the feeling good condition, while they merely walked by the rows in the neutral condition. This task was performed by a male and female pair of confederates in two of the sessions and by a female confederate in the remaining three sessions.

The coordinator also randomly divided subjects in each condition into "help" or "hinder" groups. The experimenter was told this assignment of "help" and "distract" subjects, but was was kept unaware of whether a particular row was "cookie" or "no cookie." Similarly, the coordinator was careful to withhold from the confederates information as to help or distract condition of the subjects.

A few minutes after the confederates returned following the distribution or nondistribution of cookies, the experimenter approached each subject individually and asked if and for how many 20-minute sessions the subject would serve as a confederate in a psychology experiment. In the help condition, the purpose of the experiment was given as an investigation of creativity in students at examination times, as opposed to other times during the year. The confederate was needed in this experiment to act as helper to subjects who would be attempting to conceive of novel uses for ordinary items. The confederate's aid, which involved holding and manipulating the items, was described as "something which the subjects usually found very helpful to them." In the distract condition, the job of the confederate was described as a distracter of a randomly chosen, unwitting student who happened to be studying in the library. As distracter, he would stand near the subject and drop books, make noises, rattle papers, all while the experimenter unobtrusively recorded the subject's reactions. The purpose of such an experiment was given as an investigation of distractibility of students at examination time as opposed to other times during the year. In addition, the experimenter cautioned each subject in the distract condition by saying, "I think it only fair to tell you before you decide to act as distracter, that the subjects find the distraction to be an unpleasant annoyance." Thus, in the help condition the role that the subject was invited to play was clearly that of a helper, one appreciated greatly by the creativity subjects; in contrast, the role that a confederate would play in the distract condition was clearly described as that of an annoying distracter of unsuspecting students studying in the library.

A debriefing and discussion period followed each subject's reply. Subjects' reports indicated that the independent and dependent manipulations were plausible, and that they had not been associated in the subjects' minds prior to the debriefing.

RESULTS

Since the five sessions yielded comparable results, the data were combined. Table 1 shows the proportion of subjects volunteering in each condition and the means and variances of number of minutes volunteered. A t-test for proportions was performed on the number of subjects volunteering in each condition. This test revealed the predicted

TABLE 1. STUDY I: MEANS AND VARIANCES OF AMOUNT OF TIME (IN MINUTES) VOLUNTEERED AND PROPORTION OF SUBJECTS VOLUNTEERING IN EACH CONDITION

CONDITION	HELP	DISTRACT
Cookie		
M	69.00	20.00
s^2	6923.08	1400.00
P	.69 (9/13)	.31 (4/13)
No cookie		
M	16.70	78.60
s^2	563.64	11659.34
P	.50 (6/12)	.64 (9/14)

interaction between receiving a cookie or not and volunteering to help or to distract. That is, subjects receiving cookies volunteered to help more, but to distract less, than those not receiving cookies ($t = 1.96$, $p < .05$).

For the data on number of minutes volunteered in each condition, an F test of the variances indicated that the data did not meet the assumptions of the analysis of variance ($F = 20.69$, $df = 11/13$, $p < .01$). A two-way analysis of variance was performed, however, on the transformed scores, which did meet the assumptions of the test. This analysis indicated no main effect, but did show the predicted significant interaction, with cookie subjects volunteering more time to help, but less to distract, than no-cookie subjects.

DISCUSSION

The results of this experiment indicate that in terms of both number of subjects volunteering and amount of time volunteered, subjects who have unexpectedly received cookies help more, but distract less, than do those who have not received cookies. Thus, feeling good, induced naturalistically and in a way other than via report of success, seems to lead to increased helping, and to helping specifically, rather than to general activity.

Although this finding provides evidence for the "warm glow" hypothesis—people who feel good themselves are more likely to help others—an alternative interpretation is possible. Following from a modeling or a normative explanation, cookie subjects might have been more helpful simply because they had just been exposed to a helpful model (the person passing out the cookies) who may have reminded them of norms of kindness to others. Furthermore, a few aspects of the dependent measure complicate the warm glow interpretation. Although the independent manipulation was more naturalistic than that found in many experiments, the dependent measure was one of *solicited* helpfulness. In addition, help was only volunteered, rather than actually performed.

Thus, a second study was conducted to determine whether nonsolicited, low-cost helpfulness increases following the induction of good feeling, without the good mood being directly brought about by another person. The question was, Does feeling good lead to increased helping, even if there is no helpful model? In the "dime" study, which is directed at this question and which is presented below, good feeling was induced in a subject by the discovery of an unexpected dime in the coin return slot of a pay telephone. The dependent measure was that of helping a young woman pick up papers which she had just dropped.

STUDY II

METHOD

Subjects

Subjects were 24 female and 17 male adults who made calls from designated public telephones located in enclosed shopping malls in suburban San Francisco and Philadelphia. Excluded from the subject pool were those shoppers who were not alone and those who were carrying packages.

Procedure

Telephone booths were "set up" in the following manner. The experimenter made an incomplete call, ostensibly took her dime from the return slot, and left the booth. In actuality, the dime was left in the coin return slot for a randomly selected half of these trials. Thus, subjects using such telephones received an unexpected ten cents when they checked the coin return before, during, or upon completion of their calls; these subjects constituted the experimental group. The control group was made up of individuals who used a telephone that had not been "stocked" with a dime and who therefore did not receive unexpected money.

The experimenter set up the experimental and control telephones without informing the confederate as to condition. This was done in order to eliminate any possible systematic bias in the confederate's performance of the paper dropping. The experimenter also checked to make sure that all

subjects did look in the coin return slot. Only a few subjects failed to meet this requirement, and these were not included in the data analysis. This was done in order to avoid ultimately obtaining a sample of subjects which was inadvertently selected for attention. For this reason, no subject who was at an "experimental" condition telephone and simply failed to see his dime was included in the control group.

During the call, the confederate was able to observe the outline of the subject unobtrusively by pretending to "window shop," while actually watching the subject's reflection in one of the store windows. The aim of this surveillance was simply to know when the subject was leaving the telephone. When the subject did leave, the confederate started in the same direction as the subject and, while walking slightly ahead and to the side of him or her, dropped a manila folder full of papers in the subject's path. The dependent measure was whether the subject helped the female confederate pick up the papers.

RESULTS

Table 2 shows the number of males and females helping in each condition. A Fisher exact test on the data of the females indicated a significant relationship between getting a dime and helping ($p < .005$). A similar finding ($p = .025$) was obtained for the males.

DISCUSSION

These results indicate that differential unsolicited helping occurs even when good mood is induced in an impersonal manner. The finding appears to be less pronounced for males than for females, but the smaller number of male subjects may be responsible in part for this apparent difference. Because our society has specific norms applying to this particular helping situation for males, one might have expected the behavior of the males,

TABLE 2. STUDY II: NUMBER OF PEOPLE HELPING IN EACH CONDITION

CONDITION	FEMALES		MALES	
	Helped	Did not help	Helped	Did not help
Dime	8	0	6	2
No dime	0	16	1	8

more than that of females, to reflect not only the independent manipulation but also these norms for courtesy. The data show that while no females in the control condition helped, one male in the same condition did help. However, it must also be noted that two males in the experimental condition failed to help, while no female experimental subjects failed to help. Thus, while it is true that the behavior of the males may be more complex than that of the females, the simple courtesy expectation is not supported.

The results of the two studies taken together provide support for the notion that feeling good leads to helping. Because feeling good has been generated in a variety of ways and settings, and since the type of helping measure and the source of the subject populations have also varied, this relationship seems to have some empirical gen-

erality. We recognize, however, that the question of why feeling good leads to helping, or more properly, what mediates the relationship between the two, remains to be answered. Moreover, such an answer may provide some insights into the more general and important issue of how the observed determinants of helping, such as success, feeling good, feeling bad in some circumstances, guilt, verbal contact, and the presence or absence of other people, relate to one another. That is, while these states or events may seem unrelated as determinants of helping, they may have some common aspects in that capacity. If so, then the determination of helping may be more parsimoniously understood in terms of broader concepts, such as maintenance of positive affective state, perception of costs and rewards, or both, and this possibility is now under investigation.

REFERENCES

Aderman, D. Effect of prior mood on helping behavior. Unpublished doctoral dissertation, University of Wisconsin, 1971.

Aderman, D., and Berkowitz, L. Observational set, empathy, and helping. *Journal of Personality and Social Psychology*, 1970, *14*, 141–48.

Berkowitz, L., and Connor, W. H. Success, failure, and social responsibility. *Journal of Personality and Social Psychology*, 1966, *4*, 664–69.

Isen, A.M. Success, failure, attention, and reaction to others: the warm glow of success. *Journal of Personality and Social Psychology*, 1979, *15*, 294–301.

PERSONAL RESPONSIBILITY AND ALTRUISM IN CHILDREN

GEOFFREY MARUYAMA, SCOTT C. FRASER, AND NORMAN MILLER

People do not always extend a helping hand when it is called for. This was true in the Kitty Genovese murder case, and the research studies that were spawned by that incident focused on why people fail to help in emergency situations. One of the explanations that was proposed for this bystander apathy was a diffusion of responsibility—no one felt personally responsible for coming to the aid of someone else. If so, then the reverse ought to be true: Making people feel more personally responsible should induce more helpfulness on their part. This is exactly what was done by Maruyama, Fraser, and Miller in an ingenious field experiment with Halloween trick-or-treaters. The results suggest that personal responsibility can be a critical factor for promoting generosity.

In 1970 Zimbardo proposed a three-stage model to explain the occurrence of behaviors that are normally inhibited by social norms and sanctions. The first stage focuses on antecedent conditions such as anonymity or social support from others that augment normally restrained behavior. The second stage is concerned with the process that occurs when, in response to the cues provided by the facilitating antecedent conditions, individuals are released from personal and social constraints. The release presumably reflects a reduced concern for self-evaluation and/or beliefs that personal consequences of a negative evaluation by others can be minimized. The third stage, the emergence of behaviors that Zimbardo called *deindividuated*, results from the changes in internal state produced in the second stage.

Research examining the plausibility of this deindividuation model has focused on how deindividuation can increase the occurrence of antisocial, aggressive types of behavior. However, the model should also be able to account for the occurrence or nonoccurrence of prosocial behaviors. The present study uses the Halloween paradigm to extend the applicability of the model to prosocial behavior. Groups of children trick or treating on Halloween night were asked to donate candy to hospitalized children. Personal responsibility for the amount donated was manipulated by identifying either no child, one child, or all the children within each group as responsible. We assumed that when the children entered the houses selected as experimental sites, they were in a deindividuated state and that the designation of responsibility should act to individuate them. This, in turn, should make them more willing to give their own candy to hospitalized children.

To develop our rationale for the study, we will briefly examine the deindividuation model, discuss the relation between personal responsibility and prosocial behavior, and then, consider the implications of these ideas for the Halloween paradigm.

DEINDIVIDUATION

Research examining the plausibility of Zimbardo's model generally has tended to validate it; antisocial behavior has been found to increase di-

Reprinted from *Journal of Personality and Social Psychology*, 1982, 42:4, 658–64. Copyright © 1982 by the American Psychological Association, Inc.

rectly with manipulations of anonymity, diffusion of responsibility, social support, and arousal. In addition studies concerned with children's transgressions, such as stealing candy or money, provide further support for it. A few studies, however, do report seemingly contrary findings. Recently, Diener (1979) revised the deindividuation model in order to integrate relevant findings and to provide a focus for future work. In particular, he examined the link between individuation and self-awareness and argued that it is the minimization of self-awareness that accounts for the occurrence of deindividuated behaviors. That is, deindividuation will occur only if the antecedent conditions described by Zimbardo act to block an individual's self-awareness (and self-consciousness). Diener's arguments suggest that the instances in which the model is not supported probably reflect the fact that the experimental manipulations did not act to decrease self-awareness.

PERSONAL RESPONSIBILITY AND PROSOCIAL BEHAVIOR

Prosocial behavior typically is seen as involving aspects of self-reward as well as reward that is given to others. It even has been argued that prosocial behavior is primarily hedonistic. People reward others because they expect to be rewarded in return either with tangible goods or by recognition for being kind. People expect to receive such rewards in return only to the extent that they are recognized as being responsible for having provided the necessary benefits to the person in need. In other words, insofar as receiving self-reward is tied to recognition, identification as the person responsible for providing the help is critical. In terms of this analysis, if a person is designated as personally responsible for the help given to another, the inclination to offer it should increase.

Turning to the implications of the deindividuation model, it should first be noted that societal norms generally promote altruism and that prosocial behavior is typically viewed as consistent with such norms. Therefore, from the standpoint of the deindividuation model, prosocial behavior should be reduced by deindividuation. When instead self-focus is increased, behavior that is consistent with altruistic norms should also increase. The designation of personal responsibility for the amount of help that is given to someone in need appears to be a direct means of increasing self-focus and thereby attenuating a person's level of deindividuation.

HALLOWEEN PARADIGM

Halloween provides a good natural setting for testing the application of the deindividuation model to prosocial behavior. Children who are trick-or-treating should experience many of the antecedent conditions for a deindividuated state. Their costumes generally make them anonymous; they are excited (high arousal); and, since they typically trick-or-treat with friends, they have social support and can readily diffuse responsibility for any antisocial behavior in which they engage. Certainly, the many occurrences of petty vandalism on Halloween, such as toilet papering trees and houses or soaping windows and cars, provide strong anecdotal evidence for a changed mental state. Within this setting the deindividuation model can be tested by *removing* one or more of the ingredients for a deindividuated state, thereby restoring children to a more individuated state. As argued above, making children personally responsible should increase their self-awareness and thereby make them more inclined to judge their behavior against normative standards. This, in turn, should increase the occurrence of prosocial behavior.

Because children trick-or-treat in groups that vary in size, the effects of group size warrant additional consideration. Prior studies on both deindividuation and prosocial behavior have found that subjects in larger groups more readily diffuse responsibility among group members. One interpretation of this finding is that children in larger groups are less self-focused and have less concern about negative evaluation by others. In addition, however, because groups are self-selected, their members should provide social support to one another. Thus, the larger the group, the more social support available to any individual member. These considerations argue that children in larger groups should exhibit less prosocial behavior than those in smaller ones.

METHOD

Subjects were 177 children who were trick-or-treating in 56 groups within the Los Angeles metropolitan area. They ranged in estimated age from 4 to 13 years. Groups generally had two to five persons, although some single groups had six, seven, and eight children. Eighty-nine children were identified as male, 72 as female; the sex of 16 children could not accurately be determined. Female experimenters and male raters from research classes at the University of Southern California were assigned to each of six houses chosen as experimental sites. In the first room of each house, a female met children who were trick-or-treating on Halloween night. She was the only person visible in each house. In the front room of each house, hospital posters and pictures of hospitalized children were prominently placed. The female greeted the children and allowed them to enter, leaving the door open. She individually complimented each child on his or her costume. She then informed the children that she was sorry but that she was completely out of candies. Pointing to a large poster containing pictures of hospitalized children, she then told them that she was trying to collect candies for hospitalized children who were unable to go trick-or-treating. She asked the children to donate candies to the hospitalized children by putting them into a box. The specific instructions about the donation comprised the manipulation of responsibility. The three conditions were as follows:

1. No designated responsibility. Pointing to the contribution container, the experimenter said, "Please give them as many as you want by putting the candies in the *white* box on the table. Then you can leave."

2. One child responsible. One child was arbitrarily selected by the experimenter. She pointed at the child and said, "I will put you in charge of the group here." Looking in turn at each of the other children and again pointing, she said, "She/He is the leader of the group, and I will put her/his name on the bag of candy I give tomorrow to the hospitalized children." She further said, "Here is a badge for you to be head of the group," and placed a badge on the selected child, continuing, "Please give as many candies as you all want by putting the candies in the *white* box on that table. Then you can leave."

3. Each child responsible. Pointing to each child in turn, the experimenter said, "I will be counting on you and you and you . . . I will put each of your names on the bag of candy I give tomorrow to the hospitalized children. Here is a badge for each of you to be in charge." She then placed a badge on each child, and after each badging, she said, pointing to the appropriate container, "Please put as many candies as you

want in the (*color*) box on that table. Then you can leave." In this condition a distinctively colored box was available for each individual child.

After administering the instructions, the adult left "to finish my work in the other room." The boxes were constructed so that candy contributed by any one child was not visible to other children. In no condition did the experimenter specify which child should go to the box(es) first. Also, at no time during her contact with them did she ask any of the children their names. A male rater, hidden behind a partition, unobtrusively observed the behavior of the children, recorded the donations of each child (whether the child contributed any candy and the amount of any donation), and estimated demographic characteristics of each child, such as age and sex. After the children had time to contribute and were about to leave the house, the adult returned, told the children that she had just found some more candies, and gave some to each of them. If any child asked whether the experimenter was going to write down his/her name to put on the candy, the experimenter wrote down the name of the child on a piece of paper. Between experimental sessions the rater emptied the boxes and validated his observations against the actual amount of candy given whenever possible. If the estimate could not be reconciled with the actual amount of candy, the data were discarded (scores for five individuals or two groups had to be discarded). At each house the first replication of each condition was used as an additional training session and, therefore, was omitted from the analyses; the sample size of 177 subjects excludes 20 omitted groups (i.e., three groups from each of six sites) plus two with missing data.

RESULTS

Because the manipulations were imposed on groups of children, we will first examine the group data, presenting individual data to assess effects of age (and sex) on contribution rates and to augment findings of group data. The dependent measures are (a) whether children contributed candy and (b) the amount of candy contributed. In order to examine the effects of group size, groups were classified "small" (two or three children) or "large" (four or more children).

Preliminary examination of the data addressed two issues: the overall rate of occurrence of prosocial behavior and the possibility that the average group size differed between conditions. First, the overall rate of prosocial behavior was high. In over 86 percent of the groups, each child donated at least one candy. Over 92 percent of the children donated one or more candies, and over 40 percent of the children donated three or more candies. Second, there were virtually no differences in average size of the groups in each condition and no interaction of condition by group size (large/small). Therefore, group size cannot account for any between-condition differences.

Because virtually all children contributed candy, our analyses focus on the number of candies contributed. This analysis yielded main effects for the responsibility manipulation and for group size, and no interaction. When each child was made responsible, children donated an average of 5.0 candies, compared with 3.3 candies when one child was designated as responsible and 2.2 when no child was designated as responsible. Children in large groups donated an average of only 2.0 candies, compared with 4.0 candies by children in small groups.

Individual level data found not only main effects for conditions and group size, but an interaction as well. As responsibility was increased from none to one to each child, contributions in small groups increased; mean number of candies donated was 2.44, 3.77, and 6.96, respectively. In large groups, however, the conditions did not differ; means were 1.76, 2.30, and 1.92, respectively. Further analyses comparing responsible and nonresponsible children within the one-child-responsible condition found no differences between them.

DISCUSSION

The results are consistent with the deindividuation model. They argue that processes that spontaneously occur in large groups diminish individual prosocial behavior. Furthermore, they suggest that when individuals are embedded in large groups, they are not affected by procedures that attempt to increase their contribution rates by identifying them as personally responsible; the effect of this manipulation was apparent only in smaller groups. As argued in the introduction, one plausible interpretation of this effect is that responsibility is more readily diffused in larger groups. On the other hand, as noted earlier, in self-selected groups it seems particularly likely that social support will covary directly with group size and thus provide an alternate explanation of this effect.

As well as demonstrating generalizability of the deindividuation model to prosocial behavior, the present application may make clearer its conceptual base with respect to the terms *normative* and *normal restraints*. Although Zimbardo used the two terms interchangeably, a distinction between them becomes important when examining prosocial behaviors. For example, a prosocial behavior such as contributing to a charity, although normatively encouraged, may occur with low frequency and consequently might be viewed as "normally restrained." When this latter aspect of charitable contributions is emphasized, it makes the model appear to argue that such behavior will *increase* under conditions of deindividuation. Clearly, however, the term *normative* rather than *normal* is the one that is consistent with the intent of the deindividuation model; regardless of initial frequency of a given behavior, a deindividuated state should lead to a decreased occurrence of normatively sanctioned behavior. In the present instance the uncurbed deindividuated state produced by Halloween reduced charitable donations, whereas individuating children by assigning personal responsibility to them increased their compliance with social responsibility and helping norms.

The bearing of the deindividuation model on the broader range of prosocial behaviors also warrants consideration. Although the most common forms of prosocial behavior do seem to be supported by social norms, nonnormative instances of prosocial behavior, such as one male hugging another to express his joy in seeing him, do occur. Deindividuation should facilitate rather than inhibit the occurrence of such nonnormative instances of prosocial behavior.

Finally, the fact that our own particular manipulation of responsibility did effectively increase the occurrence of normatively sanctioned behavior is interesting because it defines a boundary condition for countering the effect of diffusing responsibility. Diener et al. (1979) found that appointing an anonymous individual to be responsible increased the antisocial behaviors of the group. The assignment of responsibility in the present study, which in addition told subjects that they would be identified by name, produced the opposite effect, that is, it increased rather than decreased normatively sanctioned behavior. When taken together, these findings suggest that personal identification is a necessary ingredient if one wishes to induce greater helping by assigning individual responsibility; the mere assignment of responsibility did not increase normative behavior.

In conclusion the results provide evidence that the deindividuation model can be applied to prosocial behaviors. Not only does being identified as responsible increase the occurrence of normative prosocial behavior, but in addition its effects operate primarily in smaller groups.

REFERENCES

Diener, E. Deindividuation, self-awareness, and disinhibition. *Journal of Personality and Social Psychology*, 1979, *37*, 1160–71.

Diener, E., Fraser, S. C., Beaman, A. L., & Kelem, R. T. Effects of deindividuation variables on stealing among Halloween trick-or-treaters. *Journal of Personality and Social Psychology*, 1976, *33*, 178–83.

Zimbardo, P. G. The human choice: Individuation, reason, and order versus deindividuation, impulse, and chaos. In W. J. Arnold & D. Levine (eds.), *Nebraska Symposium on Motivation* (Vol. 17). Lincoln: University of Nebraska Press, 1970.

PROJECTS

Name _____

Date _____

7.1: WHEN DO PEOPLE HELP?

Research on altruism has tried to isolate both the personal and the situational factors that influence one person's tendency to help another. Studies have looked at the effect of the helper's mood and personality, various characteristics of the recipients, the type of aid requested, the presence of other people, and so on.

This project involves a field experiment in which you are to collect data on people's responses to an individual in need of help. The stimulus person will be obviously lost and in need of directions. The extent to which this person makes a direct or indirect request for aid may determine whether such aid will be forthcoming. Therefore, with half the subjects, this person will specifically ask for directions (direct request); with the remaining subjects, the person will make the need salient but will not specifically ask for help (indirect request). Your data should include the sex of the stimulus person and the sex of the subjects.

HYPOTHESES

1. Subjects will be more likely to help someone who makes a direct request for aid than someone who makes an indirect request.

2. Subjects will be more likely to help females than males.

3. The sex of the stimulus person and of the subjects will have an effect on stimulus-subject interaction. Most helping will occur when male subjects see a female stimulus person; least helping will occur when female subjects see a male stimulus person.

Would you propose any additional hypotheses? Would you propose any alternative hypotheses? State your hypotheses and the reasoning behind them.

PROCEDURE

The best way to handle this project is to work in teams of two. One of you will be the stimulus person; the other will be the experimenter and therefore responsible for the random assignment of subjects and for observing the subjects' responses. (You and your partner should alternate these roles periodically, so that each of you spends an equal amount of time as subject and as experimenter-observer.) Choose several areas of the campus or surrounding community where a lot of people are likely to pass by and where (if possible) there are benches on which people often sit.

In this setting, the stimulus person (who will be perusing a map and looking obviously lost) will sit down on a bench near the subject designated by the experimenter. In the indirect-request condition, the stimulus person will search briefly through the map, look around in a bewildered way, and then mumble something like, "Boy, I don't know *where* that is." The stimulus person will then wait one minute. If help is not forthcoming, he or she will then leave. In the direct-request condition, the stimulus person will go through the same sequence of actions; but after the mumbled statement, he or she will turn to the subject and say, "Excuse me. Can you tell me how to get to *X?*" In either condition, if the subject does offer help, he or she is to be thanked by the stimulus person, who then leaves.

In both conditions, the subjects' responses will be noted on the data sheet by both the stimulus person and the experimenter (who should remain standing inconspicuously nearby). Each subject's response can be coded in one of several categories: ignores stimulus person, looks at stimulus person but says nothing, says that he or she doesn't know where *X* is, tells stimulus person where *X* is, or gives stimulus person some suggestion for finding *X*. In addition, the subject's facial expression and posture can be rated by both the stimulus person and the experimenter for the degree of friendliness or hostility that was conveyed.

In addition to selecting the subjects, the experimenter will specify what request condition is to be run and will record the data. The request condition can easily be determined by the flip of a coin. Deciding at random who among many passers-by is to be the subject is a more difficult task. However, if the experimenter does not use a systematic procedure, he or she runs the risk of biasing the sample in some way (e.g., by picking only friendly-looking people as subjects). In such a field situation, it is often best to develop a "sort of random" procedure for selecting subjects. For example, the experimenter might choose some arbitrary starting point (the edge of a plaza, a row of benches) and then use a random numbers table to determine who will be the subject. If the random number 5 appeared, it would mean that the fifth person who crossed the edge of the plaza (after the experimenter had started counting) or the fifth person sitting along the row of benches would be the subject. If unforeseen circumstances make it impossible for you to use the chosen subject (e.g., the subject gets up from the bench and leaves just as the stimulus person sits down), you and your partner should wait awhile, then leave, and return a little later to do another trial. After successfully testing a subject, you and your partner should also leave the setting for a short period of time before coming back to test another subject. If you do not leave, the stimulus person's behavior will look suspicious. If you have chosen several possible locations for your study, you can move from one to another after running each trial.

Name _____

Date _____

Data Sheet

Subjects	Sex of Stimulus Person	Sex of Subject	Condition (Dr/Ir)	Response				Expression Hostile (1) to Friendly (7)
				Ignores	Looks	No Information	Helps	
1								
2								
3								
4								
5								
6								
7								
8								
9								
10								
11								
12								
13								
14								
15								
16								
17								
18								
19								
20								

ANALYSIS

Look at the pattern of your own findings, and then compare it with those of the other teams in the class.

1. Did your data support or refute the hypotheses? Explain.

2. Do your results suggest alternative hypotheses? If so, what are they?

3. Were there any confounding variables or other problems that might account for your findings? For example, might your prior knowledge of the hypotheses and the experimental condition (or your partner's prior knowledge) have affected your results?

Name _____

Date _____

7.2: ASKING FOR CHARITY

In this project, you will be making observations of one or more persons who are asking other people for money (for example, panhandlers and individuals who are asking for donations to charity). The goal is to analyze the different persuasive appeals that are being used by these solicitors and to discover which ones seem to be most effective in getting people to actually donate money. For each solicitor that you observe, describe each person who is approached (in terms of sex, age, appearance, and so forth), describe the type of appeal that is made (such as humorous, guilt-inducing, social pressure), and describe the outcome (was a donation made or not, did the donor talk to the solicitor or display any emotional feelings, and so forth).

Person asking for money: _____

Persons Approached	Type of Appeal	Result

Person asking for money: _____

Persons Approached	Type of Appeal	Result

1. What were the most successful types of appeal in terms of getting people to donate money? Why do you think they worked best?

2. Were certain types of people more likely to donate than others? If so, what do you think are the reason(s)?

3. How did people avoid making donations?

4. Based on your observations, what factors do you consider to be most crucial in the process of donation, and why?

THE SELF AND OTHERS

8

When you think about your "self"—the part of you that is your essence, your core, your very own—what do you see? Do you, like some psychoanalysts, see the self as being somewhat similar to an iceberg, with the greater part of its mass hidden beneath the surface of everyday consciousness and your behavior motivated mainly by deep impulses linked to childhood? Or do you perhaps share the view of B. F. Skinner that the self is a vacuum, a black box, an unknowable part of the organism that is motivated mainly by external environmental forces. You may also see the self as Jung saw it: an island rising above water, joined to others by a collective unconscious. Or do you see the self as a mirror reflecting the world and other people around you, or as a series of roles, rather like the layers of an onion—a ball of persons with no real substance at the core? You may share the view of Erikson and the existential philosophers, that the self is an active selector which reflects its own free will through the essential human ability to choose. If you do not see yourself as any of these things, the conceptualizations proposed by other psychologists, who have characterized the self as, among other things, a "digital computer," a "child of God," a "pilgrim," and a "godhead," may strike you as more to the point. And if none of these metaphors fits your own self-concept, then maybe, as suggested by some, you are just an "illusion" or a "ghost in the machine." Maybe in reality there is no "you" at all!

Clearly, there are many definitions of the self in everyday language and many more in the psychological literature. In addition to their dramatic-pic-

torial effect, these metaphors and definitions share the notion of the self as that part of human experience that we regard as essentially us—unique, stable, coherent, organized, consistent, and integrated. Nevertheless, most of us behave, think, and feel very differently with different people at different times. Quite appropriately, we experience and express rather different selves with our parents, friends, supervisors, and lovers. Furthermore, things such as weather, music, drugs, meditation, and even clothing can affect our self-perception.

A good example of the effects of social atmosphere on the different roles that the self must assume can be observed among people who are called to serve in the military reserves. When they arrive, they are quiet and are dressed conservatively. They may be clerks, executives, bus drivers, teachers. They may be a little overweight and perhaps have balding heads. They are likely to be preoccupied with the cares of the business or job that was left unfinished when the call for service came. Yet, within a short period of time, as they put on the old uniforms and start to carry a gun, they are transformed. Other selves emerge. The old glitter comes back to the eyes and with it the youthful expression, the old gestures, the special army vocabulary. The atmosphere is radically changed. They are loud and noisy, united—a group. They in fact begin to behave in a way that they themselves might have found rather unacceptable just a few hours earlier. Yet, they clearly have no great difficulty assuming the proper role once they have the proper uniform.

ADVICE FROM A CATERPILLAR

The Caterpillar and Alice looked at each other for some time in silence: at last the Caterpillar took the hookah out of his mouth, and addressed her in a languid, sleepy voice.

"Who are *you?*" said the Caterpillar.

This was not an encouraging opening for a conversation. Alice replied, rather shyly, "I—I hardly know, Sir, just at present—at least I know who I *was* when I got up this morning, but I think I must have changed several times since then."

"What do you mean by that?" said the Caterpillar, sternly. "Explain yourself!"

"I can't explain *myself,* I'm afraid, Sir," said Alice, "because I'm not myself, you see."

"I don't see," said the Caterpillar.

"I'm afraid I can't put it more clearly," Alice replied, very politely, "for I can't understand it myself, to begin with; and being so many different sizes in a day is very confusing."

"It isn't," said the Caterpillar.

"Well, perhaps you haven't found it so yet," said Alice: "but when you have to turn into a chrysalis—you will some day, you know—and then after that into a butterfly, I should think you'll feel it a little queer, won't you?"

"Not a bit," said the Caterpillar.

"Well, perhaps *your* feelings may be different," said Alice: "all I know is, it would feel very queer to *me.*"

"You!" said the Caterpillar contemptuously. "Who are *you?*"

From Lewis Carroll, *Alice's Adventures in Wonderland* (New York: Random House).

TRAIT SALIENCE IN THE SPONTANEOUS SELF-CONCEPT

WILLIAM J. MCGUIRE AND ALICE PADAWER-SINGER

"Who are you?" asked the caterpillar in Lewis Carroll's Alice's Adventures in Wonderland. This is a very good question indeed when one wants to find out about another person's self-perception, yet it is rarely asked by psychologists studying the self.

The study of the self is probably one of the best examples of the negative effects of researchers' preconceived notions. In far too many of the studies on self-concept, researchers presented subjects with questionnaires and dimensions that they assumed were important, only to discover ambiguous or uninteresting results. The reason for that, claim McGuire and Padawer-Singer, is that they didn't let people describe themselves the way they perceive themselves, which is, of course, what these two social psychologists did to discover "the spontaneous self-concept." Instead of structured questionnaires, they simply said to subjects, "Tell me about yourself."

In their article, McGuire and Singer show that it is possible to predict which traits will be salient for the individual. Trait salience is a function of that particular trait's distinctiveness within the individual's social environment.

The self-concept has hardly been neglected in psychological research. Fifteen years ago Wylie

W. J. McGuire and A. Padawer-Singer, Trait salience in the spontaneous self-concept, *Journal of Personality and Social Psychology*, 1976, *33:6*, 743–54. Copyright © 1976 by the American Psychological Association. Reprinted by permission of the publisher and author.

(1961) described the results of a good thousand (if not a thousand good) studies on the topic. Her more recent edition (Wylie, 1974) analyzes over a thousand studies in only the first of two volumes. This continuing fascination with the self-concept is easy to understand: What we think about ourselves is probably the central concept in our conscious lives. Yet this vast input of research effort contrasts unfavorably with the low yield of interesting findings regarding the phenomenal self. We fear it may be said of the self-concept, as it has been said of sex (by the young, at least), that only psychological research could make so inherently interesting a topic seem dull.

This low yield we attribute primarily to researchers' having measured the self-concept almost exclusively by information-losing "reactive" methods, that is, by studying subjects' reactions to a dimension chosen a priori by the researcher. Subjects are thus reduced to saying how they would think of themselves with respect to the given dimension if they happened to think of it at all, without furnishing any information on the more important question of how salient the dimension is to them.

A second limitation explaining the somewhat disappointing yield of past self-concept research is that this researcher-chosen dimension is almost always self-evaluation or self-esteem, as if our thoughts about ourselves are concerned almost entirely with how good we are. Indeed, the landmark volumes of Wylie (1961, 1974), which necessarily reflect the content of the field they analyzed, might just as appropriately have been entitled *Self-Esteem as Self-Concept*. In contrast to the past preoccupation with self-esteem, the study we report here suggests that when people are allowed more freedom in describing themselves, fewer than 10 percent of their thoughts deal with self-evaluation.

We have been urging for some years that the researcher forego this reactive approach and take a somewhat lower profile toward the participants by studying the "spontaneous" self-concept. Instead of presenting the participants with the dimension on which they must describe themselves, they can be allowed to choose the dimensions that are salient and significant to them. We feel that there is more interesting information about the self-concept in the dimensions one chooses for describing oneself than in the positions to which one assigns oneself on dimensions presented by the experimenter.

DETERMINANTS OF SPONTANEOUS SALIENCE

The determinant of spontaneous salience on which we particularly focus here is the distinctiveness of the personal characteristic in question. For several years we have been working on the problem of how people cope with informational overload. Although we pointed out that various coping strategies are available (e.g., chunking, temporary storage, parallel processing, and selectivity), our own empirical work has focused exclusively on perceptual selectivity as a means of handling informational overload. And while we have mentioned many determinants of which aspects of our perceptual field are singled out for noticing, we have concentrated on distinctiveness as a determinant of perceptual selectivity. Our guiding theoretical notion is that the person in a complex stimulus field focuses on points of maximum information, so that one selectively notices the aspects of the object that are most peculiar.

The spontaneous self-concept is a particularly appropriate domain in which to test this postulate. Each person is his or her own most complex stimulus object, both because the human being is intrinsically complex and because each of us is so familiar with our own complexities. Hence, when an internal need or external demand requires that we consider our identity (who we are, what kind of person we are), any of a vast variety of personal characteristics could occur to us. The distinctiveness theory of selective perception, when applied to this spontaneous self-concept, predicts that we notice any aspect (or dimension) of ourselves to the extent that our characteristic on that dimension is peculiar in our social milieu. For example, because the majority of our associates are right-handed, it is more likely for sinister people to notice their left-handedness than for dexterous people to think of themselves as right-handed. Again, given that a person is a black woman, she is more likely to be aware of her womanhood when she is associating with black men and of her blackness when she is associating with white women. The research reported here is designed to test this kind of prediction.

Our stress on personal distinctiveness as a determinant of what is noticed in one's spontaneous self-concept might overshadow other determinants of trait salience. To avoid complete neglect of these other factors, we shall mention briefly six other determinants of what is spontaneously salient in the self-concept. First, situational demand probably has a considerable effect. If someone says, "Tell me about yourself," the self-perceptions evoked are likely to be quite different depending on whether the question has been put by a prospective employer or by a smiling new acquaintance at a singles party. Second, stimulus intensity is probably operative because an individual is more likely to think of a more gross characteristic, such as hair color, than a more subtle one, such as shape of eyebrows, and of a broken leg rather than an ingrown toenail. Third, availability (in the sense of recency, familiarity, and expectation) will affect what is spontaneously salient to the self-concept: We are more likely, for example, to think of a current rather than an earlier activity; and a person is more likely to think of health status in response to the question "Tell me about yourself" if he or she has just visited a physician.

The three variables just mentioned are situational determinants of salience in the self-concept. To observe the equal-time provision, we must now mention three determinants which have to do with the individual's internal motivational state. A fourth determinant of salience in the self-concept is the individual's momentary need: If asked to "tell us about yourself" by the admissions officer of one's prospective college, one would probably think of one's assets and past achievements with a social desirability bias. However, asked the same question by a psychoanalyst to whom one has gone for help, one might think of one's anxieties and past difficulties, thus showing a rarer social-undesirability biased scanning. A fifth determinant is one's enduring values: Given a deeply religious Methodist and a Methodist who is rather casual about religion, the former is more likely than the latter to think of denominational membership when asked for a self-description. Past reinforcement is a sixth determinant of salience: Whether one thinks of oneself in terms of race or religion would be affected by which characteristic had been most influential in determining one's rewards and punishments in the past.

This list of determinants of what is salient in the spontaneous self-concept could be extended indefinitely or revised completely if one chose alternate bases for analysis and experiments could be devised to evaluate the effect of each. In the present study, however, we confine ourselves mainly to testing the hypothesis that the distinctiveness of one's own characteristic on a given dimension is a major determinant of whether that dimension is spontaneously salient in one's self-concept.

METHOD

Procedure and Measures

First Session. The participants were sixth graders who took part in two sessions, scheduled a week apart, during their regular classroom work. The first session was devoted to obtaining the children's spontaneous self-concepts. At a time prearranged with the teacher, the experimenters entered the classroom and announced that they were conducting the "Tell us about yourself" test. Copies of the mimeographed test booklet were distributed to each member of the class. The children were told not to put their names on the booklet and assured that no one would know who had filled out any given book. They were asked to open the booklet to the first page, which was headed "Tell us about yourself," beneath which there was a series of numbered lines. They were then told that they would have seven minutes to write down on the lines all of the things about themselves that they thought of, writing each new thing on a new line as they thought of it. They were told that they could use a single word, a couple of words, or a whole sentence (whichever they preferred) to report each thing as they thought of it. The instruction to start was then given.

After seven minutes, the children were asked to stop writing on that part of the test and turn to the next page, headed "Describe what you look like," beneath which was again a series of numbered lines. They were given similar instructions to write on these lines each of the things that came to mind in answer to the question about what they looked like. It was mentioned that they would have four minutes to answer this item. They were then told to start and allowed four minutes to respond. The seven-minute response to the first, "Tell us about yourself," item is hereafter called the *general self-concept,* and the response to the second, "Describe what you look like," item will be called the *physical self-concept.* The responses to these two items provide the dependent variable measured to test the hypotheses that the more distinctive the characteristic, the greater the likelihood that it will be salient in one's spontaneous self-concept.

Second Session. The researchers returned the following week with a more structured questionnaire entitled the "Describe yourself list" on which the participants were asked for specific information about their physical appearance (e.g., height, weight, hair color, eye color), demographic characteristics (e.g., birthdate, birthplace), and household composition. The children were given as much time as they needed to fill out this structured questionnaire about themselves. The responses to each of these specific questions provided information both on each child's own characteristic on the given dimension and about the child's classmates' distribution over the characteristics on that dimension. This information allowed scoring the independent variable to which characteristics on the dimension were common and which were distinctive in the social milieu constituted by the child's classmates. For example, each child was classified with respect to weight into either the middle half or upper or lower quarters of the class in weight; with respect to hair, into the modal color or some rarer color; with respect to sex, into the majority or the minority sex in the classroom, and so on. The distinctiveness theory was then tested by predicting, for example, that people who were found in the second session questionnaire to be unusually low or high in weight would have been more likely spontaneously to have mentioned their weight.

At the end of each of the two sessions, the children were asked to draw some design of their choice on the cover sheet of that session's booklet, and they were asked to use the same design in each session so that we could match the first and second session booklets from a given child without endangering anonymity. Matching handwriting also helped.

Sample

We wanted to test whether people think of themselves in terms of their peculiarities with respect to their significant reference groups.

We chose to study elementary school children because only at this level do the classroom groupings tend to be intact throughout the school day, thus providing a more meaningful reference group in terms of which to define characteristic peculiarity for each respondent. We collected the data while the children were in their intact classroom setting to enhance the class's status as a meaningful reference group. Because of this group administration, it was necessary that the spontaneous self-concept probes be answered in writing to avoid interference. Young children have difficulty on written tasks, so we chose to use sixth graders because they are the oldest students still within elementary schools.

All students in each of the ten classes (the advanced and a standard class from each of the five schools) were included in our sample if they attended school on both the days of our two sessions. A total of 252 students participated (class size ranged from 19 to 31), with six of the ten classes having 23, 24, or 25 students present at both sessions. There were 132 students in the advanced and 120 in the standard track; the group included 127 girls and 125 boys.

RESULTS AND DISCUSSION

Number of Characteristics Mentioned

Permissive measures like our open-ended spontaneous self-concept instrument are attractive in

that they allow respondents a great deal of freedom in expressing themselves and thus provide a large amount of information and unanticipated insights to the researcher. The disadvantage of such measures is that scoring the free responses is difficult and requires more subjective judgment on the part of the scorer than do instruments that enforce the participant's choosing responses from among a small set of predetermined alternatives.

Our procedure for scoring the two types of spontaneous self-concept protocols (the general and the physical) was to unitize each protocol and then classify each unit by a content-analysis procedure. Unitizing was achieved by dividing each protocol into individual thought elements, each of which expressed essentially one thing about the self. For example, a typical unitization is shown by the slash marks in the following paragraph:

> I am twelve years old/ I was born in South Carolina/ I have two sisters/ and a dog/ I have a babysitting job every day after school/ I am a good roller skater/ I hate arithmetic/ but I like our teacher/ My father works in a bank/ I wish I could lose some weight.

By this unitizing procedure, it was determined that the 252 students produced 2,659 units in their seven-minute response protocols to the general "Tell us about yourself" probe, or an average of 10.98 units per student. On the four-minute responses to the "Describe what you look like" physical self-concept probe, they produced 1,411 units, or an average of 5.62 units per student.

Types of Characteristics Mentioned

After each self-concept protocol was divided into units, each item was copied on a separate slip and sorted among eight major categories which included significant other people, physical characteristics, demographic characteristics, self-evaluations, school, own activities, own attitudes and miscellaneous. Each of the eight categories was divided into subcategories.

The distribution over the content-analysis categories of the 2,659 items generated by the 252 sixth graders in response to the request "Tell us about yourself" shows that almost a quarter of all of the responses fell in the habitual activities categories (recreations, daily routine, etc.). Another fifth of the items was composed of mentions of significant other people—mostly the children's parents, siblings, and friends, though pets were mentioned rather frequently. There were about half as many mentions of pets as of family members or friends, even though fewer than half of the students had pets. Hence, it might be said that given that a child has a pet, she or he is more likely to mention that pet than to mention all other family members combined. Teachers (almost always one's current teacher) were the only other category of significant others to receive frequent mention, though less frequent than one's dog, despite the fact that everyone had a teacher and only a minority had dogs. Aside from these four categories of significant others (family, friends, pets, and teachers) there were practically no other mentions of people in the life space represented by these children's spontaneous self-concepts.

The third most frequent category of mentions was one's attitudes, with particularly frequent mentions of likes and dislikes, which constituted the most popular of all 35 subcategories. There were numerous mentions also of hopes and desires (though far fewer than of likes and dislikes), especially regarding future jobs. Even though these children were only 12 years old, 18 percent of them did mention career aspirations in response to the request "Tell us about yourself."

Mentions of school constituted another 15 percent of all items (or 17 percent if we group mention of teachers here instead of with significant others). Demographic characteristics constituted 12 percent of the mentions, with age, residence, and name being the most frequent. It is interesting that in responding to the request "Tell us about yourself" 19 percent of the children mentioned their names, even though the preexperimental instructions stressed that the study was an anonymous one and that they should not write their names on top of the page. On the other hand, the specific instructions said that they should write down whatever came to mind, and for 19 percent of the children their names apparently occurred spontaneously to them and were written down, despite the inhibiting earlier instructions. Probably an even larger proportion think of their names as a salient part of their self-concept, but their giving names here was depressed due to the explicit instruction regarding anonymity. The somewhat "touchy" demographic characteristics of sex, ethnicity, and religion were relatively rare, spontaneous mention of one's sex accounting for only about 1 percent of the total items and mentions of race and especially religion rarer still.

The self-evaluation category accounted for only 7 percent of all the responses. We complained in the introduction that about 90 percent of all self-concept studies focus on that one dimension of self-evaluation or self-esteem. When asked to talk about themselves, sixth graders think about things

other than self-evaluation about 93 percent of the time; therefore, it seems a disproportionate emphasis that researchers on the self confine almost all of their studies to the other 7 percent. When the children do mention self-evaluation, it tends to be in terms of morality ("I fight too much" or "I think I behave better than most people my age") and physical ("I'm not very well coordinated" or "I'm very strong"). Considerably less frequent are intellectual self-evaluations ("I'm terrible at arithmetic" or "I'm pretty smart"), and emotional self-evaluations appear very rarely ("I cry too easily").

Mentions of physical characteristics account for about 5 percent of the total spontaneous response units, these being confined almost entirely to the four categories of hair (usually hair color), weight, height, and eyes (almost invariably eye color). A final 1 percent of the items do not fall in any of the preceding seven categories and hence are classified as miscellaneous.

Distinctiveness and Spontaneous Salience

Each of the 25 subcategories of our content analysis that were used by at least 10 percent of the participants in giving their general self-concepts was examined for possible use in testing our distinctiveness hypothesis. Seven dimensions seemed to provide a suitable test. Three were demographic characterisics, of which two (age and birthplace) were testable only with the general self-concept because they were not reported as part of the physical self-concept; and the third characteristic (sex) could be tested with both the general and the physical self-concept since it was mentioned by at least 10 percent of the participants on each instrument. The other four usable dimensions were physical characteristics (hair color, eye color, weight, and height), each of which was testable with both general and physical self-concept data because it met the 10 percent occurrence criterion on each instrument. These seven categories of spontaneously salient characteristics supplied 9 percent of all mentions of the general self-concept and 41 percent of all physical self-concept mentions.

The other categories did not lend themselves to a clear test of the distinctiveness hypothesis either because their usage was rare or was very scattered and showed different bases of analysis from child to child.

Spontaneous Mention of Age. Age was mentioned by 25 percent of the children in response to the general "Tell us about yourself" self-concept probe. The distinctiveness theory prediction is that students close to the modal age of the class are less likely to mention their age spontaneously than are younger and older children who deviate more from the modal age. On the basis of the birthdate information they provided on their second-session questionnaire, the 252 children were partitioned into those who were within six months of the modal class age versus those more than six months younger or more than six months older than the class mode. Only 19 percent of children within six months of the class modal age spontaneously mentioned their ages, while 30 percent of those who were atypically young or atypically old spontaneously mentioned their ages.

Spontaneous Mention of Birthplace. Regarding birthplace, the distinctiveness hypothesis predicts that people born at places different from that of most of their associates are more likely to think of themselves in terms of their origin than are those who share their birthplace with most of their associates. The sixth graders who participated in this study were typically born, as might be expected, in the city where the study was done, 70 percent of them having been born in this metropolis. Only 6 percent of these natives spontaneously mentioned their birthplace, whereas 22 percent of those who had been born elsewhere spontaneously mentioned their birthplaces. When we partition the respondents' birthplace distribution at a still more extreme point, namely, into those born in the U.S. and the foreign born, the difference is still more pronounced. Only 7 percent of the children born in the U.S. spontaneously mention their birthplaces while 44 percent of the foreign born do.

This birthplace confirmation shows the distinctiveness hypothesis to be rather robust since several other determinants of perceptual selectivity are pitted against it. For example, both "social desirability" and "availability" factors would tend to push the relationship in the opposite direction. Coming from somewhere else and especially being foreign born would seem to be at least slightly undesirable and a social handicap in this sixth-grade milieu. Such a disadvantage would normally motivate repression of birthplace among the outsiders rather than the heightened salience which was found. Likewise, birthplace should be more "available" for the locally born because talking about the local city is probably much more frequent and recent in everyday conversation among these children than is talking about the more distant birthplaces. Yet the data indicate that the hypothesized peculiarity effect of these latter places

apparently overcame their social undesirability and their lesser recency and frequency so that they were more salient in the spontaneous self-concept.

Spontaneous Mention of Physical Characteristics. The remaining five dimensions about which predictions can be made on the basis of the distinctiveness hypothesis can be tested with both the general and the physical self-concept data because each dimension was spontaneously mentioned by at least 10 percent of the participants in response to both "Tell us about yourself" and "Describe what you look like." The results with respect to three of these dimensions (hair color, eye color, and weight) are very similar: For each dimension about $1\frac{1}{2}$ times as many people having unusual characteristics on the dimension spontaneously mentioned it than did those with the more typical characteristics, on both the general self-concept and the physical self-concept.

On the second-session questionnaire item, which specifically requested hair color information, most of the respondents (88 percent) reported that they had brown or black hair, and the remaining 12 percent answered that their hair color was either red or blond; hence, the former two colors were defined as typical and the latter two as distinctive.

To the second-session questionnaire item on eye color, 70 percent of the respondents reported brown eyes and only 21 percent reported blue or green eyes. The remaining 9 percent mentioned gradations of eye colors that we found difficult to classify, such as brownish-blue, green-brown, and the like, and so are not included in our analysis of the spontaneous mention data. On the physical self-concept, only 56 percent of those with the typical brown eyes spontaneously mentioned the fact, while 77 percent of those with the atypical blue or green eyes spontaneously mentioned it.

Again, as regards weight, the distinctiveness hypothesis is shown to be robust because it is once again pitted against the social desirability hypothesis which predicts that being overweight or underweight would be a social detriment and, thus, suppressed in thought and underreported. Any such suppression tendency seems to have been overridden by the increased salience produced by the distinctiveness effect.

Spontaneous Mention of Sex. When we lump all ten classes together, there are almost exactly as many girls as boys among our 252 participants, 127 versus 125. But when we look at sex composition on a class-by-class basis, we find that in five of the classes, boys are in the majority, whereas girls represent the majority in the other five classes. The discrepancy is not great: The majority sex exceeds the minority by an average of three persons in these classes of over 25 students, with the within-class excess ranging from one to five persons. However, even though the excess of the majority over the minority sex in any one class is not great, it does allow us to test the hypothesis, with both general and physical self-concept data, that members of the minority sex will more often spontaneously mention their sex than will the majority sex in that class. With the physical self-concept, there was a sizable and significant difference in the direction predicted. Over the ten classes, 26 percent of members of the minority sex in any given class spontaneously mentioned their sex, whereas only 11 percent of those in the majority sex mentioned their sex, yielding a difference significant beyond the .01 level. This sizable difference in the predicted direction is especially encouraging considering that the discrepancy in numbers between the two sexes in any classroom was not great.

The results for sex might be typical of other personally and socially important demographic dimensions, such as race and religion, which we were not allowed to study directly because of reluctance to embarass any of the children or to cause political problems for the schools. As mentioned, the distinctiveness postulate's implications regarding the effect of classroom racial (or the university's religious) composition on spontaneous salience of ethnicity in one's self-concept was an issue that initially attracted us to this school study. Our selective perception theory, that a person acts like an information-encoding machine, predicts that the more one is in a minority with respect to ethnic or religious group membership, the more salient this demographic characteristic becomes in one's self-concept. The theory also predicts that in any social group, ethnicity would have more overall salience as it had more information value, namely, that ethnicity becomes more salient as increasing numbers of different ethnic groups are represented and as the group members are more equally distributed over the various ethnic groups. The effect of sex on salience, as the classroom sex

composition varied, provided an analogous test of the ethnicity and religious salience prediction. . . .

Further Directions of This Research

We are continuing this research in three directions. First, our original hypothesis, that distinctiveness is an important determinant of selective perception, is being tested in terms of our perceptions of external stimuli (other persons and non-human entities) rather than the internal self-concept. A second line of research pursues incidental findings of the present study. For example, we are testing the spontaneous self-concept of children at a wider range of ages, from first grade through twelfth grade (using individual testing so that oral responses can be obtained, thus allowing testing to extend to younger children), in order to test the developmental aspects of the salience of one's sex in one's spontaneous self-concept.

Finally, we are taking an even lower theoretical posture with respect to our data by doing a descriptive study of developmental trends in the general self-concept without regard to any single theory. That is, we are obtaining the self-concepts from first through twelfth graders, under standardized conditions, to see how the life space of the child changes in content and structure over the ages 6 through 18. Our distinctiveness postulate enabled us to make predictions about 9 percent of the material we elicited in the general self-concept. Our current, more descriptive "ecology of mind" approach allows us to deal also (admittedly, less elegantly) with the other 91 percent of the general self-concept protocols. We are attempting to describe developmental trends in what gets mentioned both as a main effect of age and in interaction with other situational and personal variables. In addition, we are interested in the structure of these responses, hoping to test notions about the structure and functioning of mind, by analyzing which items follow others in these free and spontaneous self-concepts. This work involves several cycles of tedious content analysis, and although many data have been collected, it will be some time before we turn in our accounts.

REFERENCES

Wylie, R. C. *The self-concept: A critical survey of pertinent research literature.* Lincoln: University of Nebraska Press, 1961.

Wylie, R. C. *The self-concept: A review of methodological considerations and measuring instruments.* (Vol. 1). Lincoln: University of Nebraska Press, 1974.

WHEN BELIEF CREATES REALITY: THE SELF-FULFILLING IMPACT OF FIRST IMPRESSIONS ON SOCIAL INTERACTION

MARK SNYDER

How do you come to know and like another person? Presumably, it is a fairly straightforward process in which you observe what the other person is like and then decide whether you are attracted to him or her. However, the assumption that you are the passive observer of another person's inherent charms and foibles may be quite erroneous. According to Snyder in "When Belief Creates Reality," you are more likely to be the active creator of the person you think you see. That is, your initial impression of what a person is "really" like will determine how you behave toward her or him, and your behavior will, in turn, shape the person's responses in ways that confirm your initial expectations. The lesson to be learned from this process is that what you find beautiful or ugly about another person often reflects what is beautiful or ugly about yourself.

For the social psychologist, there may be no processes more complex and intriguing than those by which strangers become friends. How do we form first impressions of those we encounter in our lives? How do we become acquainted with each other? When does an acquaintance become a friend? Why do some relationships develop and withstand the test of time and other equally promising relationships flounder and fall by the wayside? It is to these and similar concerns that my colleagues and I have addressed ourselves in our attempts to chart the unfolding dynamics of social interaction and interpersonal relationships. In doing so, we chose—not surprisingly—to begin at

the beginning. Specifically, we have been studying the ways in which first impressions channel and influence subsequent social interaction and acquaintance processes.

When we first meet others, we cannot help but notice certain highly visible and distinctive characteristics such as their sex, age, race, and bodily appearance. Try as we may to avoid it, our first impressions are often molded and influenced by these pieces of information. Consider the case of physical attractiveness. A widely held stereotype in this culture suggests that attractive people are assumed to possess more socially desirable personalities and are expected to lead better personal, social, and occupational lives than their unattractive counterparts. For example, Dion, Berscheid, and Walster (1972) had men and women judge photographs of either men or women who varied in physical attractiveness. Attractive stimulus persons of either sex were perceived to have virtually every character trait that pretesting had indicated was socially desirable to that participant population: "Physically attractive people, for example, were perceived to be more sexually warm and responsive, sensitive, kind, interesting, strong, poised, modest, sociable, and outgoing than persons of lesser physical attractiveness" (Berscheid & Walster, 1974, p. 169). This powerful stereotype

© 1977 by Mark Snyder.

This research was supported in part by National Science Foundation Grant SOC 75-13872, "Cognition and Behavior: When Belief Creates Reality," to Mark Snyder. For a more detailed description of the background and rationale, procedures and results, implications and consequences of this investigation, see M. Snyder, E. D. Tanke, & E. Berscheid, Social perception and interpersonal behavior: On the self-fulfilling nature of social stereotypes. *Journal of Personality and Social Psychology*, 1977. For related research on behavioral confirmation in social interaction, see M. Snyder & W. B. Swann, Jr., Behavioral confirmation in social interaction: From social perception to social reality. *Journal of Experimental Social Psychology*, 1978.

was found for male and female judges and for male and female stimulus persons. In addition, attractive people were predicted to have happier social, professional, and personal lives in store for them than were their less attractive counterparts. (For an excellent and comprehensive review, see Berscheid & Walster, 1974.)

What of the validity of the physical attractiveness stereotype? Are the physically attractive actually more likable, friendly, sensitive, and confident than the unattractive? Are they more successful socially and professionally? Clearly, the physically attractive are more often and more eagerly sought out for social dates. And well they should be, for the stereotype implies that they should be perceived as more desirable social partners than the physically unattractive. Thus, it should come as little surprise that, among young adults, the physically attractive have more friends of the other sex, engage in more sexual activity, report themselves in love more often, and express less anxiety about dating than unattractive individuals do. But the effect is even more general than this. Even as early as nursery school age, physical attractiveness appears to channel social interaction: The physically attractive are chosen and the unattractive are rejected in sociometric choices.

A differential amount of interaction with the attractive and unattractive clearly helps the stereotype persevere because it limits the chances for learning whether the two types of individuals differ in the traits associated with the stereotype. But the point I wish to focus on here is that the stereotype may also channel interaction so as to confirm itself *behaviorally*. Individuals appear to have different patterns and styles of interaction for those whom they perceive to be physically attractive and for those whom they consider unattractive. These differences in self-presentation and interaction style may, in turn, elicit and nurture behaviors from the target person that are in accord with the stereotype. That is, the physically attractive may actually come to behave in a friendly, likable, sociable manner, not because they necessarily possess these dispositions, but because the behavior of others elicits and maintains behaviors taken to be manifestations of such traits.

In our empirical research, we have attempted to demonstrate that stereotypes may create their own social reality by channeling social interaction in ways that cause the stereotyped individual to behave in ways that confirm another person's stereotyped impressions of him or her. In our initial investigation, Elizabeth Decker Tanke, Ellen

Berscheid, and I sought to demonstrate the self-fulling nature of the physical attractiveness stereotype in a social interaction context designed to mirror as faithfully as possible the spontaneous generation of first impressions in everyday social interaction and the subsequent channeling influences of these impressions on social interaction. In order to do so, pairs of previously unacquainted individuals (designated for our purposes as a *perceiver* and a *target*) interacted in a getting-acquainted situation constructed to allow us to control the information that one member of the dyad (the male perceiver) received about the physical attractiveness of the other individual (the female target). In this way, it was possible to evaluate separately the effects of actual and perceived physical attractiveness on the display of self-presentational and expressive behaviors associated with the stereotype that links beauty and goodness. In order to measure the extent to which the self-presentation of the target individual matched the perceiver's stereotype, naïve observer-judges who were unaware of the actual or perceived physical attractiveness of either participant listened to and evaluated tape recordings of the interaction.

Fifty-one male and fifty-one female undergraduates at the University of Minnesota participated, for extra course credit, in what had been described as a study of the "processes by which people become acquainted with each other." These individuals interacted in male-female dyads in a getting-acquainted situation in which they could hear but not see each other (a telephone conversation). Before initiating the conversation, the male member of each dyad received a Polaroid snapshot of his female interaction partner. These photographs, which had been prepared in advance and assigned at random to dyads, identified the target as either physically attractive (attractive-target condition) or physically unattractive (unattractive-target condition). Each dyad engaged in a ten-minute unstructured telephone conversation that was tape-recorded. Each participant's voice was recorded on a separate channel of the tape.

In order to assess the extent to which the actions of the female targets provided behavioral confirmation of the male perceivers' stereotypes, twelve observer-judges listened to the tape recordings of the getting-acquainted conversations. The observer-judges were unaware of the experimental hypotheses and knew nothing of the actual or perceived physical attractiveness of the individual whom they heard on the tapes. They heard only those tape tracks containing the female participants' voices. Nine other observer-judges listened to and rated only the male perceivers' voices. (For further details of the experimental procedures, see Snyder, Tanke, & Berscheid, 1977.)

In order to chart the process of behavioral confirmation of stereotype-based attributions in these dyadic social interactions, we examined the effects of our manipulation of the target's apparent physical attractiveness on both the male perceivers' initial impressions of their female targets and the females' behavioral self-presentation during their interactions, as measured by the observer-judges' ratings of the tape recordings of their voices.

The male perceivers clearly formed their initial impressions of their female targets on the basis of general stereotypes that associate physical attractiveness with socially desirable personality characteristics. On the basis of measures of first impressions that were collected after the perceivers had been given access to their partners' photographs but before the initiation of the getting-acquainted conversations, it was clear that (as dictated by the physical attractiveness stereotype) males who anticipated physically attractive partners expected to interact with comparatively cordial, poised, humorous, and socially adept individuals. By contrast, males faced with the prospect of getting acquainted with relatively unattractive partners fashioned images of rather withdrawn, awkward, serious, and socially inept creatures.

Not only did our perceivers fashion their images of their discussion partners on the basis of their stereotyped intuitions about the links between beauty and goodness of character, but the stereotype-based attributions initiated a chain of events that resulted in the behavioral confirmation of these initially erroneous inferences. Analysis of the observer-judges' ratings of the tape recordings of the conversations indicated that female targets who (unbeknown to them) were perceived to be physically attractive (as a consequence of random assignment to the attractive-target experimental condition) actually came to behave in a friendly, likeable, and sociable manner. This behavioral confirmation was discernible even by outside observer-judges who knew nothing of the actual or perceived physical attractiveness of the target individuals. In this demonstration of behavioral confirmation in social interaction, the "beautiful" people became "good" people, not because they necessarily possessed the socially valued dispositions that had been attributed to them, but because the actions of the perceivers, which were based on their stereotyped beliefs, had erroneously confirmed and validated these attributions.

Confident in our demonstration of the self-fulfilling nature of this particular social stereotype, we then attempted to chart the process of behavioral confirmation. Specifically, we searched for evidence of the behavioral implications of the perceivers' stereotypes. Did the male perceivers present themselves differently to the target women whom they assumed to be physically attractive or unattractive? An examination of the observer-judges' ratings of the tapes of only the males' contributions to the conversations provided clear evidence that our perceivers did have different interactional styles with targets of different physical attractiveness.

Men who interacted with women whom they believed to be physically attractive appeared to be more cordial, sexually warm, interesting, independent, sexually permissive, bold, outgoing, humorous, obvious, and socially adept than their counterparts in the unattractive-target condition. Moreover, these same men were seen by the judges to be more attractive, more confident, and more animated in their conversation than their counterparts. They were also considered by the observer-judges to be more comfortable in conversation, to enjoy themselves more, to like their partners more, to take the initiative more often, to use their voices more effectively, to see their women partners as more attractive, and finally, to be seen as more attractive by their partners than men in the unattractive-target condition.

It appears, then, that differences in the expressive self-presentation of sociability by the male perceivers may have been a key factor in the process of bringing out those reciprocal patterns of expression in the target women that constitute behavioral confirmation of the attributions from which the perceivers' self-presentation had been generated. One reason that target women who had been labeled attractive may have reciprocated this sociable self-presentation is that they regarded their partners' images of them as more accurate and their style of interaction to be more typical of the way men generally treated them than women in the unattractive-target condition did. Perhaps, these latter individuals rejected their partners' treatment of them as unrepresentative and defensively adopted more cool and aloof postures to cope with their situations.

Our research points to the powerful but often unnoticed consequences of social stereotypes. In our demonstration, first impressions and expectations that were based on common cultural stereotypes about physical attractiveness channeled the unfolding dynamics of social interaction and acquaintance processes in ways that actually made those stereotyped first impressions come true. In our investigation, pairs of individuals got acquainted with each other in a situation that allowed us to control the information that one member of the dyad (the perceiver) received about the physical attractiveness of the other person (the target). Our perceivers ... fashioned erroneous images of their specific partners that reflected their general stereotypes about physical attractiveness. Moreover, our perceivers had very different patterns and styles of interaction for those whom they perceived to be physically attractive and to be unattractive. These differences in self-presentation and interaction style, in turn, elicited and nurtured behaviors of the targets that were consistent with the perceivers' initial stereotypes. Targets who (unbeknown to them) were perceived to be physically attractive actually came to behave in a friendly, likable, and sociable manner. The perceivers' attributions about their targets based on their stereotyped intuitions about the world had initiated a process that produced behavioral confirmation of those attributions. The initially erroneous impressions of the perceivers had become real. The stereotype had truly functioned as a self-fulfilling prophecy:

> The self-fulfilling prophecy is, in the beginning, a *false* definition of the situation evoking a new behavior which makes the originally false conception come *true*. The validity of the self-fulfilling prophecy perpetuates a reign of error. For the prophet will cite the actual course of events as proof that he was right from the very beginning. . . . Such are the perversities of social logic. [Merton 1948, p. 195]

True to Merton's script, our "prophets," in the beginning, created false definitions of their situations. That is, they erroneously labeled their targets as sociable or unsociable persons on the basis of their physical attractiveness. But these mistakes in first impressions quickly became self-erasing mistakes because the perceivers' false definitions evoked new behaviors that made their originally false conceptions come true: They treated their targets as sociable or unsociable persons, and, indeed, these targets came to behave in a sociable or unsociable fashion. Our prophets also cited the actual course of events as proof that they had been right all along. Might not other important and widespread social stereotypes—particularly those concerning sex, race, social class, and ethnicity—also channel social interaction in ways that create their own social reality?

Any self-fulfilling influences of social stereotypes may have compelling and pervasive societal consequences. Social observers have for decades commented on and demonstrated the ways in which stigmatized social groups and outsiders may fall victim to self-fulfilling cultural stereotypes. Consider Scott's (1969) observations about the blind:

> When, for example, sighted people continually insist that a blind man is helpless because he is blind, their subsequent treatment of him may preclude his own exercising the kinds of skills that would enable him to be independent. It is in this sense that stereotypic beliefs are self-actualized. [P. 9]

All too often, it is the victims who are blamed for their own plight . . . rather than the social expectations that have constrained their behavioral options.

REFERENCES

Berscheid, E., & Walster, E. Physical attractiveness. In L. Berkowitz (ed.), *Advances in Experimental Social Psychology.* Vol. 7. New York: Academic Press, 1974.

Dion, K. K., Berscheid, E., & Walster, E. What is good is beautiful. *Journal of Personality and Social Psychology,* 1972, *24,* 285–90.

Merton, R. K. The self-fulfilling prophecy. *Antioch Review,* 1948, *8,* 193–210.

Scott, R. A. *The Making of Blind Men.* New York: Russell Sage, 1969.

Snyder, M., Tanke, E. D., & Berscheid, E. Social perception and interpersonal behavior: On the self-fulfilling nature of social stereotypes. *Journal of Personality and Social Psychology,* 1977, *35,* 656–66.

PROJECTS

Name _____

Date _____

8.1: WHO AM I?

Each of us is a unique individual, quite distinct from other people. Yet, we all have much in common. You probably have your own theory about what makes you such a special person, what characteristics, behaviors, goals, accomplishments, and so on add up to "you." But do others see the same person that you see? Would they characterize you in the same way? If they see you differently, what is the basis for their divergent perceptions? The following exercise is designed to stimulate your thinking about the multiple identities or masks that you may possess.

A. Give 10 answers to the question: Who am I? Do this quickly, writing down your answers exactly as they come to mind.

1. _____

2. _____

3. _____

4. _____

5. _____

6. _____

7. _____

8. _____

9. _____

10. _____

B. Answer the same question the way you think your father or mother (choose one) would have answered it *about you.*

1. _____

2. _____

3. _____

4. _____

5. _____

6. _____

7. _____

8. _____

9. _____

10. _____

C. Answer the same question the way you think your best friend would have answered it *about you*.

1. _____

2. _____

3. _____

4. _____

5. _____

6. _____

7. _____

8. _____

9. _____

10. _____

D. Compare your three sets of answers and indicate the following:

1. What are the similarities? _____

_____

_____

_____

_____

_____

2. What are the differences? _____

_____

_____

_____

_____

_____

3. If there are differences, in what ways are they attributable to *you?* That is, to what extent do you act differently and adopt varying roles with others?

_____

_____

_____

_____

_____

_____

4. In what ways are the differences attributable to *others?* That is, how do *their* personalities and expectations shape the ''you'' that they see?

_____

_____

_____

_____

_____

_____

5. In evaluating your self-description (Part A), indicate which of the 10 answers referred to

a. physical characteristics _____

_____

b. psychological characteristics _____

_____

   c. social roles _____

   _____

6. Now indicate the *priority* you gave to these different types of characteristics. That is, which did you list first, second, and so on? Which type of characteristics did you use to describe yourself, and what implications might this have for your conception of self?

_____

_____

_____

_____

_____

Name _____

Date _____

8.2: THE TRANSPARENT SELF

Sidney Jourard in his book, *The Transparent Self,* describes his research on self-disclosure. Some of the questions that interested him were:

Do people vary in the extent to which they disclose themselves to different target persons, such as mother, father, male friend, and female friend? What is the effect of marital status on self-disclosure to parents and friends? What is the effect of the feelings and attitudes toward particular target persons upon self-disclosure to them? For example, what is the relationship between disclosure of self to parents, and feelings and attitudes toward one's parents. Are there differences between categories of information about the self (*aspects* of self) with respect to self-disclosure? Do we tend to disclose some aspects of self more fully than others? Are there ascertainable racial differences with respect to self-disclosure? Are there sex differences regarding self-disclosure?

In order to investigate these questions, the *Self-Disclosure Questionnaire,* a 60-item questionnaire, was devised. The items are classified in groups of ten within each of six more general categories of information (aspects) about the self. We chose five items out of each category.

The answer sheet you have been given has columns with the headings "Mother," "Father," "Male Friend," and "Female Friend." Read each item on the questionnaire, and then indicate on the answer sheet the extent to which you have talked about that item to each person—that is, the extent to which you have made yourself known to that person. Use the following rating scale:

0: Have told the other person nothing about this aspect of me.
1: Have talked in general terms about this item. The other person has only a general idea about this aspect of me.
2: Have talked in full and complete detail about this item to the other person. He or she knows me fully in this respect and could describe me accurately.
X: Have lied or misrepresented myself to the other person so that he or she has a false picture of me.

The numerical entries are summed (Xs are counted as zeros), yielding totals which constitute the self-disclosure scores.

For your project—either as a class or as an individual—you can compare, like Jourard did, males to females, marrieds to singles, different target people, or different aspects of self-disclosure.

The Self-Disclosure Questionnaire	Mother	Father	Male Friend	Female Friend
Attitudes and Opinions				
1. What I think and feel about religion; my personal religious views.				
2. My views on the present government—the president, government, policies, etc.				

The Self-Disclosure Questionnaire	Mother	Father	Male Friend	Female Friend

3. My personal views on sexual morality—how I feel that I and others ought to behave in sexual matters.

4. My personal standards of beauty and attractiveness— what I consider to be attractive in a woman—man.

5. My feeling about how parents ought to deal with children.

Tastes and Interests

1. My favorite foods, the ways I like food prepared, and my food dislikes.

2. My favorite reading matter.

3. The kinds of movies that I like to see best; the TV shows that are my favorites.

4. My tastes in clothing.

5. My favorite ways of spending spare time, e.g., hunting, reading, cards, sports events, parties, dancing, etc.

Work (or studies)

1. What I find to be the worst pressures and strains in my work.

2. What I feel are *my* shortcomings and handicaps that prevent me from working as I'd like to, or that prevent me from getting further ahead in my work.

3. What I feel are my special strong points and qualifications for my work.

4. My ambitions and goals in my work.

5. How I really feel about the people that I work for, or work with.

Money

1. Whether or not others owe me money; the amount, and who owes it to me.

2. All of my present sources of income—wages, fees, allowance, dividends, etc.

3. My total financial worth, including property, savings, bonds, insurance, etc.

	Mother	Father	Male Friend	Female Friend

The Self-Disclosure Questionnaire

4. My most pressing need for money right now, e.g., outstanding bills, some major purchase that is desired or needed.

5. How I budget my money—the proportion that goes to necessities, luxuries, etc.

Personality

1. The aspects of my personality that I dislike, worry about, that I regard as a handicap to me.

2. The facts of my present sex life—including knowledge of how I get sexual gratification; any problems that I might have; with whom I have relations, if anybody.

3. Whether or not I feel that I am attractive to the opposite sex; my problems, if any, about getting favorable attention from the opposite sex.

4. Things in the past or present that I feel ashamed and guilty about.

5. What it takes to hurt my feelings deeply.

Body

1. My feelings about different parts of my body—face, legs, hips, waist, weight, chest or bust, etc.

2. Any problems and worries that I had with my appearance in the past.

3. Whether or not I now have any health problems— e.g., trouble with sleep, digestion, female complaints, heart condition, allergies, headaches, piles, etc.

4. Whether or not I have any long-range worries or concerns about my health, e.g., cancer, ulcers, heart trouble.

5. My feelings about my adequacy in sexual behavior— whether or not I feel able to perform adequately in sex relationships.

SOCIAL COGNITION

9

You have heard the old saying, "Beauty is in the eye of the beholder." That is, our judgments of beauty are based on the way we think about things. There are no universal, hard-and-fast characteristics of people or objects that are beautiful in and of themselves. Psychologists extend this argument to say that most of *reality* is in the eye—and mind—of the beholder. What we see in the world around us is as much the product of our personal biases, thoughts, and feelings as it is of what physically exists. Our perceptions are not a passive reflection of the environment; rather, they are the result of an active process of selecting, organizing, and interpreting various bits of information. We actually shape and create our reality, although we are often not aware of how much we do so. (Optical illusions provide one way of exploring the nature of this active, creative process. See, for example, the box on this topic.) As Lewis Mumford said, "What was once called the objective world is a sort of Rorschach ink blot, into which each culture, each system of science and religion, each type of personality, reads a meaning only remotely derived from

the shape and color of the blot itself" ("Orientation to Life," *The Conduct of Life,* 1951).

Social psychologists are particularly interested in people's perceptions of other people. We all make judgments about others and have different attitudes and feelings toward them. But where do these judgments come from? How do we know that a person is kind, aggressive, aloof, or trustworthy? How can we tell whether a person's compliment is sincere or merely currying favor? What is the basis for the good or bad feelings that we have about different people? We tend to assume that our reactions reflect what these people are really like. But in fact, they indicate a lot about what *we* are like. Our own expectations and attitudes bias what we see of other people and lead us to make certain interpretations about their behavior. We often see what we are prepared to see, either by focusing on particular characteristics of the person and ignoring others or by distorting what we remember about him or her. Nevertheless, these perceptual biases are also very valuable because they help us to organize and make sense of the chaotic mass of information that constantly bombards us.

THE EYE OF THE UMPIRE

Three baseball umpires were comparing notes on how they called balls and strikes. Because the outcome of a game may depend upon a single decision by the umpire, the question arose of how objective such decisions are.

"Well," said the first umpire, "I crouch in real tight behind the catcher, keep my eyes fixed on the ball at all times, and then when the ball is thrown, *I call it as it is.*"

"No, that's not right," replied the second ump. "I do what you do until

the pitcher throws the ball, and then *I call it as I see it.*"

The third ump smiled, "You guys are both wrong," he said. "I crouch down and keep my eye on the ball, too. But after the pitch, *it ain't nothing until I call it.*"

SOCIAL ROLES, SOCIAL CONTROL, AND BIASES IN SOCIAL-PERCEPTION PROCESSES

LEE D. ROSS, TERESA M. AMABILE, AND JULIA L. STEINMETZ

Suppose we see an employer giving authoritative commands to employees and loudly reprimanding someone who has made a mistake. What personal attributions are we likely to assign him or her? We will probably judge the employer to be someone who is authoritarian, rigid, cold, and insensitive to people's feelings. Thus, we would be very surprised if we discovered that same person to be warm and affectionate toward family and friends, a volunteer worker at a local charity, and so forth. What we have failed to recognize here is that the on-the-job behaviors are part of the social role of being a boss, and are not necessarily reflective of inner traits. The individual may even feel uncomfortable about publicly rebuking someone, but will do it because that is what a boss is supposed to do. Even though social roles can have an enormous influence on people's behavior, their power is not well recognized by outside observers. In the experiments reported in this article, Ross, Amabile, and Steinmetz demonstrate how this insensitivity to the power of social roles can bias the judgments we make.

Interpersonal encounters provide an important informational basis for self-evaluation and social judgment. Often, however, our performances in such encounters are shaped and constrained by the social roles we must play. Typically, roles confer unequal control over the style, content, and duration of an encounter; such social control, in turn, generally facilitates displays of knowledge, skill, insight, wit, or sensitivity, while permitting the concealment of deficiencies. Accurate social judgment, accordingly, depends upon the perceiver's ability to make adequate allowance for such role-conferred advantages and disadvantages in self-presentation.

The thesis of the present paper, and of the research it reports, is a simple one: In drawing inferences about actors, perceivers consistently *fail* to make adequate allowance for the biasing effects of social roles upon performance. The specific empirical demonstration reported here dealt with the particular roles of "questioner" and "answerer" and with the biased perceptions of general knowl-

edge that result from the arbitrary assignment and fulfillment of these roles. Subjects participated in a general knowledge "quiz game," in which one person was assigned the role of questioner and the other the role of answerer, or "contestant." The questioner first composed a set of challenging general knowledge questions and then posed them to the contestant; both participants (and, in a subsequent reenactment, a pair of observers) were then required to rate the questioner's and contestant's general knowledge.

It should be emphasized that the role-conferred advantages and disadvantages in self-presentation of general knowledge in the quiz game were neither subtle nor disguised. Questioners were allowed and encouraged to display their own wealth of general knowledge by asking difficult and esoteric questions, and their role, of course, guaranteed that they would know the answers to the questions asked during the quiz game. The contestant's role, by contrast, prevented any such selective, self-serving displays and made displays of ignorance virtually inevitable. In a sense, the arbitrary assignment and fulfillment of roles forced participants to deal with nonrepresentative and highly biased samples of the questioners' and contestants' general knowledge.

The primary experimental prediction was that the perceivers of the quiz game—the participants

L. D. Ross, T. M. Amabile, and J. L. Steinmetz. Social roles, social control, and biases in social-perception processes. *Journal of Personality and Social Psychology*, 1977, 35:7, 485–94. Copyright © 1977 by the American Psychological Association. Reprinted by permission of the publisher and author.

themselves and observers as well—would form relatively positive impressions of the questioners' general knowledge and relatively negative impressions of the contestants' knowledge. This prediction, it should be reemphasized, follows from the expectation that perceivers would consistently underestimate, and/or make inadequate allowance for, the biasing effects of the questioners' and contestants' roles upon their ability to display general knowledge advantageously.

EXPERIMENT 1: CONTESTANTS' AND QUESTIONERS' PERCEPTIONS

In Experiment 1, subjects performed the arbitrarily assigned roles of questioner or contestant in an oral quiz of general knowledge. In the experimental condition, questioners asked questions that they had composed themselves; in a yoked control condition they posed questions formulated by a previous questioner. All of the subjects rated their own general knowledge and that of their partners after the quiz session was completed, and then again after taking a written general knowledge quiz prepared by the experimenter.

METHOD

Subjects and Role Assignment

Eighteen male pairs and 18 female pairs of subjects were recruited from an introductory psychology class at Stanford University for a "quiz game" experiment. Upon their arrival at the laboratory, subjects were met by a same-sex experimenter, who explained that the study dealt with the processes by which "people form impressions about general knowledge." The experimenter then introduced the quiz format and explained that one subject would be given the "job of contestant" and the other the "job of questioner." The random and arbitrary nature of the role assignment was then made obvious to the subjects by having them each choose one of the two cards ("Questioner" or "Contestant") that had been shuffled and placed face down before them.

Questioner and Contestant Roles

The questioner and contestant in each session were seated at separate tables in the same room. Each received oral instructions and each heard the instructions given to his or her partner. These oral instructions were supplemented with more detailed written descriptions of their tasks and roles.

Twelve pairs of subjects of each sex participated in the *experimental* condition. In this condition, the questioners were instructed to compose ten "challenging but not impossible" questions for the contestant. They were cautioned to avoid both easy questions (e.g., the number of days in the month of April) and unfair questions (e.g., the name of the questioner's brother) and to draw from any area in which they had interest or expertise ("for example, movies, books, sports, music, literature, psychology, history, science, etc."). The questioner was instructed to complete, in ten or fifteen minutes, ten questions that could be answered in a word or two and to ask the experimenter for help if he or she had any problems. To aid the questioner in this task the experimenter offered a few sample questions (e.g., "What is the capital of New Mexico?") and suggested some possible areas or question formats (e.g., "You can ask about something you read in the news, or ask about the geography of a particular state, or ask what is the largest or the highest, etc.").

During the period in which the questioner composed difficult quiz items, the contestant also engaged in a question-preparation task. However, the contestant's task involved composing easy questions that would be irrelevant to subsequent advantages and disadvantages in self-presentation. The experimenter's instructions to the contestant emphasized the difference in tasks:

> Your job, as "contestant," will be to answer the questions that the questioner is now composing. Right now, however, we would like you to "warm up" for the quiz game by composing some questions of your own. These questions won't be used during this experiment; they're just for you to get into the spirit of our study. The questioner's instructions tell him or her to compose ten challenging questions of the type that are used in TV game shows. However, we want you to compose ten questions that are relatively *easy*, questions that could be answered by 90 percent of high school freshman.

Six pairs of subjects of each sex participated in the *control* condition. In this condition, both questioners and contestants were informed that for the quiz session, the questioner would ask questions prepared beforehand by another individual. Here, both the participants spent 15 minutes before the quiz preparing "easy general knowledge questions"; that is, their preparation task was identical to that of the contestants (but not that of the questioners) in the experimental condition. Again, both participants were fully aware of the details of each other's preparation and quiz game tasks.

The preparation period was followed by the quiz game: As described earlier, questioners in the experimental condition posed their own questions to the contestants; in the control condition, each questioner posed items prepared by someone else. It should be emphasized that the contestants were always aware of whether or not the questions were prepared by their own questioner or by someone else. During the quiz the questioner faced the contestant and waited about 30 seconds for the contestant's response to each question, acknowledging correct responses and supplying them when the contestant failed to answer or answered incorrectly. To minimize extraneous self-presentation evidence concerning general knowledge, all participants were instructed to say nothing beyond the questioning and answering demanded by their assigned roles.

Throughout the quiz session, the experimenter recorded all responses given by the contestant, and made certain that the two participants properly fulfilled their roles. At the conclusion of the session, the experimenter noted aloud the number of correct responses made by the contestant.

Dependent Measures and Concluding Procedures

Immediately following the quiz game, the participants rated themselves and their partners on several scales anchored at "much better than average" and "much worse than average." The two most relevant measures required participants to rate themselves and their partners on general knowledge "compared to the average Stanford student."

The experimental session concluded with a detailed account by the experimenter of research hypotheses and postulated biases, along with a request that subjects not discuss the study's procedures and purposes with potential subjects.

RESULTS

Contestants' Performances

The quiz sessions of Experiment 1 were designed to confer a self-presentation advantage upon questioners relative to contestants. Thus it was intended and anticipated that contestants would be unable to answer most of the questions posed by the questioners. This precondition for testing our primary hypothesis was reasonably well met; overall, contestants correctly answered a mean of only 4.0 out of ten questions posed by questioners. This low performance rate was consistent with the level of difficulty of many of the questions asked (e.g., "What do the initials W. H. in W. H. Auden's name stand for?" and "What is the longest glacier in the world?").

General Knowledge Ratings

The principal dependent measures were ratings of general knowledge completed immediately following the quiz game. The results for experimental and yoked-control subjects in Experiment 1 are reported in Table 1.

Several comparisons reveal the extent to which the main experimental hypothesis was confirmed. In 18 of the 24 experimental-condition pairs, the contestant's self-rating was less positive than the questioner's self-rating, and in only four cases was the reverse true. Similarly, in 18 of 24 cases (with only five reverses) the contestants rated their questioners more positively than questioners rated their contestants.

An examination of the differences between

TABLE 1. MEAN RATINGS OF GENERAL KNOWLEDGE OF QUESTIONERS AND CONTESTANTS ON QUESTIONNAIRE IMMEDIATELY FOLLOWING QUIZ GAME

	MEASURE		
CONDITION	SUBJECT'S RATING OF SELF	SUBJECT'S RATING OF PARTNER	SELF-PARTNER DIFFERENCE
Experimental (n = 24)			
Questioner	53.5	50.6	2.9
Contestant	41.3	66.8	−25.5
Difference	12.2	−16.2	
Control (n = 12)			
Questioner	54.1	52.5	1.6
Contestant	47.0	50.3	−3.3
Difference	7.1	2.2	

Note: All ratings were made on 100-point scales. A higher number indicates more general knowledge relative to other Stanford students.

subjects' self-ratings and their ratings of their partners can clarify these results. These scores reveal that the contestants rated themselves far inferior to their questioners, while the questioners rated themselves slightly superior to their contestants. Furthermore, 20 contestants rated themselves inferior to their questioners, and only a single contestant rated himself superior to his questioner; on the other hand, 12 questioners rated themselves superior and 9 questioners rated themselves inferior to their contestants. These data leave little doubt that it was the contestants and not the questioners whose social perceptions were distorted by the fulfillment of the assigned roles.

Results from the control condition further illustrate the nature and degree of these distortions. The control-group questioners, it will be recalled, were denied the opportunity to display their own stores of esoteric knowledge to their contestants. Instead, they were limited to asking questions prepared by someone else. Control-condition contestants, accordingly, were less prone than experimental-condition contestants to rate themselves negatively in relation to their partners. Control-condition questioners, by contrast, produced ratings of self and partner that were virtually indistinguishable from those of experimental-condition questioners.

EXPERIMENT 2:
OBSERVERS' PERCEPTIONS

A second demonstration experiment exposed observers to close simulations of the interactions that had occurred between questioners and contestants in Experiment 1. Experiment 2 thus permitted comparison of the observers' relatively impersonal and objective assessments with those of the two personally involved actors in Experiment 1. The experimental prediction paralleled that of Experiment 1. It was predicted that observers, like the actors themselves, would make inadequate allowance for role-conferred advantages and disadvantages in personal presentation and, in so doing, would judge the contestants to be inferior in general knowledge to the questioners.

METHOD

Personnel and Procedures

Two female confederates were recruited to simulate the 12 sessions from Experiment 1 involving the female pairs in the experimental group. Each simulation was observed by one male and one female undergraduate and each of the original sessions was simulated twice (thereby allowing the two confederates to alternate questioner and answerer roles). A total of 48 subjects, 24 males and 24 females, were recruited from the introductory psychology class to serve as observers in Experiment 2.

The subjects were led to believe that the simulation was authentic—that they personally just happened to be the ones randomly assigned to the role of observers, that the two confederates just happened to receive the two participant roles, and that the quiz game was genuine rather than contrived. The assignment of roles was accomplished through a procedure similar, at least from the subjects' viewpoint, to that followed in Experiment 1. That is, all four participants picked a card at random from among those four shuffled and placed face down before them. All of the cards, in fact, read "Observer": The confederates simply claimed that their cards had read "Questioner" and "Contestant" as dictated by the experimental design.

The simulation unfolded just as the experimental sessions had in Experiment 1. Upon oral instructions from the experimenter (heard by the observers), the confederate playing the role of questioner pretended to compose ten items for the quiz session, while the contestant pretended to prepare a set of easy questions. During this question-preparation period, the observer subjects also composed easy questions in the manner previously described for Experiment 1 contestants. The questioner's quiz questions and the contestant's responses were identical to those that had been recorded in Experiment 1 for the original pair of subjects. During the quiz session, the subjects watched the participants closely, without speaking, as instructed by the experimenter.

After the quiz simulation, the observers rated the contestant's and questioner's general knowledge. In virtually all respects the experimenter's instructions and descriptions of purpose were unchanged from Experiment 1.

RESULTS

Observers' impressions of the participants in the quiz game showed the same bias that was evident in the participants' own perceptions. Overall, the questioner is seen as tremendously knowledgeable; the contestant is seen as only slightly less knowledgeable than the average Stanford student (see Figure 1).

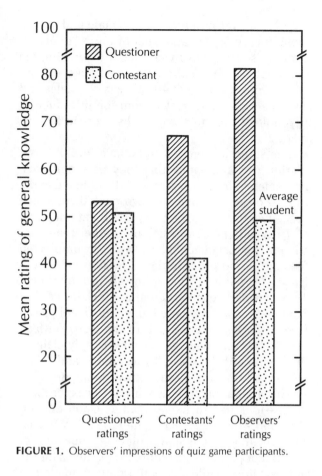

FIGURE 1. Observers' impressions of quiz game participants.

These results further support and clarify the findings for Experiment 1: In a sense, the observers necessarily shared the perspective of the contestants. Like the contestants, the observers almost certainly found that they were unable to answer the difficult questions posed by the questioners. What the observers, like the contestants, failed to recognize was that the questioners did not possess any superiority in general knowledge—they merely had exploited the opportunity to choose the particular topics and specific items that most favorably displayed their general knowledge.

GENERAL DISCUSSION

Attribution Error and Sampling Bias

The two experiments reported here clearly demonstrate that social perceivers may fail to make adequate allowance for the role-conferred advantage in self-presentation enjoyed by questioners relative to contestants. This failure was demonstrated by contestants and by observers but not by questioners. When the questioner's role retained

its title but lost its self-presentation advantage (i.e., in the control condition), the distortion in judgment disappeared.

A conception of the social perceiver as an "intuitive psychologist" who must draw inferences from the social data he samples, stores, retrieves, and analyzes (cf. Ross, 1977) suggests an interpretation of the demonstration experiments reported in the present paper. Ratings of general knowledge were made on the basis of data furnished during the quiz game. In fact, it is apparent that distorted judgments about the participants in the game were based on highly unrepresentative data samples, systematically *biased* to favor the questioner. Consider the quiz items prepared by the questioners. These surely were the most biased samples imaginable of their general knowledge; indeed, an item was presented to a contestant (and to observers) only if the questioner both knew the answer *and* anticipated that the contestant would be unlikely to know it. The present findings suggest that this tremendously biased sample of the questioner's knowledge was nevertheless treated by the contestant and by subsequent observers as reasonably representative. These raters apparently failed to make adequate allowance for the fact that, had the role assignments been reversed, the contestants could have just as easily prepared questions that would have stumped their questioners and revealed their own knowledge to best advantage.

Judgments about the Questioner

The contestants and observers alike had access to only one sample of the questioner's general knowledge, that flattering sample of ten difficult questions prepared for the quiz game. The contestants and observers knew, of course, that the relevant sample was not random; indeed, they knew precisely how it was drawn and why it was biased. Nevertheless, they consistently rated the questioners as highly knowledgeable.

The questioners, by contrast, were not forced to rely uniquely upon the ten-item sample available to contestants and observers. The questioners had a lifetime of experience and social comparison to draw upon in assessing their own knowledge; moreover, they were aware of the vast areas of ignorance they had passed over in searching for optimal topics and specific items. It is consistent with our analysis, therefore, that questioners did not rate themselves as superior to the average of their peers.

Judgments about the Contestant

The sample of the contestant's knowledge provided by the quiz game was not really biased or unrepresentative. It was a reasonably random sample of his or her ability to answer relatively difficult and obscure general knowledge questions. As our analysis would dictate, the questioners and observers rated the contestant, overall, as "average" in general knowledge. It is interesting to note that the contestant did downgrade his or her own knowledge somewhat as a result of the quiz-game experience. This probably resulted not from any distortion in self-perception but rather from the basis of comparison (i.e., the "average Stanford undergraduate") used in the rating. The contestant might have been led to overestimate the knowledge of the population from whom his partner was sampled on the basis of this one vivid and concrete experience.

Social Roles and Social Perceptions

The phenomenon demonstrated in the two present experiments has clear implications for role-constrained encounters outside the laboratory. In fact, the specific relationship between advantaged questioners and disadvantaged contestants has obvious parallels within academic settings. Teachers consistently enjoy the prerogatives of questioners and students typically suffer the handicaps of answerers (although some students leap at opportunities to reverse these roles). Consider, as a particularly dramatic instance, the role-constrained encounters that characterize the typical dissertation "orals." The candidate is required to field questions from the idiosyncratic and occasionally esoteric areas of each examiner's interest and expertise. In contrast to the examiners, the candidate has relatively little time for reflections and relatively little power to define or limit the domains of inquiry. In light of the present demonstrations, it might be anticipated that the typical candidate leaves the ordeal feeling more relief than pride, while his or her examiners depart with increased respect for each others' insight and scholarship. Such evaluations, of course, may often be warranted; however, they may also reflect in whole or in part the inadequate allowance made for advantages and disadvantages in personal presentation. Perhaps an alternative procedure for the oral examination, one in which the candidate first posed questions for his examiners and then corrected their errors and omissions,

might yield more elated candidates. Such a procedure might also produce examiners more impressed with the candidate and less impressed with each other.

The present demonstrations dealt with encounters between questioners and answerers, but there are countless other contexts in which social roles bias interpersonal encounters and, consequently, interpersonal judgments. The basis for role-differentiated behavior in an encounter may be formal, as in the interactions between employers and employees, or it may be informal, as in the encounters between a domineering individual and a reticent one. Regardless of its basis, however, this role differentiation creates unequal control and unequal opportunity for advantaged self-presentation. Thus the employer can discuss his personal triumphs, avocations, and areas of expertise without risk of interruption while the employee enjoys no such opportunity. Similarly, the domineering partner in a friendship can determine whether poetry or poker will furnish the arena for personal presentation, and the choice is apt to be self-serving. Again, we do not contend that the participants or relevant observers are oblivious to the inequality of the participants' opportunities for advantageous self-presentation. Rather, we contend that the social judgments of the disadvantaged and of relevant observers will reveal inadequate *allowance* or *correction* for such inequalities.

It is important to resist premature generalizations and conclusions based on the present specific demonstrations. Nevertheless, if subsequent research demonstrates a more general tendency for disadvantaged social participants and observers to make inadequate allowance for the self-presentation advantages of role and rank, the implications may be all too clear. Individuals who, by accident of birth, favorable political treatment, or even their own efforts, enjoy positions of power, also enjoy advantages in self-presentation. Observers of such social interactions and the disadvantaged participants (although not the advantaged ones, if the present results are representative) are apt to underestimate the extent to which the seemingly positive attributes of the powerful simply reflect the advantages of social control. Indeed, this distortion in social judgment could provide a particularly insidious brake upon social mobility, whereby the disadvantaged and powerless overestimate the capabilities of the powerful who, in turn, inappropriately deem members of their own caste well-suited to their particular leadership tasks.

REFERENCES

Ross, L. The intuitive psychologist and his short-comings: Distortions in the attribution process. In L. Berkowitz (ed.), *Advances in Experimental Social Psychology* (Vol. 10). New York: Academic Press, 1977.

OPTICAL ILLUSIONS

Perception, whether of people, objects, or events, concerns the way we interpret information received from the environment and then organize it into meaningful patterns. This process of information gathering and analysis forms the basis of all our agreed-upon knowledge of the universe, yet most of the time we take it for granted. Indeed, we usually pay attention to our perceptual processes only when our senses are jarred by unexpected or ambiguous features of the objects and events we encounter, as indicated in the common expression of surprise, *"I can't believe my eyes."*

Three different types of optical illusions are shown on p. 209. All three examples contain elements that play tricks on the perceiver. It is through such devices as these simple illusions that scientists have come to a better understanding of how our perceptual processes work under normal conditions. One thing is clear—our expectations of the ways things are supposed to be can make it difficult, if not impossible, for us to experience things as they really are; and so, what our eyes witness and transmit to the brain may be quite unreliable information. In order to grasp what is going on in the figures and sentences that follow, you probably should not believe your eyes.

(For an explanation of the illusions, see p. 210).

(1)

Can you find the end of the top staircase?

(2)

Can you read this sentence out loud correctly?

A BIRD IN THE
THE HAND IS WORTHLESS.

Using only your eye, count the number of F's in the sentence below.

Fascinating fairytales of faraway lands are the fertilizer for the fructification of the creative minds of the future.

(3)

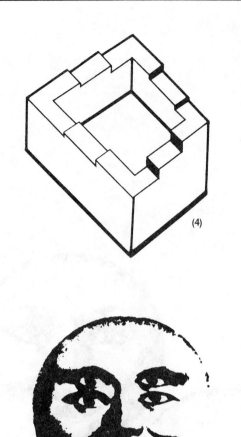

(4)

(5)

In the lithograph (1), M. C. Escher used a classic example of an irrational figure (4) to form the staircase on the top of the building. Though most of the monks in the picture are climbing stairs endlessly, there are two who refuse to take part in this meaningless exercise. Escher said that sooner or later they would be brought to see the error of their nonconformity and would join their fellow monks.

By duplicating the eyes and mouth on the faces (2), a "conflict" of grouping is created. At first glance you probably saw only a normal number of features, since the eye finds it difficult to interpret unfamiliar repetitions in familiar figures.

The tricky phrase that makes up the first part of the third illusion (3) contains the word "the" twice, one after the other. But because the two "thes" appear on separate lines, the lazy eye ignores the second one and rushes to finish the sentence. Seeing the word "worthless" (instead of the familiar ending to this phrase) confuses some people so much that even on second glance the illusion goes undiscovered.

The second deceptive sentence contains eleven F's. If you counted only eight, you probably skipped the word "of," which appears three times. We read "of" as "ov" and thus tend to overlook the "f" in the word.

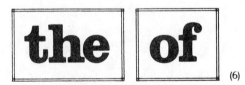

the of

(6)

PSYCHOLOGY OF THE EYEWITNESS

ROBERT BUCKHOUT

The creative aspect of the perceptual process can be valuable, but it can also be detrimental. In a situation in which a premium is placed on completely accurate observation, perceptual biases can cause problems. The courtroom presents just such a situation. There, the goal is to determine "the truth, the whole truth, and nothing but the truth." To accomplish that goal, witnesses are called to testify under oath about the facts of a case. There is often conflicting testimony about those facts, but that is not necessarily the result of deliberate misrepresentation. Even with the best of intentions to be completely objective, witnesses are not, and cannot be, infallible. Just as, in the famous parable, three blind men gave totally different (but "truthful") descriptions of an elephant, many witnesses may give differing accounts of an incident as a function of the way in which they perceived it. Their personal biases and expectations may lead them to make different judgments about a person or recall different aspects of the event. They are being truthful in their reports, but it is the truth as they saw it. The subjective and creative qualities of their perceptions and memories may have distorted the content of that report.

In "Psychology of the Eyewitness," Buckhout presents a thorough analysis of the limitations and possible pitfalls of courtroom evidence. He draws on a wide variety of studies to demonstrate the applicability of person perception research to the real-life situation of legal proceedings. Although there is as yet no adequate alternative to eyewitness testimony, a recognition and understanding of the errors that an eyewitness may make would surely aid in making the justice system more sensitive to its human frailty.

If you see an auto accident or witness a murder, and are then asked to describe what you saw, there is no one who can create an instant replay in slow motion for you. You depend upon your memory with all its limitations—a fact which may be of minor importance in your ordinary daily activities. If you are unreliable, if you shade the truth in describing what you saw, it matters little. But when you are called in as a witness to a crime, the situation escalates in importance. A person's life or an institution's reputation may be at stake. You may be asked to report what you saw in excruciating detail as if you were a videotape recorder.

In court, the written transcript contains your replay of the events. The prosecutor will attempt to show that you have perfect recall; the defense attorney will try to show, by cross-examining you vigorously, that your "tape recorder" is defective. The stakes are high because in modern courts eyewitness testimony is more highly valued than alibi testimony or "circumstantial" evidence. Uncritical acceptance of eyewitness testimony seems to be based on the fallacious notion that the human observer is a perfect recording device—that everything that passes before his or her eyes is recorded and can be "pulled out" by sharp questioning or "refreshing one's memory." In a categorical statement, which psychologists rarely make, I argue that this is *impossible*—human perception and memory function effectively by being selective. A human being has no particular need for perfect recall; perception and memory are decision-making processes affected by the totality of a person's abilities, background, environment, attitudes, motives, and beliefs, and by the methods used in testing recollection of people and events.

As I work in criminal courts, I'm aware of a fundamental clash of conceptions—the nineteenth-century vs. the twentieth-century view of a person. The nineteenth-century view—embodied in psychophysics—asserted a scientific parallel between the mechanisms of the physical world and the mechanisms of the brain. The courts in the United States accept this nineteenth-century thinking quite readily—as does much of the public. However, modern psychologists have developed a conception of a whole human being as an information processing mechanism which is far more complex than the one in the nineteenth-century model. Unfortunately, research psychologists, who began by studying practical problems (functionalism), have become more esoteric in their research and less visible in the real world.

I regard the human observer as an active rather than a passive observer of the environment; motivated by (a) a desire to be accurate in extracting meaning from the overabundance of information which affects the senses; and (b) a desire to live up to the expectations of others and stay in their good graces, a factor which makes the eye, the ear, and other senses social as well as physical organs.

In our laboratory experiments on the physical capabilities of the eye and the ear, we speak of an "ideal observer," by which we mean a subject who would respond cooperatively to lights and tones with unbiased ears and eyes much like a machine. However, the ideal observer does not exist. In other words, the "ideal observer" is a convenient fiction. Great effort and expense are put into the design of laboratories to provide an "ideal physical environment" free of distractions to enable the observer to concentrate. Such ideal environments can be approached only in a laboratory; in the real world they are seldom, if ever, found. The non-machine-like human observer copes reasonably effectively in uncontrolled environments with a perceptual capability which fits the nature of a social being. The witness to a crime is engaged in what can be described as "one-shot perception."

In a machine we would expect that what comes out (the report) would be a direct function of what goes in (the input or stimulus). However, human perception can be characterized in terms of the phrase: "The whole is greater than the sum of the parts." This characterization reflects the ability of the human observer to take the fragments of information to which he or she has time to pay attention (i.e., actively reduce the information), and to reach conclusions based on his or her prior experience, familiarity, biases, expectancy, faith, desire to appear certain, etc. Most human observers, for example, look at the moon and see a sphere—despite their inability to verify the shape of the unseen side. The conclusion, in psychological

terms, is a decision efficiently arrived at and independent of the physical evidence which is incomplete.

As an eyewitness to crime, the fallible human observer is usually in a less than ideal environment. He or she is subject to factors which I believe inherently limit a person's ability to give a complete account of what took place or to identify the persons involved with complete accuracy.

The thrust of my research has been to learn about and describe (in a form useful to the criminal justice system) those factors which affect both the *recall* of events by a witness and his or her subsequent ability to make an *identification*. I've ventured into the courtroom in some 30 criminal trials discussing the following factors as they relate to eye-witness accounts.

STRESS

"I could never forget what he looked like!" This common statement expresses the faith that people have in their memory—even under stress. When a person's life or well-being is threatened, a stress pattern known as the General Adaptional Syndrome (GAS) can be expected to occur in varying degrees. . . . This pattern is due to an increase in adrenaline levels and involves increased heart rate, breathing rate, and higher blood pressure. The end result is a dramatic increase in available energy, making the person capable of running fast, fighting, lifting enormous weight—taking the steps necessary to ensure safety or survival.

But, if you are under extreme stress, you will be a less reliable witness than you would be normally. Research shows that observers are less capable of remembering details, less accurate in reading dials, less accurate in detecting signals when under stress. They are paying more attention to their own well-being and safety than to nonessential elements in the environment. My research with trained Air Force flight crew members confirms that even highly trained people became poorer observers when under stress. They never can forget the stress and what hit them; the events, being highly significant at the time, can be remembered. But memory for details, clothing worn, colors, etc., is not as clear. Time estimates are especially exaggerated under stress.

You might test this idea by asking a few people where they were in 1963 when they first heard the news of the assassination of President John F. Kennedy. Chances are they will recall vividly where they were and who they were with. But can they describe what they or the persons with them were wearing? Can those who witnessed the killing of Lee Harvey Oswald on television describe the people next to the killer? These are logical questions—seemingly trivial—but if you were asking them in court, would you be willing to agree that the witness might have been too concerned with more important things to pay attention?

PRIOR CONDITIONING AND EXPERIENCE

Psychologists have done extensive research on how *set,* or expectancy, is used by the human observer to make judgments more efficiently. In a classic experiment done in the 1930s, observers were shown a display of playing cards for a few seconds and asked to report the number of aces of spades in the display.[1] Most observers reported only three, when actually there were five. Two of the aces of spades were colored red instead of the more familiar black color. The interpretation was given that since people were so familiar with black aces of spades, they did not waste time looking carefully at the display. Thus efficiency, in this case, led to unreliable observation. In many criminal cases, the prior conditioning of the witness may enable him to report facts or events which were not present but which should have been. Our research also indicates that white observers show better recognition of white people than of black people in a lineup. Recent research supports the proposition that observers have better recognition of people of their own race.

PERSONAL BIASES AND STEREOTYPES

Expectancy in its least palatable form can be found in the case of biases or prejudices held by a witness. A victim of a mugging may initially report being attacked by "niggers," and may, because of limited experience as well as prejudice, be unable to tell one black man from another ("they all look alike to me"). In a classic study of this phenomenon, observers were asked to take a brief look at a drawing of several people on a subway train.[2] In the picture, a black man was seated and a white man was standing with a knife in his hand. When questioned later, observers tended to report having seen the knife in the hand of the black man.

Prejudices may be racial, religious, or based on physical characteristics such as long hair, dirty clothes, status, etc. All human beings have some stereotypes upon which they base perceptual judgments; stereotypes which lead not only to prejudice, but are a means of making decisions more efficiently. A witness to an auto accident may save thinking time by reporting his well-ingrained stereotype about "women drivers." But these shortcuts to thinking may be erroneously reported and expanded upon by an eyewitness who is unaware that he or she is describing a stereotype rather than the events which actually took place. If the witness's biases are shared by the investigator taking the statement, the report may reflect their mutual biases rather than what was actually seen.

UNFAIR TEST CONSTRUCTION

The lineup and the array of photographs used in testing the eyewitness's ability to identify a suspect can be analyzed as fair or unfair on the basis of criteria which most psychologists can agree on. A fair test should be designed carefully so that, first, all items have an equal chance of being selected by a person who didn't see the suspect; second, the items are similar enough to each other and to the original description of the suspect to be confusing to a person who is merely guessing; and last, the test is conducted without leading questions or suggestions from the test giver.

All too frequently, I have found that lineups or photographic arrays are carelessly assembled, or even rigged in such a way as to make the eyewitness identification test completely unreliable. If, for example, you present five pictures, the chance should be only 1 in 5 (20 percent) that any one picture will be chosen on the basis of guessing; but frequently, a single picture of a suspect may stand out. In the Angela Davis case, one set of nine pictures used to check identification contained three pictures of the defendant taken at an outdoor rally, two mug shots of other women showing their names, one of a 55-year-old woman, etc. It was so easy for a witness to rule out five pictures as ridiculous choices, that the "test" was reduced to four pictures—including three of Davis. This means that witnesses had a 75 percent chance of picking out her picture, whether they had seen her or not. Such a "test" is meaningless to a psy-

---

[1] J. S. Bruner and L. J. Postman, On the perception of incongruity: A paradigm, *Journal of Personality* 18 (1949): 206–223.

[2] G. W. Allport and L. J. Postman, in *Transactions of the New York Academy of Sciences* 8 (1945): 66.

chologist and probably tainted as an item of evidence in court.

Research on memory has also shown that if one item in the array of photos is uniquely different (in dress, race, height, sex, photographic quality, etc.), it is more likely to be picked out and attended to. A teacher making up a multiple-choice test designs several answers which sound or look alike to make it difficult for a person who doesn't know the right answer to succeed. Police lineups and photo layouts are also multiple-choice tests. If the rules for designing fair tests are ignored by authorities, the tests become unreliable.

So far I've presented the research framework on which I've built my testimony in court as an expert witness. The framework is built on the work of the past, much of which is familiar to a working psychologist, but is hardly the day-to-day conversation of adult Americans who become jurors. Some of the earliest psychologists, notably Münsterberg . . . , had written the essence of this analysis as far back as the beginning of this century. But there was a nagging gap between the controlled research settings which yield data on basic perceptual processes and some very important questions about perception in the less well controlled, but real world. Thus our laboratory and field studies are designed to evaluate eyewitness accuracy and reliability after seeing simulated crimes where we have a good record of the veridical (real) events for comparison. I began with a more detailed version of an experiment which Münsterberg and others had conducted over 65 years ago.

AN EXPERIMENTAL STUDY OF THE EYEWITNESS

In order to study the effects of eyewitness testimony in a somewhat realistic setting, we staged an assault on a California State University campus, in which a distraught student "attacked" a professor in front of 141 witnesses. We recorded the entire incident on videotape so that we could compare the veridical event with the eyewitness reports. After the attack we took sworn statements from each witness, asking them to describe the suspect, the incident, and the clothes worn (essentially a free recall process). We also asked for a confidence rating (0–100 percent) in their description. Another outsider, of the same age as the suspect, was on the scene.

Table 1 shows a comparison of the known characteristics of the suspect and the averages of the descriptions given by the witnesses. It is clear that

TABLE 1. COMPARISON OF AVERAGE DESCRIPTIONS BY 141 EYEWITNESSES WITH ACTUAL DESCRIPTION OF SUSPECT AND EVENTS

	KNOWN CHARACTERISTICS		AVERAGED DESCRIPTIONS
Duration of incident	34	sec	81.1 sec
Height	69.5	in	70.4 in
Weight	155	lb	180 lb
Age	25	yr	22.7 yr
Total accuracy score	28	pts	7.4 pts

the witnesses gave very inaccurate descriptions, a fact which has been demonstrated so often in this type of experiment that professors of psychology use this as a demonstration of the unreliability of the eyewitness. People tend to overestimate the passage of time—in this case by a factor of almost $2\frac{1}{2}$ to 1. The weight estimate was 14 percent higher, the age was underestimated, and the accuracy score—made up of points for appearance and dress—was only 25 percent of the maximum possible total score. Only the height estimate was close; but this may be due to the fact that the suspect was of average height. People will often cite known facts about the "average" man when they are uncertain—inaccurate witnesses' weight estimates correlate significantly with their own weight.

We then waited seven weeks and presented a set of six photographs to each witness individually, creating four conditions in order to test the effects of biased instructions and unfair testing on eyewitness identification. There were two kinds of instructions: Low Bias, in which witnesses were asked only if they recognized anybody in the photos; and High Bias, where witnesses were told that we had an idea of who the assailant was, and we made a plea for them to find the attacker in the photos. There were two types of photo spreads, using well-lit frontal views of young men the same age as the suspect. In the nonleading photospread (Figure 1), all six photos were neatly set out, with the same expression on all faces and similar clothing worn by all men. In the biased photo spread (Figure 2), the photo of the actual assailant was placed crooked in the array, and the suspect wore different clothing and had a different expression from the other photos. We thus violated good testing practice for the sake of comparison.

The results indicated that overall only 40 percent of the witnesses correctly identified the assailant; 25 percent of the witnesses identified the wrong man—an innocent bystander who had been

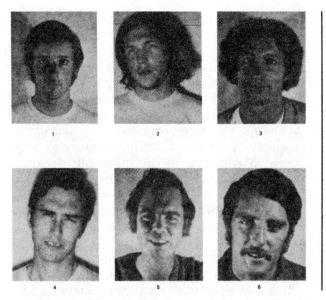

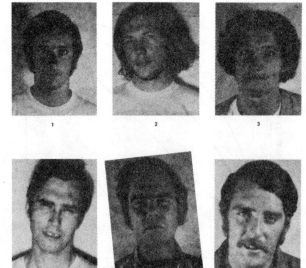

FIGURE 1. Example of a reasonably unbiased photo-spread lineup used in testing eyewitnesses to an assault. Number 5 was the perpetrator.

Confidence level

0-10-20-30-40-50-60-70-80-90-100%

FIGURE 2. Example of a biased photo-spread lineup used in testing witnesses to an assault.

Confidence level

0-10-20-30-40-50-60-70-80-90-100%

at the scene of the crime. Even the professor who was attacked picked out the *innocent* man from the photos as his attacker! Of those correctly identifying the assailant, the highest percentage correct was found in the condition where there was a combination of a biased set of photos and biased instructions. In some of our recent research we have tested the same photo spreads with a group of nonwitnesses, who also picked out suspect number 5. We thus demonstrated how the violation of good testing practices could lead to unreliable eyewitness identifications in a fairly realistic setting.

Our conclusions in this study were as follows. First, the reports of over 100 eyewitnesses to a crime were so highly unreliable that if an investigation began to find the person most witnesses described, the likelihood is high that attention would focus on the wrong person. Second, in following police procedures for testing identification through photographs, the presence of biased instructions and leading sets of photos can increase the percentage of witnesses who end up picking the photo toward which the authorities are already biased. Third, if the police are biased toward an innocent man, the presence of biased instructions and a leading set of photos could increase the likelihood that the wrong person would be identified.

Our more recent research is guided by the "signal detection" paradigm. This choice was made because signal detection theory evolved in psychophysics as a means of coping with the empirical fact that the observer's attitude "interferes" with the accurate detecting, processing, and reporting of sensory stimuli. An ideal observer has a clear distinction in mind as to what a signal (stimulus) is and what it is not. The task usually is to say whether a signal (e.g., a tone of a particular frequency) is present or not. The experimenter always presents the subject with some background noise, but only on half the trials will a low strength signal (the tone) also be present. In deciding whether the trial consists of noise alone or contains a signal, the subject employs a criterion which is influenced by individual factors such as personality, experience, anticipated cost or reward, or motivation to please or frustrate. The experimenter keeps track of both hits (correct "yeses") and false alarms (incorrect "yeses"), thus providing a quantitative estimate of the observer's criterion for judging his or her immediate experience. A very cautious person might have very few false alarms and a high number of hits, indicating that "yes" is being used sparingly. A less cautious observer might say "yes" most of the time, increasing the proportion of false alarms to hits.

In our experiment, we presented 20 to 25 state-

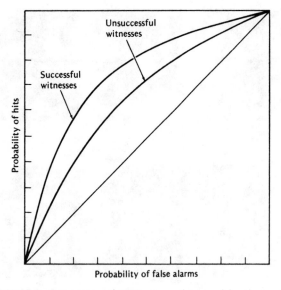

FIGURE 3. Comparison of ROC curves of successful and unsuccessful eyewitnesses where successful d′ = 1.18 and unsuccessful d′ = 0.74.

ments about the crime which were true and the same number which were false. The witness indicated yes or no and gave a confidence rating as well. We end up with a record of hits and false alarms based on the witness's recall of the crime. These data are combined statistically to produce Receiver Operating Characteristic (ROC) curves as shown in Figure 3. The straight line would be generated by a person or group whose hits and false alarms were equal—indicating that responses have no relationship to the facts. The sharper the curve, the more cautious the observer. The greater the area under the curve, the more sensitive was the witness to the difference between a true and a false statement. Our current studies indicate that the witnesses with better ROC curves in the laboratory perform more accurately in recognizing the suspect in a lineup. This observer sensitivity function enables us to test various hypotheses on how environmental conditions, stress, bias in interrogation, sex, and social milieu affect the accuracy and reliability of an eyewitness. Thus, we

are on the way toward developing a standardized test of eyewitness sensitivity, accuracy, and reliability.

One basic change has occurred in our research strategy. Instead of staging the crimes "live" in the classroom, we are using color and sound movies of carefully staged crimes. In part, we did this for control, but more importantly, the time of the apathetic bystander to a crime appears to have passed. Staging even an innocuous purse-snatching became dangerous for our "perpetrators" as a number of the (bigger) witnesses began to take off in hot pursuit of the purse-snatcher. No research is worth that much realism (at least my suffering assistants didn't think so)!

With the ROC curve as a measure of the sensitivity of witnesses, we can explore the extent to which biasing factors commonly encountered in court cases affect identifications. In our early studies, we found that witnesses who were ultimately successful in recognizing the suspect in a good lineup had shown high observer sensitivity scores during recall. People with low observer sensitivity scores tended to give height and weight descriptions which correlated with their own stature—confirming our belief that when pressured to give a description, witnesses fabricate their responses in the meaningful way that a perception researcher would expect.

We plan to refine the test, giving witnesses the chance to see several crimes. In this way we can check general reliability of a witness and test a number of hypotheses which police officers hold regarding older witnesses, women as witnesses, members of different racial and economic groups, etc. Thus, in one sense, we are just beginning a large research program which came from the real world to be absorbed into the laboratory—and changed the laboratory. Soon we hope to emerge from the laboratory and to bring the results back to the real world where they belong—and hopefully to utilize psychological knowledge to make eyewitness identification a more reliable and much fairer element in the judicial process.

PROJECTS

Name _____

Date _____

9.1: PERCEPTION OF MOTIVATIONS

This project is intended to give you an opportunity to evaluate fellow students and then to compare your evaluations with theirs. It lists several possible reasons why students decide to attend a particular college. Use the following scale to rate how important you think each of these reasons was in his or her choice of school: Rate one or two people (whose names will be given to you by your instructor) on 1 = not at all important, 2 = slightly important, 3 = moderately important, 4 = quite important, and 5 = extremely important.

Person being evaluated _____

Reason for choosing this college	Importance of reason (1–5)
Parental wishes	
Desire to get away from home	
Good scholastic reputation	
Good location	
Desire to find a marriage partner	
Good social life	
Ease of getting admitted	

Person being evaluated _____

Reason for choosing this college   Importance of reason (1–5)
_____

Parental wishes

Desire to get away from home

Good scholastic reputation

Good location

Desire to find a marriage partner

Good social life

Ease of getting admitted

Comments on the comparison between the two persons

Name _____

Date _____

9.2: ACTOR AND OBSERVER

According to Jones and Nisbett (1971), people make different attributions about themselves than about others. When they are evaluating their own behavior as *actors*, they are more likely to attribute it to external situational variables. However, when they are *observers* of someone else's behavior, they are more likely to attribute that action to internal personality traits. This exercise is designed to gather some data in order to test the validity of that proposition.

Collect a series of ratings from several people (students from another class, roommates), and record their responses on the data sheet. These ratings are evaluations of the characteristic behaviors of two other people and a self-evaluation. Each of the behaviors ("assertive," "calm," and so on) should be rated as follows: "yes" (this behavior is definitely characteristic of this person), "no" (this behavior is definitely *not* characteristic of this person), and "depends" (sometimes "yes," sometimes "no"—it depends on the situation). For ease of recording, use the abbreviations Y, N, and D.

First, have your subjects rate someone that they like very much. Ask them to think of that person and then to rate him or her on the set of behaviors, indicating how characteristic (or uncharacteristic) each is. It is easiest if you read off the behaviors one by one and mark down the subjects' responses. Then ask the subjects to think of someone that they dislike very much. Repeat the procedure. Finally, ask the subjects to rate themselves.

Now recode your data so that you can compare the frequency of trait responses (Y + N) with the frequency of situation responses (D). If the Jones-Nisbett hypothesis is correct, you should have found that subjects gave more trait responses for themselves. If there are exceptions to this pattern, how do you account for them? For example, what types of behavior did the subjects attribute to their own personalities rather than to the situations?

Data Sheet

Individual Ratings

		Assertive	Calm	Talkative	Impulsive	Kind	Optimistic	Cynical	Self-confident
S_1	Liked other								
	Disliked other								
	Self								
S_2	Liked other								
	Disliked other								
	Self								
S_3	Liked other								
	Disliked other								
	Self								
S_4	Liked other								
	Disliked other								
	Self								

Combined Ratings

	Assertive	Calm	Talkative	Impulsive	Kind	Optimistic	Cynical	Self-confident
Other (liked and disliked)								
No. trait ratings (Y and N)								
No. situation ratings (D)								
Self								
No. trait ratings (Y and N)								
No. situation ratings (D)								

SEX ROLES

10

There have been many attempts to explain the origin of our sex roles. Since this is a social-psychological textbook and the articles chosen for this chapter are presenting a social-psychological perspective, we would like, in this brief introduction, to present some of the other attempts to explain the differences between males and females, namely the biological, genetic, and évolutionary perspectives. These different explanations have dominated the field for many years, and social psychologists have tried to respond to them in their research.

On the biological level, the initial sex determination occurs at the moment of conception. If the sperm carries an X chromosome the XX combination will create a female; if it carries a Y chromosome the XY combination will create a male. If the hormone testosterone is later produced or introduced (during the third prenatal month), the male sex organ will develop. If no male hormone is present, the female sex structure will develop. And yet Money and Ehrhardt, in their classic book, *Man and Woman, Boy and Girl* (1979), conclude that human beings are bipotential in their psychosexual identity and that sex roles depend on both the external and the internal environment. Money and Ehrhardt present many clinical cases to support their conclusion that the sex of assignment, which is the sex one's parents raise one to be, is the single most important variable in the development of gender identity, a variable which can override the influence of genes, hormones, and external organs.

On the sociobiological level, Symons, in his book, *The Evolution of Human Sexuality* (1979), posited that sex differences are related to different reproductive strategies in the sexes, which originate in the difference between their original sex cells,

the sperm and the egg. Because men produce a large number of sperm, their reproductive strategy is to have many sexual partners and transient relationships. Women, because they have a small supply of eggs and must carry a child for at least nine months, require stable relations with a good provider.

The evolutionary perspective posited a different origin of sex roles. Darwin, in his book, *The Descent of Man and Selection in Relation to Sex* (1871), argued that evolution itself dictated an increasing sexual differentiation, in that each sex perfected the characteristics most suitable to its role and function. Male traits so generated included superior courage, intelligence, and resourcefulness, while female traits so generated included a passive maternalism.

But most famous is probably Freud's statement that "anatomy is destiny," in which he claimed that a child's sex role development is based on unconscious reaction to anatomical differences. When a little boy of about three discovers that a female does not have a penis, he becomes afraid of losing his. This castration anxiety forces him to repress his desire for his mother and identify with his father. A little girl, on the other hand, upon discovering she does not have a penis, envies a male and feels inferior. She rejects her mother, and eventually compensates for her penis envy by desiring a child.

In contrast to the biological and evolutionary perspectives, social psychologists have made a strong case for the overriding importance of socialization over biological and anatomical features in determining sex-typed behavior. The articles we chose to include in this chapter present, in one way or another, this social-psychological perspective.

YOU ARE WHAT YOU SAY

"Women's language" is that pleasant (dainty?), euphemistic, never-aggressive way of talking we learned as little girls. Cultural bias was built into the language we were allowed to speak, the subjects we were allowed to speak about, and the ways we were spoken of. Having learned our linguistic lesson well, we go out in the world, only to discover that we are communicative cripples—damned if we do, and damned if we don't.

If we refuse to talk "like a lady," we are ridiculed and criticized for being unfeminine. ("She thinks like a man" is, at best, a left-handed compliment.) If we do learn all the fuzzy-headed, unassertive language of our sex, we are ridiculed for being unable to think clearly, unable to take part in a serious discussion, and therefore unfit to hold a position of power.

It doesn't take much of this for a woman to begin feeling she deserves such treatment because of inadequacies in her own intelligence and education.

. . .

In the area of syntax, . . . there is one construction, in particular, that women use conversationally far more than men: the tag question. A tag is midway between an outright statement and a yes-no question; it is less assertive than the former, but more confident than the latter.

A *flat statement* indicates confidence in the speaker's knowledge and is fairly certain to be believed; a *question* indicates a lack of knowledge on some point and implies that the gap in the speaker's knowledge can and will be remedied by an answer. For example, if, at a Little League game, I have had my glasses off, I can legitimately ask someone else: "Was the player out at third?" *A tag question*, being intermediate between statement and question, is used when the speaker is stating a claim, but lacks full confidence in the truth of that claim. So if I say, "Is Joan here?" I will probably not be surprised if my respondent answers "no"; but if I say, "Joan is here, isn't she?" instead, chances are I am already biased in favor of a positive answer, wanting only confirmation. I still want a response, but I have enough knowledge (or think I have) to predict that response. A tag question, then, might be thought of as a statement that doesn't demand to be believed by anyone but the speaker, a way of giving leeway, of not forcing the addressee to go along with the views of the speaker.

Another common use of the tag question is in small talk when the speaker is trying to elicit conversation: "Sure is hot here, isn't it?"

But in discussing personal feelings or opinions, only the speaker normally has any way of knowing the correct answer. Sentences such as "I have a headache, don't I?" are clearly ridiculous. But there are other examples where it is the speaker's opinions, rather than perceptions, for which corroboration is sought, as in "The situation in Southeast Asia is terrible, isn't it?"

While there are, of course, other possible interpretations of a sentence like this, one possibility is that the speaker has a particular answer in mind—"yes" or "no"—but is reluctant to state it baldly. This sort of tag question is much more apt to be used by women than by men in conversation. Why is this the case?

The tag question allows a speaker to avoid commitment, and thereby avoid conflict with the addressee. The problem is that, by so doing, speakers may also give the impression of not really being sure of themselves, or looking to the addressee for confirmation of their views. This uncertainty is reinforced in more subliminal ways, too. There is a peculiar sentence intonation-pattern, used almost exclusively by women, as far as I know, which changes a declarative answer into a question. The effect of using the rising inflection typical of a yes–no question is to imply that the speaker is seeking confirmation, even though the speaker is clearly the only one who has the requisite information, which is why the question was put to her in the first place:

(Q) When will dinner be ready?
(A) Oh . . . around six o'clock?

It is as though the second speaker were saying, "Six o'clock—if that's okay with you, if you agree." The person being addressed is put in the position of having to provide confirmation. One likely consequence of this sort of speech pattern in a woman is that, often unbeknownst to herself, the speaker builds a reputation of tentativeness, and others will refrain from taking her seriously or trusting her with any real responsibilities, since she "can't make up her mind," and "isn't sure of herself."

Such idiosyncrasies may explain why women's language sounds much more "polite" than men's. It is polite to leave a decision open, not impose your mind, or views, or claims, on anyone else. So a tag question is a kind of polite statement, in that it does not force agreement or belief on the addressee. In the same way a request is a polite command, in that it does not force obedience on the addressee, but rather suggests something be done as a favor to the speaker. A clearly stated order implies a threat of certain consequences if it is not followed, and—even more impolite—implies that the speaker is in a superior position and able to enforce the order. By couching wishes in the form of a request, on the other hand, a speaker implies that if the request is not carried out, only the speaker will suffer; noncompliance cannot harm the addressee. So the decision is really left up to the addressee. The distinction becomes clear in these examples:

Close the door.

Please close the door.

Will you please close the door?

Won't you close the door?

DOONESBURY   **by Garry Trudeau**

THE INFLUENCE OF DIFFERENTIAL SOCIALIZATION ON THE PERSONALITY DEVELOPMENT OF MALES AND FEMALES

JEANNE H. BLOCK

While men and women have much in common, they differ in some important ways—psychologically as well as physically. Gender differences in personality and cognitive development are often well known, but not always well understood in terms of their origin. In this article, Block proposes that these differences arise from the different social contexts in which boys and girls grow up. In a variety of ways, both subtle and obvious, boys are given more opportunities for independent problem-solving and exploration, while girls are more closely supervised and restricted in their experiences. According to Block, the effects of these social contexts are profound. Boys and girls are led to think differently about the world around them and to use different strategies for dealing with that world.

In attempting to understand the nature of the psychological differences between the sexes and the extent to which these differences, within the confines set by biological predispositions, may be influenced by sex-differentiated socialization emphases, we closely reviewed and evaluated the voluminous literature bearing on sex-related differences and parental socialization practices. Our conclusions, derived from the literature on sex

Adapted from J. H. Block, Personality development of males and females: the influence of differential socialization. APA master lecture, 1979. Copyright © 1979 by American Psychological Association. Reprinted by permission.

differences and including recent empirical researches and our own longitudinal study, are presented here. These gender differences in psychological functioning are then related to the sex-differentiated socialization practices experienced by males and females. It is the contention of this paper that (1) males and females grow up in psychological contexts that are importantly different, and (2) these differing contexts have decisive implications for the subsequent psychological functioning of males and females. Finally, an organizing rubric for integrating some of the empirical findings surrounding sex differences is offered, and the implications of this conceptualization for the cognitive heuristics developed by males and females are explored.

SEX-RELATED DIFFERENCES IN PERSONALITY

The gender differences in personality considered here may be grouped into seven conceptual domains: aggression, activity, impulsivity, susceptibility to anxiety, achievement-related behaviors, self-concept, and social relationships.

Attempts to distill the literature in any area are always difficult and controversial, particularly when inconsistencies characterize many of the research findings. Data in psychology are often fragile, ephemeral, and unreproducible. In the area of sex differences, the attempt to develop and convey conclusions is particularly hazardous, not only because of problems characterizing the data base, but also because the topic of sex differences has become politicized. Conclusions drawn may have a consequential effect on social policies and, therefore, on people. Conclusions represent inferences, and reasonable people may well differ in the inferences drawn from a body of data. In reaching the conclusions that follow, converging empirical evidence for divergence between the sexes across studies, using samples representing different age levels and/or incorporating different modes of assessment, has been sought. However, it shall be remembered that the differences being summarized emerge from studies comparing, for the most part, mean levels of response for males and females. A focus on mean-response levels tells us little about the pattern or organization existing among variables in males and females. A focus on differences also tends to ignore the degree of overlap characterizing score distributions and neglects the many similarities existing between males and females.

Aggression

Research findings surrounding aggression are perhaps the most consistent in the literature, demonstrating that males are more aggressive than females, and from an early age. Males engage in more rough-and-tumble play, attempt more often to dominate peers, engage in more physical aggression, exhibit more antisocial behavior, prefer television programs with more aggressive content, and, depending upon context, are more competitive than females. Results demonstrating the greater aggressiveness of males have been obtained in the laboratory and in naturalistic settings, and generalize to the animal kingdom, as well.

Activity Level

Research findings surrounding gender differences in activity level are less compelling than those found with respect to aggression. When significant results are found, boys typically score higher on activity indices than girls, and this directional pattern is also typically found in studies when comparisons fail to achieve conventional significance levels. Males have also been observed to be more curious and to engage in more exploratory behaviors. Maccoby and Jacklin (1974) note, "In the age range from three to six there is a clear trend for boys to show more curiosity and exploratory behavior . . ." (p. 144). Boys engage in more manipulation of objects and play more than girls in outdoor areas. Studies of older boys and adult males show that they perceive and describe themselves as more daring and adventurous than females. Consistent with males' greater adventurousness is the set of findings demonstrating, in an enormous and representative sample, that boys had significantly more accidents requiring emergency medical treatment at every age level between 4 and 18 years. While activity and exploration have been shown to be sensitive to environmental and social contexts, the accrued findings suggest that males are both more active and engage in more exploratory behaviors than females.

Impulsivity

While impulsivity is related conceptually to both the expression of aggression and exploratory behavior, it encompasses other kinds of behaviors as well, which have proven to be sex discriminating. When impulsivity is defined broadly to include lesser control of impulse, the inability to delay gratification, and over-reactivity to frustration, males have been found to be more impulsive than females. Males tend to be more mischievous and are more likely to manifest more behavior problems related to undercontrol of impulse, such as temper tantrums, stealing, and disruptive behaviors, than girls. The assessment of impulse control in adults is complicated by the difficulty of designing controlled laboratory studies. While some naturalistic studies have been done in which, for example, the automobile-driving behaviors of adult males and females have been observed systematically and found to reflect both greater impatience and impulsivity on the part of male drivers than female drivers, the data base surrounding impulsivity in adulthood is somewhat thin.

Susceptibility to Anxiety

A constellation of findings suggests females are more fearful, manifest greater anxiety, and have less confidence in their abilities than males. Females score higher on self-report measures of anxiety, expect to do less well than males on problem-solving tasks, judge the adequacy of their performance less favorably than males, blame their failures on lack of ability more often than males, who blame their failures on lack of motivation. Females also attribute their successes to luck more often than males, who attribute their successes to ability. The lesser sense of competence characteristic of female adolescents extends into adulthood as well. Females who were studied as they aged from 18 to 26 years demonstrated a decrease in ego sufficiency, while males during the corresponding period showed an increase in their perceived sense of competence.

Related to the greater susceptibility to anxiety found among females is the finding that women score higher on measures of social desirability and, at least at the younger ages when compliance to adults is studied, females are found to be more compliant. Behaving in socially approved ways represents both a cooperative orientation and an effective strategy for warding off anxiety engendered by anticipation of disapproval from peers or adults. Also related to the findings surrounding anxiety is the greater tendency of females to yield to group pressures in experiments designed to assess influenceability. Eagly (1978) recently reviewed the literature on suggestibility and influenceability, and concluded that females in group situations characterized by uncertainty are more influenced by peer pressures than males. While recognizing that situational factors, such as the nature of the targeted task and the constituency of the group, may affect results in studies on influenceability, the conclusions that females are more socially conforming still appear warranted.

Achievement

Studies in human achievement often reveal inconsistent, sex-specific results. Accordingly, it is difficult to summarize this large and complex body of data with regard to gender differences. Females, relative to males, feel less confident in problem-solving situations and tend to underestimate their level of performance. They do not differ, however, in being less persistent or less motivated in achievement-relevant situations. Instead, it appears that females are *differently* motivated than males. The achievement of males is stimulated under challenging, ego-involving situations, whereas these same situational factors do not facilitate—and may even impair—the performance of females. L. Hoffman (1972) suggested that affiliative and achievement needs of females are in conflict, and that when achievement threatens interpersonal acceptance, anxiety is aroused to the detriment of performance. It also appears that the presence or absence of an adult in the achievement setting has a sex-differentiated effect, facilitating the performance of females and having little effect on the performance of males. These observations accord with those of L. Hoffman in suggesting that social (adult) approval may subserve achievement in females to a greater extent than males. Further evidence for sex-related motivational differences in the achievement domain is provided by Spence and Helmreich (1978), who distinguish four achievement areas—work, mastery, competitiveness, and personal unconcern. Their results demonstrate significant sex differences on the mastery and competitiveness scales, with males scoring higher, and on the work scale, with females scoring higher. The results of numerous studies suggest that the constellation of personality variables and situational factors associated with achievement in women appear to be reliably different from the set of factors associated with achievement in men.

Potency of the Self-Concept

Not only do males appear to feel more confident in problem-solving situations, but their self-concept includes feelings of greater personal efficacy as well. Males show less evidence than females of "learned helplessness" in achievement situations, and results of studies on young children indicate that the opportunity to exert control over external events is a more salient issue for boys than for girls. Data indicating the greater tendency of males to score higher on the lie and defensiveness scales of psychological inventories also suggest the self-images of males, in contrast to those of females, include stronger feelings of being able to control (or to manipulate) the external world—even if by occasional dissimulation. Males describe themselves as more powerful, ambitious, energetic, and as perceiving themselves as having more control over external events than females. The self-descriptions of males, more than of females, include concepts of agency, efficacy, initiative, and instrumentality—all reflections of a self-concept in which potency and mastery are important components. In contrast, females describe themselves as more generous, sensitive, nurturing, considerate, and concerned for others. The self-concepts of females emphasize interpersonal values and communion, conservation, and expressiveness, and deemphasize competition and mastery.

Social Orientations

Social behaviors of the two sexes have been found to diverge in a number of areas. M. Hoffman (1977) reviewed the psychological studies of empathy and concluded that clear sex differences exist, with females being the more empathic sex. That is, females, on the average, tend to manifest more vicarious and veridical affective responses in reaction to another person's feelings than males. Reviewing the results of 75 studies of the interpretation of nonverbal cues, Hall (1978) concluded that females more accurately discern emotions from nonverbal cues than males. Among college students, females engage in significantly more prosocial extra-curricular activities. Considering social groups and friendship patterns, females appear to be more affiliative, to be more cooperative, and to develop more intensive social relationships in contrast to the more extensive relationships developed by males. Girls were observed to play more often in small groups while boys tended to play in large groups. Females also, more than males, maintain greater proximity to other persons as reflected in measures of eye contact, distance, and physical contact. Wheeler and Nezleck (1977) examined the daily records of social interactions of entering university students for two weeks at the beginning and at the end of the academic year and found evidence of a different patterning in the social interactions of males and females. Entering college women not only so-

cialized more intensively in the new environment than males, but they also made greater use of their same-sex best friend to help them deal with the stimulation (and anxiety) experienced in the new situation than did males. That friendship groups serve different needs in males and females is suggested by Rubin (1980), who notes that boys view the group as a collective entity, emphasizing solidarity, loyalty, and shared activities, while girls perceive the group as an intimate network, emphasizing the sharing of confidences and support. Females, across cultures and across species, also appear to express more interest in babies and to engage in more nurturing behaviors. Both data derived from self-reports and from observational studies provide considerable evidence that women are more interpersonally oriented than men, who appear to have a more individualistic, instrumental orientation to the world.

Having presented conclusions about sex-related differences in several different areas of personality functioning, the socio-cultural contexts and the socialization emphases experienced over the childhood and adolescent years by contemporary males and females next will be considered. The psychological milieus in which the development of boys and of girls takes place are examined because it seems likely that particular sex-differentiated parental emphases and societal pressures contribute to the psychological sex differences identified.

SEX-DIFFERENTIATED SOCIALIZATION

Parental Self-Reports of Child-Rearing Emphases

Looking first at parental socialization values, we (1979) summarized the results of six studies in which the self-described child-rearing orientations of mothers and fathers were compared. The overall conclusions provided evidence: (1) for sex-differentiated parental socialization behaviors, (2) for specific, consistent sex-of-parent and sex-of-child interaction effects, (3) for the increase in sex differentiation in socialization with the increase in the age of the child, and (4) for relatively consistent sex-related socialization values of mothers and fathers across socioeconomic levels, educational levels, and cultural backgrounds.

With respect to the socialization of sons, we reported that the self-described child-rearing emphases of both mothers and fathers in several independent samples press achievement and competition more on their sons than on their daughters. In addition, both parents encourage their sons, more than their daughters, to control the expression of affect, to be independent, and to assume personal responsibility. They employ punishment more with their sons than with their daughters. Furthermore, fathers appear more authoritarian in their rearing of their sons: They are more strict, firm, endorsing of physical punishment, less tolerant of aggression directed toward themselves, and less accepting of behaviors deviating from the traditional masculine stereotype.

The self-described child-rearing emphases of parents of daughters indicate that the parent–daughter relationship, in contrast to the parent–son relationship, is characterized by greater warmth and physical closeness, greater confidence in the trustworthiness and truthfulness of their daughters, greater expectation by both mothers and fathers of "ladylike" behavior, greater reluctance to punish daughters, and greater encouragement to reflect upon life. Additionally, mothers of daughters tend to be more restrictive of their daughters and to engage in closer supervision of their activities.

Observational Studies of Parental Behaviors

Even in the first year of life, sex-differentiated parental interactions with infants have been observed. One implicative area in which parents of boys and parents of girls have been observed to differ is in the frequency of their contingent responding to behaviors initiated by their child. In the feeding situation, mothers were observed to be more responsive and attentive to signals from their male infants than to their female infants. Both mothers and fathers have been observed to react more contingently to the vocalizations of boys than to the vocalizations of girls. These apparent differences in contingent responding noted in infancy appear to continue through the childhood years. It has been shown in numerous studies at different age levels that boys not only receive more negative feedback, including physical punishment, from parents, but they appear to receive more positive feedback as well.

Differences in contingency experiences in the interpersonal realm are augmented by differences in the contingent possibilities afforded by the toys parents provide their boys and girls. Boys are given a greater variety of toys than girls, and there are important differences in the kinds of toys parents provide for boys and girls. Boys' toys, more than girls' toys, afford inventive possibilities, encourage manipulation, and provide more explicit feedback from the physical world. Girls' toys, on the other hand, tend to encourage imitation, are more often used in proximity to the caretaker, and provide less opportunity for variation and innovation. Differences in the toy preferences of boys and girls have been documented in numerous studies. The developmental implication of these differences in toy preference and availability only recently has been explored. Differential exposure to toys with dissimilar characteristics predisposes toward different play and problem-solving experiences for boys and girls, experiences which may have implication for later cognitive development.

In addition to being more contingently responsive to actions initiated by males than by females, parents have been observed also to provide more physical stimulation for boys than for girls. Male infants are held and aroused more and they are also given more stimulation for gross motor activity. In Yarrow's (1975) study of mother–infant interactions, mothers of males were observed to interact more frequently with their male infants, at higher intensity levels, and with richer, more varied behaviors. These observational studies, demonstrating that infant boys are given more stimulation than girls, are consistent with the sex-related socialization differences in the encouragement of exploratory behaviors found in later childhood.

Studies of sex-differentiated parental socialization behaviors generally report that boys are given more freedom to explore than girls. Girls have been observed to play more proximally to their mothers, to be allowed fewer independent excursions from home, to be encouraged by their mothers to follow them about the house, and to be more closely supervised in their activities. The differential assignment of household chores to boys and to girls also reflects proximity differences, since boys more often are given chores taking them out of the house and/or farther away from home while girls are assigned homebound chores of cleaning, helping around the house, babysitting, chores increasing the salience of the family milieu. Chodorow (1974) argues that the different social contexts experienced by boys and by girls over the childhood years account for the development of many psychological sex differences, particularly those reflecting the greater embeddedness of women in social networks in contrast to the more individualistic, mastery-emphasizing activities of men.

Turning to systematic studies of parent–child interactions observed in standard settings, further evidence for sex-differentiated parental behaviors is found. In one of our studies, the separate teaching behaviors of fathers and of mothers were videotaped, observed, and independently rated. Greater sex differentiation in the teaching behaviors of fathers than of mothers was found, a finding consistent with other observations showing that fathers exert greater pressure than mothers for sex-appropriate behaviors. With their sons, fathers set higher standards, attended to the cognitive elements of the tasks, and placed greater emphasis on achievement in the teaching–learning situation. With their daughters, fathers focused more on the interpersonal aspects of the teaching situation—encouraging, supporting, joking, playing, and protecting. Day (1975) found a similar sex-differentiated pattern in adults' teaching behaviors in an experiment where the investigator manipulated the presumption of the sex of her two-year-old subjects. Adults, particularly males, provided more goal-directed reinforcements to presumed boys and expected them to do significantly better on the tasks than presumed girls. Presumed girls were given more compliments and encouragement. Together, these results indicate that adults, particularly fathers, act in more instrumental, task-oriented, mastery-emphasizing ways with their sons and in more expressive, less achievement-oriented, dependency-reinforcing ways with their daughters.

The lesser paternal emphasis on achievement and mastery in girls is reflected also in maternal behaviors. Mothers of girls have been observed to provide help in problem-solving situations more than mothers of boys, even when their help is not required. Mothers respond with more positive effect to bids for help from girls than from boys and provide girls more immediate physical comfort after a frustrating experience. Not only do parents appear to deemphasize independent achievement with their daughters, but also may devalue their daughters' efforts as well. Studying communication patterns within families, Greif (1979) found that parents interrupt their daughters more often than their sons, and mothers are interrupted more frequently than fathers. Interruptions may convey a meta-message suggesting the idea that females are considered less important, less worthy of respect. Such meta-messages may well have a detrimental influence on the development of confidence and self-esteem in women.

Studies of Sex-Differentiated Teacher Behaviors

To the extent that sex-related differences in family socialization patterns are echoed in the behaviors of teachers, the sex-typed behaviors of males and females are given more extensive reinforcement. Considerable evidence for such reinforcement in the classroom exists. Observations of nursery

school teachers' behaviors demonstrate in several studies that boys are given more attention, both positive and negative, than girls (Serbin, O'Leary, Kent, and Tonick, 1973). Serbin et al. also found differences in the responses given to boys and to girls in reaction to solicitation behaviors: Teachers were not only more likely to respond to boys, but they responded in more helpful ways, providing more specific information. Other researches report similar findings. A recent study of teaching behavior with fifth-grade children solving concept-evaluation problems is distressing in its implications for intellectually advantaged girls (Frey, 1979). In this investigation, teaching behaviors of men and women tutors were recorded as they taught boys and girls assigned to one of two ability levels (high and moderate achievement). Of the four groups of pupils, *girls in the high achievement-condition received the lowest levels of supportive, ego-enhancing feedback*; they also received significantly fewer laudatory attributional statements and significantly more disparaging attributional statements. The findings from this study cohere with those from other researches of sex-differentiated teacher behavior where teachers have been observed to interact more with boys, to give boys more positive feedback, and to direct more criticism toward girls. Even at the university level, lesser reinforcement of the cognitive achievements of female students is reported. Survey studies of student and faculty attitudes reveal that the intellectual aspirations of female students are taken less seriously by professors. The greater attrition of women in higher education may reflect, among other factors, the pernicious effects of this pattern of discouragement and negative reinforcement of females' intellectual activities, a pattern identified at all educational levels—from nursery school through college. These results from the home, laboratory, and classroom settings suggest that girls, even high-achieving girls, are given less encouragement for their efforts than are their male peers. Gender differences in confidence, self-concept, and problem-solving behaviors may well derive from these home and classroom experiences that often discourage and denigrate the efforts of females.

In addition to specific teacher behaviors, the larger school context reinforces gender differences and traditional sex-role behaviors as well. Males hold the more prestigious positions in the school system; female teachers are less professionally identified and committed; schoolyards tend to be sex-segregated as a function of the different activity preferences of boys and girls; and classroom chores tend to be allocated in a sex-differentiated way. Further, on the playground, the games in which boys and girls spontaneously participate are sex-differentiated and diverge in their formal characteristics. Lever (1976) analyzed the formal characteristics of games played on the playground by boys and girls and found that girls participated in highly structured, turn-taking games which are regulated by invariable procedural rules, include fewer players, and less often require contingent strategies. Boys' games, while rule-governed, reward initiative, improvisation, and extemporaneity, involve teams made up of a number of peers, and encourage both within-team cooperation and between-team competition. These sex-differentiated experiences with games also may be expected to influence importantly both social development and approaches to problem solving.

These differences in teacher behaviors, institutional arrangements, and peer activities accentuate differences between males and females and reinforce the sex-differentiating socialization behaviors of parents by extending the network of sex-differentiating socializing agents beyond the family, thus providing continuity in the experiences of the child from the home to the larger world.

In summary, there appears to be appreciable sex-differentiated socialization at home and at school, allowing boys greater freedom to explore and encouraging curiosity, independence, and the testing of oneself in achievement and other competitive settings. This socialization pattern tends to extend the experiences of males. For females, the socialization process discourages exploration, circumscribes spheres of activity, stresses proprieties, and emphasizes close supervision, thus restricting the experiences of females. Access to experience and the opportunity actively to engage the world have been shown by numerous investigators to influence cognitive development. It would be expected, therefore, that the sex-differentiated socialization practices described would influence the cognitive and personality development of males and females. In the next section, some conceptual implications of the diverging experiences of boys and girls will be considered from a developmental perspective.

IMPLICATIONS OF SEX-DIFFERENTIATED SOCIALIZATION

In an earlier article (Block, 1973), attention was directed to the implications of different conceptions of gender roles for personality development. In that article ways in which the socialization of traditional gender roles affects the development

of ego structures in males and in females was considered. In the present paper, building on the evidence cited in earlier sections, the focus now shifts to the implications of sex-related differences in socialization for cognitive development.

Applying a developmental perspective to the gender differences observed, it is proposed that the sex-differentiated socialization and parental "shaping" behaviors affect boys and girls in ways that importantly influence the deep structure of their cognitive development. Three fundamental, early bases for later cognitive development are identified and related to the socialization patterns noted as differentially characterizing the sexes. The three anlagen on which so much of subsequent cognitive development hinges are: (1) the child's premises about the responsivity of the world to his or her actions; (2) the child's opportunities to "experiment with nature"; and (3) the child's strategies for responding to discrepant, disconfirming experiences.

Premises About the Responsivity of the World to One's Actions

Experience with contingency relationships has been shown to have important cognitive consequences. Contingency understandings were found to be related to general developmental level, goal-direction, and exploratory behaviors of infants. To the extent that modes of processing information and the enduring cognitive structures resulting therefrom derive from the child's early experiences with contingency relationships in the physical and social worlds, parent-child interactions and "shaping" behaviors that are sex differentiating with respect to contingency experience can assume appreciable significance.

Earlier, in summarizing the literature on sex-differentiated socialization, it was noted that boys more than girls receive contingent responding in the form of attention, responsivity, and both encouraging and critical feedback from parents and teachers. Boys are given toys with more feedback potential and participate in games requiring contingent strategies. These earlier and more frequent experiences of boys with contingency relationships may be expected to benefit motivation, goal orientation, and development of awareness of the evocative role they play in eliciting effects from the environment. These early experiences of efficacy (and the sense of efficacy) can help build the personality and cognitive foundations on which later instrumental competence depends. It is posited that boys more than girls, as presently socialized in this culture, are helped to develop a premise system that presumes or anticipates mastery and instrumental competence.

The Opportunity to "Experiment with Nature"

Piaget (1970) has reminded us that "each time one prematurely teaches a child something he [she] could have discovered for him[her]self, the child is kept from inventing it and consequently from understanding it completely" (p. 715). Sigel and Cocking (1976) draw attention to the effects of insufficient parental "distancing" on the development of children's representational thought. They propose that adult distancing behaviors promote the child's active engagement in problem solving and increase the likelihood that the child will encounter discrepancies between experience and expectation which cannot be assimilated readily. Such discrepancies place demands on the child to alter approach, reexamine earlier understandings, and modify premises—that is, to develop new cognitive structures. Data from several sources converge in suggesting that socialization practices fostering proximity, discouraging independent problem solving by premature or excessive intervention, restricting exploration, and discouraging active play may impede the child's achievement of the cognitive recognitions and fluencies that represent the essence of cognitive development.

It was earlier noted that boys more than girls are reared in ways encouraging of curiosity, independence, and exploration of the environment—behaviors requisite for the kind of experimentation deemed critical by Piaget and others for the development of cognitive structures. In contrast, the more restrictive child-rearing practices characterizing parents of girls (such as emphasis on physical proximity, expectations of "ladylike" behaviors, close supervision, and provision of help in problem-solving situations) lessen the opportunity for girls to engage in active experimentation with the environment, to encounter discrepancies, and to engage in solution efforts. It is posited that boys more than girls, then, as presently socialized in this culture, are afforded greater opportunities for "discovering," "examining," and "understanding" the world in which they must live.

Cognitive Strategies for Responding to Discrepant Experiences

The notions of cognitive assimilation and cognitive accommodation are widely known in devel-

opmental psychology, largely due to Piaget. The process of assimilation involves the fitting of new information or experience into preexisting cognitive schemas; the process of accommodation involves the modification and the formation of cognitive schemas capable of encompassing new information or experience at variance with prior understandings. While the adaptation to new experience, according to Piaget (1970), always and simultaneously requires both assimilation and accommodation as two sides of one coin, the usage of the concepts here departs from Piaget in separating these two cognitive strategies. Of course, all individuals use both modes of processing experience at different times in rapid succession and under different circumstances. Nevertheless, it is useful to consider the preferred or dominant mode, assimilation or accommodation, characterizing a person. Further, if the assimilative mode has a built-in priority over the accommodative mode, it becomes of interest to ascertain the personal point at which an individual abandons continuing efforts at assimilation to begin the task of creating a new and integrative accommodation. In reacting to new experiences failing to conform to the expectations generated from existing schemata, some persons have an ability (and even an insistence) to see if they can encompass the new information in ways that require little or no modification of previously established premises. Other persons encountering new experiential inputs have a greater readiness (and even preference) to leave cognitive schema that do not mesh readily with the new information and to move on to the formulation of new and sufficient meaning-making structures.

Both assimilation and accommodation may be seen as serving an adaptive evolutionary function. Assimilation conserves existing structures, sometimes in creative ways, providing continuity with the past and perpetuating cultural and familial traditions and historical values. Accommodation results in the creation, sometimes unnecessarily, of new adaptive modes, thus fostering social innovation and cultural change. When both modes of processing experience are available to the individual, and when they can be invoked in context-responsive ways, problem-solving effectiveness is broadened. Overreliance on either strategy for processing disconfirming information will prove dysfunctional if it is out of phase with the real world. The use of procrustean and perseverative methods to fit, shape, or mold new perceptions into preexisting schemata can result in a projective, distorted, oversimplified, rigid approach to the world, while premature jettisoning of established schemata and zealously sought or passively accepted redefinition of premises may result in an ahistorical, compartmentalized, overly situational, standardless, impulsive approach to the world.

The literature reviewed earlier suggests females grow up in a more structured and directive world than males. Parental supervision, restrictions on exploration, household chores assignments, proximity emphases, and the more frequent—sometimes unnecessary—help provided girls in problem solving situations combine to create a more canalized and more predictable environment for girls than for boys. Encounters with the world outside the home are both less extensive and more controlled than in the case of boys. Contributing also to the more structured world of girls is the greater structure of their preferred play activities which, more than the play of boys, involves model availability, instruction, and rule governance. At older ages, the games preferred by girls also are more structured and make fewer demands for improvisation than the games of boys, which often reward extemporaneity and the ability to take advantage of a momentarily advantageous situation. Relatively structured environments, in contrast to those less structured, have been found to elicit less creativity and more compliance in children, to be associated with less task engagement, and to be related to intolerance of ambiguity. These differences in the learning environments experienced by girls and by boys can be expected to have powerful and general effects on the cognitive strategies invoked at times when expectations fail.

It is posited that girls, more than boys, are socialized in ways encouraging the use of assimilative strategies for processing new information while boys, more than girls, are socialized in ways that encourage the use of accommodative strategies when confronted with informational inputs discrepant with prior understandings. Further, it is suggested that girls, more than boys, are slower to leave efforts to cognitively assimilate for efforts to cognitively accommodate. Socialization practices creating relatively structured environments, more common in the case of females, emphasize the adaptive rewards of efforts to be assimilative and to discourage the anxiety-inducing efforts of innovative accommodation. Boys, experiencing a less predictable world where *ad hoc* strategies are frequently demanded, are pressed more often to reexamine and even to abandon structures proving ineffective. Success in inventive *ad hoc* solutions, over time, would be expected to benefit boys' self-confidence and their freedom to assume the risk of seeking to restructure.

Admittedly, empirical evidence supporting the proposition that males and females differ in their preferred modes for dealing with new informational inputs is sparse. This formulation, however, is consonant in interesting ways with Lynn's (1962) characterization of the differences in both the *nature* and the *process* of identification for males and for females. Lynn postulated that the task of achieving identification for each sex requires separate methods of learning, methods paralleling the two kinds of learning tasks—problem mastery and lesson learning.

Lynn suggests that the availability of the mother and the visibility of her daily activities provide the daughter with an opportunity to observe, to imitate, and to identify with specific aspects of the mother's role. Therefore, the daughter's task of achieving identification with the mother and developing a feminine gender-role orientation can be viewed as a profound instance of lesson learning. The son's task of achieving identification with the father, however, is complicated by two factors: the necessity of shifting from an initial identification with the mother to the father (a task requiring early accommodation) and the lesser visibility of the father's day-to-day activities outside the home. The opportunity for imitative or template lesson learning is less available to the son and, therefore, the task of achieving identification with the father and developing a masculine gender-role orientation requires extrapolation and can be considered an instance of problem learning. This is consistent with Lynn's formulation in that the relationship between assimilation and lesson learning and the relationship between accommodation and problem learning are apparent.

In addition to the support for the present argument afforded by Lynn's discussion of the identification process and its sex-differential implications for learning, some—albeit limited—empirical justification can be cited as well. Research findings demonstrating the greater conservation of females in problem-solving situations are pertinent. A set of findings surrounding categorization behavior demonstrates that females have narrower category boundaries than males. In summarizing the results of several categorization studies, Silverman (1970) notes, "Females are more disposed than males *to accept the basic structure of a stimulus configuration* [italics added] and to elaborate it only minimally" (p. 84). With regard to cognitive problems requiring restructuring or breaking set, data are quite clear in showing that females score lower. Assessments of cognitive risk-taking have found females to be more conservative in their judgments than males. A study by Duck (1975), seeking to identify factors associated with friendship patterns, demonstrates that the basis for friendships in girls, but not in boys, is similarity in psychological constructs. The importance of familiar, well-tried pathways for females is to be seen also in a study by Harter (1975), who found that girls spent more time than boys on a task after reaching a learning criterion, particularly under the condition of social reinforcement. Boys, on the other hand, spent more time on unsolvable problems, seeking to find the key to solution. It is suggested that these results (demonstrating females' greater adherence to the midrange in categorization studies, lesser inclination to restructure in set-breaking problems, greater conservativism in judgments involving risk-taking, preference for friends sharing similar psychological characteristics, and preference for staying with mastered tasks) are consistent with the assimilative mode of dealing with new experience. As such, they offer support for the proposition that females, to a greater extent than males, rely on assimilative strategies while males tend more often to manifest accommodative strategies in problem-solving situations.

While there has not yet been research directly evaluating preferences for assimilative as compared to accommodative strategies, results of the foregoing studies are suggestive. A necessary next step is to test the tenability of the conjectures offered here. Until targeted research begins to be available and can be brought to bear on the proposition, the heuristic conjecture that boys, more than girls, are presently socialized in this culture to invoke the process of cognitive accommodation [while girls more than boys are presently socialized to invoke the process of cognitive assimilation] would appear to assimilate many of the data, and other more informal observations, on the different ways the sexes tend to resolve disconfirming experiences.

In overall summary, it has been proposed that sex-differentiated socialization practices influence the cognitive development of males and females in several ways that, separately and in sum, provide more opportunity for independent problem solving in a variety of contexts for males than for females. The differential provision for the two sexes to engage actively the larger world outside the familiar and protected home environment is seen as creating different premises about the world, as developing different competencies, and as reinforcing the use of different cognitive heuristics for dealing with new experience.

REFERENCES

Block, J. H. Conceptions of sex role: Some cross-cultural and longitudinal perspectives. *American Psychologist,* 1973, *28,* 512–26.

Block, J. H. Another look at sex differentiation in the socialization behavior of mothers and fathers. In J. Sherman and F. L. Denmark (eds.), *Psychology of women: Future directions of research.* New York: Psychological Dimensions, 1979.

Block, J. H., & Block, J. The role of ego-control and ego-resiliency in the organization of behavior. In W. A. Collins (ed.), *Minnesota Symposia on Child Psychology,* Vol. 13. Hillsdale, N.J.: Lawrence Erlbaum Associates, 1980.

Chodorow, N. Family structure and feminine personality. In M. Z. Rosaldo & L. Lampere (eds.), *Women's culture and society.* Stanford, Cal.: Stanford University Press, 1974, pp. 43–66.

Day, K. Differences in teaching behavior in adults as a function of sex related variables. Doctoral dissertation, University of Washington, 1975.

Duck, S. W. Personality similarity and friendship choices by adolescents. *European Journal of Social Psychology,* 1975, *5,* 351–65.

Eagly, A. H. Sex differences in influenceability. *Psychological Bulletin,* 1978, *85,* 85–116.

Frey, K. S. Differential teaching methods used with girls and boys of moderate and high achievement levels. Paper presented at the meeting of the Society for Research in Child Development, San Francisco, March 1979.

Greif, E. Sex differences in parent-child conversations: Who interrupts whom? Paper presented at the meeting of the Society for Research in Child Development, San Francisco, March 1979.

Hall, J. A. Gender effects in decoding nonverbal cues. *Psychological Bulletin,* 1978, *85,* 845–57.

Harter, S. Developmental differences in the manifestation of mastery motivation on problem-solving tasks. *Child Development,* 1975, *46,* 370–78.

Hoffman, L. W. Early childhood experiences and women's achievement motive. *Journal of Social Issues,* 1972, *28,* 129–55.

Hoffman, M. L. Sex differences in empathy and related behaviors. *Psychological Bulletin,* 1977, *84,* 712–22.

Lever, J. Sex differences in games children play. *Social Problems,* 1976, *23,* 478–87.

Lynn, D. B. Sex-role and parental identification. *Child Development,* 1962, *33,* 555–64.

Maccoby, E. E., & Jacklin, C. N. *The psychology of sex differences.* Stanford, Cal.: Stanford University Press, 1974.

Piaget, J. Piaget's theory. In P. H. Mussen (ed.), *Carmichael's Manual of Child Psychology.* New York: John Wiley & Sons, 1970.

Rubin, Z. *Children's friendships.* Cambridge, Mass.: Harvard University Press, 1980.

Serbin, L. A., O'Leary, K. D., Kent, R. N., & Tonick, I. J. A comparison of teacher response to the preacademic and problem behavior of boys and girls. *Child Development,* 1973, *44,* 796–804.

Sigel, I. E., & Cocking, R. R. Cognition and communication: A dialectic paradigm for development. In M. Lewis & L. Rosenblum (eds.), *Communication and language: The origins of behavior,* Vol. 5. New York: John Wiley & Sons, 1976.

Silverman, J. Attentional styles and the study of sex differences. In D. I. Mostofsky (ed.), *Attention: Contemporary theory and analysis.* New York: Appleton-Century-Crofts, 1970.

Spence, J. T., & Helmreich, R. L. *Masculinity & femininity: Their psychological dimensions, correlates, & antecedents.* Austin, Tex.: University of Texas Press, 1978.

Wheeler, L., & Nezlek, J. Sex differences in social participation. *Journal of Personality and Social Psychology.* 1977, *35,* 742–54.

SEX TYPING AND ANDROGYNY

SANDRA BEM, WENDY MARTYNA, AND CAROL WATSON

Androgyny is a Greek word comprised of two parts: andro, meaning male, and gyn, meaning female. To the Greeks, androgyny meant the presence of female and male characteristics in a single organism—the hermaphrodite. The contemporary use of the word androgyny, mostly inspired by the work of Sandra Bem, is psychosocial rather than physio-sexual. It refers to the presence of both masculine and feminine characteristics in the same individual. In her previous work, Bem showed that androgynous individuals of both sexes display "masculine" independence when under pressure to conform, as well as "feminine" nurturance when playing with a kitten. In contrast, sex-typed individuals were deficient in one of these behaviors; androgynous individuals were able to be either feminine or masculine, whenever the particular response was appropriate, thus documenting the liberating effect of androgyny.

In the present article, which was written in collaboration with Martyna and Watson, Bem attempted to replicate that previous work and further explore the role played by sex typing and androgyny in the expressive domain of behavior.

Both historically and cross-culturally, masculinity and femininity have represented complementary domains of positive traits and behaviors. . . . Masculinity has been associated with an "instrumental" orientation, a cognitive focus on getting the job done or the problem solved, whereas femininity has been associated with an "expressive" orientation, an affective concern for the welfare of others and the harmony of the group.

More recently, scholars in a number of disciplines have begun to concern themselves with the concept of psychological androgyny, a term which denotes the integration of both masculinity and femininity within a single individual. The concept of psychological androgyny implies that it is possible for an individual to be both masculine and feminine, both instrumental and expressive, both agentic and communal, depending upon the situational appropriateness of these various modalities; and it further implies that an individual may even blend these complementary modalities into a single act, being able, for example, to fire an employee if the circumstances warrant it, but to do so with sensitivity for the human emotion that such an act inevitably produces.

Empirical research on the concept of androgyny is now beginning to appear in the psychological literature. For example, a more androgynous view of oneself has recently been found to be accompanied by greater maturity in one's moral judgments and by a higher level of self-esteem. In our own laboratory studies, we have found that androgynous individuals not only perform cross-sex behavior with little reluctance or discomfort but display both "masculine" independence when under pressure to conform as well as "feminine" nurturance when given the opportunity to interact with a baby kitten.

However, for many individuals, traditional sex roles still produce an unnecessary and perhaps even dysfunctional pattern of avoidance, which prevents the possibility of androgyny from ever becoming a reality. For example, in the study by Bem and Lenney (1976), sex-typed individuals not only actively avoided a wide variety of simple, everyday activities (like nailing two boards together or winding a package of yarn into a ball) just because those activities happen to be stereotyped as more appropriate for the other sex, but they also reported discomfort and even some temporary loss of self-esteem when actually required to perform such activities.

Moreover, this pattern of avoidance is not limited to simple, everyday behaviors but appears to constrict the individual's instrumental and expressive functioning as well. Thus, whereas androgynous individuals in the Bem (1975) study displayed high levels of both masculine independence and feminine nurturance, nonandrogynous individuals did not. Rather, masculine males were low in nurturance, and feminine males were low in independence.

Like the nonandrogynous males, the nonandrogynous females were also constricted, but their behavioral patterns were more complicated. As anticipated, masculine females were quite independent, but they were not significantly less nurturant toward the kitten than were androgynous females. Hence, it could not be concluded that the masculine woman was low in her expressive functioning. But it was the behavior of the feminine woman that was the most surprising and the most constricted. Not only was the feminine woman low in independence but she was also low in her nurturance toward the kitten. Of course, it is possible that feminine women might simply find animals unappealing for some reason and that they might therefore display much greater nurturance if they were given the opportunity to interact with another human being rather than with a kitten.

The current investigations represent a further exploration of the expressive domain. In an attempt to give the feminine women a fairer test of their expressive functioning, two additional studies were carried out. Because we wished to clarify whether the feminine woman's low level of nurturance was unique to her interaction with animals, both of these studies were designed to be genuinely interpersonal situations in which the subjects' nurturant sympathies were more likely to be aroused. In addition, because it also seemed possible that feminine women might be insufficiently assertive to act out their nurturant feelings if the situation required that they take responsibility for initiating the interaction, the second study was designed not only to be genuinely interpersonal but also to place the subject in a more passive role that would require very little initiative or improvisation and in which there would be virtually no ambiguity about what a subject ought to do if he or she wished to be nurturant. Accordingly, the first study gave the subject the opportunity to interact with a human baby, and the second required the subject to listen to a fellow student who openly shared some of his or her unhappy emotions.

EXPERIMENT 1

METHOD

Subjects

Subjects were 84 undergraduates (half males and half females) from Stanford University who participated in the experiment during the winter and spring quarters of 1974. All of the subjects had taken the Bem Sex Role Inventory at the beginning of the quarter, and all had experienced relatively little prior interaction with babies. One third of the subjects had been preselected as masculine, one third as feminine, and one third as androgynous on the basis of the androgyny t ratio, a difference score that measures the extent to which subjects distinguish between masculine and feminine personality characteristics in their self-descriptions.

Also participating in the study were 14 babies (10 males and 4 females), each of whom interacted with one representative of each of the six different sex roles. During the experimental sessions, however, each baby was dressed in sex-neutral clothing and was randomly assigned to be introduced to all six subjects either as "David" or as "Lisa." The babies ranged in age from $4\frac{1}{2}$ to 7 months. Naturally, great care was taken to protect the health and well-being of all of the babies who participated.

Dependent Variables

Subjects were solicited for a study of social responsiveness in infants and were then left alone with a baby for a period of ten minutes while we observed the interaction from behind a one-way mirror. Specifically, the subject's behavior was time sampled every ten seconds by one of three female coders, all of whom were blind with respect to the subject's sex role and all of whom observed an approximately equal number of masculine, androgynous, and feminine subjects of each sex. For each subject, the coder made sixty 3-second observations. The following six behaviors were coded as present or absent: Was the subject smiling directly at the baby? Was the subject talking to the baby? Was the subject kissing or nuzzling the baby? Was the subject holding the baby chest to chest? Was the subject stimulating the baby in a way that involved touching (e.g., tickling, patting, stretching)? Was the subject stimulating the baby in a way that did not involve touching (e.g., shaking a rattle, squeaking a toy)? These behavioral measures were all highly reliable, with two independent coders agreeing perfectly on over 90 percent of the observations for each measure. Moreover, because only nonphysical stimulation was negatively correlated with the other behaviors ($r = -.13$), a summary measure of behavioral nurturance was constructed by averaging together the standard score equivalents of the remaining five behaviors.

In order to derive a summary measure of subjects' self-reported feelings of nurturance toward the baby, we also averaged together the subject's ratings on seven written questions asked at the end of the study. These questions asked such things as how positive the subject's feelings were toward the baby and how much the subject wanted to be affectionately responsive to the baby.

RESULTS

The two orthogonal comparisons to be tested were the following: (a) that feminine and androgynous subjects would both be significantly more nurtur-

ant to the baby than masculine subjects and (b) that feminine and androgynous subjects would not differ significantly from one another in this regard.

The results revealed a significant main effect of the subject's sex role, with mean scores of $-.19$, $-.15$, $+.18$, and $+.16$ for the undifferentiated, masculine, androgynous, and feminine subjects, respectively. Moreover, planned comparisons indicated that as predicted, masculine subjects were significantly less nurturant toward the baby than feminine or androgynous subjects, and furthermore, that feminine and androgynous subjects did not differ significantly from one another.

Although these supplementary results can only be seen as suggestive, they do serve to replicate conceptually our earlier finding that feminine and androgynous males were more nurturant toward a kitten than masculine males; they also suggest that the feminine woman's low level of nurturance was situation specific and probably resulted from having her interact with an animal rather than with another human being.

EXPERIMENT 2

The supplementary results of Experiment 1 offer tentative support to the hypothesis that feminine and androgynous subjects of both sexes are more nurturant than masculine subjects. Experiment 2 represents an attempt to test this hypothesis still further. Because it seemed possible that feminine women might be most capable of acting out all of their nurturant feelings in a situation where they did not have to take responsibility for initiating and sustaining the interaction, as they had to do with both the kitten and the baby, the situation in Experiment 2 was designed not only to be genuinely interpersonal but also to place the subject in a more passive or responsive role. Accordingly, Experiment 2 was designed to evoke sympathetic and supportive listening on the part of the subject but, at the same time, did not require the subject to play an active or initiating role in the interaction.

METHOD

Subjects

Subjects were 84 undergraduates (half males and half females) from Stanford University who participated in the experiment during the spring quarter of 1974. All had taken the Bem Sex Role Inventory at the beginning of the quarter, with one third of each sex preselected as masculine, one third as feminine, and one third as androgynous on the basis of the androgyny *t* ratio.

Three undergraduate experimenters and four undergraduate confederates also participated in the study. They interacted with subjects of their own sex only, were blind with respect to the subjects' sex roles, and interacted with approximately equal numbers of masculine, androgynous, and feminine subjects.

Procedure

Two males or two females, one of whom was a subject and one of whom was a confederate, participated together in a study whose alleged purpose was to find out "whether you begin to feel close to another person primarily because of the things you learn about the other person, or primarily because of the things you tell that other person about yourself." The two "subjects" drew lots to allegedly determine who would take the role of "talker" and who, the role of "listener," but in fact, the confederate always served as the talker and the subject always served as the listener. The experimenter explained that the talker's role was simply to talk about himself or herself for approximately ten minutes. The talker was told to begin with some general background information and, at the experimenter's signal, to move on to more personal material. In contrast, the listener's role was primarily to listen. Thus, the listener was allowed to ask questions or make comments but never to shift the focus of the conversation to himself or herself.

After explaining the role of talker and listener, and after pointing out that he or she would be able to hear the conversation from behind the one-way mirror, the experimenter left the room. At that point, the talker began, somewhat shyly and nervously, to deliver a memorized script. The first half of the script dealt with relatively casual background information (e.g., major, hometown, summer job, new apartment, etc.), whereas the second half was more personal. In general, the talker described himself or herself as a recent and rather lonely transfer student to Stanford University. He or she talked about problems such as missing old friends, the difficulty of making new friends now that cliques had already been established, and having to spend more time alone than he or she would have liked. In short, the talker described feelings common to many new transfer students. He or she did not seem neurotic, just somewhat

isolated, and rather pleased to have this opportunity to share some of his or her feelings with another person.

After the talker had finished, the experimenter returned with questionnaires for the two "subjects" to fill out. He or she mentioned that the experiment was now over and that the subjects were no longer expected to play the roles of talker and listener. The subjects were then left alone in the room again while they filled out their questionnaires.

After they had both finished filling out their questionnaires but before the experimenter had returned to the room, the confederate/talker turned to the subject and said, "I really feel better after talking to you. It's too bad we didn't get a chance to talk longer." This statement was designed to provide the subject with his or her only opportunity to be responsive outside of the listener role. Following the subject's response, the experimenter returned to the room and began the debriefing process.

Dependent Variables

As in Experiment 1, a summary measure of behavioral nurturance was developed by averaging together the standard score equivalents of five individual behaviors. The five behaviors were as follows:

1 and 2. *Head nods and facial reactions (nonverbal responsiveness):* Listeners who nodded their heads or changed their facial expression in response to what the talker was saying seemed, in most instances, to be listening to the talker and to be involved. Accordingly, the experimenter time-sampled the subject's behavior every 15 seconds and recorded whether or not each of these two behaviors occurred. Both measures were highly reliable, with two independent coders agreeing perfectly on over 93 percent of the 40 five-second observations for each behavior.

3. *Verbal responsiveness:* Although the listener was instructed to keep the focus of the conversation on the talker, he or she was allowed to ask questions and to make comments. Moreover, if the subject had said nothing during the entire ten minutes, the interaction would have been very strained and the talker would have been made to feel extremely uncomfortable. Accordingly, the interaction was recorded on audiotape and was later scored for the subject's

number of verbalizations. This measure was highly reliable, with a correlation of $+.92$ between two independent coders.

4. *Positive reaction to the talker's implicit request for further contact:* The subject's response to the statement, "I really feel better after talking to you; it's too bad we didn't get a chance to talk longer," was coded into one of five categories: (1) no response, (2) acknowledgement that the talker had spoken, (3) sympathetic response, (4) interest expressed in getting together again, and (5) specific time offered for getting together again. Independent coding yielded 100 percent perfect agreement on this measure.

5. *Degree of nurturance as perceived by others:* Both the experimenter and the confederate/talker independently rated the subject on a 5-point scale in terms of "how nurturant" he or she had been to the talker. Because they agreed within a single scale point on 96 percent of the subjects, their ratings were averaged together.

In addition, in order to derive a summary score of subjects' self-reported feelings of nurturance toward the talker, we also averaged together the subject's ratings on four written questions that asked "how close" the subject felt to the talker, "how much of a real identification or empathy" he or she felt with the talker, "how concerned" he or she felt about the talker, and "how eager" he or she would be to talk to the talker "in a real situation (not an experiment)." The scale ranged from 1 (not very much) to 6 (extraordinarily).

RESULTS

The two orthogonal comparisons to be tested were as follows: (a) that feminine and androgynous subjects would both be more nurturantly responsive to the talker than would masculine subjects and (b) that feminine and androgynous subjects would not differ significantly from one another in this regard.

The first rows of Tables 1 and 2 present the mean scores on the composite measure of behavioral nurturance for the masculine, androgynous, and feminine males and females, respectively. As the tables suggest, there was a significant main effect of the subject's sex role for this measure, with mean nurturance scores of $-.29$, $+.04$, and $+.25$ for the masculine, androgynous, and feminine subjects, respectively. Moreover, planned

TABLE 1. MALE NURTURANCE TOWARD A LONELY FELLOW STUDENT

	SUBJECT		
MEASURE	MASCU-LINE	ANDROGY-NOUS	FEMI-NINE
Summary			
Observed nurturance	$-.43$	$-.04$	$+.05$
Self-reported nurturance[a]	3.45	3.80	3.64
Individual			
Global rating[b]	2.6	3.0	3.1
Verbalizations	42.1	56.1	60.4
Behavioral offer[b]	3.1	3.5	3.3
Head nods[c]	17.1	18.3	19.9
Facial reactions[c]	8.7	10.4	11.4

Note. For all subjects, $n = 14$.
[a]Max = 6.
[b]Max = 5.
[c]Max = 40.

comparisons indicated that, as predicted, masculine subjects were significantly less nurturant than feminine or androgynous subjects, and furthermore, that feminine and androgynous subjects did not differ significantly from one another.

An analysis of the individual measures that were scored during the subject's interaction with the talker provides a close-up of what behaviors most differentiated the three groups of subjects. The lower portions of Tables 1 and 2 display the means for each of these measures. The overall analyses of variance revealed significant or near-significant

TABLE 2. FEMALE NURTURANCE TOWARD A LONELY FELLOW STUDENT

	SUBJECT		
MEASURE	MASCU-LINE	ANDROGY-NOUS	FEMI-NINE
Summary			
Observed nurturance	$-.16$	$+.11$	$+.43$
Self-reported nurturance[a]	3.59	3.45	4.13
Individual			
Global rating[b]	2.8	3.1	3.3
Verbalizations	51.6	61.8	64.1
Behavioral offer[b]	2.9	3.1	3.4
Head nods[c]	19.6	22.9	27.1
Facial reactions[c]	12.5	12.2	15.0

Note. For all subjects, $n = 14$.
[a]Max = 6.
[b]Max = 5.
[c]Max = 40.

main effects of the subject's sex role for head nods, for verbalizations, and for the global rating of nurturance given to the subject by the experimenter and the talker. In addition, planned comparisons for each of these measures indicated that masculine subjects were significantly less nurturant than feminine or androgynous subjects, in each comparison; and furthermore, that feminine and androgynous subjects did not differ significantly from one another. Finally, with respect to subjects' self-reported feelings of nurturance toward the talker, feminine women described themselves as feeling significantly more nurturant than androgynous women.

DISCUSSION

Instrumental and Expressive Functioning

As noted in the introduction to this article, the two studies reported here represent an attempt to broaden the empirical base upon which our earlier conclusions about sex typing and androgyny were founded. Although the results that emerged from the reanalysis of the baby study can only be seen as suggestive by themselves, the two studies taken together conceptually replicate the low nurturance of the masculine male, and even more importantly, they demonstrate that the low nurturance of the feminine female does not extend beyond her interaction with animals.

In addition, we would now like to pull together all of our findings on the instrumental and expressive domains in an attempt to reach some tentative conclusions about the effects of sex typing and androgyny. We will begin with the men because their data have been so consistent. Quite simply, only androgynous males were high in both the instrumental and the expressive domains; that is, only androgynous males were found to stand firm in their opinions as well as to cuddle kittens, bounce babies, and offer a sympathetic ear to someone in distress.

In contrast, the feminine male was low in independence, while the masculine male was low in nurturance. Because at least one-third of college-age males are classified as masculine, it is noteworthy that masculine males were lower in nurturance than androgynous or feminine males whether they were interacting with a kitten, a baby, or a lonely fellow student. In other words, they were relatively low in nurturance in all the diverse situations that we designed to evoke their more tender emotions—to tug, if only a little, on their heartstrings.

The results for women are less consistent, but the same general pattern emerges. Only androgynous women were high in both independence and nurturance; feminine women were low in independence; and masculine women were (in two situations) low in nurturance. Thus, for both men and women, sex typing does appear to restrict one's functioning in either the instrumental or the expressive domains. Masculine individuals of both sexes are high in independence but low in nurturance, and feminine individuals of both sexes are high in nurturance but low in independence. In contrast, androgynous individuals of both sexes are capable of being both independent and nurturant, both instrumental and expressive, both masculine and feminine.

REFERENCES

Bem, S. L. Sex role adaptability: One consequence of psychological androgyny. *Journal of Personality and Social Psychology,* 1975, *31,* 634–43.

Bem, S. L., & Lenney, E. Sex typing and the avoidance of cross-sex behavior. *Journal of Personality and Social Psychology,* 1976, *33,* 48–54.

PROJECTS

Name _____

Date _____

10.1: ATTITUDES TOWARD WOMEN QUESTIONNAIRE

The following exercise is to be carried out in the field and then discussed and evaluated in the classroom. Its goal is to give you some data on the ways in which men and women evaluate their attitudes toward women. Pick two people you know and consider to be either highly liberated in terms of their attitudes toward women or not. (They may, of course, be of either sex.) Give them the Attitudes Toward Women Questionnaire and record their answers. After you have completed the interviews, write down any other comments you may have about the scale, the interviewees, and your own feelings and attitudes.

Scoring procedure for the questionnaire: Items are scored 0 to 3, with high scores indicating a profeminist, egalitarian attitude. Possible scores range from 0 to 45.

INTERVIEW COMMENTS

Interview A: _____

_____

_____

_____

_____

_____

_____

_____

_____

Interview B: _____

_____

_____

_____

_____

_____

_____

_____

_____

_____

Sex _____

Age _____

Interview

The statements listed below describe attitudes different people have toward the roles of women in society. There are no right or wrong answers, only opinions. Your are asked to express your feeling about each statement by indicating whether you (A) agree strongly, (B) agree mildly, (C) disagree mildly, or (D) disagree strongly.

1. Swearing and obscenity are more repulsive in the speech of a woman than a man.

A	B	C	D
Agree strongly	Agree mildly	Disagree mildly	Disagree strongly

2. Under modern economic conditions with women being active outside the home, men should share in household tasks such as washing dishes and doing the laundry.

A	B	C	D
Agree strongly	Agree mildly	Disagree mildly	Disagree strongly

3. It is insulting to women to have the "obey" clause remain in the marriage service.

A	B	C	D
Agree strongly	Agree mildly	Disagree mildly	Disagree strongly

4. A woman should be as free as a man to propose marriage.

A	B	C	D
Agree strongly	Agree mildly	Disagree mildly	Disagree strongly

5. Women should worry less about their rights and more about becoming good wives and mothers.

A	B	C	D
Agree strongly	Agree mildly	Disagree mildly	Disagree strongly

6. Women should assume their rightful place in business and all the professions along with men.

A	B	C	D
Agree strongly	Agree mildly	Disagree mildly	Disagree strongly

7. A woman should not expect to go to exactly the same places or to have quite the same freedom of action as a man.

A	B	C	D
Agree strongly	Agree mildly	Disagree mildly	Disagree strongly

8. It is ridiculous for a woman to run a locomotive and for a man to darn socks.

A	B	C	D
Agree strongly	Agree mildly	Disagree mildly	Disagree strongly

9. The intellectual leadership of a community should be largely in the hands of men.

A	B	C	D
Agree strongly	Agree mildly	Disagree mildly	Disagree strongly

10. Women should be given equal opportunity with men for apprenticeship in the various trades.

A	B	C	D
Agree strongly	Agree mildly	Disagree mildly	Disagree strongly

11. Women earning as much as their dates should bear equally the expense when they go out together.

A	B	C	D
Agree strongly	Agree mildly	Disagree mildly	Disagree strongly

12. Sons in a family should be given more encouragement to go to college than daughters.

A	B	C	D
Agree strongly	Agree mildly	Disagree mildly	Disagree strongly

13. In general, the father should have greater authority than the mother in the bringing up of children.

A	B	C	D
Agree strongly	Agree mildly	Disagree mildly	Disagree strongly

14. Economic and social freedom is worth far more to women than acceptance of
    the ideal of femininity, which has been set up by men.

A	B	C	D
Agree strongly	Agree mildly	Disagree mildly	Disagree strongly

15. There are many jobs in which men should be given preference over women in
    being hired or promoted.

A	B	C	D
Agree strongly	Agree mildly	Disagree mildly	Disagree strongly

Name _____

Date _____

10.2: CONFRONTATION THROUGH ROLE PLAYING

The goal of the following exercise is to demonstrate, through role-playing techniques, some of the issues discussed in this chapter. Familiarize yourself with the background information and the issues presented below until you feel you could comfortably play either role in a confrontation between the principal and the superintendent. You will then be prepared to proceed with the exercise. The roles of principal and superintendent will be assigned by your instructor, who will explain the circumstances of the confrontation.

BACKGROUND INFORMATION

COMMUNITY: About 60,000 people. Conservative values with respect to education. A typical community for its size.

SUPERINTENDENT: Has doctorate in school administration. Twenty years in public education. On present job for five years; came from outside of state. Has made progress improving schools, but moves cautiously.

JUNIOR HIGH SCHOOL PRINCIPAL: Has master's degree in school administration. Second principalship. Total of five years in school administration; nine years in public education. On present job for two years. Came from another state. Predecessor retired after thirty-five years as teacher and principal (fifteen years as principal of the school in question).

SCHOOL: Three years old; modern construction; modern equipment; traditional curriculum.

FACULTY: About equally divided according to age, experience, philosophy, methodology, and so on.

ISSUES

VANDALISM: Apparently increasing. Maintenance staff reports repeated calls for service to ceiling tiles, lavatory partitions, mirrors, marks on walls, blocked sinks, broken faucets.

DISCIPLINE: Disciplinary referrals are running high (there are usually two or three students waiting for the assistant principal). The secretaries complain about the noise; parents are upset when they come into school. Fighting occurs every few days. In addition, food is thrown in cafeteria, and cafeteria workers say students complain rudely about food and are generally impolite.

FACULTY: Older faculty complain about "permissiveness"; they say that the school was run better by former principal, that students knew where they stood. They question need to promote more classroom discussions, student projects, and the like. Young faculty want to move ahead; they enjoy the freedom of the school. Their classrooms tend to be noisier than those of most of the staff veterans because they encourage a greater number of discussions and projects.

PARENTS: There have been several letters to the editor in the local paper in recent months regarding disciplining of students and apparent lack of firmness; the letter writers want less talking to students and more action. Some parents complain that the veteran teachers are frequently unfair in dealing with students; they like most of the young staff and its methods but are quick to criticize its weaknesses.

GROUP INFLUENCE

11

The group is essential to human survival be-cause, without other people, the individual cannot function and develop. As we noted in our introduction to Chapter 5, people need each other for a variety of reasons, and it is through various kinds of groups that one person gains access to others. Whether it is small or large, formal or informal, each group to which a person belongs can have a tremendous impact on his or her life.

Groups can increase individuals' chances for survival, promote their welfare, protect their rights, and establish a basis for validation of their beliefs. However, membership in a group can also make the individual susceptible to social influences that encourage irrational or destructive behavior. The group pressures that cause us to obey the command to "love thy neighbor" are intimately related to the pressures that prompt us to reject those who are different from ourselves. Clearly, all groups have the potential for both good and ill.

Research on groups was at the core of social psychology in its early years. However, the "cognitive revolution" in psychology has led many researchers away from interindividual processes to the study of intraindividual processes, such as perception, attribution, and information-processing. Group research has also suffered from being very complex and costly to carry out. Nevertheless, new and innovative developments have been taking place in the study of the dynamics of social groups. With the growing interest in applied social psychology, more studies have been conducted with naturally occurring groups, such as juries, encounter groups, political demonstrations, and crowds.

CREATIVE PROBLEM SOLVING AS A RESULT OF MAJORITY VERSUS MINORITY INFLUENCE

CHARLAN JEANNE NEMETH AND JOEL WACHTLER

How are our individual judgments and decisions affected by the judgments of others? This question is at the heart of an enormous amount of research literature on social influence processes. Most of the studies have investigated how a position held by a majority of the group can influence an individual member. The classic conformity studies by Asch demonstrate the persuasive power that a majority holds, even when it is incorrect. But what about a minority position in the group? Does it ever influence individuals' judgments, and if so, how? According to Nemeth and Wachtler, the difference between majority and minority influence is not simply a quantitative one. Rather, there is a qualitative difference in the process of minority versus majority influence. To support their argument, the authors present the results of an experiment on problem solving and show that, while there was more conformity to the majority position, the minority stimulated greater creativity in subjects' responses.

For at least two decades, the area of social influence has been dominated by an interest in the conformity process—that is, the movement of an individual or a minority of individuals toward the position advocated by the majority. Much of this concentration on the conformity aspect of social influence is due to the classic and important work of Asch (1955) who demonstrated that individuals will abdicate the information from their own senses in favor of the position espoused by a majority of individuals. Research on this phenomenon of conformity has been considerable, the focus of such research being primarily on the reasons for conformity versus independence—when do individuals conform to the majority view or resist it? More recently, however, there has been an awareness that conformity and independence are not the only possible reactions to a majority opinion. The minority may actively promote its position and influence the majority. Thus, the bi-directionality of influence between majority and minority has been noted and emphasized.

With the recognition that both the majority and minority may exercise influence, an obvious question arises as to whether or not these processes are governed by the same principles or whether they are quite different modes of influence. Some researchers argue that the same principles govern these two processes. Latané and Wolf (1981), for example, theorize that both majority and minority influence are a multiplicative function of strength, immediacy and numbers of its members. Thus, majority and minority influence differ in degree but not in the nature of the influence process. Most of the theory and research, however, argue and provide evidence for the contention that the processes are indeed quite different. The fact that it is a minority view, the fact that the source of influence is a minority rather than a majority has considerable consequences. Let us first argue this assertion from a theoretical point of view.

Theoretically, majority influence has been considered to be based on dependency. The minority is *dependent* upon the majority for information about reality. It is also *dependent* upon the majority for approval or at least not disapproval. These two forms of dependency have been termed informational and normative influence, respectively. Both such bases of influence by a majority depend on numbers and clearly point to the advantages held by a given majority. The more the numbers the greater the information about social reality and the more people there are to give approval or disapproval.

Minority influence, on the other hand, does not have the numbers for such dependencies. Rather, the influence exerted by a minority is theorized as stemming from an appropriate behavioral style. It requires time. It depends on the orchestration and patterning of verbal and nonverbal cues exhibited by the minority in espousing its position. Specifically, a behavioral style that conveys consistency and confidence has been emphasized. Such consistency is presumed to create both a cognitive and social conflict. On the one hand, it attests to the confidence with which a position is held and thus causes a consideration of the possible correctness of the position. On the other hand, it conveys an unwillingness to compromise, thus creating a social conflict.

It is this distinction between conflict at the level of the stimulus or issue (that is, its correctness) and conflict at the level of response (that is, the interpersonal level) that has been used to underscore a difference between majority and minority influence. Moscovici (1976) argues that majority influence occurs mainly at the response or interpersonal level while minority influence occurs mainly at the stimulus or correctness level. One consequence of such a distinction is that influence by a minority should occur at a private, even latent, level while influence by a majority should be particularly powerful at the public or manifest level.

The empirical evidence, by and large, supports such a contention. Majorities tend to exert more public influence than minorities. Studies on majority influence, for example, report over 30 percent responses in conformity with a majority, while studies in minority influence report considerably less public influence. However, majority influence is rarely evident at the private level. In con-

---

trast, influence by a minority at the manifest or public level tends to be accompanied by private change.

More dramatically, there is evidence that minority influence occurs at a latent level even when subjects do not show public or manifest influence. Subjects exposed to a minority who consistently judges blue slides to be "green" may show little or no movement to the "green" position publicly. Yet they will call more "blue-green" stimuli "green" on a subsequent perception task. Subjects showing that same lack of public movement to the "green" position will nonetheless report an afterimage consistent with "green" after being exposed to a minority who consistently judges the stimuli as green. This latter phenomenon was found only for conditions where the influence was a minority.[1] It was not found when the source of influence was a majority. Subjects exposed to a confederate who consistently espouses a low compensation for a personal injury victim may not publicly change their opinion on the amount of compensation. However, they choose much lower amounts of compensation on *other* personal injury cases.

Empirical data point to still other distinctions between majority and minority influence. One involves the importance of time. Conformity is often manifest on the first few trials or in the first few minutes of discussion. Minority influence is rarely evident in these first trials or first minutes of discussion. Consistent with this is the repeated finding of a sizeable "group effect" in minority influence, that is, members of the majority in a given group show similar patterns of influence. They tend to "move together." Further, this movement tends to occur on the last half of the trials rather than the first half.

Still other experimental data underscore the differing perceptions of the opposing faction as a function of their majority versus minority status. In a majority influence setting, individuals are placed into conflict with a majority who unanimously disagrees with them. In such a situation, they tend to assume that the others (the majority) must be right and they, the naive subjects, must be wrong. In contrast, when a minority is in disagreement, members of the majority assume the minority is relatively incompetent or inaccurate.

They also consistently dislike the minority *even if* the minority is influential. A consistent minority, however, is also seen as more confident.

From the foregoing, one can construct quite different patterns for these two forms of influence. First, we argue that there is much more stress created by a disagreeing majority than a disagreeing minority. When one is faced with a majority who disagrees with oneself, one is concerned immediately about both the correctness of one's own position and the likelihood of disapproval from the majority. . . . A person starts with a presumption that the majority may be correct and even if one is not convinced that they are accurate, one is motivated to show public agreement for the sake of approval. The subject essentially has a decision to make. Does he move to the majority or rest independent? That decision may come from an assessment of who is correct, the majority or the subject him or herself. It may also come from a motivation to avoid disapproval regardless of the perceived correctness of the majority position.

According to the early Asch study (1951), subjects apparently make such a decision. Some conform; some remain independent. Further, they appear to make this decision quite early and behave quite consistently with that decision over the trials. The immediacy and power of a disagreeing majority is a situation of great stress for the subject. Further, the world of alternatives has been reduced to two and ultimately, the subject must make a decision whether to follow the majority or rest independent—a decision that involves both interpersonal aspects of approval as well as stimulus aspects of correctness.

Minority influence, on the other hand, appears to involve quite a different process. At first, the disagreeing minority is regarded with derision. When the minority refuses to compromise but, rather, insists on its position with consistency, he or she is perceived less negatively and, in fact, is accorded dynamic perceptions of confidence. After the passage of time which allows the behavioral consistency to become evident, sometimes one person from the majority moves to the minority position. When that occurs, the process "snowballs" and members of the majority tend to move together. However, there are a number of groups in which no public movement to the minority position is evident. We assume that this is due, in part, to the unfavorable consequences of being in a minority position. However, the influence still occurs, though at a latent level. Many subjects who show no public movement will nonetheless show

---

[1] It should be pointed out that these results have been contested in a replication by Doms and Van Avermaet (1980).

substantive private change in related beliefs or in the perception of the stimulus.

Thus, we hypothesize that subjects exposed to a minority view will be under considerably less stress than those exposed to the majority view. The minority simply does not have the immediate impact of a majority. However, we assume that their impact is related to behavioral consistency. If the minority is that confident, if they are willing to incur the unfavorable consequences of nonconformity, perhaps there is something to their position. The consideration of that viewpoint and its correlate of reconsideration of one's own viewpoint is, we believe, a starting point for creativity. If one looks to the stimulus or looks to the issue in an attempt to understand the minority's persistent position, one can perhaps find other facets of the stimulus or issue; one can perhaps find novel solutions, even those not proposed by the minority.

In majority influence, one is forced to make a decision between two alternatives and the pressure to conformity is quite high. In minority influence, the pressure is considerably less but one is motivated to reassess the situation, to reconsider both one's own position and that proposed by the minority. Thus, the likelihood of finding still other solutions or positions is increased. The preceding descriptions are obviously quite speculative but they are consistent with the array of theoretical and empirical evidence to date and provide us with a number of hypotheses about the potentially creative contribution of a persistent minority.

The emphasis on novel solutions is a departure from the usual definition of influence as a change towards the position espoused. However, change towards a position other than that originally held and other than that espoused is another form of influence. We hypothesize that the former is more typical of majority influence and the latter is more typical of minority influence. Specifically, we predict that when the influencing agent is a member of the majority, subjects will be in great conflict and will choose between following the majority exactly or remaining independent. When the influencing agent is a member of the minority, we predict that subjects will reassess the positions; they will be under less stress; and they will be prone to adopting a novel position (i.e., a position different from that originally held and different from that espoused). Thus, we predict that subjects will be more likely to conform exactly to the majority position than to the minority position.

However, subjects will show more creativity when exposed to the consistent minority. They should find new solutions, hopefully better or correct solutions.

In addition to the above hypotheses regarding differential reactions to a majority versus a minority, we explored the importance of this majority or minority being correct versus incorrect. Most studies investigate movement towards an incorrect position and it is an empirical question as to whether or not this variable affects influence and whether it interacts with the majority or minority status of the influencing agent. One would assume that correctness would foster influence but we left this as an empirical question.

METHOD

Procedure

Overview. Subjects were shown a series of slides with a standard figure on the left and a group of six comparison figures on the right. Three of these comparison figures contained the standard and three did not. One comparison figure was "easy" (named by a large percentage of subjects) and the other five were difficult. Depending on the experimental condition, a majority or minority of confederates judged the standard as embedded in the easy comparison figure and in one of the difficult comparison figures. Again depending on condition, they were either correct or incorrect in their judgment. Subjects were asked to identify all the comparison figures, if any, that contained the standard. Subsequent to the experimental sessions they were asked to complete a questionnaire reporting moods and perceptions of the confederates.

Specifics. Subjects were 162 male undergraduates in an introductory psychology course who volunteered to participate in an experiment on "visual perception." These subjects were placed in one of four experimental conditions or a control. Nine groups were run in each of the five conditions. Each of the groups consisted of six persons, some of whom were subjects and others of whom were confederates of the experiment. The confederates were all male undergraduates randomly assigned to the groups. In the "majority" conditions, two subjects and four confederates comprised the group. In the "minority" conditions, there were four subjects and two confederates in the group. In the control condition, six subjects constituted the group. There were two "majority" and two "minority" conditions, one in which the majority of four (or minority of two) gave correct judgments and one in which they gave an incorrect judgment.

The task for the subjects and confederates was to identify any and all of the six comparison figures which contained a given standard figure. The figures were taken from the hidden patterns test Cf-5 of the Educational Testing Service (adapted from *Designs* by C. C. Thurstone). Subjects were shown eight slides in which the standard was on the left and the six comparison figures were on the right. The standard was the same for all eight slides. Of the six comparison figures, one was very "easy" for subjects to detect the embedded figure. It consisted of the standard figure in a right-side up position with very few superfluous lines. Pretesting on 128 subjects showed that 77 percent of the subjects chose the "easy" figure as containing the standard. The other comparison figures were difficult; two contained the embedded figure (difficult correct) and three did not contain the embedded figure (difficult incorrect). "Difficulty" was achieved by adding many superfluous lines, darkening some lines, or having the standard on its side or upside down. Pretesting of the 128 subjects indicated that only 15 percent chose a "difficult correct" figure and 8 percent chose a "difficult incorrect" figure.

In the experimental conditions, the confederates either judged the standard to be embedded in the "easy" comparison figure and in a "difficult correct" figure (right conditions) or they judged the standard to be in the "easy" comparison figure and in a "difficult incorrect" figure (wrong conditions). Confederates gave the same difficult right or wrong answers when in the majority or minority conditions. Thus, there were four experimental conditions as follows:

Minority right: The minority of two confederates judged the standard to be in both the "easy" figure and a "difficult correct" comparison figure.

Minority wrong: The minority of two confederates judged the standard to be in both the "easy" figure and a "difficult incorrect" comparison figure.

Majority right: The majority of four confederates judged the standard to be in both the "easy" figure and a "difficult correct" comparison figure.

Majority wrong: The majority of four confederates judged the standard to be in both the "easy" figure and a "difficult incorrect" comparison figure.

As each group of six entered the room, they were assigned seats such that the confederates in the "majority" conditions took the first, second, fourth, and fifth seats. The confederates in the "minority" conditions took the first and fourth seats. Subjects gave their answers orally in the order of seating. Four categories of responses were used to classify the figures chosen. One category was the "easy" response. A second was the other response chosen by the confederates (either correct or incorrect). A third was a choice of a "novel correct" comparison figure—that is, a figure that contained the standard but was not suggested by the confederates. The fourth category was a choice of a "novel incorrect" figure—that is, one that did not contain the standard and was not suggested by the confederates. Each slide consisted of three correct and three incorrect figures. Subsequent to the judgments of embedded figures, subjects were asked to complete a questionnaire on moods and perceptions of the confederates. The mood scales revolved around the issue of stress (e.g., awkward, embarrassed, fearful) and the perceptions of the confederate centered on issues of competence, confidence, and liking.

Analyses were computed for the behavioral responses of choosing the "easy" solution only, for "exact following" (i.e. making the same two responses as made by the confederates), for percentage of "novel correct" responses and for percentage of "novel incorrect" responses (number chosen divided by number available). The hypotheses were that subjects would "follow" the majority more than the minority but that the minority would induce reassessment and thus foster more novel or creative responses. If this is a creative process rather than mere guessing, it should be reflected in the number of novel correct judgments but not in the number of novel incorrect judgments. Analyses were also computed for the mood scales and perceptions of the confederates.

RESULTS

All analyses used the group mean as the datum. Thus, the responses of two naive subjects in the "majority" conditions, four naive subjects in the "minority" conditions and six naive subjects in

TABLE 1.

	MAJORITY		MINORITY		
	RIGHT	WRONG	RIGHT	WRONG	CONTROL
"Easy" response only	5.61	4.67	5.19	5.50	6.39
Exact following	1.44	1.94	0.67	0.58	—
% novel correct	2.47	5.55	9.26	7.02	3.92
% novel incorrect	1.45	1.85	3.50	2.22	1.93
% novel	1.74	3.82	5.12	4.77	2.78

the control condition were averaged over the eight trials. The group mean was used since subjects are not independent of one another in a given group.

Since we started with the assumption that the control group would be more likely to choose the "easy" figure only, we computed a 5-level one-way ANOVA on choosing "easy only," that is, the "easy" figure but no other figure was judged to contain the standard (see Table 1). This analysis was significant with a subsequent t-test showing the control to be significantly different from the experimental groups. None of the experimental groups differed from each other with regard to choosing "easy only."

Our next hypothesis concerned the likelihood of subjects following the majority more than the minority—that is, choosing the exact figures suggested by the confederates. A 2 × 2 ANOVA found a significant main effect for majority versus minority conditions on this "exact following." Subjects followed a majority more than a minority. No main effect was found for the right versus wrong conditions, nor was there any interaction between the two variables.

A third hypothesis concerned the likelihood of making a novel response—that is, one that was not suggested by the minority or majority, but one which was correct. For this, we used "percentage novel correct" judgments—that is, the number of novel correct figures chosen by the subject divided by the number of novel correct figures that were possible. The mean for the group was the datum. Both minority conditions showed a significantly higher percentage of "novel correct" responses than the majority conditions or the control; neither of the majority conditions differed from the control conditions. We also computed a 2 × 2 ANOVA on "percentage correct novel" responses and found a significant main effect for majority versus minority conditions and a marginal significance for the interaction between majority/minority and right/wrong. The marginal interaction is due to a tendency for a majority to

induce more novel correct responses when they are incorrect rather than correct while there is a nonsignificant trend for the minority to induce more novel correct responses when they are correct rather than incorrect. No main effect was found for the right/wrong conditions.

With regard to the "percentage novel incorrect" answers—that is, the number of novel incorrect figures chosen by the subject divided by the number of novel incorrect figures that were possible, the 5-level one-way ANOVA did not show a significant main effect. The 2 × 2 ANOVA showed no significant main effects nor a significant interaction.

Consistent with the previous two findings, we found a significant main effect for the number of "novel" responses, both correct and incorrect. Both minority conditions showed more "novel" responses than either the majority conditions or the control. The majority conditions did not differ from the control. A 2 × 2 ANOVA showed a significant main effect for majority/minority. Subjects exposed to the minority gave more novel responses than those exposed to the majority.

For the questionnaire, planned contrasts between the majority and minority conditions were calculated. Subjects reported that they felt more awkward, more embarrassed, and less happy in the majority conditions than in the minority conditions. They also reported a tendency to feel more fearful and frustrated in the majority conditions than in the minority conditions. Subjects reported being more angry and less happy when the confederates were "right" rather than "wrong." As a check on the manipulation of "right/wrong," subjects reported that the confederates found a higher percentage of "all possible correct responses" and that they less often selected a comparison figure which did not contain the standard when they were "right" rather than "wrong." With regard to perceptions of the confederates, group means of subjects' perceptions of the confederates within a given group were used. Subjects reported that minority confederates found a lower "percentage of all possible correct responses'' stood out more, were less concerned "about agreeing with the others in the group,'' were more "independent'' and that "when the group disagreed,'' more "of the disagreement was due'' to the minority individuals.

DISCUSSION

Our experimental situation consisted of asking subjects to find any and all of the comparison figures in which a standard figure was embedded. We chose a situation where subjects alone would tend to choose the comparison figure that was easy—that is, most subjects could tell that the comparison figure contained the standard. This is corroborated by the finding that the control group was more likely to judge only the "easy'' comparison figure relative to all the experimental groups. We then predicted that the subjects exposed to a majority who gave a judgment in addition to the "easy'' one would follow that majority more than they would follow a minority who gave the same judgments. This was confirmed by a significant main effect for majority/minority conditions on the "exact following'' dependent variable. Subjects followed the majority more exactly than they did a minority. However, as predicted, subjects exposed to a minority were influenced in a different way. They made novel judgments—that is, they chose figures which were not suggested by the confederates. However, such a tendency to make novel responses was not just guessing. Importantly, they chose "novel'' comparison figures which were correct. There were no significant differences between conditions on the number of comparison figures which were "novel'' but incorrect. This "creative'' finding of correct solutions that tend to be undetected when subjects are alone or when they are faced with a disagreeing majority, is, we believe, one of the more interesting consequences of facing a persistent minority and points to the possibility of a creative contribution of conflict when posed by a minority.

Majority influence on the other hand is seen to force a decision between two alternatives, the position of the majority or the information from one's own senses. Subjects either conformed exactly to the majority or tended to remain independent. They did not show a significant tendency to find "novel'' solutions and, in particular, they did not tend to find "novel correct'' solutions. Subjects in the majority conditions differed from their control counterparts mainly on the dimension of conformity in its traditional sense. The majority is very effective in gaining "exact following'' from subjects. In contrast, subjects exposed to a minority were less likely to follow the minority exactly but, as indicated previously, they were more likely to find novel solutions and, in particular, novel solutions that were correct.

Correctness of position appeared to have little effect on majority or minority influence. Whether the majority or minority was correct or incorrect had little impact on "exact following.'' However, there was an interesting, though marginal, finding with regard to the correctness of the position interacting with the majority/minority variable on the number of "novel correct'' responses. The "just short of significance'' interaction was due to a tendency for the majority to induce more novel correct responses from the subjects when they were incorrect rather than correct; the tendency to find novel correct responses as a consequence of minority influence was not significantly affected by the correctness of their position.

Though necessarily speculative at this point, this finding is consistent with our general premise that the majority reduces the world of alternatives to two—their position and that of the subject. When they are incorrect, however, they may induce some attempt to explore novel alternatives. If a number of people can be wrong, perhaps the situation or stimulus is more complicated than one imagined. Even if such a process is evident, it appears not to have a force equivalent to that exerted by the minority. Comparing the condition where the majority is correct versus incorrect, subjects go from "just below'' the control groups in "percentage novel'' responses to "just above'' the control groups. Even when the majority is incorrect, the tendency to find novel solutions is not significantly different from the control.

The important comparisons between majority and minority influence, however, are in the different types of influence that are exerted. The majority exerts a powerful pressure to conform. Subjects report feeling more awkward, embarrassed, fearful, frustrated and less happy in the majority influence conditions. They also tend to follow the majority more than do the minority—follow in the sense of giving the same judgments as those espoused by the majority. Apart from conformity in the sense of "exact following,'' the majority influence conditions are quite similar to the controls. In contrast, we expected and found that the subjects in the minority influence situation would be less stressed, prone to judge the minority as incorrect, but to be stimulated to peruse the entire situation and, in the process, find novel and correct solutions. They report that the minority gave fewer correct answers but they also saw them as independent, standing out, not concerned about disagreement. They followed them less in the traditional sense of influence, but more importantly, they found novel solutions which were correct, solutions that would have gone undetected without the influence of the minority.

In our emphasis on the creative contribution of conflict generated by a minority and the potential hindering of creative problem solving caused by a majority who reduces the world of alternatives to two, we are underscoring our belief that the processes of influence exerted by a majority versus a minority are indeed quite different. We are also arguing and underscoring the definition of influence as broader than adopting the position of the influencing agent or even moving towards it. One can be influenced to reanalyze a problem and, in the process, perhaps function more creatively and accurately.

REFERENCES

Asch, S. E. Effects of group pressure upon the modification and distortion of judgment. In H. Guetzkow (ed.), *Groups, leadership, and men*. Pittsburgh, Pa.: Carnegie Press, 1951.

Asch, S. Opinions and social pressure. *Scientific American*, 1955, *193*, 31–35.

Doms, M., and Van Avermaet, E. Majority influence, minority influence, and conversion behavior: A replication. *Journal of Experimental Social Psychology*, 1980, *16*, 283–92.

Latané, B., and Wolf, S. The social impact of majorities and minorities. *Psychological Review*, 1980, *88*, 438–53.

Moscovici, S. *Social influence and social change*. New York: Academic Press, 1976.

CROWD SIZE AS A FACTOR IN THE PERSUASION PROCESS: A STUDY OF RELIGIOUS CRUSADE MEETINGS

JAMES W. NEWTON AND LEON MANN

The phenomenon of crowd behavior has fascinated social scientists and philosophers for many years. The way in which individuals get caught up in a larger group and act in concert, sometimes doing things they would never do on their own, led LeBon to postulate the presence of a "group mind." Although this concept is no longer a popular one, researchers have shown a renewed interest in understanding the dynamics of crowd behavior. One argument has been that crowds can affect the process of persuasion by moderating the impact of the communicator on the audience. To investigate this issue, Newton and Mann studied religious crusade meetings where thousands of people came to hear an evangelist. Their question was: Does the size of the crowd affect how persuasive the evangelist is? According to their data, the answer is yes, and the authors speculate on why this might be so.

Reprinted from the *Journal of Personality and Social Psychology*, 1980, *39:5*, 874–83. Copyright © 1980 by The American Psychological Association, Inc.

The social influence perspective on collective behavior is concerned with changes that occur in individual conduct as a function of belonging to or coming in contact with a crowd. Field research on collective behavior has shown that crowd or audience size is a key variable mediating some social influence processes. For example, large crowds exert more influence than small crowds in drawing or attracting outsiders and in recruiting new members. However, there is no conclusive evidence on crowd size as a factor affecting the persuasion of crowd members who have been urged to change their opinions or to take action.

It is conceivable that increases in crowd size may moderate social influence processes within the crowd so as to either enhance or hinder a communicator's persuasive efforts.[1] Consider a formal meeting or rally in which the speaker advocates a course of action before a generally sympathetic audience. As the crowd grows, the effects of social facilitation, social support, modeling of responses, and pressure toward conformity could enhance the speaker's influence. Alternatively, in a large crowd the speaker's influence attempt may be weakened because each member is relatively inconspicuous to the speaker and the relationship between speaker and audience is remote and impersonal.

Although crowd size per se may affect the person's responsiveness to an influence attempt, it is also possible that the composition of large crowds may be responsible for apparent changes in crowd responsiveness to a speaker. For example, one "convergence" explanation would hold that the apparent responsiveness of large crowds is due to an influx of large numbers of partisan supporters who come prepared to respond to the speaker. Another convergence explanation would argue that large crowds function as a magnet for certain types of people who are highly susceptible to influence. These explanations are not mutually exclusive, of course, and it is possible that influence and composition factors are jointly responsible for increases in responsiveness to a speaker's appeal in large crowds.

We postulate that in general when crowd members assemble voluntarily to hear a speaker, there will be a positive relationship between crowd size and influence.[2] That is, the larger the crowd, the greater the proportion of its membership who will be persuaded to adopt the speaker's recommen-

dation. To test the hypothesized enhancement effect of large crowds, we shall examine data gathered during religious crusade meetings organized by the Billy Graham Evangelistic Association. Religious crusades are well suited to this purpose for the following reasons:

1. A crusade consists of many meetings, each one following a standard format. This enables data to be collected from a large sample of similar crowds.

2. Meetings often vary in size from fewer than 1,000 people to over 80,000, ensuring a wide range for examining the effects of different crowd sizes.

3. The "inquiring" response the evangelist attempts to elicit—that is, coming forward at the end of the sermon to make a public "decision" for Christ—is a socially significant act with potentially important consequences for both the individual and the evangelical movement.

Previous Data on Billy Graham Rallies

There are some fragmentary data on the effects of the size of crusade crowds on inquiring. Argyle and Beit-Hallahmi (1975) provide statistics from Billy Graham's crusade meetings in Britain, 1954–1955, and note that the proportion of the audience who became inquirers appeared to increase as a function of the size of the audience. For example, the proportion of the audience making "decisions" at the first eight meetings at Harringay, London, in 1954 was 2.04 percent, based on an average meeting size of 10,000, whereas the proportion making "decisions" at the following 25 meetings was 2.37 percent, based on an average meeting size of 12,000 (computed from data in Colquhoun, 1955). Statistics on crowd response during Graham's Seattle crusade (May 1976) also suggest a positive relationship between crowd size and the proportion coming forward to make public "decisions" for Christ. Calculations based on a report in the *Seattle Post Intelligencer* (Smith, 1976) reveal the following crowd sizes and associated percentages of "inquirers" for the eight crusade meetings: 49,600—2.8 percent (based on five meetings); 51,000—3.5 percent; 61,000—4.2 percent; and 74,000—9.4 percent.

Although there are indications of a positive relationship between crowd size and the proportion of inquirers, it is clear that the statistics from both Graham's British crusade (1954–1955) and his Seattle crusade (1976) must be regarded with great caution. The figures are not given for each meeting

---

[1]Latané, B. *Theory of social impact.* Paper presented at the 21st International Congress of Psychology, Paris, July 1976.

[2]This would not be the case, of course, if those attending the meeting had attended intentionally to disrupt the speaker or for some purpose other than to learn the evangelist's message.

separately, but are frequently grouped and averaged, thereby obscuring possible reversals in the relationship. In addition, there is some evidence that large crowds may actually inhibit inquiring. Data reported by Latané (Note 1), based on 37 Graham rallies held in 1970, reveal a negative relationship (r = −.41) between crowd size and percentage inquiring for Christ. Latané's data pose difficulties for our hypothesis, because the 37 rallies he reports span a wide range of crowd sizes (from fewer than 3,000 to over 140,000), and the percentage of inquirers is given for each rally separately.

The purpose of the present study was to determine whether reliable data from a number of crusades would reveal a consistent relationship between the attendance at crusade meetings and the proportion of inquirers for Christ.

The Data Base

Staff members of the Billy Graham Evangelistic Association (BGEA) routinely prepare a statistical profile for each crusade. People who know the capacity of each section of the meeting site count the occupants of each section while each meeting is in progress. Statistics on inquirers are compiled immediately after each meeting by a team of volunteers working from cards the inquirers have filled out with the aid of trained counselors. A summary sheet is drawn up for each meeting, showing the total attendance with breakdowns on inquirers by classification (Salvation, Assurance, Rededication, or Other), sex, and age group.

The BGEA staff provided complete sets of summary sheets for four crusades in Australia: Billy Graham's crusade of April–May 1979 in Sydney and Leighton Ford's crusades of March 1979 in Adelaide and Illawarra and October 1978 in Melbourne. Although we have no way to assess the accuracy of these data, we were impressed by the technical proficiency of the BGEA organization, and we are confident that the organization strives for accuracy. There is no reason to suspect the presence of systematic errors in the data that might generate spurious patterns of association between crowd size and inquiring.

The data made available to us included total attendance and limited information on inquirers but no information on other crowd members. Determination of the social psychological dynamics underlying a relationship between crowd size and inquiring would require information from samples of all attenders at crusade meetings as well as additional information on inquirers. Neverthe-less, these data did provide a basis for clarifying key issues to be addressed if and when more extensive data become available.

Data Analysis

One strategy for data analysis would be to combine the four crusades, treating all meetings as comparable elements of a single sample. However, there are strong arguments in favor of analyzing each crusade separately. The Graham and Ford crusades differed in several respects: (a) Preparations for Graham's Sydney crusade began three years in advance, whereas Ford's crusades had about one year of preparation; (b) Graham's smallest meeting (9,000) was larger than Ford's largest meeting (8,500), so factors associated with crusade organization and the two evangelists' personal styles cannot be separated from the effects of crowd size; (c) Graham's mean percentage of inquirers (4.61) was significantly higher than Ford's (2.07). In addition, the crusades occurred in different parts of Australia under local conditions about which we have little information. Accordingly, the data will be presented for each crusade separately and then common patterns will be identified.

Study 1: Billy Graham in Sydney. A total of 491,500 people attended Graham's 20 meetings at a large racetrack in Sydney in 1979. The attendance was 9,000 at the smallest meeting and 85,000 at the largest meeting with a mean attendance of 24,575. Overall, 4.61 percent of those attending made public decisions for Christ. Of these inquirers, 53 percent were female and 72 percent were under 26 years of age.

Contrary to the hypothesis, the overall relationship between meeting size and the percentage of the audience who came forward to make a decision was negative, $r(18) = -.41$. However, close inspection indicates no uniform negative relationship across the range of crowd sizes. It suggests a changing pattern, characterized by a positive relationship in the range of 9,000 to 22,000, which gives way to a negative relationship for crowds between 25,000 and 85,000. A check on meeting dates revealed an interesting fact: The size of the meeting and the day of the week on which it occurred were systematically related. All of the smaller meetings (9,000–22,000 people) took place on weekdays, meetings in the middle of the size distribution took place on Saturdays (25,000–32,000), and the largest meetings took place on

Sundays (38,000–85,000). When the data were analyzed for these day-of-the-week groups separately, distinct patterns were apparent. The relationship between crowd size and the percentage inquiring was positive for the 13 weekday meetings, and for the four Sunday meetings. The three Saturday meetings showed a slight negative trend.

Since none of these correlations was statistically significant, it would be premature at this point to speculate about the possible dynamics of the relationship between crowd size and responsiveness to the evangelist's call. The data suggest, however, that factors associated with the day of the week moderate the effects of crowd size.

Study 2: Leighton Ford Crusades in Australia. Further opportunities to test the crowd influence hypothesis were provided by three crusades led by Leighton Ford (Graham's brother-in-law) in Australia in 1978 and 1979. Ford held eight meetings in Adelaide and 12 meetings in Illawarra in March 1979 and 17 meetings in Melbourne in October 1978. The availability of data from these crusades is important because they enable a test of crowd enhancement and resistance effects taking into account differences between evangelists' styles and crusade attendance.

RESULTS

Combining the Data

It is possible to combine the results from the four crusades to determine whether a significant relationship occurs for the set altogether. When the correlation coefficients for weekday meetings in the four crusades are combined, the result is significant, revealing a reliable positive relationship between crowd size and inquiring on weekdays. In two of the four crusades, there were too few Saturday and Sunday meetings to permit computation of correlation coefficients (Adelaide and Illawarra), and therefore we are unable to combine probabilities for weekend meetings.

Who Are the Inquirers?

The Billy Graham Evangelical Association counselors classified the inquirers into four groups according to information on their "decision cards": (a) Salvation—virtually new converts who accept Christ as Savior and Lord; (b) Assurance—people with a tenuous prior religious involvement who seek assurance of salvation; (c) Rededication—believers who are reaffirming their commitment; (d)

Others. Salvation, a "first time" decision, is the most interesting of the categories from a social influence perspective because it entails a much greater psychological step than either rededication or assurance. Consistently, across crusades salvation inquirers constituted approximately half of the total inquirer group. There were more female than male inquirers in each crusade, and the majority of inquirers were young people.

Let us first consider the relationship between the percentage of inquirers in the crowd and the composition of the inquirer group. Stouffer tests showed reliable positive correlations between increases in the percentage inquiring and the proportion of salvation inquirers, the proportion of females, and the proportion of young people. In other words, in crowds where there was a relatively high proportion of inquirers, more of these people were salvation inquirers, females, and young people.

When data from the Melbourne crusade were omitted (in Melbourne crowd size was not positively related to inquiring), combined probabilities for the three remaining crusades revealed significant positive relationships between crowd size and the proportions of salvation inquirers, females, and young people.

In sum, our analysis of changes in the composition of the inquirer group has drawn attention to salvation inquirers—those making a first commitment—and to females and young people as the principal contributors to higher rates of inquiring. Larger crowds have greater proportions of salvation inquirers than smaller crowds, and in larger crowds the proportions of female and young inquirers increase. Since we lack data on individual inquirers, we cannot assess the extent to which these groups overlap. It is possible, for example, that most of the increase in inquiring in larger crowds is due to a higher proportion of young females in the salvation category.

DISCUSSION

It was hypothesized that the evangelist's persuasive effect on the audience would be enhanced by the presence of a large crowd. The rationale for this hypothesis is derived from analysis of the following influence processes associated with the leader–audience situation.

1. The presence of a large crowd reinforces and confirms the evangelist's prestige as a religious figure and communicator. The communicator's

prestige increases a listener's motivation to accept his or her message.

2. In large audiences, the example set by those who first answer the evangelist's call is more compelling to people who are inclined to go forward but are hesitant. Let us assume that 1 percent of any crusade gathering is predisposed to respond readily to the speaker's request. For the undecided members of the audience, the sight of 1 percent of 100,000 people (i.e., 1,000) moving forward creates a more powerful magnet than the sight of 1 percent of 1,000 people (i.e., 10) moving forward. As people observe and imitate the responses of others, a kind of "contagion" or "snowballing" effect occurs. Religious counselors, whose role it is to proceed to the platform as the inquirers move forward, add to the impression of a continuous flow of people responding spontaneously to the evangelist's call. This contributes to the snowballing effect in large crowds. Lang and Lang (1960) note that Graham's appeal for inquirers during one crusade referred explicitly to imitation and social support: "To make a decision . . . was to join something larger than one's self; everybody's doing it, why not you? *How many,* Graham asked, will be new people tonight? Come to the platform—*hundreds* are coming" (Lang and Lang, 1960, p. 424; italics in original).

3. The mere presence of many others produces arousal and excitement that tends to energize the expression of dominant responses. If the person's dominant inclination is to go forward, then the larger the crowd, the greater the social facilitation of that response.

4. Aspects of the evangelist's own performance when preaching to a large crowd may contribute to an enhancement effect. The evangelist may be more inspired, and therefore more inspiring, when addressing a large audience. Also, the evangelist may deliberately strive for greater effect when addressing large audiences, bearing in mind impact on the wide media audience.

Data from four evangelistic crusades did reveal a reliable positive relationship between crowd size and inquiring for meetings held on weekdays. A pattern of higher attendance without higher inquiring rates distinguished weekend meetings from weekday meetings, so that separate analyses were required. There was suggestive evidence that crowd size and inquiring may be positively correlated for Saturdays and Sundays as well as weekdays.

The limitations of our data prevented us from establishing the basis of the relationship between crowd size and inquiring. As we have pointed out, it may be due to enhancement of the evangelist's influence by social influence processes, or it may be due to a tendency for larger crowds to include higher proportions of people whose independent predisposition is to go forward as inquirers. Alternatively, enhanced influence and factors related to crowd composition may be jointly responsible. Larger crowds may strengthen the influence forces to which crowd members are subject and may also include more people who are highly susceptible to social influence. Yet another possibility, suggested in Allport's (1924) classic treatment of crowd behavior, is a convergence-social facilitation model. Allport contended that the prime mechanism in collective behavior is the gathering of people with similar predispositions whose co-presence facilitates the release and expression of their predispositions. Finally, it is possible that all of these factors contribute to increased responsiveness to influence attempts in larger crowds. Resolution of this issue must remain a matter for future research with more extensive data.

The proportion of first-time inquirers (those in the salvation category) was greater when inquiring rates were higher and in larger crowds. This finding contradicts the notion that increased inquiring may reflect greater activity by committed Christians who have come to help make the crusade impressive as a massive religious event and who "boost the numbers" for the media audience by joining the inquirer group. Whether large crowds enhance the evangelist's persuasiveness or simply attract more potential first-time inquirers, then, the evidence is that large crowds provide a context conducive to more successful evangelism.

Several studies have reported that females and young people consistently make up the majority of inquirers at crusade meetings. In Billy Graham's crusades in England in 1954–1955, two thirds of the inquirers were female, and 60 percent were under 19 years of age. In a 1970 Graham crusade meeting in Tennessee, 53 percent of the inquirers were female, and 73 percent were under 20 years of age. Similarly, in the Australian crusades the majority of inquirers were female and young. Our data showed that the proportions of females and young people increased with higher inquiring rates and in larger crowds. These two groups were therefore the main contributors to increased inquiring associated with crowd size. Without data on the composition of crusade crowds as a whole, we cannot determine whether this pattern was due to greater responsiveness to influence or increased attendance by females and young people at larger meetings. However, previously reported sex and age differences in susceptibility to social influence encourage the view that increased inquiring by females and young people in larger crowds may result from their greater tendency to respond to influence processes, which in turn may gain strength as crowd size increases. There is evidence that females are more responsive than males to influence attempts in face-to-face situations and to persuasive communications. In general, conformity declines from adolescence to adulthood. It has also been found that people under 20 years of age show greater attitude change following persuasive communications than older people do. It seems unlikely that changes in the inquiring rate for young people simply mirror their proportions in the crowd, since previous studies have reported that the proportion of young people among the inquirers far exceeds their representation in the audience as a whole.

We suspect that the tendency for weekend meetings to have higher attendance but not higher inquiring rates than weekday meetings was a consequence of their special composition. The doubling and sometimes tripling of attendance on weekends may be due largely to the presence of greater numbers of committed Christians (who are much less likely to become inquirers), as well as casual observers. Crusade staff members whom we interviewed believed that weekend crowds included many more church members than weekday crowds—people who traveled to the crusade meeting after morning church services or attended the meeting in lieu of regular services. These changes in composition would mean that on Saturdays and Sundays the *absolute* number of inquirers could increase with crowd size while the *proportion* of inquirers increased only slightly or actually decreased.

Analysis of the data from Ford's Melbourne crusade (in which crowd size and inquiring were negatively correlated, although not significantly) pointed toward crowd composition as the principal moderator of responsiveness to the evangelist's message. Although these findings cannot be conclusively interpreted without data on the attenders as a whole, they suggest that in Melbourne larger crowds had higher proportions of older, male Christians. A pattern of this sort could be produced by unusual publicity procedures or arrangements for organized transportation of church members to particular meetings.

In conclusion, when the crusade data included sufficient numbers of comparable meetings to permit the appropriate analysis (i.e., weekday meetings), a positive relationship between crowd size and inquiring was demonstrated. There is reason to suspect that this relationship would also hold for Saturdays and Sundays. First-time inquirers (those whose decisions should be least affected by prior religious commitment or church affiliation and most affected by the evangelist's influence) increased within the inquirer group as a function of crowd size, as did the proportions of females and young people. These results are consistent with the hypothesis that influence is enhanced when persuasive appeals are made to large audiences of people whose attendance is voluntary and generally motivated by favorable attitudes toward the speaker. However, they can also be explained by postulating that crowd size is associated with increasing attendance by females, young people, and prospective first-time inquirers. Further field studies on religious crusades in which both attenders and inquirers are surveyed, as well as experimental studies involving audiences of varying sizes, are needed to determine the social psychological basis for the relationship between crowd size and responsiveness to an appeal and to clarify the reliability and magnitude of the effect.

REFERENCES

Argyle, M., & Beit-Hallahmi, B. *The social psychology of religion.* London: Routledge & Kegan Paul, 1975.

Lang, K., & Lang, G. E. Decisions for Christ: Billy Graham in New York City. In M. Stein, A. J. Vidich, & D. M. White (eds.), *Identity and anxiety.* Glencoe, Ill.: Free Press, 1960.

Smith, K. Graham parts with warning. *Seattle Post Intelligencer,* May 17, 1976.

ON LEADERS

What is a leader—the controller of history and personal fortune or a pawn of fate, history's slave? Machiavelli and Tolstoy express opposing views on the subject.

How Far Human Affairs are Governed by Fortune[1]

I am not unaware that many have held and hold the opinion that events are controlled by fortune and by God in such a way that the prudence of men cannot modify them, indeed, that men have no influence whatsoever. Because of this, they would conclude that there is no point in sweating over things, but that one should submit to the rulings of chance. This opinion has been more widely held in our own times, because of the great changes and variations, beyond human imagining, which we have experienced and experience every day. Sometimes, when thinking of this, I have myself inclined to this same opinion. Nonetheless, so as not to rule out our free will, I believe that it is probably true that fortune is the arbiter of half the things we do, leaving the other half or so to be controlled by ourselves. I compare fortune to one of those violent rivers which, when they are enraged, flood the plains, tear down trees and buildings, wash soil from one place to deposit it in another. Everyone flees before them, everybody yields to their impetus, there is no possibility of resistance. Yet although such is their nature, it does not follow that when they are flowing quietly one cannot take precautions, constructing dykes and embankments so that when the river is in flood it runs into a canal or else its impetus is less wild and dangerous. So it is with fortune. She shows her power where there is no force to hold her in check; and her impetus is felt where she knows there are no embankments and dykes built to restrain her. . . .

We see that some princes flourish one day and come to grief the next, without appearing to have changed in character or any other way. This I

believe arises, first because those princes who are utterly dependent on fortune come to grief when their fortune changes. I also believe that the one who adapts his policy to the times prospers, and likewise that the one whose policy clashes with the demands of the times does not. It can be observed that men use various methods in pursuing their own personal objectives, such as glory and riches. One man proceeds with circumspection, another impetuously; one uses violence, another stratagem; one man goes about things patiently, another does the opposite; and yet everyone, for all this diversity of method, can reach his objective. It can also be observed that with two circumspect men, one will achieve his end, the other not; and likewise two men succeed equally well with different methods, one of them being circumspect and the other impetuous. This results from nothing else except the extent to which their methods are or are not suited to the nature of the times. Thus it happens that, as I have said, two men, working in different ways, can achieve the same end, and of two men working in the same way one gets what he wants and the other does not. This also explains why prosperity is ephemeral; because if a man behaves with patience and circumspection and the time and circumstances are such that this method is called for, he will prosper; but if time and circumstances change he will be ruined because he does not change his policy. Nor do we find any man shrewd enough to know how to adapt his policy in this way; either because he cannot do otherwise than what is in character or because, having always prospered by proceeding one way, he cannot persuade himself to change. Thus a man who is circumspect, when circumstances demand impetuous behaviour, is unequal to the task, and so he comes to grief. If he changed his character according to the time and circumstances, then his fortune would not change.

History and Great Leaders[2]

Man lives consciously for himself, but is an unconscious instrument in the attainment of the historic, universal, aims of humanity. A deed done is irrevocable, and its result coinciding in time with the actions of millions of other men assumes an historic significance. The higher a man stands on the social ladder, the more people he is connected with and the more power he has over others, the more evident is the predestination and inevitability of his every action.

"The king's heart is in the hands of the Lord."

A king is history's slave.

History, that is, the unconscious, general, hive life of mankind, uses every moment of the life of kings as a tool for its own purposes.

. . .

Chance, millions of chances, give Napoleon power, and all men, as if by agreement, collaborate to confirm that power. Chance forms the characters of the rulers of France, who submit to him; chance forms the character of Paul I of Russia, who recognizes his power; chance puts the Duc d'Enghien in his hands and unexpectedly impels him to assassinate him—thereby convincing the mob by the most cogent of means that he has the right since he has the might. Chance contrives that though he bends all his efforts toward an expedition against England (which unquestionably would have ruined him) he never executes this plan, but fortuitously falls upon Mack and the Austrians, who surrender without a battle. Chance and genius give him the victory at Austerlitz: and by chance all men, not only the French but all Europe, except England, which takes no part in the events about to occur—forget their former horror and detestation of his crimes, and now recognize his authority, the title he had bestowed upon himself, and his ideal of glory and grandeur, which seems splendid and reasonable to them all.

. . .

The invasion courses eastward and reaches its final goal—Moscow. The capital is taken; the Russian army suffers heavier losses than the opposing army suffered at any time during previous wars from Austerlitz to Wagram. But all at once, instead of *chance* and the *genius* that had so consistently led him by an unbroken series of successes to the predestined goal, a succession of counter *chances* occur—from the cold in his head at Borodino to the frosts, and the spark that set fire to Moscow—and instead of *genius*, stupidity and unprecedented baseness are displayed.

The invaders flee, turn back, flee again, and now the *chances* are not for Napoleon but consistently against him.

[1] From *The Prince* by Niccolò Machiavelli, translated by George Bull (Penguin Classics, 1961), pp. 130–131, 132. Copyright © George Bull, 1961. Reprinted by permission of Penguin Books Ltd.
[2] From *War and Peace* by Leo Tolstoy, translated by Ann Dunnigan. Copyright © 1968 by Ann Dunnigan. Reprinted by arrangement with The New American Library, Inc., New York.

THE THIRD WAVE

RON JONES

It has often been noted that a group can transcend its individual members and become an entity that may act in ways contrary to the normal individual behavior of those members. This effect may result from the establishment of new norms (combined with the group's power to enforce conformity to them), from diffusion of responsibility, and from feelings of anonymity. "The Third Wave" is a vivid account of a group movement that took on a life of its own, far exceeding the intentions of its creator. A week-long experiment designed to enhance the students' understanding of Nazi Germany quickly became far too real, sucking in almost everyone who came in contact with it. Although Jones has not written a social-psychological analysis, his article illustrates a number of group processes at work and shows how they can be simultaneously attractive and destructive.

For years I kept a strange secret. I shared this silence with two hundred students. Yesterday I ran into one of those students. For a brief moment it all rushed back.

Steve Coniglo had been a sophomore student in my world history class. We ran into each other quite by accident. It's one of those occasions experienced by teachers when they least expect it. You're walking down the street, eating at a secluded restaurant, or buying some underwear, when all of a sudden an ex-student pops up to say hello. In this case it was Steve running down the street shouting, "Mr. Jones, Mr. Jones." In an embarrassed hug we greet. I had to stop for a minute to remember. Who is this young man hugging me?

He calls me Mr. Jones. Must be a former student. What's his name? In the split second of my race back in time Steve sensed my questioning and backed up. Then he smiled and slowly raised a hand in a cupped position. My God. He's a member of the *Third Wave*. It's Steve, Steve Coniglo. He sat in the second row. He was a sensitive and bright student. Played guitar and enjoyed drama.

We just stood there exchanging smiles when, without a conscious command, I raised my hand in curved position. The salute was given. Two comrades had met long after the war. The *Third Wave* was still alive. "Mr. Jones, do you remember the Third Wave?" I sure do; it was one of the most frightening events I ever experienced in the classroom. It was also the genesis of a secret that I and two hundred students would sadly share for the rest of our lives.

We talked and laughed about the Third Wave for the next few hours. Then it was time to part. It's strange: you meet a past student in these chance ways. You catch a few moments of your life, hold them tight, then say good-bye, not knowing when and if you'd ever see each other again. Oh, you make promises to call each other, but it won't happen. Steve will continue to grow and change. I will remain an ageless benchmark in his life, a presence that will not change. I am Mr. Jones. Steve turns and gives a quiet salute, hand raised upward in the shape of a curling wave. Hand curved in a similar fashion, I return the gesture.

The Third Wave. Well at last it can be talked about. Here I've met a student, and we've talked for hours about this nightmare. The secret must finally be waning. It's taken three years. I can tell you and anyone else about the Third Wave. It's now just a dream, something to remember. No, it's something we tried to forget. That's how it all started. By strange coincidence I think it was Steve who started the Third Wave with a question.

We were studying Nazi Germany, and in the middle of a lecture I was interrupted by the question. How could the German populace claim ignorance of the slaughter of the Jewish people? How could the townspeople, railroad conductors, teachers, doctors, claim they knew nothing about concentration camps and human carnage? How can people who were neighbors and maybe even friends of the Jewish citizen say they weren't there when it happened? It was a good question. I didn't know the answer.

In as much as there were several months still to go in the school year and I was already at World War II, I decided to take a week and explore the question.

STRENGTH THROUGH DISCIPLINE

On Monday, I introduced my sophomore history students to one of the experiences that characterized Nazi Germany: discipline. I lectured about the beauty of discipline. How an athlete feels having worked hard and regularly to be successful at a sport. How a ballet dancer or painter works hard to perfect a movement. The dedicated patience of a scientist in pursuit of an idea. It's discipline, that self-training, control, the power of the will, the exchange of physical hardships for superior mental and physical facilities, the ultimate triumph.

To experience the power of discipline, I invited—no, I commanded—the class to exercise and use a new seating posture. I described how proper sitting posture assists concentration and strengthens the will. In fact I instructed the class in a mandatory sitting posture. This posture started with feet flat on the floor, hands placed flat across the small of the back to force a straight alignment of the spine. "There, can't you breathe more easily? You're more alert. Don't you feel better?"

We practiced this new attention position over and over. I walked up and down the aisles of seated students pointing out small flaws, making improvements. Proper seating became the most important aspect of learning. I would dismiss class, allowing them to leave their desks, and then call them abruptly back to an attention sitting position. In speed drills the class learned to move from standing position to attention sitting in fifteen seconds. In focus drills I concentrated attention on the feet being parallel and flat, ankles locked, knees bent at ninety-degree angles, hands flat and crossed against the back, spine straight, chin down, head forward. We did noise drills in which talking was allowed only to be shown as a distraction. Following minutes of progressive drill assignments the class could move from standing positions outside the room to attention sitting positions at their desks without making a sound. The maneuver took five seconds.

It was strange how quickly the students took to this uniform code of behavior. I began to wonder just how far they could be pushed. Was this display of obedience a momentary game we were all playing, or was it something else? Was the desire for discipline and uniformity a natural need, a societal instinct we hide within our franchise restaurants and TV programming?

I decided to push the tolerance of the class for regimented action. In the final twenty-five minutes of the class I introduced some new rules. Students must be sitting in class at the attention position before the late bell; all students must carry pencils and paper for note-taking; when asking or answering questions students must stand at the side of their desk; the first words given in answering or asking a question are "Mr. Jones." We practiced short "silent reading" sessions. Students who responded in a sluggish manner were reprimanded and in every case made to repeat their behavior until it was a model of punctuality and respect. The intensity of the response became more important than the content. To accentuate this, I requested answers to be given in three words or less. Students were rewarded for making an effort at answering or asking questions. They were also acknowledged for doing this in a crisp and attentive manner. Soon everyone in the class began popping up with answers and questions. The involvement level in the class moved from the few who always dominated discussions to the entire class. Even stranger was the gradual improvement in the quality of answers. Everyone seemed to be listening more intently. New people were speaking. Answers started to stretch out as students usually hesitant to speak found support for their effort.

As for my part in this exercise, I had nothing but questions. Why hadn't I thought of this technique before? Students seemed intent on the assignment and displayed accurate recitation of facts and concepts. They even seemed to be asking better questions and treating each other with more compassion. How could this be? Here I was enacting an authoritarian learning environment, and it seemed very productive. I now began to ponder not just how far this class could be pushed but how much I would change my basic beliefs toward an open classroom and self-directed learning. Was all my belief in Carl Rogers to shrivel and die? Where was this experiment leading?

STRENGTH THROUGH COMMUNITY

On Tuesday, the second day of the exercise, I entered the classroom to find everyone sitting in silence at the attention position. Some of their faces were relaxed with smiles that come from pleasing the teacher. But most of the students looked straight ahead in earnest concentration, neck muscles rigid, no sign of a smile or a thought or even a question, every fiber strained to perform the deed. To release the tension I went to the chalkboard and wrote in big letters, "STRENGTH THROUGH DISCIPLINE." Below this I wrote a second law, "STRENGTH THROUGH COMMUNITY."

While the class sat in stern silence, I began to talk, lecture, sermonize about the value of community. At this stage of the game I was debating in my own mind whether to stop the experiment or continue. I hadn't planned such intensity or compliance. In fact I was surprised to find the ideas on discipline enacted at all. While debating whether to stop or go on with the experiment, I talked on and on about community. I made up stories from my experiences as an athlete, coach, and historian. It was easy. Community is that bond between individuals who work and struggle together. It's raising a barn with your neighbors; it's feeling that you are a part of something beyond yourself, a movement, a team, *La Raza*, a cause.

It was too late to step back. I now can appreciate why the astronomer turns relentlessly to the telescope. I was probing deeper and deeper into my own perceptions and the motivations for group and individual action. There was much more to see and try to understand. Many questions haunted me. Why did the students accept the authority I was imposing? Where is their curiosity or resistance to this martial behavior? When and how will this end?

Following my description of community I once again told the class that community, like discipline, must be experienced if it is to be understood. To provide an encounter with community I had the class recite in unison, "Strength through Discipline. Strength through Community." First I would have two students stand and call back our motto, then add two more, until finally the whole class was standing and reciting. It was fun. The students began to look at each other and sense the power of belonging. Everyone was capable and equal. They were doing something together. We worked on this simple act for the entire class period. We would repeat the mottos in a rotating chorus or say them with various degrees of loudness. Always we said them together, emphasizing the proper way to sit, stand, and talk.

I began to think of myself as a part of the experiment. I enjoyed the unified action demonstrated by the students. It was rewarding to see their satisfaction and excitement to do more. I found it harder and harder to extract myself from the momentum and identity that the class was developing. I was following the group dictate as much as I was directing it.

As the class period was ending, and without forethought, I created a class salute. It was for class members only. To make the salute you brought your right hand up toward the right shoulder in a curled position. I called it the Third Wave salute because the hand resembled a wave about to top over. The idea for the three came from beach lore that waves travel in chains, the third wave being the last and largest of each series. Because we had a salute, I made it a rule to salute all class members outside the classroom. When the bell sounded, ending the period, I asked the class for complete silence. With everyone sitting at attention, I slowly raised my arm and with a cupped hand I saluted. It was a silent signal of recognition. They were something special. Without command the entire group of students returned the salute.

Throughout the next few days students in the class would exchange this greeting. You would be walking down the hall when all of a sudden three classmates would turn your way, each flashing a quick salute. In the library or in gym, students would be seen giving this strange hand jive. You would hear a crash of cafeteria food only to have it followed by two classmates saluting each other. The mystique of thirty individuals doing this strange gyration soon brought more attention to the class and its experiment into the German personality. Many students outside the class asked if they could join.

STRENGTH THROUGH ACTION

On Wednesday, I decided to issue membership cards to every student that wanted to continue what I now called the experiment. Not a single student elected to leave the room. In this the third day of activity there were forty-three students in the class. Thirteen students had cut other classes to be a part of the experiment. While the class sat at attention, I gave each person a card. I marked three of the cards with a red x and informed the recipients that they had a special assignment to report any students not complying with class rules. I then proceeded to talk about the meaning of action. I explained how discipline and community were meaningless without action. I discussed the beauty of taking full responsibility for one's action, of believing so thoroughly in yourself and your community or family that you will do anything to preserve, protect, and extend that being. I stressed how hard work and allegiance to each other would allow accelerated learning and accomplishment. I reminded students of what it felt like being in classes where competition caused pain and degradation, of situations in which students were pitted against each other in everything from gym to reading, of the feeling of never acting, never being a part of something, never supporting each other.

At this point students stood without prompting and began to give what amounted to testimonials. "Mr. Jones, for the first time I'm learning lots of things." "Mr. Jones, why don't you teach like this all the time." I was shocked! Yes, I had been pushing information at them in an extremely controlled setting, but the fact that they found it comfortable and acceptable was startling. It was equally disconcerting to realize that complex and time-consuming written homework assignments on German life were being completed and even enlarged on by students. Performance in academic skill areas was significantly improving. They were learning more. And they seemed to want more. I began to think that the students might do anything I assigned. I decided to find out.

To allow students the experience of direct action I gave each individual a specific verbal assignment. "It's your task to design a Third Wave banner." "You are responsible for stopping any student that is not a Third Wave member from entering this room." "I want you to remember and be able to recite by tomorrow the name and address of every Third Wave member." "You are assigned the problem of training and convincing at least twenty children in the adjacent elementary school that our sitting posture is necessary for better learning." "It's your job to read this pamphlet and report its entire content to the class before the period ends." "I want each of you to give me the name and address of one reliable friend that you think might want to join the Third Wave. . . ."

To conclude the session on direct action I instructed students in a simple procedure for initiating new members. It went like this: A new member had only to be recommended by an existing member and issued a card by me. Upon receiving this card the new member had to demonstrate knowledge of our rules and pledge obedience to them. My announcement unleashed a fervor of effort.

The school was alive with conjecture and curiosity. It affected everyone. The school cook asked what a Third Wave cookie looked like. I said chocolate chip, of course. Our principal came into an afternoon faculty meeting and gave me the Third Wave salute. I saluted back. The librarian thanked me for the thirty-foot banner on learning that she placed above the library entrance. By the end of the day over two hundred students were admitted into the order. I felt very alone and a little scared.

Most of my fear emanated from the incidence of tattling. Although I formally appointed only three students to report deviate behavior, approximately twenty students came to me with reports about how Allan didn't salute or Georgene was talking critically about our experiment. This incidence of monitoring meant that half the class now considered it their duty to observe and report on members of their class. Within this avalanche of reporting one legitimate conspiracy did seem under way.

Three women in the class had told their parents all about our classroom activities. These three young women were by far the most intelligent students in the class. As friends they chummed together. They possessed a silent confidence and took pleasure in a school setting that gave them academic and leadership opportunity. During the days of the experiment I was curious how they would respond to the equalitarian and physical reshaping of the class. The rewards they were accustomed to winning just didn't exist in the experiment. The intellectual skills of questioning and reasoning were nonexistent. In the martial atmosphere of the class they seemed stunned and pensive. Now that I look back, they appeared much like the child with so-called learning disability. They watched the activities and participated in a mechanical fashion. Whereas others jumped in, they held back, watching.

In telling their parents of the experiment they set up a brief chain of events. The rabbi for one of the parents called me at home. He was polite and condescending. I told him we were merely studying the German personality. He seemed delighted and told me not to worry, he would talk to the parents and calm their concern. In concluding this conversation I envisioned similar conversations throughout history in which the clergy accepted and apologized for untenable conditions. If only he had raged in anger or simply investigated the situation, I could point the students to an example of righteous rebellion. But no. The rabbi became a part of the experiment. In remaining ignorant of the oppression in the experiment he became an accomplice and advocate.

By the end of the third day I was exhausted. I was tearing myself apart. The balance between role playing and directed behavior became indistinguishable. Many of the students were completely into being Third Wave members. They demanded strict obedience of the rules from other students and bullied those that took the experiment lightly. Others simply sunk into the activity and took self-assigned roles. I particularly remember Robert. Robert was big for his age and displayed very few academic skills. Oh, he tried harder than anyone I know to be successful. He handed in elaborate weekly reports copied word for word from the reference books in the library. Robert is like so many kids in school that don't excel or cause trouble. They aren't bright, can't make the athletic teams, and don't strike out for attention. They are lost, invisible. The only reason I came to know Robert at all is that I found him eating lunch in my classroom. He always ate lunch alone.

Well, the Third Wave gave Robert a place in school. At last he was equal to everyone. He could do something, take part, be meaningful. That's just what Robert did. Late Wednesday afternoon I found Robert following me and asked what in the world was he doing. He smiled (I don't think I had ever seen him smile) and announced, "Mr. Jones, I'm your bodyguard. I'm afraid something will happen to you. Can I do it, Mr. Jones, please?" Given that assurance and smile I couldn't say no. I had a bodyguard. All day long he opened and closed doors for me. He walked always on my right, just smiling and saluting other class members. He fol-

lowed me everywhere. In the faculty room (closed to students) he stood at silent attention while I gulped some coffee. When accosted by an English teacher for being a student in the "teachers' room," he just smiled and informed the faculty member that he wasn't a student, he was a bodyguard.

STRENGTH THROUGH PRIDE

On Thursday I began to draw the experiment to a conclusion. I was exhausted and worried. Many students were over the line. The Third Wave had become the center of their existence. I was in pretty bad shape myself. I was now acting instinctively as a dictator. Oh, I was benevolent. And I daily argued with myself on the benefits of the learning experience. By this, the fourth day of the experiment, I was beginning to lose my own arguments. As I spent more time playing the role, I had less time to remember its rational origins and purpose. I found myself sliding into the role even when it wasn't necessary. I wondered if this doesn't happen to lots of people. We get or take an ascribed role and then bend our life to fit the image. Soon the image is the only identity people will accept. So we become the image. The trouble with the situation and role I had created was that I didn't have time to think where it was leading. Events were crushing around me. I worried for students doing things they would regret. I worried for myself.

Once again I faced the thoughts of closing the experiment or letting it go its own course. Both options were unworkable. If I stopped the experiment, a great number of students would be left hanging. They had committed themselves in front of their peers to radical behavior. Emotionally and psychologically they had exposed themselves. If I suddenly jolted them back to classroom reality, I would face a confused student body for the remainder of the year. It would be too painful and demeaning for Robert and the students like him to be twisted back into a seat and told it's just a game. They would take the ridicule from the brighter students that participated in a measured and cautious way. I couldn't let the Roberts lose again.

The other option of just letting the experiment run its course was also out of the question. Things were already getting out of control. Wednesday evening someone had broken into the room and ransacked the place. I later found out it was the father of one of the students. He was a retired air force colonel who had spent time in a German prisoner of war camp. Upon hearing of our activity he simply lost control. Late in the evening he broke into the room and tore it apart. I found him that morning propped up against the classroom door. He told me about his friends that had been killed in Germany. He was holding onto me and shaking. In staccato words he pleaded that I understand and help him get home. I called his wife and with the help of a neighbor walked him home. We spent hours later talking about what he felt and did, but from that moment on Thursday morning I was more concerned with what might be happening at school.

I was increasingly worried about how our activity was affecting the faculty and other students in the school. The Third Wave was disrupting normal learning. Students were cutting class to participate, and the school counselors were beginning to question every student in the class. The real gestapo in the school was at work. Faced with this experiment exploding in one hundred directions, I decided to try an old basketball strategy. When you're playing against all the odds, the best action to take is to try the unexpected. That's what I did.

By Thursday the class had swollen in size to over eighty students. The only thing that allowed them all to fit was the enforced discipline of sitting in silence at attention. A strange calm is in effect when a room full of people sit in quiet observation and anticipation. It helped me approach them in a deliberate way. I talked about pride. "Pride is more than banners or salutes. Pride is something no one can take from you. Pride is knowing you are the best. ... It can't be destroyed."

In the midst of this crescendo I abruptly changed and lowered my voice to announce the real reason for the Third Wave. In slow, methodic tone I explained what was behind the Third Wave. "The Third Wave isn't just an experiment or classroom activity. It's far more important than that. The Third Wave is a nationwide program to find students who are willing to fight for political change in this country. That's right. This activity we have been doing has been practice for the real thing. Across the country teachers like myself have been recruiting and training a youth brigade capable of showing the nation a better society through discipline, community, pride, and action. If we can change the way that school is run, we can change the way that factories, stores, universities and all the other institutions are run. You are a selected group of young people chosen to help in this cause. If you will stand up and display what you have learned in the past four days ..., we can change

the destiny of this nation. We can bring it a new sense of order, community, pride, and action, a new purpose. Everything rests with you and your willingness to take a stand."

To give validity to the seriousness of my words I turned to the three women in the class who I knew had questioned the Third Wave. I demanded that they leave the room. I explained why I acted and then assigned four guards to escort the women to the library and to keep them from entering the class on Friday. Then in dramatic style I informed the class of a special noon rally to take place on Friday. This would be a rally for Third Wave members only.

It was a wild gamble. I just kept talking, afraid that if I stopped, someone would laugh or ask a question and the grand scheme would dissolve in chaos. I explained how at noon on Friday a national candidate for president would announce the formation of a Third Wave Youth Program. Simultaneous to this announcement over 1,000 youth groups from every part of the country would stand up and display their support for such a movement. I confided that they were the students selected to represent their area. I also questioned if they could make a good showing, because the press had been invited to record the event. No one laughed. There was not a murmur of resistance. Quite the contrary. A fever pitch of excitement swelled across the room. "We can do it!" "Should we wear white shirts?" "Can we bring friends?" "Mr. Jones, have you seen this advertisement in *Time* magazine?"

The clincher came quite by accident. It was a full-page color advertisement in the current issue of *Time* for some lumber products. The advertiser identified his product as the Third Wave. The advertisement proclaimed in big red, white, and blue letters, "The Third Wave is coming." "Is this part of the campaign, Mr. Jones?" "Is it a code or something?"

"Yes. Now listen carefully. It's all set for tomorrow. Be in the small auditorium ten minutes before twelve. Be seated. Be ready to display the discipline, community, and pride you have learned. Don't talk to anyone about this. This rally is for members only."

STRENGTH THROUGH UNDERSTANDING

On Friday, the final day of the exercise, I spent the early morning preparing the auditorium for the rally. At eleven-thirty students began to ant their way into the room; at first a few scouting the way and then more. Row after row began to fill. A hushed silence shrouded the room. Third Wave banners hung like clouds over the assembly. At twelve o'clock sharp I closed the room and placed guards at each door. Several friends of mine posing as reporters and photographers began to interact with the crowd, taking pictures and jotting frantic descriptive notes. A group photograph was taken. Over two hundred students were crammed into the room. Not a vacant seat could be found. The group seemed to be composed of students from many persuasions. There were the athletes, the socially prominents, the student leaders, the loners, the group of kids that always left school early, the bikers, the pseudo hip, a few representatives of the school's Dadaist clique, and some of the students that hung out at the laundromat. The entire collection, however, looked like one force as they sat in perfect attention. Every person focusing on the TV set I had in the front of the room. No one moved. The room was empty of sound. It was as if we were all witness to a birth. The tension and anticipation were beyond belief.

"Before turning on the national press conference, which begins in five minutes, I want to demonstrate to the press the extent of our training." With that, I gave the salute. It was followed automatically by two hundred arms stabbing a reply. I then said the words "Strength through Discipline." It was followed by a repetitive chorus. We did this again and again. Each time the response was louder. The photographers were circling the ritual, snapping pictures, but by now they were ignored. I reiterated the importance of this event and asked once more for a show of allegiance. It was the last time I would ask anyone to recite. The room rocked with a guttural cry: "Strength through Discipline."

It was 12:05. I turned off the lights in the room and walked quickly to the television set. The air in the room seemed to be drying up. It felt hard to breathe and even harder to talk. It was as if the climax of shouting souls had pushed everything out of the room. I switched the television set on. I was now standing next to the television, directly facing the room full of people. The machine came to life, producing a luminous field of phosphorous light. Robert was at my side. I whispered to him to watch closely and pay attention for the next few minutes. The only light in the room was coming from the television, and it played against the faces in the room. Eyes strained and pulled at the light, but the pattern didn't change. The room stayed deathly still, waiting. There was a mental tug of war between the people in the room and

the television. The television won. The white glow of the test pattern didn't snap into the vision of a political candidate. It just whined on. Still the viewers persisted. There must be a program. It must be coming on. Where is it? The trance with the television continued for what seemed like hours. It was 12:07. Nothing. A blank field of white. It's not going to happen. Anticipation turned to anxiety and then frustration. Someone stood up and shouted.

"There isn't any leader, is there?" Everyone turned in shock, first to the despondent student and then back to the television. Their faces held looks of disbelief.

In the confusion of the moment I moved slowly toward the television. I turned it off. I felt air rush back into the room. The room remained in fixed silence, but for the first time I could sense people breathing. Students were withdrawing their arms from behind their chairs. I expected a flood of questions but instead got intense quietness. I began to talk. Every word seemed to be taken and absorbed.

"Listen closely. I have something important to tell you. Sit down. There is no leader! There is no such thing as a national youth movement called the Third Wave. You have been used, manipulated, shoved by your own desires into the place you now find yourself. You are no better or worse than the German Nazi we have been studying.

"You thought that you were the elect, that you were better than those outside this room. You bargained your freedom for the comfort of discipline and superiority. You chose to accept the group's will and the big lie over your own conviction. Oh, you think to yourself that you were just going along for the fun, that you could extricate yourself at any moment. But where were you heading? How far would you have gone? Let me show you your future."

With that I switched on a rear screen projector. It quickly illuminated a white drop cloth hanging behind the television. Large numbers appeared in a countdown. The roar of a Nuremberg rally blasted into vision. My heart was pounding. In ghostly images the history of the Third Reich paraded into the room: the discipline; the march of super race; the big lie; arrogance, violence, terror; people being pushed into vans; the visual stench of death camps; faces without eyes; the trials; the plea of ignorance. I was only doing my job, my job. As abruptly as it started, the film froze to a halt on a single written frame: "Everyone must accept the blame. No one can claim that they didn't in some way take part."

The room stayed dark as the final footage of film flapped against the projector. I felt sick to my stomach. The room sweated and smelled like a locker room. No one moved. It was as if everyone wanted to dissect the moment, figure out what had happened. As though awakening from a dream and deep sleep, the entire room of people took one last look back into their consciousness. I waited for several minutes to let everyone catch up. Finally questions began to emerge. All the questions probed at imaginary situations and sought to discover the meaning of this event.

In the still-darkened room I began the explanation. I confessed my feeling of sickness and remorse. I told the assembly that a full explanation would take quite a while. But it was important to start. I sensed myself moving from an introspective participant in the event toward the role of teacher. It's easier being a teacher. In objective terms I began to describe the past events.

"Through the experience of the past week we have all tasted what it was like to live and act in Nazi Germany. We learned what it felt like to create a disciplined social environment, to build a special society, to pledge allegiance to that society, to replace reason with rules. Yes, we would all have made good Germans. We would have put on the uniform, turned our head as friends and neighbors were cursed and then persecuted, pulled the locks shut, worked in the 'defense' plants, burned ideas. Yes, we know in a small way what it feels like to find a hero, to grab quick solutions, to feel strong and in control of destiny. We know the fear of being left out, the pleasure of doing something right and being rewarded, of being number one, of being right. Taken to an extreme we have seen and perhaps felt what these actions will lead to. We each have witnessed something over the past week. We have seen that Fascism is not just something those other people did. No, it's right here, in this room, in our own personal habits and way of life. Scratch the surface, and it appears. It is something in all of us. We carry it like a disease. It is the belief that human beings are basically evil and therefore unable to act well toward each other, a belief that demands a strong leader and discipline to preserve social order. And there is something else—the act of apology.

"This is the final lesson to be experienced. This last lesson is perhaps the one of greatest importance. This lesson was the question that started our plunge in studying Nazi life. Do you remember the question? It concerned a bewilderment at the German populace claiming ignorance and noninvolvement in the Nazi movement. If I remember the question, it went something like this: 'How could the German soldier, teacher, railroad conductor, nurse, tax collector, the average citizen claim at the end of the Third Reich that they knew nothing of what was going on? How can a people be a part of something and then claim at the demise that they were not really involved? What causes people to blank out their own history?' In the next few minutes and perhaps years you will have an opportunity to answer this question.

"If our enactment of the Fascist mentality is complete, not one of you will ever admit to being at this final Third Wave rally. Like the Germans, you will have trouble admitting to yourself that you came this far. You will not allow your friends and parents to know that you were willing to give up individual freedom and power for the dictates of order and unseen leaders. You can't admit to being manipulated, to being a follower, to accepting the Third Wave as a way of life. You won't admit to participating in this madness. You will keep this day and this rally a secret. It's a secret I shall share with you."

I took the film from the cameras of the three photographers in the room and pulled the celluloid into the exposing light. The deed was concluded. The trial was over. The Third Wave had ended.

I glanced over my shoulder. Robert was crying. Students slowly rose from their chairs and without words filed into the outdoor light. I walked over to Robert and threw my arms around him. Robert was sobbing, taking in large, uncontrollable gulps of air. "It's over." "It's all right." In our consoling each other we became a rock in the stream of exiting students. Some swirled back to momentarily hold Robert and me. Others cried openly and then brushed away tears to carry on. Human beings circling and holding each other, moving toward the door and the world outside.

For a week in the middle of a school year we had shared fully in life. And as predicted we also shared a deep secret. In the four years I taught at Cubberley High School no one ever admitted to attending the Third Wave rally. Oh, we talked and studied our actions intently. But the rally itself. No. It was something we all wanted to forget.

PROJECTS

Name _____

Date _____

11.1: MAKING DECISIONS

The goal of this project is to compare the ways in which an individual and a group make decisions. You will be the individual decision maker; you will also be a part of the group, which will be made up of several people in your class. Your instructor will assign people to these small groups.

The decisions concern three different personal dilemmas, which are described on the following pages. The central character in each situation is faced with two possible courses of action. One alternative is more desirable than the other, but it always involves greater risk.

1. Read each situation and determine the *lowest* probability that you consider acceptable for the central character to pursue the more desirable alternative. For example, if you think the alternative should be attempted only if it is sure to work, check the answer "the chances are 10 in 10 that the alternative will succeed." However, if you think the alternative should be tried when the odds are even, check the answer "the chances are 5 in 10." Read each situation, and indicate your own decision.

> Mr. C., a competent chess player, is participating in a national chess tournament. In an early match he draws the top-favored player in the tournament as his opponent. Mr. C. has been given a relatively low ranking in view of his performance in previous tournaments. During the course of his play with the top-favored man, Mr. C. notes the possibility of a deceptive though risky maneuver which might bring him a quick victory. At the same time, if the attempted maneuver should fail, Mr. C. would be left in an exposed position and defeat would almost certainly follow.
>
> Imagine that you are advising Mr. C. Listed are several probabilities or odds that Mr. C's deceptive play would succeed. *Please check the lowest probability that you would consider acceptable for the risky play in question to be attempted.*

_____ The chances are 0 in 10 that the play would succeed (i.e., the play is certain to fail).

_____ The chances are 1 in 10.

_____ The chances are 2 in 10.

_____ The chances are 3 in 10.

_____ The chances are 4 in 10.

_____ The chances are 5 in 10.

_____ The chances are 6 in 10.

_____ The chances are 7 in 10.

_____ The chances are 8 in 10.

_____ The chances are 9 in 10.

_____ The chances are 10 in 10 that the play would succeed (i.e., the play is certain to succeed).

> Ms. G. is currently a college senior who is very eager to pursue graduate study in chemistry leading to the Doctor of Philosophy degree. She has been accepted by both University X and University Y. University X has a worldwide reputation for

excellence in chemistry. While a degree from University X would signify outstanding training in the field, the standards are so rigorous that only a fraction of the degree candidates actually receive the degree. University Y, on the other hand, has a much less prestigious reputation in chemistry, but almost everyone admitted is awarded the Doctor of Philosophy degree, so the degree carries much less esteem than the corresponding degree from University X.

Imagine that you are advising Ms. G. Listed are several probabilities or odds that Ms. G. would be awarded a degree at University X, the one with the greater prestige. *Please check the lowest probability that you would consider acceptable to make it worthwhile for Ms. G. to enroll in University X rather than University Y.*

_____ The chances are 0 in 10 that Ms. G. would receive a degree from University X.

_____ The chances are 1 in 10.

_____ The chances are 2 in 10.

_____ The chances are 3 in 10.

_____ The chances are 4 in 10.

_____ The chances are 5 in 10.

_____ The chances are 6 in 10.

_____ The chances are 7 in 10.

_____ The chances are 8 in 10.

_____ The chances are 9 in 10.

_____ The chances are 10 in 10.

Mr. I. is the captain of College X's football team. College X is playing its traditional rival, College Y, in the last game of the season. The game is in its final seconds and Mr. I.'s team, College X, is behind by three points. College X has time to run one more play. Mr. I., the captain, must decide whether it would be best to settle for a tie score with a play which would be almost certain to work or whether he should try a more complicated and risky play which would bring victory if it succeeded, but defeat if it failed.

Imagine that you are advising Mr. I. Listed are several probabilities or odds that the risky play will work. *Please check the lowest probability that you would consider for the play to be attempted.*

_____ The chances are 0 in 10 that the risky play will work.

_____ The chances are 1 in 10.

_____ The chances are 2 in 10.

_____ The chances are 3 in 10.

_____ The chances are 4 in 10.

_____ The chances are 5 in 10.

_____ The chances are 6 in 10.

_____ The chances are 7 in 10.

_____ The chances are 8 in 10.

_____ The chances are 9 in 10.

_____ The chances are 10 in 10.

2. After participating in the group discussion and decision making, list the group's decisions. Then list your individual decisions.

	Group	Individual	Riskier Decision
Situation 1			
Situation 2			
Situation 3			

3. In the third column of question 2, indicate whose decision was riskier for each situation (i.e., had the lower probability): group, individual, or no difference. Is there any pattern to these results? For example, was one set of decisions riskier than the other? Compare your own results with those of the other people in class. Do these overall findings suggest a group-individual difference in riskiness?

4. If there is an apparent difference between group and individual decisions, how do you explain it? What sorts of things happened during the group discussion that might have led you to support a decision different from the one you made on your own?

Name _____

Date _____

11.2: CROWD BEHAVIOR

The purpose of this project is to observe and compare different types of crowds. Select two settings in which a crowd will gather for a similar purpose—in this case, to hear music. For example, you might choose a rock concert and a concert of classical music. During the concerts, observe the audience and rate their behavior on several global dimensions. Since you cannot observe everybody all the time, your ratings should be based on a general survey of the entire audience as a single unit. Make ratings at several different points during the concert (and be sure they are the same points for both concerts—such as, at the end of a musical selection, during intermission, and so forth).

Concert 1		Time 1	Time 2	Time 3
Amount of talking	(1 = little or none, 5 = a lot)			
Amount of shouting	"			
Amount of physical movement	"			
Amount of physical contact and touching	"			
Amount of audience participation (singing, humming along, dancing, waving in time to the music, etc.)	"			
Other				

Concert 2		Time 1	Time 2	Time 3
Amount of talking	(1 = little or none 5 = a lot			
Amount of shouting	"			
Amount of physical movement	"			
Amount of physical contact and touching	"			
Amount of audience participation (singing, humming along, dancing, waving in time to the music, etc.)	"			
Other	"			

1. What behavior patterns characterized each concert?

2. What do you think might have caused these behavioral differences?

3. How would you characterize the mood or "group feeling" of each of these audiences? How are these related to the audience behavior?

4. What are some implications of your analysis for other sorts of crowd situations?

THE ENVIRONMENT
AND BEHAVIOR

12

People have long been aware that their environment has an effect on their feelings and behavior. For example, it is commonly believed that the weather can influence one's moods. We have all heard or made remarks such as "Rainy days get me down" or "I feel happy when the sun is shining." Spring fever and spring madness on college campuses and elsewhere often begin with the first warm days following a cold and dreary winter. Hot temperatures are thought to exacerbate interpersonal aggression, and moonlight has often been linked to mental problems (see the boxed excerpt "The Moon and the Mind"). Work, home, and play environments are also viewed as instrumental to psychological well-being. How many times have you heard someone say, "I hate to work in an inner office without windows" or "Those endless walls of institutional green get me depressed" or "I always feel cheery in a room full of plants"?

In recent years, these presumed connections between the physical environment and personal experience have been subjected to careful study by psychologists and other social scientists. The exciting new research being done in this area has important implications for shaping and improving the settings in which we live.

THE MOON AND THE MIND

The belief in the effects of the moon on the human mind dates from ancient times and has survived rather obstinately. The following little experience will serve both as a sample and as evidence of how alive this belief is today, in our midst.

Our little party was standing on the terrace of the suburban home, admiring the yellow disk of the moon which was shining bright and full from a cloudless summer night sky. Suddenly our young hostess exclaimed, "Oh dear I forgot to pull the shades in Tommy's room!" and, explaining, she added, "The poor child has his bed right near the window; the moon must be shining right on his face." Later, when she returned, someone made a skeptical remark as to the alleged harmful effect of the moon on the sleeper, but our hostess stood firm in her conviction, and two or three of the guests, both men and women, spoke up in her defense. "No, it is quite true," said a middle-aged businessman from a midwestern city, "to have the moon shine on your face when you sleep, is bad; particularly for children. It gives them bad dreams and nightmares, and I have heard that some people with a delicate nervous system even become insane."

. . . From the oldest times 'lunacy' (from the Latin luna = moon) was closely associated with the moon, both in etiology and clinical manifestations. The origins of this belief, so widespread and persistent, lose themselves far back in ancient history. Both the Old and the New Testament mention the moon in connection with mental derangement. Later this relation became a commonplace. Plutarch, in the first century, said, "Everybody knows that those who sleep outside under the influence of the moon are not easily awakened, but seem stupid and senseless." Pliny the Elder asserted that the "moon produces drowsiness and stupor in those who sleep under her beams." And even before their time Hippocrates had written, "As often as one is seized with terror and fright and madness during the night, he is said to be suffering from the visitation of Hecate [moon goddess]."

Novelists and poets have also made frequent mention of this belief. Charles Dickens created the term 'a mooner,' signifying "one who wanders or gazes idly or moodily about as if moonstruck.". . . Byron, too, used the word 'moon-struck,' T. Adams, English writer of the 17th century, mentions 'a moonsick head,' and Ben Jonson 'the mooning.' Shel-

273

ley spoke of 'moon-madness ' Richard Brome, in *Queen and Concubine,* blamed a 'moon-flaw' for an exalted condition of one of his heroes. . . .

There actually seems to be no country or culture where the belief in the moon's effect upon the human mind has not prevailed at some time or other, and frequently still does. "It is dangerous to sleep in the moonlight," say the French peasants. Or, "It is not well to gaze fixedly at the moon," goes a saying among the Bedouins, or the German country people think that "When the moon shines into the window, the maid breaks many pots."

From J. F. Oliven, "Moonlight and Nervous Disorders: A Historical Study," *American Journal of Psychiatry,* 1943, 99, 579–84. Copyright © 1943, the American Psychiatric Association. Reprinted by permission.

STRESS AND THE ENVIRONMENT

ANDREW BAUM, JEROME E. SINGER, AND CHARLENE S. BAUM

Although we all know what it feels like to be stressed, most of us are unable to define it clearly. Baum, Singer, and Baum define stress as a process in which environmental events or forces, called stressors, threaten an organism's existence and well-being, and the organism responds to this threat. In recent years, the subject of stress has become increasingly popular. One of the major contributors to the growing popularity of the subject of stress has been the work of Dr. Hans Selye. Selye was the first scientist to study stress in a systematic way. In his classic book (first published in 1956), The Stress of Life, Selye argued that long-term exposure to an environmental stressor, and to a repeated demand to cope with such a stressor, can deplete the body's adaptive resources and lead to physical dysfunction.

In this article Baum, Singer, and Baum review the most current literature on the effect of environmental stresses on the functioning of the individual. When talking about characteristics of the environment, they organize their discussion around three important variables—source, transmission, and audience.

Stress has become a popular concept for explaining a wide variety of outcomes, mostly negative, that otherwise seem to defy explanation. In the scientific realm, stress has been used as a psychological precursor of illness, as a result of any number of conditions, or as a catch-all for anxiety reactions, discomfort, and the like. It is also fashionable to attribute erratic or unexplainable behavior of friends and acquaintances to the fact that "they are under a lot of stress." From a cursory reading of psychological and medical texts and from simply listening to people, one can derive a fairly broad definition of stress. Yet, despite its general use, stress refers to a process that is not only specific, but also central to the relationship between people and their surroundings.

Stress is a process in which environmental events or forces, called stressors, threaten an organism's existence and well-being and the organism responds to this threat. The stress reaction, replete with commonly known symptoms such as fear, anxiety, and anger, is only part of this process. It is probably the most easily recognized, but in many cases may simply represent "side-effects" of the main attraction—perceiving a threat, coping with it, and adapting to it. This adaptation sequence is almost a daily routine—our lives can be characterized as constant adaptation to sudden change or gradual evolution of our surroundings. Sometimes these changes are minor and we can adapt to them without even being aware of them. At other times, however, these changes can be severe and clearly threatening.

Reprinted with permission from *Journal of Social Issues,* Vol. 37, No. 1 (1981), 4–35. © 1981 by the Society for the Psychological Study of Social Issues.

SOURCES OF STRESS

Lazarus and Cohen (1977) have considered three general classes of stressors. The first, cataclysmic phenomena, refers to sudden, unique and powerful single events or clusters of related occurrences affecting large numbers of people. Many of these have been studied, including natural disaster and relocation. These fairly obvious examples do not represent an exhaustive listing; one could consider the Arab oil embargo of 1973–74 or the present gasoline shortfalls as stressors of this magnitude.

A second class of stressors include those powerful events that challenge adaptive abilities in the same way as cataclysmic events, but affect fewer people. This distinction is important, since affiliative and socially comparative behaviors have been identified as styles of coping with a focused, specific threat and social support has been shown to moderate the effect of stress. In the first category, people are able to share distress with others undergoing the same difficulties. In this case, fewer people are involved resulting in fewer people with whom to share. These events include response to illness, death, significant loss, or losing one's job.

Lazarus and Cohen refer to the third group of stressors as "daily hassles"—those stable and repetitive problems encountered in daily life that typically do not present great adaptive difficulty. Many of these are more chronic than the stressors described above, including job dissatisfaction, neighborhood problems, and commuting. Crowding, especially that encountered in one's neighborhood, in transportation settings, and in residential buildings, may also be considered to be chronic or often repeated stressors. In dormitory settings, for example, it is unlikely that a single episode of unwanted contact presents severe adaptive demands. Rather, the cumulation of instances of unwanted contact and loss of control appears to be responsible for the stress and withdrawal that have been observed. Similarly, people can cope with individual episodes of noise even if it is uncontrollable, but the cumulative effects of chronic exposure to noise appear to be more severe.

These distinctions involve differences on a number of dimensions. Some stressors are acute, affecting large numbers of people and requiring major adaptive responses. Other stressors may be more chronic, but may still tend to be short-term, may require more adaptive energy, affect large numbers of people *but on an individual basis*, and do not require great amounts of adaptive energy. They may not even be readily identifiable, as in the case of air pollution. Yet, the chronicity of this last group may result in these stressors having deceptively severe consequences. Because of regular and prolonged exposure to them, they may not be perceived as severe, but they may require far more adaptive responses *over time* than other stressors. If we think of these background stressors as generally pushing an individual's adaptive abilities towards their limit, or committing people to make allocations of resources that are not easily changed, they may gradually reduce an individual's ability to cope with subsequent, acute stressors.

Kiretz and Moos (1974) have proposed other ways of viewing stressors, [such as] the magnitude of adjustment required, the kind of adjustment, perceptions of control, and valence as important mediators of stress.

One thing that is apparent in this listing of ways of classifying stressors is that some are intrusive, physical and universally threatening (such as natural disaster) while others are more culturally determined, less universal and more psychosocial in nature. Crowding and spatial invasion are examples of the latter. Responses to varying densities and proximities are specific to cultural norms and meanings. Similarly, certain aspects of different occupations and work settings, such as the degree of control, responsibility, or redundancy in the job, can evoke stress. These kinds of stressors are clearly more imbedded in the psychological processes involved in appraisal, and are less universal, than such things as earthquakes or floods. The psychosocial medium in which some events are conveyed make them different and, in some cases, more destructive.

It is therefore important to distinguish between physical and psychological stressors. Clearly, physical agents such as pollution, climate, temperature, and natural disasters have a direct effect on us (although the relation between such effects and the physical agent may be complex, as in the case of heat stress). At the same time, however, stress responses can be evoked by changes and challenges that are experienced in daily life, by disruption of one's habits (e.g., by crowding or unpredictable noise) or culturally-governed mores, by obstacles and hindrances placed before us through malfunction of social systems, or by deprivation or loss experienced in life. In short, noxious agents may be anything from a virus to a vicissitude.

APPRAISAL OF STRESSORS

As one would expect of "transmission" variables, factors that mediate interpretation of stressors are both environmental and psychological in nature. For example, individuals with a great wealth of resources for coping (e.g., money, friends, material) may be less likely to appraise events as threatening and, as a result, be less affected by the stressor. Thus, the upper-middle-class resident of a large city may be less likely to experience difficulty as a result of urban stressors than will a poorer resident of the same city, or may be less likely to be exposed to these aversive urban conditions at all. Although the availability of resources often provides a buffer between the individual and the stressor, concern about air pollution is positively correlated with socioeconomic status. Since higher SES persons are generally more insulated from many highly visible urban stressors, they may have more freedom to concern themselves with less obvious ones.

Attitudes towards the sources of stress will also mediate responses. If we believe that a stressor will cause no permanent harm, our response will probably be less extreme than if its danger carries the threat of lasting harm. At a more psychological level, perceptions of control, social support and other characteristics of the person exposed to the stressor will affect the appraisal of different stressors. While an exhaustive review of these mediating factors will not be attempted here, we will selectively consider some of the variables that affect the transmission of stress and, in effect, link the source with the response by the recipient.

Attitudes Towards Stressors

Attitudes and beliefs about stressors are important filters in the perception and appraisal of stressors. In early studies of psychological stress, for example, Lazarus and his colleagues were able to affect the appraisal of stressful stimuli by manipulating information that caused subjects to have different beliefs about what they were viewing. Similarly, opinions about the limitations fostered by stressors and the consequences of demands they impose will mediate response.

High levels of noise are generally regarded as potent environmental stressors. Although noise levels in areas surrounding airports are highly correlated with noise annoyance reported by residents of these areas and exposure to airport noise has been shown to have deleterious effects on children, the direct relationship between noise and annoyance is generally not strong. Tracor (1971) found that individual annoyance ratings were more highly correlated with several attitudinal measures than they were with various indices of physical exposure to noise; and, in his review of the literature, Davis (1975)[1] notes that noise levels alone can only explain between one-tenth and one-third of the variability in individual annoyance. Several studies suggest that the addition of attitudinal measures increases the predictability of annoyance to between 58 percent and 65 percent.

Fear of nearby airplane crashes seems to be the single most powerful predictor of individual annoyance in response to airport noise. In two different samples, Leonard and Borsky (1979) found correlations between fear and annoyance. Two surveys conducted among residents near Heathrow Airport indicated that a sizeable percentage perceived a danger from nearby crashes: 42 percent in 1961 and 38 percent in 1967. It is interesting to note that fear decreased during a time period in which there was a substantial increase in air traffic. Although the authors hypothesized that fear decreased as a result of the increase in number of respondents who had flown in commercial aircraft, it is possible that the increased exposure of residents to air traffic without accidents or crashes during the interim period was also an important factor in producing some decrease in levels of fear. Prior experience has been shown to be a determinant of response to a stressor, as each subsequent episode either exacerbates stress or facilitates coping and adaptation. Such adaptation may sometimes be physiological as well as psychological.

An analogy may be drawn to residents of Richland, Washington, site of the oldest U.S. atomic facility, the Hanford Project, which has been in operation since 1945. Although they live on the edges of a 570 square mile nuclear park that houses 75 percent of the radioactive wastes in the United States, the residents of Richland express great feelings of confidence and safety. Richland is a one-industry town: the nuclear industry. The economic well-being of the town is inextricably linked with the Hanford Project, and this is probably the strongest determinant of the residents' overwhelmingly pro-nuclear opinions and the relative absence of (reported) stress due to the proximity of such an extensive nuclear reservation. Consistent with this, Evans and Jacobs (1981) report that

---

[1]Davis, C. E. *Attitudinal mediation of annoyance to transportation noise.* Unpublished manuscript, 1975.

employees of industries identified as major polluters are generally less concerned than most other people about the consequences of air pollution.

Perception of Risk and Danger

The perception of risks associated with a stressor and the nature of the threats or dangers posed by it will also mediate appraisal of the stressor. Assessment of risk appears to be influenced by certain biases in perception that may be related to cognitive limitations in information processing. Simon (1957) has considered a theory of "bounded rationality," asserting that decision makers must necessarily construct simplified models of the world to be able to deal with all of it. These models are inevitably influenced by the attitudes and characteristics of the individuals who have constructed them. They are not veridical with objective reality, and rest upon general inferential rules, guidelines, or heuristics that simplify difficult mental calculations.

In situations in which evidence of a certain degree of risk or danger is not immediately available, individuals are likely to use heuristics to estimate degree of danger. The need for certainty and confidence often leads to biases in judgment. Under some conditions, when people are able to make predictions about events (i.e., they have enough information to do so), some degree of uncertainty is desirable. In such instances, absolute certainty makes prediction obvious, meaningless, and seemingly trivial. However, uncertainty is aversive when predictions cannot be made with any expected accuracy, and in order to reach a decision and reduce uncertainty, people may give undue weight to dramatic instances, or overestimate the reliability of data from small samples. The result of such bias is often a deficit in probabilistic judgments. Thus, when Hynes and Vanmarcke (1976) asked geotechnical engineers to specify upper and lower limits for the height at which an embarkment would cause a clay foundation to collapse, not one of the expert estimates successfully enclosed the true failure height. Biases in judgment made in the absence of adequate information often lead to decisions made primarily to reduce uncertainty. Information may be distorted or simply denied, as among flood victims, some of whom denied that their area might be flooded again by believing that the flood had been a freak occurrence or by placing great emphasis on new forms of flood control.

Another heuristic relevant to risk perception is availability. People generally believe an event is more likely to occur if they can imagine it or recall examples of it. While the availability heuristic may be useful in evaluating events that occur frequently, its application to rare events can lead to distortions in judgment. The availability bias is especially relevant to stress that may or may not accompany proximity to nuclear power plants such as Three Mile Island. Atomic bombs and the Cold War, books and movies depicting nuclear holocaust, and the antinuclear portion of the American public have all served to create vivid images of nuclear disaster in our minds. It has been noted that attempts to impress the public with the low probability of a reactor accident may have the reverse effect. While a speaker may be discussing the improbability of a number of different factors that could result in a nuclear accident, the audience may be shocked by the realization that so many things could go wrong. A more mundane instance is reflected by the relatively large amounts of money that public agencies spend for aircraft safety compared to auto safety—in effect implying that a life lost in a dramatic plane crash was more valuable than one lost in a commonplace auto wreck. Other research findings support the notion that dramatic threats may be overestimated as to real danger potential and may therefore evoke stress reactions of greater magnitude. Perceived risk appears to depend, in part, on how dramatic the events in question are, and response to these events seems to be based on potential for danger rather than likelihood of threat. Thus, the steady but largely unnoticed pollution of the atmosphere by industries, transportation, heating systems, and the like evokes a lower level response than it should; while the likelihood of suffering some effect of pollution is high for most people, the consequences are neither dramatic nor even apparent. The potential danger of air pollution is probably judged to be low by many people, even though the likelihood of being affected by pollution is fairly high. Perception of risk, attitudes, and other influences on the appraisal of a stressor can exert an influence on whether an event is seen as threatening, the extent of arousal and intensity of coping, and the degree of concern and attention given to the event.

Dispositional Variables

Factors related to individuals' prior experiences and predispositions are also important in mediating the effects of stressors. The existence of per sons with "high stress" or "high risk" personalities, for example, has been indicated by a number of studies. Grinker and Spiegel (1945) noted that only a relatively small number of air combat crews serving during World War II ever developed serious or diagnosable stress-related ailments. Some of the airmen studied had previously established neuroses that made them more susceptible to the stress of battle. This vulnerability notion has been used often in more recent research, providing an explanation for selective onset of schizophrenia, illness, and other stress-related disturbances. One index of vulnerability in crowded situations is a person's preferences and needs with regard to interindividual distancing. People who prefer large amounts of space between themselves and others are more susceptible to the effects of spatial density than are those who can get along with less space.

Coping styles or behavior patterns have also been identified, and these styles appear to affect the ways in which events are appraised as well as which types of coping are involved. Work on a number of these dimensions, such as repression-sensitization, arousal seeking, screening and denial has indicated that people differing along them may interpret situations differently. A study by Davis and Baum, for example, suggests that individuals who cope with overload by screening and setting priorities on demands are less susceptible to the effects of social density than are people who do not cope in this way.

Glass (1976) has described a particularly vivid instance of this kind of predisposition. Individuals who manifest a Type A behavior pattern are people who respond to stress as if it were control-threatening and interpret any threats to control as stressful. Their appraisal of events is particularly sensitive to anything that might reduce their control over a situation. The time urgency, competitiveness, and hostility that accompany this response, together with the enhanced likelihood of experiencing stress and physiological concomitants of that stress, make Type As more at risk for coronary heart disease (Glass, 1976). It is tempting to speculate that this behavior pattern might make people more reactive and susceptible to stressors such as crowding or noise of which loss of control may be a direct antecedent or cause.

Control

Perceived control is a powerful mediator of stress, providing a sense of being able to cope effectively,

predict events, and determine what will happen. Unfortunately, data on the effects of perceived control are not available for all potential stressors. For example, there is little research on the relationship between control and heat stress; however, the relationship between control and other stressors has been studied extensively. Glass and Singer (1972) considered the effects of perceived controllability in their studies of stress due to noise, finding that predictable or controllable noise exacted smaller costs in adaptation. The perception that the noise might be accurately anticipated or even turned off if so desired facilitated adaptation with minimal aftereffects. Subsequently, others found the same relationship for stress due to crowding. Providing control reduced crowding stress.

Whether control has these effects by influencing appraisal of the stressor is a matter for speculation. One study bears on this point. Subjects who were given perceived control over shocks reported less discomfort than did subjects who did not "control" the intensity or administration of the shock. This was so even though all subjects actually received the same number and intensity of shocks. The perception of control seemed to affect perception of the stressor used in that study.

Somewhat more direct evidence of control influencing appraisal of stressors comes from the growing literature on cognitive control. By providing subjects with information about a stressor prior to subjects' exposure to it, researchers have been able to reduce the threat appraisal made when the stressor is experienced. Some studies have considered medical settings, and have found that the stress of surgery or of unusual medical procedures can be reduced by providing patients with accurate expectations of what they will feel. By giving normative information about sensations to patients, researchers have provided them with "road maps" telling them what they should experience. As a result, when these sensations are experienced they will not be appraised as abnormal or frightening. Other studies have found that accurate expectations also reduce crowding stress. Inaccurate or violated expectations of crowding result in some negative response, but appear quickly remedied when people realize what has happened and form new expectations.

On a broader level, perceived control may also be a very important prerequisite for meaningful social change. Evans and Jacobs (1981) discuss the relationship between public apathy towards air pollution abatement and the belief that individuals have little or no control over such pollution.

If most of the population believes that a given stressor is beyond their control, they will be less likely to attempt ameliorative actions.

THE STRESS RESPONSE

Despite the sometimes overwhelming nature of stressors, or the likelihood that they will be appraised as threatening, stress cannot be defined without reference to the response made by the organism. These physiological, cognitive, and social reactions or effects are therefore an important aspect of the stressor-stress process.

Physiological responses to stress may be both specific and nonspecific and may be chronic or acute. Those responses that are shortlived, either because adaptation is achieved or because the stressor was brief, resemble a mobilization response. When frightened by a loud noise or exposed to a highly threatening but rapidly unfolding situation (e.g., we see a car heading right for us at high speed, and it speeds by just missing us), the organism is alerted to the danger and readies itself to respond. However, when stress responses are repeated or prolonged, the alarm reaction no longer functions. If adaptation is not achieved, prolonged arousal can lead to tissue damage and diseases of exhaustion (Selye, 1956/1976).

Stress can cause cognitive deficits as well as improved performance. Cognitive deficits may in turn be caused by behavioral strategies that are used for coping—the person exposed to loud noise may "tune out" or narrow his or her field of attention. At this level, response may become more specific to the stressor being experienced. Behavioral aspects of the stress response may often reflect the specific causes of discomfort as the organism copes with the stressor.

Coping behavior seems to be directly related to characteristics of the source of stress. People may respond to crowding caused by a surfeit of people by withdrawing and avoiding social contacts, while they may respond to crowding caused by inadequate amounts of space by becoming aggressive. By the same token, they may respond to job loss actively if the loss was caused by a lack of effort or ability, or may become helpless under certain conditions. Coping with victimization appears to be specific to different levels of self-blame and the type of strategy taken also seems to be related to the kind of problems confronted during exposure to a stressor.

Aftereffects, on the other hand, are not always specific to certain stressors. These effects, defined as consequences that are experienced after exposure to a stressor has terminated, fit into Selye's (1956/1976) notion of limited adaptive energy. As exposure to stress increases, the adaptive reserves are depleted, causing aftereffects and reductions of subsequent coping ability. Evidence for the existence of poststressor effects comes from a number of sources, including research on the effects of noise and electric shock. However, explanations for these effects are not as clear.

Aftereffects that have been associated with stress include decreases in cognitive functioning and reduced tolerance for frustration, aggressiveness, helplessness, decreased sensitivity to others, and withdrawal. They also seem to be sensitive to perception of control with fewer aftereffects following experiences in which participants felt that they had control. However, evidence for aftereffects as costs of the adaptive process is equivocal, although consideration of effort expended during adaptation may better reflect this relationship. In addition to psychic costs, aftereffects may represent persistent coping responses, the effects of restricted cue utilization or narrowing of attention, or symptoms of learned helplessness.

Perhaps most important among aftereffects is the simple effect stress seems to have on ability to adapt in the future. Calhoun's (1970) discussions of crowding included "refractory periods" during which organisms recover from interactions with others, and several studies have suggested that repeated or prolonged exposure to stress can reduce one's ability to cope. Support for this position has also come from studies of adjustment to life change. This work has suggested that there are physiological and psychological costs associated with adaptation, especially when events that require adjustment or adaptation are clustered together in time. When people must adapt to a number of changes of varying magnitude, either serially or at once, ease and success of adjustment decrease and adaptation becomes increasingly difficult. If the amount of adjustment required is large enough, it may render the individual unable to cope and lead to severe consequences.

Illness and death are clear examples of the most severe consequences of stress. Again, the psychosocial determinants of this stress are important. The interaction of people, one with another, has been viewed as an important aspect of the effects of population density. Unwanted interaction and inability to regulate contact have been implicated as a cause of behavioral and physiological dysfunction among humans and animal populations. Population density has also been associated with health in a number of settings. In one study, stress associated with population density appeared to contribute to death rates.

Studies of stress and illness also provide evidence of negative effects of stress. Traditionally, illness has been viewed as a biological phenomenon, the result of specific physiological dysfunction or invasion by some foreign substance. However, there appear to be diseases that do not fit within a strict biomedical model. Diseases of "life style," such as heart disease, seem to be related to patterns of coping. Hypertension, heart disease, and the like are not contagious; they do not seem to be caused by germs, microbes or other simple infectious-like mechanisms. Rather, they develop over the course of a person's life and are contributed to by a number of factors, including diet, working habits, whether or not we smoke, and how we respond to stress.

Research on the relationships between stress and illness has been conducted in several settings and at different levels. Early research, for example, considered the stress of the mass bombings of London beginning in 1940 during World War II, and stress associated with the German concentration camps has also been studied. Many survivors of these brutalities showed relatively permanent adjustment problems, elevated blood pressures during initial exposure and greater physical illness later, and a greater incidence of premature or sudden death than people their age who were not confined (Cohen, 1953).

More recent studies reveal another example of stress related illness and death. Research conducted at the space center at Cape Kennedy during the last years of this country's moon program considered base employees who monitored moon missions from the ground. These workers, in addition to having high-pressure jobs, were also exposed to a rather stressful paradox. Their goal was to put a man on the moon, a highly rewarding end in and of itself. But they knew that once a successful mission was completed, the program would be cut back and eventually discontinued. Thus, these workers were pushed to do difficult jobs so that the United States could land men on the moon, with the ultimate payoff being unemployment. Increased rates of alcoholism and divorce were observed as pressure to complete the mission increased. More seriously, there was a spontaneous increase in sudden deaths among the relatively young workers. These deaths, presumably caused by heart failure, were nearly 50 percent more frequent than the average for that age group. The sudden deaths peaked as the space program was being phased out.

As was mentioned earlier, there may exist a stress-prone personality that renders some people more susceptible to the consequences of stress. In the space program studies, most workers did not die, but were able to cope with the stress they experienced without such a dramatic toll. Kasl and Cobb's (1970) research on stress associated with job loss also found that only some subjects became ill, but a greater proportion were affected than one would expect based on averages for the age groups studied. Following loss of job, some subjects showed an increase in blood pressure, ulcers and swollen joints. Some evidence of incipient diabetes and atherosclerosis was also found in blood samples of men who had recently lost their jobs.

Although these and other studies may have methodological weaknesses that have led to some questioning of these findings, the evidence does suggest some linkages between stress and physical illness. Environmental events or interpretations of them that lead to perceptions of threat or danger can generate stress responses, and prolonged exposure to such stimuli can result in physiological dysfunction or death. However, the link between stress and illness is still, for the most part, unexplained.

CONCLUDING COMMENTS

Our organization of stress research includes three components: a source, a transmission, and a recipient. Several points can be emphasized. First, the three components are interactive. So, for example, recipients can modify a stressor directly—they can turn off a noise or leave a densely populated room—or they can reappraise the nature of the stressor, deciding that although dense with people, the room is neither noisy nor crowded. Second, some stressors, such as extremely high temperature, may override the recipient's use of defense mechanisms and may produce debilitating reactions despite resistance. Third, appraisal and coping mechanisms may span periods of time longer than just the application of the stressor; evaluation processes may begin well in advance, may be affected by the recipient's personal history, and may persist to influence evaluation of future stressors. Fourth, although many stresses are triggered by a noxious agent, it is not always possible to identify such an agent, or even specify the circumstances under which such an agent or pathogen is present. Indeed, several types of anxiety may be defined as a source of psychological stress in which no apparent agent is present. Fifth, one of the interesting and underresearched questions of the stress field is the relation between positive affect and stress. Are the reactions to a positive stressor the same as to a negative one? Does defining a wild car ride as a thrill and not a danger change only the appraisal?

The environment is the source of a number of stressors. These initiate a variety of reactions. Some of these are physiological; others are psychological. They range from endocrine secretion to com-

plicated appraisals and evaluations of the sources. Transmission events such as control intervene between the source and the recipient. Few investigators attempt to study all aspects of the process simultaneously, and still fewer do so successfully. Yet many studies, which on the surface are dissimilar, can be fundamentally related to the same underlying model. This essay has attempted to make those relations explicit, at least for those studies conventionally considered environmental.

REFERENCES

Calhoun, J. B. Space and the strategy of life. *Ekistics*, 1970, *29*, 425–37.

Cohen, E. A. *Human behavior in the concentration camp.* New York: W. W. Norton, 1953.

Evans, G. W., & Jacobs, S. V. Air pollution and human behavior. *Journal of Social Issues*, 1981, *37*(1), 95–125.

Glass, D. C. *Behavior patterns, stress, and coronary disease.* Hillsdale, N.J.: Lawrence Erlbaum Associates, 1976.

Glass, D. C., & Singer, J. E. *Urban Stress: Experiments on noise and social stressors.* New York: Academic Press, 1972.

Grinker, R. R., & Spiegel, J. P. *Men under stress.* New York: McGraw-Hill, 1945.

Hynes, M., & Vanmarcke, E. Reliability of embarkment performances predictions. *Proceedings of the ASCE Engineering Mechanics Division Specialty Conference.* Waterloo, Canada: University of Waterloo Press, 1976.

Jonsson, E., & Sorenson, S. On the influence of attitudes toward the source on annoyance reactions to noise: An experimental study. *Nordisk Hygiensk Tidskrift*, 1967, *48*, 35–45.

Kasl, S. V., & Cobb, S. Blood pressure changes in men

undergoing job loss: A preliminary report. *Psychosomatic Medicine*, 1970, *32*, 19–38.

Kiretz, S., & Moos, R. H. Physiological effects of social environments. *Psychosomatic Medicine*, 1974, *36*, 96–114.

Lazarus, R. S., & Cohen, J. B. Environmental stress. In I. Altman & J. F. Wohlwill (eds.), *Human behavior and environment* (Vol. I). New York: Plenum, 1977.

Lazarus, R. S., Opton, E. M., Norrikos, M. S., & Rankin, N. O. The principle of shortcircuiting of threat: Further evidence. *Journal of Personality*, 1965, *33*, 622–35.

Leonard, S., & Borsky, P. N. A causal model for relating noise exposure, psycho-social variables and aircraft noise annoyance. In W. Ward (ed.), *Proceedings of the International Congress on Noise as a Public Health Problem.* Washington, D.C.: Environmental Protection Agency, 1973.

Seyle, H. *The Stress of Life.* New York: McGraw-Hill, 1956/ 1976.

Tracor, Inc. *Community reaction to aircraft noise*, Vol. I. Washington, D.C.: National Aeronautics and Space Administration, *NASA Report CR-1761*, 1971.

RESEARCH HIGHLIGHT

COLLEGE CLASSROOM ECOLOGY

A decade ago Robert Sommer and his colleagues studying classroom ecology reported that participation rates and grades were higher for students sitting in the front rows and center aisles of college classrooms. However, since students chose their own seats, these findings could be seen as reflecting either or both of two processes:

Becker, F. D., Sommer, R., Bee, J. & Oxley, B. College classroom ecology. *Sociometry*, 1973, *36*, 514–25; Knowles, E. S. A comment on the study of classroom ecology: A lament for the good old days. *Personality and Social Psychology Bulletin*, 1982, *8:2*, 357–61; Griffith, C. R. A comment upon the psychology of the audience. *Psychological Monographs*, 1921, *30:136*, 36–47.

(a) student self-selection, where smarter, more talkative, or more interested students chose front and center seats, or (b) ecological influence, where some aspects of the seating position produced greater participation, better learning, and higher grades. Recent studies have attempted to test between the self-selecting and ecological hypothesis. However, current research, according to Eric Knowles, who reviewed it recently, fails to match the quality and interest of a little known 60-year-old study. In 1921, Coleman R. Griffith studied approximately 20,000 grades achieved by students alphabetically assigned to seats in various lecture classes. His findings indicated that "the accomplishments of students in the front rows is from 3 percent to 8 percent less than that of students in the middle of the room. . . . There is still a more marked difference—approximately 10 percent—between the grades in the middle of the room and the grades found in one or two rows at the rear" (p. 39). Griffith's explanation used what he called a "social integration" feature: "physical compaction and the interests and activities of a group polarized toward the speaker tend to knit together the main body of an audience in a way that is not possible for individuals seated near the borders of the group" (p. 46).

THE EXPERIENCE OF LIVING IN CITIES: A PSYCHOLOGICAL ANALYSIS

STANLEY MILGRAM

The condition of America's cities is currently the topic of much controversy. The rising costs of municipal services, the increased crime rate, the deterioration in the quality of public education, and the problems of overcrowding and pollution are only some of the difficulties that must be dealt with. New York City's financial crisis is an extreme example of these urban woes, but many other cities are approaching crisis points. City life offers many advantages, such as greater access to the arts, education, and entertainment. But for many people, these advantages are offset by the grave problems that are also part of city life, and they have been relocating to the suburbs and rural areas in increasing numbers, seeking a better life.

But what constitutes "a better life"? In large part, the phrase is used in a psychological sense to refer to a life-style that allows people to feel secure, happy, relaxed, and in control of their destiny. To the extent that the urban life mitigates against these feelings, it is viewed as something from which to escape. In "The Experience of Living in Cities," Milgram analyzes city life from a psychological point of view, examining various factors that distinguish the urban experience from the rural experience and the different behaviors of city dwellers and their small-town counterparts. Rather than agreeing with the cliché that "city slickers" are a different breed of folk, Milgram suggests that the behavior of urban residents reflects a variety of adaptations to the "overload" situations, encounters, and other stimuli that are a part of everyday life in a city.

From *Science*, Vol. 167 (March 13, 1970), 1461–68. Copyright © 1970 by the American Association for the Advancement of Science. Reprinted by permission.

When I first came to New York it seemed like a nightmare. As soon as I got off the train at Grand Central I was caught up in pushing, shoving crowds on 42nd Street. Sometimes people bumped into me without apology; what really frightened me was to see two people literally engaged in combat for possession of a cab. Why were they so rushed? Even drunks on the street were bypassed without a glance. People didn't seem to care about each other at all.

This statement represents a common reaction to a great city, but it does not tell the whole story. Obviously, cities have great appeal because of their variety, eventfulness, possibility of choice, and the stimulation of an intense atmosphere that many individuals find a desirable background to their lives. Where face to face contacts are important, the city is unparalleled in its possibilities. It has been calculated by the Regional Plan Association (1969) that in Nassau county, a suburb of New York City, an official can meet 11,000 others with whom he may do business within 10 minutes of his office by foot or car. In Newark, a moderate-sized city, he could see more than 20,000 persons. But in midtown Manhattan an office worker can meet 220,000 persons within 10 minutes of his desk. There is an order of magnitude increment in the communication possibilities offered by a great city. That is one of the bases of its appeal and, indeed, of its functional necessity. The city provides options that no other social arrangement permits. But there is a negative side also, as we shall see.

Granted that cities are indispensable in a complex society, we may still ask what contribution psychology can make to understanding the experience of living in them. What theories are relevant? How can we extend our knowledge of the psychological aspects of life in cities through empirical inquiry? If empirical inquiry is possible, along what lines should it proceed? In short, where do we start in the construction of urban theory and in laying out lines of research?

Observation is the indispensable starting point. Any observer in the streets of midtown Manhattan will see: (a) large numbers of people, (b) high density, and (c) heterogeneity of population. These three factors need to be at the root of any socio-psychological theory of city life, for they condition all aspects of our experience in the metropolis. Wirth (1938), if not the first to point to these factors, is nonetheless the sociologist who relied most heavily on them in his analysis of the city. Yet, for a psychologist there is something unsatisfactory about Wirth's theoretical variables. *Numbers, density,* and *heterogeneity* are demographic facts, but they are not yet psychological facts. They are external to the individual. Psychology needs an idea that links the individual's

experience to the demographic circumstances of urban life.

One link is provided by the concept of *overload.* This term, drawn from systems analysis, refers to the inability of a system to process inputs from the environment because there are too many inputs for the system to cope with, or because successive inputs come so fast that Input A cannot be processed when Input B is presented. When overload is present, adaptations occur. The system must set priorities and make choices. Input A may be processed first while B is kept in abeyance, or one input may be sacrificed altogether. City life, as we experience it, constitutes a continous set of encounters with adaptations to overload. Overload characteristically deforms daily life on several levels, impinging on *role performance,* evolution of *social norms, cognitive functioning,* and the *use of facilities.*

The concept has been implicit in several theories of urban experience. Simmel (1950) pointed out that since urban dwellers come into contact with vast numbers of people each day, they conserve psychic energy by becoming acquainted with a far smaller proportion of people than their rural counterparts and by maintaining more superficial relationships even with these acquaintances. Wirth (1938) points specifically to "the superficiality, the anonymity, and the transitory character of urban social relations," and to the loss of community, which produces "the state of *anomie,* or the social void." Simmel notes as well that the high density of cities encourages inhabitants to create distance in social contacts to counteract the overwhelming pressures of close physical contact. The greater the number and frequency of human contacts the less time, attention, and emotional investment one can give to each of them, thus, the purported blasé and indifferent attitude of city dwellers toward each other.

One adaptive response to overload, therefore, is that *less time is given to each input.* A second adaptive mechanism is that *low priority inputs are disregarded.* Principles of selectivity are formulated so that the investment of time and energy is reserved for carefully defined inputs (e.g., the urbanite disregards a drunk, sick on the street, as he purposefully navigates through the crowd.) Third, *boundaries are redrawn in certain social transactions so that the overloaded system can shift the burden to the other party in the exchange;* for example, harried New York bus drivers once made change for customers, but now this responsibility has been shifted to the client who must have the exact fare ready. Fourth, *reception is blocked off prior to entering a system;* city dwellers increasingly use unlisted telephone numbers to prevent individuals from calling them, and a small but growing number resort to keeping the telephone off the hook to prevent incoming calls. More subtly, one blocks inputs by assuming an unfriendly countenance, which discourages others from initiating contact. Additionally, *social screening devices are interposed between the individual and environmental inputs* (in a town of 5,000 anyone can drop in to chat with the mayor, but in the metropolis organizational screening devices deflect inputs to other destinations). Fifth, the *intensity of inputs is diminished by filtering devices* so that only weak and relatively superficial forms of involvement with others are allowed. Sixth, *specialized institutions are created to absorb inputs that would otherwise swamp the individual* (e.g., welfare departments handle the financial needs of a million individuals in New York City, who would otherwise create an army of mendicants continuously importuning the pedestrian). The interposition of institutions between the individual and the social world, a characteristic of all modern society and most acutely present in the large metropolis, has its negative side. It deprives the individual of a sense of direct contact and spontaneous integration in the life around him. It simultaneously protects and estranges the individual from his social environment.

In summary, the observed behavior of the urbanite in a wide range of situations appears to be determined largely by a variety of adaptations to overload. We shall now deal with several specific consequences of responses to overload, which come to create a different tone to city and town.

SOCIAL RESPONSIBILITY

The principal point of interest for a social psychology of the city is that moral and social involvement with individuals is necessarily restricted. This is a direct and necessary function of excess of input over capacity to process. Restriction of involvement runs a broad spectrum from refusal to become involved in the needs of another person, even when the person desperately needs assistance (as in the Kitty Genovese case), through refusal to do favors, to the simple withdrawal of courtesies (such as offering a lady a seat, or saying "sorry" when a pedestrian collision occurs). In any transaction more and more details need to be dropped as the total number of units to be processed increases and assaults an instrument of limited processing capacity. There are myriad specific situations dealing with social responsibility. Specific incidents can be ordered in terms of two dimensions. First, there is the dimension of the importance of the action in question. Clearly, intervening to save someone's life rates higher than tipping one's hat, though both imply a degree of social involvement with others. Second, one may place any specific incident in terms of its position on a social-anomic continuum. Thus, in regard to courtesy expressions, a person may extend courtesies (the social end of the continuum) or withhold them (the anomic end). Anomic conditions, up and down the spectrum, are said to characterize the metropolis in comparison with the small town.

The ultimate adaptation to an overloaded social environment is to totally disregard the needs, interests, and demands of those whom one does not define as relevant to personal need satisfaction, and to develop optimally efficient means of identifying whether an individual falls into the category of friend or stranger. The disparity in treatment of friends and strangers ought to be greater in cities than towns; the time allotment and willingness to become involved with those who can make no personal claim on one's time will be less in cities than in towns.

Bystander Intervention in Crises

The most striking deficiencies in urban social responsibility occur in crisis situations, such as the Genovese murder in Queens. As is well known, in 1964, Catherine Genovese, coming home from a night job in the early hours of an April morning, was stabbed repeatedly over an extended period of time. Thirty-eight residents of a respectable New York City neighborhood admitted to having witnessed at least part of the attack but none went to her aid or called the police until after she was dead. Milgram and Hollander (1964) analyzed the event in these terms:

> Urban friendships and associations are not primarily formed on the basis of physical proximity. A person with numerous close friends in different parts of the city may not know the occupant of an adjacent apartment. This does not mean that a city dweller has fewer friends than does a villager, or knows fewer persons who will come to his aid; however, it does mean that his allies are not constantly at hand. Miss

Genovese required immediate aid from those physically present. There is no evidence that the city had deprived Miss Genovese of human associations, but the friends who might have rushed to her side were miles from the scene of her tragedy.

Further, it is known that her cries for help were not directed to a specific person; they were general. But only individuals can act, and as the cries were not specifically directed, no particular person felt a special responsibility. The crime and the failure of community response seem absurd to us. At the time, it may well have seemed equally absurd to the Kew Gardens residents that not one of the neighbors would have called the police. A collective paralysis may have developed from the belief of each of the witnesses that someone else must surely have taken that obvious step [p. 602].

More than just callousness prevents bystanders from participating in altercations between people. A rule of urban life is respect for other people's emotional and social privacy, perhaps because physical privacy is so hard to achieve. And in situations for which the standards are heterogeneous, it is much harder to know whether taking an active role is unwarranted meddling or an appropriate response to a critical situation. If a husband and wife are quarreling in public, at which point should a bystander step in? On the one hand, the heterogeneity of the city produces substantially greater tolerance of behavior, dress, and codes of ethics than does the small town, but this diversity also encourages people to withhold aid for fear of antagonizing the participants or crossing an inappropriate and difficult-to-define line.

Moreover, the frequency of demands present in the city gives rise to norms of noninvolvement. There are practical limitations to the Samaritan impulse in a major city. If a citizen attended to every needy person, if he were sensitive to and acted on every altruistic impulse that was evoked in the city, he could scarcely keep his own affairs in order.

Favor Doing Based on Trust

We may now move away from crisis situations to less urgent examples of social responsibility; for it is not only in situations of dramatic need, but in the ordinary, everyday willingness to lend a hand, that the city dweller is said to be deficient relative to his small-town cousin. The comparative method must be employed in any empirical examination of this question. A commonplace so-

cial situation is staged both in an urban setting and a small town, a situation to which a subject can respond either by extending help or withholding it. The responses in town and city are then compared.

One factor in the purported unwillingness of urbanites to extend themselves to strangers may well be their heightened sense of physical and emotional vulnerability—a feeling that is supported by urban crime statistics. A key test for distinguishing between city and town behavior, therefore, is how city dwellers compare with town dwellers in offering aid that increases their personal vulnerability and requires some trust of strangers. Altman, Levine, Nadien, and Villena (1969) devised a study to compare city and town dwellers in this respect. The criterion used in their study was the willingness of householders to allow strangers to enter their homes to use the telephone. Individually the investigators rang doorbells, explained that they had misplaced the address of a friend nearby, and asked to use the phone. The investigators (two males and two females) completed a total of 100 requests for entry in the city and 60 in the small towns. The results gleaned from middle-income housing developments in Manhattan were compared with data gathered in several small towns in Rockland County, outside of New York City (Stony Point, Spring Valley, Ramapo, Nyack, New City, and West Clarkstown).

As Table 1 shows, in all cases there was a sharp increase in the proportion of entries gained by an investigator when he moved from the city to a small town. In the most extreme case the investigator was five times more likely to gain admission to a home in a small town than in Manhattan. Although the female investigators had noticeably

TABLE 1. PERCENTAGE OF ENTRIES BY INVESTIGATORS FOR CITY AND TOWN HOMES

INVESTIGATOR	CITY (n = 100)	SMALL TOWN (n = 60)
Male		
1	16	40
2	12	60
Female		
1	40	87
2	40	100

higher levels of entry in both cities and towns than the male investigators, all four students did at least twice as well in gaining access to small-town homes than they did to city homes, suggesting that the city–town distinction overrides even the predictably greater fear of male strangers than of female ones.

The lower level of helpfulness by city dwellers seems due in part to recognition of the *dangers* of Manhattan living, rather than to mere indifference or coldness. It is significant that 75% of all city respondents received and answered messages either by shouting through closed doors or by peering through peepholes; in the towns, by contrast, about 75% of the respondents opened the doors, with no barriers between themselves and the investigator.

Supporting the investigators' quantitative results was their general observation that the town dwellers were noticeably more friendly and less suspicious than the city dwellers. Even city dwellers who allowed the investigators to use the phone appeared more ill at ease than their town counterparts; city dwellers often refused to answer the doorbell even when they were at home; and in a few cases city residents called the security police of the housing development. In seeking to explain the sense of psychological vulnerability city dwellers feel, above and beyond differences in actual crime statistics, Altman et al. (1969) point out that for a village resident, if a crime is committed in a neighboring village, he may not perceive it as personally relevant, though the geographic distance may be small. But a criminal act committed anywhere in the city, though miles from the city-dweller's home, is still verbally located within the city, "therefore . . . the inhabitant of the city possesses a larger vulnerable space."

Civilities

Even at the most superficial level of involvement, the exercise of everyday civilities, urbanites are reputedly deficient. Persons bump into each other and frequently do not apologize. They knock over another person's packages, and, as often as not, proceed on their way with a grump, rather than taking the time to help the victim. Such behavior, which many visitors to great cities find distasteful, is less common, we are told, in smaller communities where traditional courtesies are more likely to be maintained.

In some instances it is not simply that in the city traditional courtesies are violated; rather, the cities develop *new norms of noninvolvement.* They are so well defined and so deeply a part of city life that *they* constitute the norms people are reluctant to violate. Men are actually embarrassed to give up a seat on the subway for an old woman; they will mumble, "I was getting off anyway," instead of making the gesture in a straightforward and gracious way. These norms develop because everyone realizes that in situations of high-density people cannot implicate themselves in each other's affairs, for to do so would create conditions of continual distraction that would frustrate purposeful action.

The effects of overload do not imply that at every instant the city dweller is bombarded with an unmanageable number of inputs, and that his responses are determined by the input excess at any given instant. Rather, adaptation occurs in the form of the gradual evolution of norms of behavior. Norms are created in response to frequent discrete experiences of overload; they persist and become generalized modes of responding. They are part of the culture of the metropolis, and even newcomers may adapt to these manners in the course of time.

Overload on Cognitive Capacities: Anonymity

It is a truism that we respond differently toward those whom we know and those who are strangers to us. An eager patron aggressively cuts in front of someone in a long movie line to save time only to confront a friend; he then behaves sheepishly. A man gets into an automobile accident caused by another driver, emerges from his car shouting in rage, then moderates his behavior on discovering a friend driving the other car. The city dweller, when moving through the midtown streets, is in a state of continual anonymity vis à vis the other pedestrians. His ability to know everyone he passes is restricted by inherent limitations of human cognitive capacity. A continual succession of faces briefly appears before him then disappears. Minimal scanning for recognition occurs, but storage in long-term memory is avoided. (No one has yet calculated the number of faces scanned in a day by the typical midtown worker.)

The concept of "anonymity" is a shibboleth of social psychology, but few have defined it precisely or attempted to measure it quantitatively in order to compare cities and towns. Anonymity is part of a continuous spectrum ranging from total anonymity at one end to full acquaintance at the other, and it may well be that measurement of the precise degrees of anonymity in cities and towns would help to explain important distinctions between the quality of life in each. Conditions of full acquaintance, for example, offer security and familiarity, but they may also be stifling because the inhabitant is under continuous scrutiny by people who know him. Conditions of complete anonymity, by contrast, provide freedom from routine social ties, but they may also create feelings of alienation and detachment.

One could investigate empirically the proportion of activities in which the city dweller and town dweller are known by others at given times in their daily lives, and, if known, with what proportion of those the urbanite and town dweller interact. At his job, for instance, the city dweller may know fully as many people as his rural counterpart. While not fulfilling his occupational or family role, however—say, in traveling about the city—the urbanite is doubtlessly more anonymous than his rural counterpart. (One way to measure the difference in degrees of anonymity would be to display the picture of a New York inhabitant at a busy midtown intersection. One could offer a significant reward to any passerby who could identify the person pictured. Calculation of the total number of passersby during a given period, coupled with the proportion who could identify the picture, provides one measure of urban anonymity. Results could then be compared with those gleaned by displaying the picture of a town dweller on the main street in his town. This test could also be used to define a person's "neighborhood boundary," that area within which a high proportion of people could identify the inhabitant's picture.)

Limited laboratory work on anonymity has begun. An experiment by Zimbardo (1969) tested whether the social anonymity and impersonality of the big city encourage greater vandalism than found in small towns. . . . Zimbardo arranged for one car to be left for 64 hours near the New York University campus in the Bronx and a counterpart to be left near Stanford University in Palo Alto. The license plates on both cars were removed and the hoods opened, to provide "releaser cues" for potential vandals. The results were as expected: The New York car was stripped of all moveable parts within the first 24 hours, and was left a hunk of metal rubble by the end of three days. Unexpectedly, however, most destruction occurred during daylight hours usually under scrutiny by observers, and was led by well-dressed, white adults. The Palo Alto car was left untouched.

Another direction for empirical study is the investigation of the beneficial effects of anonymity. Impersonality of city life breeds its own tolerance for the private lives of inhabitants. Individuality and even eccentricity, we may assume, can flourish more readily in the metropolis than in the small town. Stigmatized persons may find it easier to lead comfortable lives without the constant scrutiny of neighbors.

Role Behavior in Cities and Towns

Another product of urban "overload" is the adjustment in roles made by urbanites in daily interactions. As Wirth has said: "Urbanities meet one another in highly segmental roles. . . . They are less dependent upon particular persons, and their dependence upon others is confined to a highly fractionalized aspect of the other's round of activity." This tendency is particularly noticeable in transactions between customers and those offering professional or sales services: The owner of a country store has time to become well acquainted with his dozen-or-so daily customers; but the girl at the checkout counter of a busy A & P, handling hundreds of customers a day, barely has time to toss the green stamps into one customer's shopping bag before the next customer has confronted her with his pile of groceries.

In his stimulating analysis of the city, *A Communications Theory of Urban Growth*, Meier (1962) discusses several adaptations a system may make when confronted by inputs that exceed its capacity to process them. Specifically, Meier states that according to the principle of competition for scarce resources the scope and time of the transaction shrink as customer volume and daily turnover rise. This, in fact, is what is meant by the brusque quality of city life. New standards have developed in cities about what levels of services are appropriate in business transactions.

The research on this subject needs to be guided by unifying theoretical concepts. As this section of the paper has tried to demonstrate, the concept of overload helps to explain a wide variety of contrasts between city and town behavior: (a) the differences in *role enactment* (the urban dwellers' tendency to deal with one another in highly segmented, functional terms; the constricted time and services offered customers by sales personnel); (b) the evolution of *urban norms* quite different from traditional town values (such as the acceptance of noninvolvement, impersonality, and aloofness in urban life); (c) consequences for the urban dweller's *cognitive processes* (his inability to identify most of the people seen daily; his screening of sensory stimuli; his development of blasé attitudes toward deviant or bizarre behavior; and his selectivity in responding to human demands); and (d) the far greater competition for scarce *facilities* in the city (the subway rush, the fight for taxis, traffic jams, standing in line to await services). I would suggest that contrasts between city and rural behavior probably reflect the responses of similar people to very different situations, rather than intrinsic differences between rural personalities and city personalities. The city is a situation to which individuals respond adaptively.

REFERENCES

Altman, D., Levine, M., Nadien, M., & Villena, J. "Trust of the stranger in the city and the small town" (unpublished research, Graduate Center, City University of New York, 1969).

Meier, R. L. *A communications theory of urban growth.* Cambridge: MIT Press, 1962.

Milgram, S., & Hollander, P. Paralyzed witnesses: The murder they heard. *The Nation,* 1964, *25,* 602–04.

Regional Plan Association (1969). The second regional plan. *The New York Times,* June 15, 1969, 119, Section 12.

Simmel, G. The metropolis and mental life. In K. H. Wolff (ed.), *The sociology of George Simmel.* New York: The Free Press, 1950. (Originally published: *Die Grosstadte und das Geistesleben die Grossstadt.* Dresden: v. Zahn & Jaensch, 1903.)

Wirth, L. Urbanism as a way of life. *American Journal of Sociology,* 1938, *44,* 1–24.

Zimbardo, P. G. The human choice: Individuation, reason and order vs. deindividuation, impulse and chaos. *Nebraska Symposium on Motivation,* Lincoln, Neb.: University of Nebraska Press, 1969.

PROJECTS

Name _____

Date _____

12.1: MENTAL MAPS

Milgram has proposed the concept of "psychological maps" to study people's perceptions of the city environment. You can adapt this technique to gain some insight into your own and others' perceptions of your college campus. Basically, the technique involves drawing a map of the campus. The emphasis should be on representing the campus as the person sees it, not on geographical accuracy. First, draw your own map of the campus. Then select two acquaintances who might have different relationships to the campus (e.g., an athlete and a scholar, a freshman and a senior), and ask each of them to draw a map of the campus. Do not let them see any of the other maps before they draw their own.

1. Are there certain landmarks or boundaries that are included on all three maps? If so, what are they?

2. Are certain parts of the campus overrepresented on the maps or drawn in more detail than other parts? If so, do these special parts of the maps reflect the interests and activities of the particular map maker? For example, did the scholar note all the libraries; whereas the athlete drew the various playing fields and sports facilities?

3. What aspects of the campus environment are *not* represented on the maps?

4. Aside from omissions, are there any other patterns of distortion in the maps? If so, what are they?

*Name*_____

*Date*_____

12.2: THE PROFESSORIAL ENVIRONMENT

The physical environment that surrounds a person can, without conscious intent or cognition, influence behavior and social interaction. Such things as the arrangement of furniture can encourage or discourage contact and intimacy and can indicate status differences (e.g., limiting the immediacy of contact is a very effective means of conveying high status). Thus, one professor's office may sometimes look cold and impersonal; whereas another's is friendly and casual, depending on furniture placement. In situations in which it is important to establish good rapport and intimacy, a seating arrangement that encourages immediacy is critical.

The goal of this project is to explore the relationship between the physical layout of various professors' offices and the general friendliness of those professors. In order to do that, you should first establish criteria for evaluating the office environment and the professor's rapport with students. You might consider such variables as the placement of the desk (along the side of the wall or as a barrier between student and professor), the type and placement of chairs, and the amount of open space and such variables as availability (how many office hours the professor has and whether he or she is keeping them), the physical distance between the student's and the professor's chairs, and the amount of eye contact between professor and student. Decide on five criteria for evaluating the office environment and five criteria for evaluating the professor's rapport with students, and list them on the data sheet. Then visit the office of three different professors (whom you have previously met) to talk about some topic of interest. Rate both the office and the professor's rapport with you according to your set of criteria.

Name _____

Date _____

Data Sheet

Variables	Professor A	Professor B	Professor C

Environment

1. _____

2. _____

3. _____

4. _____

5. _____

Rapport

1. _____

2. _____

3. _____

4. _____

5. _____

Comments

Name＿＿＿＿＿＿＿＿＿＿＿＿＿＿＿＿＿＿＿＿＿

Date＿＿＿＿＿＿＿＿＿＿＿＿＿＿＿＿＿＿＿＿＿

1. Look at the pattern of ratings, and speculate on possible relationships between environment and behavior (e.g., how the placement of a desk can reduce personal contact).

2. Compare your criteria and your ratings with those of other people in your class. What hypotheses do your collective ratings suggest?

3. According to your own hypotheses, what would be the ideal office environment for promoting student-professor rapport? What would be the ideal environment for hindering it?

SOCIAL PROBLEMS AND APPLICATIONS

13

Social psychology has been called upon more extensively than most other branches of psychology to apply its knowledge to solving social problems. Many within as well as outside the profession have maintained that social psychologists should actually do something about a problem rather than study it for its own sake. In fact, social psychology began largely as an applied discipline. During the 1930s and 1940s, when social psychology emerged as a distinct field of study, research was either inspired by current social issues (e.g., reducing prejudice or understanding the dynamics of fascist leadership) or designed for direct use during World War II (e.g., studies of persuasion and propaganda techniques). After the war, social psychologists attempted to enhance the reputation of their discipline by turning away from applied research and concentrating on pure research.

Today, however, the pendulum seems to be swinging back toward applied research. Although not yet a mass movement, there is a tendency among more and more social psychologists to consider the pros and cons of doing applied research.

An increasing number of studies are being done on such topics as psychology and law, health psychology, environmental psychology, and political psychology. New journals and professional organizations are being developed in these areas, and some graduate schools are providing specific training in applied research.

This growing trend might be seen by some as a return to social psychology's roots. Kurt Lewin, the "father" of social psychology, had a demonstrated commitment to action research and to the application of social psychological theory to social issues, and the current generation of researchers seems to be emulating his model. Others might argue that the movement toward application is a recent one, developing in response to the social turmoil of the 1960s and the challenge by the American Psychological Association's president, George Miller, to "give psychology away." Regardless of the interpretation, it seems clear that applied research on social problems is a thriving and ever gorwing part of modern-day social psychology.

SOME REFLECTIONS UPON LOSING OUR SOCIAL PSYCHOLOGICAL PURITY

JEROME E. SINGER AND DAVID C. GLASS

Most social psychologists have been trained to do basic research, and that training shapes the questions they ask, the expectations they have, and the methods they use. When they decide to move into applied research, they may find that it is not simply a matter of applying their basic approach to a different type of problem. Instead, there is a whole new set of issues that face the investigator, and the actual process of doing research takes a different form. This contrast between basic and applied research is strikingly illustrated in the article by Singer and Glass. They describe how they studied the social problem of urban stress, including their initial involvement with the problem, their choice of method for the study, and their theoretical explanations of stress as a social phenomenon. Rather than presenting the results of their studies (which are contained in their book Urban Stress), they give the reader a look at how applied research is done and how it differs from pure research.

The eminent British mathematician, G. H. Hardy, was widely quoted outside of mathematical circles for his famous comment, "I have never done anything useful." And if his pre-World War II remark was interesting at the time it was uttered, it is even more curious now, for it turns out that Hardy was triply wrong. He was wrong in the most literal sense in that time and technology combined in his undoing; his work in number theory provided the basis for the solution of several problems in circuitry and switching theory. He was also wrong in a general historical sense. He was engaged in creating products of the intellect and his mathematics, like other artistic creations, have always, at least in Western society, been found useful enough to command both respect and support from the larger society. It would be a strange culture or age that did not cherish some purely aesthetic endeavors. This may seem to be somewhat of a quibble, but since we are only one or two years away from seeing many of the best products of our universities discarded for having failed to meet some vague criterion of relevance, it is worth restating the point that there is a satisfaction, elegance, and utility to "pure" work. Finally, at the heart of the matter, Hardy was most seriously and perniciously wrong in all that his statement implied; that is, there was something a little suspect, déclassé, or even tawdry about research or scholarship which had a direct application. It is impossible and even irrelevant to determine whether Hardy was merely an echo of his times or a formulator of opinions; he was probably a little of both. What is important to note is that his succinct statement of the mathematician's scorn of the engineer as a mere technician somehow found its way into the graduate training of the social psychologists of our generation.

Our rallying cry was not Hardy's mot, but Lewin's ("There is nothing so practical as a good theory!"), which we shrewdly managed to distort into an equivalent meaning. Our interpretation was simple: if theory was good, it was certainly better to stay in its rarefied domain than to deal with less useful, nongeneral, applied problems. And the very structure of the world around us, from the prize fellowships to the honors given to our faculty advisors, echoed the same theme: to be a major contribution a study must deal with basic, not applied, problems.

There was, of course, some backsliding and some ambivalence to these dictums. After all, didn't many respectable social psychologists work on applied problems during the second world war? Yet their success only reinforced our attitudes: we could do significant applied work if we wished to, but without the pressure of a national emergency we did not wish to. But we did go into the field occasionally. It was nice to be able to show that dissonance theory works in discount houses or in automobile salesrooms, but once again the focus was on the theory, not the sales.

. . .

The point of our introduction is not that we were misguided, saw the light, and then reformed, but rather that a set of inappropriate values guided our training and early research styles. Paradoxically, we now believe that our training and experiences devoted to the pursuit of the pristine have been precisely the best set of tools for the study of applied social problems. The future training goal, of course, is to impart these skills with a more humane set of values.

. . .

THE APPLIED ORIENTATION

The theme of this presentation is unusual because it concerns the natural history of the conduct of the research rather than a description of the research per se.

Reprinted, with deletions, from M. Deutsch and H. A. Hornstein (eds.), *Applying Social Psychology* (Hillsdale, N.J.: Lawrence Erlbaum Associates, 1975). By permission of the Social Science Research Council and the authors.

The Rotten City and Why Do People Love to Live There?

About a half dozen years ago, we were engaged in a series of conversations filled with the usual sort of small talk that passes for conversation among social psychologists when we discovered that we shared a curiosity about an inconsistency of life in New York City. Just at the time when many newspapers and magazines were printing a spate of articles bemoaning the worsening plight of the cities and highlighting every conceivable peril, we were struck by the fact that several of our friends were striking Faustian bargains, selling their souls, as it were, to remain in the city. We were, of course, aware of the advantages of city life, with its conveniences and opportunities, as well as of its disadvantages. The question that intrigued us was how people managed to cope with urban stress. We could understand how people could value a city's attractions enough for them to outweigh its repugnancies, but how were people able to manage with the problems, such as crowding, noise, bureaucracy, garbage, traffic, crime, etc., which even the most ardent urbanophile could hardly deny. Our first statement of the problem was simple: "How do people cope with urban stress?"

What Precisely Was Our Problem?

One way of attacking our problem was to begin by consulting those studies dealing with stress. At this stage of our work, they were of little help as most stress research dealt with specific and identifiable stressors and we were considering amorphous and all-enveloping living conditions. So we made our first decision to delimit our study to specific stressors. Hopefully, we would conduct investigations on a wide variety of stressors moving sequentially on to new ones as we solved the problems of the old. But, for a start, we decided to investigate the effects of noise and of bureaucracy on people and spent most of our efforts investigating noise.

Without much discussion, we settled early on the laboratory as the place to start, not because we thought that lab work was superior to field studies, but because of two practical reasons. First, most of our training and experience was in conducting lab studies, and, in an area where we had so little previous work to guide us, we thought that it would be better to avoid, at the start, those techniques in which we were relative neophytes. Second, our immediate resources and our assistants were already at work in the laboratories

and the couching of the problems in laboratory frameworks seemed a way to save us from that almost interminable tooling-up process that seems to plague most of our new research endeavors. In retrospect, it may be that we made the right decision for the wrong reasons. We had no need to worry about our field study capabilities. Most veteran investigators have learned the general strategy of doing research, and a questionnaire in the home is not all that different from one in the laboratory. Similarly, it is not that hard to start a field study and, conversely, one can spend as much time fiddling with polygraphs as with any field instrument.

The best reason for our having started in the laboratory was our comparative ignorance of the field. It was our belief that a laboratory study, with its relatively well-defined variables, would soon reveal whether or not there are any results. An initial field study, packed with every variable which we at first believed would have any impact, would have swamped us with data. In short, we felt that not all the possible internal analyses attempted in the name of "salvage" could really convince us that our failed study actually did succeed, while an ill-defined survey, for example, could generate enough data to keep us and our staff of programmers happy for months blithefully unaware of the study's outcome. When we finally did engage in field research, the studies were focused, small in scope, and well addressed to specific problems isolated by our preliminary laboratory work. Just as confirmation in the field adds generalization to the more restricted lab results, those very same lab studies impart a certain elegance to the field studies. In any event, having decided almost by default to start in the lab, exactly what did we want to study?

Enjoy Now, Stress Later

We started our design of the noise studies with an attack on the related literature. This turned out to be a Herculean task and if we had resolved to exhaust the literature before starting, we would still be reading. Even now, a good seven years after we have begun our projects, we still find and are directed to studies we have overlooked or to journals of whose existence we were unaware. But in the material we did read, two seemingly unrelated facts caught our attention. Almost all the studies reviewing the effects of noise upon humans showed that there were very few times and very rare conjunctions of circumstances in which noise produced any direct behavioral deficits. This conclusion, soundly documented, was at odds not only with our own experience and intuition, but also with that of the public at large who were busily forming antinoise committees, with environmentalists who were waging suit against airport expansions, and with almost all social critics from the futurists to the Cassandras. Our initial resolution of this dilemma was to take a biological model of stress and adaptation proposed by Selye[1] and metaphorically adapt it to our problem. Selye pointed out that for many physical stressors, organisms are able to adapt, but that they pay a cost of adaptation such that the stressor's effects are revealed in later activities. We reasoned that noise could function in much the same way. People in a noisy environment learn to cope with it, but . . . they pay a psychic price for this adaptation which only surfaces in their later activities. Thus, a worker in a noisy office learns to work in a fashion such that his production is equal to that of a colleague in a quieter setting, but he, unlike his sheltered counterpart, is more apt to yell at his family and kick the dog when he returns home from work in the evening.

This cost of adaption hypothesis, although ultimately much revised by our cumulative findings, was the thread upon which we hung the conception of our studies. . . . Our start then, came not from social psychology, but from an odd mixture of human performance studies, evolutionary biology, and urban journalism.

Adding Social Psychology

We ran an initial study and we were fortunate enough to obtain the results that we had hypothesized and intuited; that is, our subjects did adapt to the stressor of noise; after a short period of time, their performance under intense noise stress was no different from that of control subjects performing identical tasks in the absence of noise. Yet at the same time we were able to show that those people who had worked under noise stress manifested aftereffect deficits. They did not perform as well on tasks administered in quiet, after the noise session was over, as did the controls. Encouraging as this finding was, there were three corollary results that added to our interest. One was the fact that physical intensity of the noise

was not as powerful a factor as originally supposed. The second interesting result was that the context and interpretation of the situation in which the noise was presented had a greater impact upon the subjects than the characteristics of the noise itself. The third related finding of interest was that there was a lack of coordination between the subjects' ratings of the noise and its effects upon their behavior; . . . in fact, there were no direct performance differences between differing loudnesses. And the magnitude of the aftereffects was a function of social-cognitive factors and not of perceived irritation.

Taken together these factors greatly heartened us, for they enabled us to define the problem of noise stress (and by both analogy and subsequent study, urban stress, in general) in terms relating to social psychology, not audition and psychoacoustics. We were able to redefine and narrow our major goal into the study of what social and cognitive factors meliorate or exacerbate the aversive aftereffects of a noise stress.

How to Put Context in Its Place

The nonphysical factor which we had included in our first study concerned predictability, whether or not the noise bursts the subjects heard were possible to anticipate. For half of our subjects, the bursts came at fixed intervals, that is, at regular times and of regular duration. For the other half of the subjects, the bursts were of unequal length and occurred at random intervals during the experimental session. . . . This cognitive variable overrode the effects of intensity. But it immediately presented us with three problems, any one of which could provide the basis for a series of coordinated studies. Our interest in all three of these facets and our appreciation of the large number of questions raised by the results of the first study made us unwilling to concentrate on any one aspect, so we engaged in a four-pronged research effort starting with a continuation of our original problem.

1. Since any experiment is unlikely to be definitive in the sense that it discounts all possible alternatives to the proposed explanation of the data, it was necessary for us to explore what kinds of predictability and circumstances influenced the effects of noise. These studies did not extend our findings to more general conclusions, but they enabled us to demonstrate the robustness of our results, to sharpen our

[1]Hans Selye, *The stress of life* (New York: McGraw-Hill, 1956).

theoretical explanations, and to eliminate possible methodological flaws.

2. Having opened the phenomenon of noise-produced behavioral deficits to the possibility of cognitive modification, if not cognitive control, we proceeded to explore other cognitive factors that would also modify the social environment sufficiently to show moderating effects upon the noise stress. Ultimately, we studied five such variables in some depth. These were predictability, controllability, relative deprivation, necessity, and expectation.

3. As we began to examine the cumulative results of our experiments, not unexpectedly we found it necessary to modify our initial theoretical position. Our initial Selyean position required that subjects adapt to a stressor in order to study aftereffects. We had some reason to question whether or not adaptation was a necessary phase for the production of deleterious aftereffects. Consequently, we conducted several experiments to explore the implications of our preliminary theorizing. These studies, which were an important link in our reasoned explanations of the noise phenomena, would have never been conceived of at the start of our project.

4. We had originally begun our speculations about the general effects of urban stress, but partly out of convenience much of our early work consisted of laboratory studies of noise. As that part of our program developed, we broadened our investigations to keep pace with our speculations by engaging in laboratory studies of bureaucracy, economic discrimination, field studies of noise, and aspects of the stresses in automobile traffic, street litter, and garbage.

FITTING THE THEORY TO THE DATA

As our research progressed, we found ourselves engaged in a reversal of our usual processes of explanation. In most previous circumstances, we had undertaken studies to test a hypothesis or to decide between two or more counterposed ones. When the data had been collected, our analytical task was to ascertain how well it fit each postulated theory. Granted that there was still plenty of room for internal analyses, fiddling with the data, and stretching of our points, our fundamental strategy was still to look for an answer to a question of the sort, "Were we right in expecting events to occur for the reasons we originally proposed?" When we switched to applied problems, our ques-

tions, and hence, our way of thinking underwent a change. We asked, "Now that we have created an effect, what caused it?"

The reason for this inversion is not difficult to understand. In most laboratory studies, the experimental situation has been specifically created to be a credible realization of the theory's preconditions. It does not matter that the situation has no exact real world counterpart. . . . But in dealing with a laboratory recreation of an actual world event, a high degree of abstraction is impossible. Unless the problem is well defined and demarcated—and the interesting ones never are—you never know whether the features neglected in your abstract are the most important. The experimenter's ingenuity is put to the test to create a workable replica of the social problem in the lab. It is no great surprise, then, that when his experimental design satisfies the requirement of matching an actual situation, it no longer can neatly be described by any single existing theory. Our own procedure was to speculate, with a mixture of reason, intuition, and common sense, about what could cause the phenomena we hoped to create. When we produced an effect, we then respeculated; modifying, adding, and discarding theory when necessary.

THE WORLD IS A THEORETICAL BAZAAR

We got our theory from wherever we could find it. Because our problems were so complex, usually we were as likely to find explanatory help outside the domain of social psychology as within it. Most of our efforts were attempts at a synthesis of rags and snatches of ideas and concepts from a variety of sources. As a result our receptivity to the ideas and reactions of our colleagues was much greater than when we were engaged in the relatively single-minded pursuit of an hypothesis test. For example, we learned more from the reactions to our own colloquia during this research than before; not that the proportion of dunderheads and self-propagandists in our audiences had changed, but rather, since we were no longer talking about a somewhat narrow social psychological problem, but a much broader social one, people in our audiences from a wider variety of backgrounds and interests could contribute with possible explanations, disconfirmations, and related studies.

A need for more techniques and a wider command of the psychological literature also developed because it was the problems instead of the experimental designs which placed the limits on what we had to study. It is possible for an investigator to go through a career in social psychology without once being concerned with personality measurement; that is, the ability to randomize subjects across conditions will usually allow him to ignore any potential influence from a personality factor. However, when looking at an actual problem in the real world, rarely have people been assigned different lots in life by a random process. To study some of these nonrandom conditions one must either be able to create a manipulated analogue of the factor involved or somehow to measure and adjust for it. And in field studies, the situation is even more acute. As a result, the references in our work are rather diverse with respect to theory, methods, and content. It is our feeling that it is as creative to weave a tapestry out of old and varied theoretical strands as to produce a new theory out of whole cloth. And we have some historical justification in the belief that any newly proffered idea was probably proposed earlier by someone else. There are professional genealogists in psychology who, on request, can trace any idea back to Aristotle, the Talmud, or the Ming Dynasty as the occasion demands. And as Aristotle was expounding on the nature of the dramatic event, some fellow Athenian was probably remarking that Ab of the Urs thought of it first. Be that as it may, whatever the aesthetic or intellectual value of our procedures, they were the only ones which we were able to use.

APPLIED SOCIAL PSYCHOLOGY IS LIKE EATING SALTED PEANUTS

Our original conception of our research program was broadly conceived and the choice of starting with the study of noise was, we believed, just the first step in the study of a wide range of urban stressors. But if starting was difficult, stopping was even harder. Our book, *Urban Stress*, contains about two dozen experiments; all but three of them deal with some aspect of noise as a stressor. Yet when we review what we know and don't know about noise, either by ourselves or with colleagues, it becomes painfully obvious that even within our limited framework we have only scratched the surface.

There is no necessary reason why the problem of stopping should be confined to applied work; surely basic researchers may spend their lives on a single problem. But the situation is more troublesome for the applied social psychologist. The basic researcher essentially is trying to document

a theory. He can stop his studies when the facts give him sufficient confidence in the veracity of his conjectures. If others deem him intellectually irresponsible for not fully proving his speculations, it is between him and his ego ideal to settle. For an applied problem, the criterion of when the solution is complete is a more difficult one for two reasons. More social consensus is involved in determining whether the proposed solution is satisfactory and the issue of social responsibility is involved; that is, a researcher who chooses to investigate some applied area, particularly one of a general social nature, has made a self-declaration of social involvement and concern. This declaration is inconsistent, dissonant, if you will, with the act of abandoning the research before the completion of the problem.

WHAT WE DID: A REPRISE

We have been somewhat discursive in discussing our studies of a problem in applied social psychology, and somehow that is only fitting, for we are merely recapitulating our discursive experiences with the problem. In retrospect, however, there may be more order than we realized in our procedures because now that we are studying stressors other than noise, we can see the same steps being repeated. In brief, the following order represents the chronology of our method of attacking a problem:

1. Find a problem that interests us. Discuss it at length informally in its various aspects until we can agree on the facet of major interest.

2. Speculate, if possible in an informed manner, on the reasons for the occurrence of the phenomena. Read the most salient of the relevant literature. Since a theory is usually not possible at this point, arrive at a working speculation.

3. Try to create a laboratory simulation for the conditions of the problem. The theory at this point is flexible enough to defer to the requirements of making the simulation faithful to the original problem.

4. Run some studies to see if your original hunch has any validity. You may find it necessary to engage in more replication than formerly because parameters as well as relationships are under investigation.

5. Review your theory and cast a critical eye at your findings. Scavenge around wherever you

299

can for usable explanations. Examine your work for different kinds of loose ends.

6. Expand the scope of your work by generalizing to other similar studies on related problems, and try to find field tests of your current theoretical beliefs. Contrast the results of these different procedures.

7. Don't make your current explanations too irrevocable. Continue to be sensitive to new possibilities of both explanations and unexplored aspects of the basic problem.

8. Try to arrive at a socially responsible balance between the intractability of the problem and the requirements of your own nervous system for variety when deciding to leave the problem for other pursuits.

Let us repeat that this procedural résumé is what we actually did, and as such reflects our biases, predilections, and strengths and weaknesses as researchers. We think that our experience has some didactic value as a loose informal guide to the application of social psychology but that preferences for starting work in the laboratory, the field, or elsewhere should of necessity be determined by the nature of the problems and the particular research preferences of the investigators.

SOME SERENDIPITOUS COCKTAIL PARTY BENEFITS

One disadvantage of being a pure social psychologist is that you can never do anybody any good. When schmoozing with friends about the real world, the best you can do as a professional is to make extrapolations which may or may not be plausible. You may be ingenious enough to think of a possible way . . . to predict the winner of a chessmatch through an analysis of ordinal position of birth, but it's pretty hard to take yourself seriously. One of the advantages of dealing with applied social psychology is that the problems are real ones and lend themselves to immediate application. So when the neighborhood coffee klatch starts talking about how dismal life in the cities has become and the horrors of the impending new jetport, you find that you actually know something. G. H. Hardy notwithstanding, that is a very satisfying feeling.

SOCIAL COGNITION AND HEALTH

SHELLEY E. TAYLOR

Social psychologists who do work on important social problems usually take the approach of applying theories and knowledge to the issue of concern. For example, how can principles of person perception help us understand the dynamics of eyewitness testimony? Can research on small-group processes explain what occurs in jury deliberations? Does attribution theory enlighten us on how people cope with a sudden illness? Such applications of social-psychological theory can indeed be very useful for gaining insights into these issues and developing proposals on how to deal with them more effectively. In her article, Taylor provides a number of good illustrations of this sort of application in the area of health psychology. However, she demonstrates that the relationship between theory and social problem can go the other way, as well. The problem itself can have important implications for a theory by testing its assumptions, pointing out its limitations, suggesting modifications and extensions of it, and so forth. In other words, research on social problems can have theoretical benefits, as well as practical ones.

For the first eight years of my career as a social psychologist, I did laboratory experiments in social cognition, primarily in the area of attribution theory. Social cognition research has an intrinsically fascinating quality, like a Chinese puzzle, in that there is a great sense of intellectual satisfaction when one has designed a clever experiment or solved a difficult problem. After a while, however, that satisfaction pales from time to time when one wonders what difference the results make, except to 50 or 60 other people in social cognition.

Several years ago I became interested in health psychology and simultaneously began to question whether the laboratory-derived theories of social cognition have any applicability in the real world. As a consequence, I tried to apply some of those theories to how people think about their health and their health care. One of the first results of that effort has been a large-scale study of cancer survivors that I and my collaborators, Rosemary Lichtman and Joanne Wood, have been conducting for the last one and one-half years. I would like to share with you some of the preliminary results of that research.

The study involves intensive interviews and questionnaire data on 78 women who have had breast cancer. In addition, we are usually also able to interview a significant other ($N = 61$), most commonly the spouse. We picked breast cancer for several reasons. First, it is the major cause of death among American women and hence constitutes a major health problem. Second, it is the most common cancer, and so there are lots of available patients. Third, it is a cancer with a good prognosis, and so there are lots of survivors. Our women range in age from 27 to 82; the average is 53. This is the usual age range for breast cancer patients, although our sample includes a fair number of younger women, reflecting the fact that breast cancer now has a younger onset than was true as recently as ten years ago. About half of our women have had their breast cancer treated through a mastectomy, which involves removal of the breast and sometimes also the adjacent lymph nodes; the remainder have been treated with a lumpectomy, which requires just the removal of the lump itself and is usually followed up by radiation therapy and/or chemotherapy. Most of the women have had their cancer surgery within the last four years.

All of our patients are from a three-physician practice in the San Fernando Valley area of Los Angeles. Compared with the normal population, our sample is somewhat more middle and upper class and somewhat more likely to be Jewish. However, interestingly enough, the breast cancer population is also biased in those ways, although not to the degree that our sample is. We wanted

Reprinted from Shelley E. Taylor, "Social Cognition and Health," *Personality and Social Psychology Bulletin*, Vol. 8, No. 3 (September 1982), 549–62. © 1982 by the Society for Personality and Social Psychology, Inc., with permission of Sage Publications, Inc.

a study of survivors of breast cancer and therefore initially hoped to interview only women who had small tumors that had not spread (Stage 1 cancer) and who were currently symptom-free. Cancer, of course, is not a terribly reliable disease; and as a consequence we do have some metastatic cancer patients, that is, patients in whom the disease has spread. However, the majority have a good prognosis. Reflecting our interest in studying survivors, since the study commenced we have had no deaths in our sample, but babies have been born to two of our women.

Procedurally, we contacted these women and their families through their physician and then visited them in their homes. Our interview takes approximately an hour and a half and covers background information; the theories they hold about where their cancer came from; their emotional adjustment to cancer; whether or not they believe they have control over their cancer; relationships with friends, spouse, and family; life changes; and compliance, among other topics. In addition, we leave with them an hour-long questionnaire that includes standardized measures of adjustment. The significant-other interview is somewhat shorter, lasting approximately 45 minutes, but it covers most of the same topics and is also followed by a questionnaire similar to the woman's.

For the remainder of the article I would like to sketch out our findings that are relevant to four theoretical approaches within social psychology and social cognition. The first is *attribution theory*, in which we ask, do patients make attributions, what attributions do they make, and what attributions lead to better adjustment? The second is *psychological control*. We ask, do cancer patients feel they have control over their cancer and its treatment and, if so, does that help them adjust? The third is *social comparison*. Do cancer patients compare their ability to cope with that of other women, if so, to whom, and how do those comparisons make them feel? The fourth is *victimization*. Are patients rejected and isolated by friends and family because of the threat of cancer?

ATTRIBUTION THEORY

Attribution theory is the study of why and how people go about constructing causal explanations for what happens to them. Some of its basic principles are that people engage in attributional search when they experience a sudden disruption in the environment, and that what attribution they ultimately make has important consequences for their emotional state and functioning. Consider the plight of the cancer patient who, having lived a relatively healthy and blameless life in most cases, must now try to understand why she has developed the most dreaded of diseases. It is hard to imagine a more disruptive change. Attributions, accordingly, were one of the central foci of our interviews with cancer patients.

We posed three questions: "Do cancer patients make attributions for their cancer?" "What attributions do they make?" "What attributions are the most functional from a psychological standpoint?" On the first question the majority of cancer patients do come up with some causal explanation for their cancer, in fact 95 percent do. In order to have a comparison group against which to evaluate this rate, we also asked the significant others if they had a causal explanation for their wives' or friends' cancer. Again, the majority do, as would be expected, since the significant others as well as the patients have experienced sudden disruption in their lives. Nonetheless, their rate of making causal explanations is somewhat less, about 70 percent.

On the question, "What attributions do they make?" we need to distinguish between our sophisticated patients and our unsophisticated ones. The majority of our cancer patients were quite sophisticated in their background knowledge of cancer, some because they were married to individuals who worked in medicine, a few because they themselves were in medicine as nurses or medical secretaries, and still others because they had read a great deal of literature on their own, sometimes including the medical literature. Among the sophisticated group, stress was most commonly mentioned as the cause of cancer, usually some specific stressful event such as the death of a family member; stress-based explanations arise in about one-third of our cases. Specific carcinogens were next. These ranged widely and included ingested substances such as primarin (an estrogen replenisher used in treating menopause), DES, or birth control pills. In other cases, women mentioned environmental hazards such as having lived near a chemical dump, a nuclear testing site, or a copper mine. These explanations show up in a little under one-third of our cases.

The third explanation, which arose in about one-quarter of the cases, was heredity. This explanation sometimes raises problems in the family that I will mention again later. Finally, diet, especially one high in protein and fats and low in vegetables, is mentioned in about 10 percent of the cases.

A reason why it is important to remember that this is a relatively sophisticated group arises in comparing the explanations that our patients offered for their cancer with those of other patient samples. For example, Beth Meyerowitz, in a pilot study of women in Fresno, found a high proportion of women who attributed their cancer to God's will or God's desire to test them, a relatively infrequent attribution in our group. Her population was heavily Catholic and working class, whereas our population is more heavily Jewish and middle class, and thus the difference in frequency in explanation undoubtedly reflects these cultural factors.

The causal explanations of the more naive patients are by far more interesting from a psychological standpoint. I am struck by the fact that our scientific theories of causal attribution make fairly elaborate assumptions about the processes that people undergo in trying to infer causality. What is therefore notable among the patients with relatively little knowledge about cancer is how simple their explanations for cancer are, and how those explanations illustrate relatively simple principles of causality.

The basic features of naive causal explanation, of course, is that causes always precede outcomes. This is perhaps the most fundamental aspect of both scientific and naive conceptions of causality, and it is virtually never contradicted in even the most simple of causal explanations. A second implicit principle of causality is that causes precede outcomes in fairly close temporal proximity. The notion of delayed causality may require somewhat more knowledge about particular types of causes. People who are ill-informed about the fact that cancers may grow for 15 or 20 years before they are detectable will often make the assumption that some recent event caused their cancer. For example, one woman we interviewed believed that her breast cancer had been caused by an automobile accident in which she was involved several days before she found her lump, and went so far as to consult a lawyer about suing the other driver for her cancer before being disabused of this idea.

Another naive notion of causality is that causes lead to effects in close spatial proximity. Often breast cancer patients will isolate a cause that involves some trauma to that particular area of the breast where the malignancy developed. For example, one of our women had worked at the National Fireworks for several years. She was a short woman, and when she was packing shells into the casing she had trouble getting leverage on the shells; so she would push the shell into the casing using the upper part of her ribcage. She ultimately developed a breast lesion on the lower side of the breast on that side, and believed it had been the continual pressure to the breast that had caused it.

Causes resemble effects. For example, people generally assume that big effects are produced by big causes and little effects are caused by little causes. Cancer is, of course, a big effect, and one would anticipate that it is attributed to a major cause. We find this principle illustrated even among our sophisticated patients. For example, of the patients who believed that their cancer was caused by stress, few think it was produced by small, cumulative, day-to-day hassles. Rather, they are more likely to mention some significant stressful event, which is most commonly the death of a parent or child or a particularly unpleasant divorce.

Representative causes are often attributed to effects. In trying to find an explanation for a situation, people will look at similar outcomes and infer that the cause of the current outcome is similar to the causes for those previous outcomes. For example, women who do not know much about the causes of cancer will often attribute a malignant lump to some sort of blow to the breast, since lumps are usually caused by blows. One woman believed her cancer had begun when a boy at her pool threw a frisbee that hit her in the breast. Another, who was a salesperson in a women's clothing store, believed the constant bumping of hangers against her breast as she carried clothes over her arm had caused the malignancy.

Frequency or consistency of outcome can influence perceptions of causality, such that frequent co-occurrences of two events may be seen to have a cause-effect relationship. One woman, for example, inferred that there was something carcinogenic about her golfing club since four of her acquaintances there had also developed breast cancer. Finally, under many circumstances, people seem to look for a single cause of an event rather than a confluence of causes that may have combined to produce the event. Having one cause debunked by a physician or friend, a patient may look for another single cause, rather than considering multiple factors, such as stress, a virus, the contributing role of heredity, and an environmental carcinogen. Multiple causality more commonly characterizes the explanations of our more sophisticated patients.

To summarize, it is among the most naive cancer patients that we can learn most about the process of attributing causality. What I find striking is the elegant simplicity of these causal analyses compared to the relative complexity of the analyses that we frequently attribute to the social perceiver in our theories of attributional process-

ing. This is not to say that these simple principles have not received research attention. They have, but primarily in the literature on children's attributions. Adults have been characterized as moving beyond these very simple principles to include understanding of distal or delayed causality, multiple causality, and other more complex causal rules. It is unquestionably the case that adult perceivers have this ability, at least about some causal domains. Whether they have it about most domains and whether or not they characteristically use it is another question. Our theoretical ventures, then, might be well served by returning to the level of naive explanation.

The most important question about attributions, of course, is whether or not particular patterns of attributions lead to more successful coping than others, and it is to this question that I want to turn now, drawing first on the literature concerning psychological control.

PSYCHOLOGICAL CONTROL

There is now substantial laboratory and field evidence linking feelings of psychological control to improved adjustment to noxious events, such as noxious medical procedures and noxious disorders themselves. In her review article, Suzanne Thompson (1981) isolates four kinds of control: information control, cognitive control, behavior control, and what she terms retrospective control. Retrospective control is the feeling of control that can be regained by taking personal responsibility for causing a negative event that has already transpired. For example, Janoff-Bulman (1979) reports that rape victims will often blame themselves for the rape in a possible effort to restore feelings of control and that they would be able to forestall a recurrence of the event. Bulman and Wortman (1977), in their study of paraplegic and quadriplegic victims of accidents, suggested that the fairly high rate of self-blame among these victims may reflect their need to reassert control by assuming responsibility for the event that caused their problems. Thus, from this perspective, self-blame for an event like cancer should lead to better psychological adjustment.

However, the psychodynamic perspective makes exactly the opposite prediction that self-blame leads to poor adjustment because of the guilt that is produced. Which theory is right?

One of our questions asked women to attribute their cancer to one of four things: themselves, some other person, the environment, or chance. Overall, the greatest number of attributions were made to chance, followed by the environment. A relatively small proportion attributed their cancer exclusively to themselves (17 percent) and only a very few attributed it to some other person (5 percent). (When some other is blamed for the cancer, it is always either one's doctor or one's ex-husband!) We had also asked several questions about whether or not the woman believed that she had control over the *course* of her cancer once it was detected, such as whether or not it would recur. In contrast to the question about initial causality, a more substantial number of women do believe that they have control over the *course* of their cancer. For some, this control consists of carefully monitoring and watching their body so that they seek treatment as soon as they detect any irregularity. For others, it consists of generally staying healthy through proper diet and exercise. For a third group it consists of maintaining a positive attitude. And for a fourth group it consists of using imaging, meditation, self-hypnosis, and other psychological techniques to forestall a recurrence of their cancer.

The combined results of these two sets of questions tapping, on the one hand the perceived causes for the cancer, and on the other hand perceived responsibility for the course of cancer once it is detected, raises the conceptual importance of distinguishing between responsibility for initial causes and responsibilities for solutions. Many of our women seem to be getting the best of both worlds and thus support the predictions of both theories. They avoid the potential guilt of self-blame by blaming chance or environmental factors for the cause of the cancer, but gain the psychological advantage of feelings of control by assuming that they have some influence over the course of their cancer now that it has been detected.

The importance of psychological control also emerges when we look at how these women approach their follow-up care. Because there is relatively little information about adherence to medical regimen among cancer patients, . . . we devoted a substantial portion of our interview to these issues. We were concerned, first, with whether or not cancer patients comply with their adjuvant therapy, namely radiation therapy and chemotherapy. We also examined compliance with what might be seen as discretionary advice, such as practicing breast self-examination, practicing arm exercises, and refraining from smoking. Finally, we examined these women's use of nontraditional techniques for controlling the side effects of therapy such as imaging, relaxation, and meditation.

Noncompliance, generally, is an important medical problem. Estimates of the rate of noncompliance vary from a low of about 8 percent to a high of 93 percent, depending upon the type of treatment recommendation. Compliance with chemotherapy and radiation in our sample, however, is extremely high. In fact, patients appear quite startled by the idea that they might not comply. The typical respondent had missed one visit for a good reason, which had subsequently been rescheduled. Because this rate of compliance is considerably higher than is typically found in studies of adherence, we cross-checked our data with the physician. He concurred that approximately 98 percent of his patients are compliant with chemotherapy and radiation therapy.

Compliance with all forms of what may be seen as discretionary advice is considerably lower: practice of arm exercises to restore arm use, stopping smoking, and breast self-examination. These compliance data parallel those from other studies: Advice that is seen as "discretionary" or "lifestyle"-related is not as strongly followed as advice that is seen by patients as "medical." In the case of breast self-examination (BSE), this is quite a problem. Ninety-eight percent of all breast cancer is self-detected, and with a group that is high risk, like ours, BSE is one of the few techniques of control over their cancer that patients have, and one would expect them to practice it.

One possible reason for noncompliance is that these women do not see BSE as a source of control. In contrast to dietary changes or stress reduction, which they may believe will keep the cancer from recurring, all BSE does is tell them that something is there. Thus, finding a lump wouldn't help them, it would only confirm the worst. In addition, since it is hard to distinguish a lump from all the normal breast lumpiness, the technique may only raise anxiety without providing any useful information.

By far the most interesting data on adherence have to do with the practice of nontraditional techniques for controlling the side effects of chemotherapy and radiation therapy, techniques such as imaging, relaxation, meditation, and self-hypnosis. Although not all of our women practice such behavior, a significant minority does. For example, one woman who was undergoing radiation therapy would imagine that there was a protective shield keeping her body from being burned by the radiation. Another woman imaged her chemotherapy as powerful cannons that blasted away pieces of the dragon, cancer. Another simply focused her attention on healing, with the instruction to her body, "Body, cut this shit out." Our interest in these nontraditional forms of "therapy" stems, in part, from the skepticism of some surgeons and oncologists regarding their use. Not only do some doubt that such techniques are effective, an understandable skepticism; many fear that when patients turn to nontraditional therapies, they abandon their medically recommended procedures.

What we found debunked this fear. Only two of our patients using nontraditional techniques rejected any aspect of their follow-up-care, and that is fewer than is the case among women who do not use psychological or nontraditional techniques. When asked if the use of such techniques made them more or less inclined to comply with their traditional therapy, and whether they saw these techniques as better, worse, or just different from their traditional therapy, most said that they believed the psychological techniques were just different from their traditional therapy and that both were necessary to accomplish a cure. Furthermore, the techniques appear to be successful. The majority of women who practice some nontraditional form of psychological control report that they are able to tolerate the side effects of the radiation therapy and chemotherapy better by using them, and no one reports worsened adjustment. Incidentally, these women have developed use of these techniques on their own. None was formally trained through an adjuvant therapy intervention or by their oncologist. Rather, at least in several cases, they try out several possibilities—imaging, meditation, or self-hypnosis—and hit on one that works for them.

We are very pleased with these results and believe that use of these nontraditional techniques should be encouraged to offset the negative effects of adjuvant therapies. This is all the more important, since adjuvant therapy, especially chemotherapy, can be the true horror in the cancer treatment process for many women.

SOCIAL COMPARISON

One of the intrinsically fascinating questions about cancer patients is how they evaluate their own adjustment to cancer. We can assume that if someone thinks she is dealing badly with cancer, this will be an added strain on what may be an already difficult life, whereas if she feels she is adjusting well, that belief can be a source of satisfaction and pride. This question was examined closely by Joanne Wood in our own research. Drawing on the work of Wortman and Dunkel-Schetter (1979), she hypothesized that whether or not women believed they were coping well with their cancer would

depend in part upon the type of contact they had had with other women who had had cancer, how well they thought these other women had coped with their cancer, and whether or not they thought they were doing as well as these other comparison women.

There are two important types of comparison women. One group is the supercoper, the women whom the media parade as adjusting well and going on to achieve great things in their lives. Marvella Bayh, Shirley Temple Black, Betty Ford, and Maggie Kuhn (the head of the Gray Panthers) come to mind. Reach to Recovery volunteers also fall into this category. Preselected for being well-adjusted and instructed to communicate a picture of good psychological health, they visit a woman immediately after her surgery and provide her with information and some counseling. The second possible comparison group is normal women who are adjusting in an average way to the consequences of breast cancer and surgery.

Women who have exposure only to supercoper models may find their own responses to breast cancer lacking, in that they themselves have had bouts of depression, periods of self-doubt and pessimism, difficulty readjusting to their lives, and temporary or even permanent difficulties with family or friends. Consequently, their self-esteem may suffer from such comparisons. In contrast, women who have had extensive contact with other patients, through a support group or casual encounters, might see themselves as better adjusted because they can see that most women share some of these same experiences.

We investigated the social comparison process by asking an extensive set of questions about the nature of our patients' contacts with other women through the media (books, TV movies, magazine and newspaper articles), and their personal contacts, such as knowledge of fellow patients, participation in a support group, and contact with a Reach to Recovery volunteer. We also asked whether they had formed any impression about how these others had coped, whether they compared themselves to these women, and how they felt they were adjusting by comparison.

Our results revealed several interesting findings. First, there is a lot of variability in contacts. For example, some women read everything they find in the media while others scrupulously avoid it. Some have been to support groups, others have not. More important, regardless of type of comparison available, virtually all of our women feel that they are doing "somewhat better" than other women who are coping with breast cancer.

The literature on social comparison, of course, predicts the opposite: that individuals compare themselves with people who are doing slightly better than they are; although one comes off as psychologically disadvantaged, one may gain useful information from the upward comparison. Our women, instead, appear to be making downward comparisons, in that they come off as psychologically somewhat advantaged. There is a resolution. Some research on social comparison indicates that this pattern of downward comparisons is particularly likely to occur under conditions of threat. This point suggests that our women may be selecting their comparisons to preserve their self-esteem, rather than letting their self-esteem be determined by who is readily available for comparison.

The second point of interest is that relatively few of our women actually compare themselves with the women they learn about vicariously through the media. In fact, some of our women specifically reject media figures as comparison objects by pointing out "they're rich, they're prominent, they have husbands," and the like. Instead, they almost always mention one or two women with whom they have had specific contact or about whom they have a great deal of personal information, such as fellow patients, relatives, or a personal acquaintance.

Third, there is a tendency among some of our respondents to describe extreme examples of coping outcomes, for example, to bring up cases with which they are familiar of women who have had a terrible time coping with cancer, or to bring up instances of women who coped well and went on to lead healthy, happy, productive lives. To put it another way, these women seem to be defining the end points of the coping continuum, imagining the very best possible outcomes and the very worst possible coping outcome of the cancer bout. Again, the social comparison literature is helpful here. It suggests that when people are asked to make social comparisons on a dimension about which they have relatively little information, rather than picking someone similar as a basis for comparison, they will often choose people embodying the extremes in an apparent effort to gain some knowledge of the dimension itself. By implication, of course, these results suggest that women have a very ill-formed idea of what adequate coping with cancer is.

In summary, the preliminary results of our efforts to understand cancer patients' social comparisons suggest, first, that they are making downward comparisons instead of upward ones and hence are behaving like individuals in other settings who are under threat. Second, they seem to lack knowledge about coping, testing out the nature of the coping dimension itself by seeking information about the extremes of the coping dimension rather than making comparisons that place themselves on the dimension at one point or another. And finally, they seem to be defining the range of appropriate comparisons quite narrowly. They tend to compare themselves with one or two individuals rather than a set of individuals with which they had contact, and they tend to compare themselves with people about whom they have specific, personal, first-hand information rather than with people about whom they have indirect information.

We believe these results have direct relevance to interventions with cancer patients. Instead of presenting patients with supercoper models as Reach to Recovery does, our results suggest that patients might be better off having contact with more similar, average women who did have occasional personal or family problems following their cancer bout, but who are now doing better.

VICTIMIZATION

The final theoretical perspective I will apply to our cancer results is victimization. Wortman and Dunkel-Schetter (1979), in particular, have advanced the position that cancer patients are often victims within their own families and among their friends; according to this perspective, cancer raises such fear and anxiety among others that cancer patients are rejected, often isolated, and unable to talk about the issues that are disturbing to them. Certainly there are echoes of this perspective in the media. Job discrimination against cancer patients is a reality; their insurance coverage may be withdrawn; or cancer patients may be falsely isolated by others who fear that they will catch cancer from them. Accordingly, we asked our patients a number of questions about this issue, tapping whether or not they felt they had been treated differently by friends, family, and relatives after their cancer. In addition, we specifically examined the husband-wife relationship and relationships between the woman and her children for signs of these kinds of problems. We also asked if there had ever been circumstances under which they had been surprised by a show of support from friends, relatives, or family.

Overall, we found very little support for the victimization hypothesis. Some patients reported that their relationship with one friend or relative or with a couple had deteriorated because those particular individuals were not able to cope with cancer. However, quite the opposite pattern was more common. Most of our patients reported great surprise at the extensive support that their co-workers, neighbors, and other friends provided. It was not uncommon for patients to come home from the hospital and find that their meals had been cooked, there were flowers around the house, or that chores that they would normally have accomplished themselves had been taken on by other people. On occasion, friends or neighbors would come in to help out with arm exercises and changes of dressing. Overall, the amount of support reported was substantial.

We were surprised by the difference in our results compared with those obtained by Wortman and Dunkel-Schetter and accordingly looked for some factor that might explain the difference. A conversation with them leads us to believe that a partial answer lies in the sample used. Wortman and Dunkel-Schetter based their inferences heavily on cancer patients who participated in support groups. In contrast, among our women only two had participated for any significant length of time in a cancer support group. Others had gone to one or two meetings, but had decided the support group experience was not for them. One hypothesis, then, is that the experience of rejection from others may act as an impetus for joining a support group, but that overall, relatively few cancer patients experience this kind of rejection.

However, this is not to suggest that everyone welcomes the returning cancer patient and her problems with open arms. There are unquestionably areas of awkwardness and strain that develop when the cancer patient attempts to share her thoughts with family members and friends. The most common experience we uncovered was that cancer patients themselves generally think of cancer as a continuing threat they they can never fully escape, whereas family members and close friends are inclined to think of it as a crisis that has now passed. Family members and friends seem to give the cancer patient a latitude of time during which they expect the cancer patient to be somewhat upset, to dwell on the issue, and to have needs that require communication. After this period of time, however, they expect the cancer patient to put the problem behind her; in contrast, cancer patients quite realistically see a cancer threat as something that is looming over their heads at least for the next five years and probably for the rest of their lives. They may accordingly want to share some

of these fears with family members who discourage such discussion on the grounds that it is negative, pessimistic thinking. Rarely, however, is this reported by our women to be a major problem; rather, it seems to constitute a modest strain.

The second case in which we commonly find ongoing difficulty as a consequence of the cancer experience is in the mother-daughter relationship, when the mother is the cancer patient and has one or more adolescent or postadolescent daughters. Although it is by no means the case that every mother-daughter relationship is affected negatively, a substantial proportion of relationships do change, with mother and daughter growing more distant and have more difficulty communicating. It is hard to identify the causes of this deterioration; it seems to come from several sources. One possibility is that the mother, finding that her husband is not as willing as she had hoped to talk about the cancer, turns to her daughter in the expectation that she may be able to serve that function and leans on her more than the daughter is able to tolerate. The daughter may of course already be threatened by the mother's cancer, not only because her mother is ill, but because her own risk of developing cancer is now apparent. She may resent her mother for putting her at risk and pull away from her mother precisely at the point when her mother needs her most.

Let me reiterate, however, that despite these and other sources of strain, the experience of the cancer patient generally seems to be one of substantial support rather than widespread rejection. My suspicion is that the victimization perspective may have characterized the cancer patient's experience as recently as a few years ago. However, as more is known about cancer, as the cure rates improve, and as more individuals have direct contact with cancer, the unrealistic fears may diminish, allowing a very basic compassion to emerge.

CONCLUSION

I would like to conclude by again posing the question, what can social psychological theories, particularly those concerned with social cognitions, tell us about how people think about health and illness? On the one hand, we found these tools extremely useful in identifying areas for closer investigation. The theories gave us hypothesis-testing directions in what could otherwise have been merely an intrinsically interesting descriptive process. On the other hand, none of the theories applied in precisely the ways that the theory would have led us to believe. Instead, the cancer context defined dimensions that the theories had not always anticipated, occasionally pointed out problems with the theories, and clearly identified problems in the cancer experience that needed further consideration. For example, our results on social comparisons indicate that women may well have a relatively poor idea of what adequate coping with cancer is and hence seek individuals at the extremes of the dimension in an effort to try to undersand what it means to cope with cancer. As mentioned earlier, perhaps by providing more information about how other average people cope with cancer, this apparent lack of information can be handled. In the case of control it is clear that we need to make a separation between control for the cause of an event and control for the solution of an event. This distinction echoes current work by Philip Brickman and his associates (in press)

and suggests that the psychological and social consequences of attributions for causes versus solutions of a problem like cancer may be very different. In short, the application of social psychological theory to a social problem like cancer is a two-way street, with the theories providing novel perspective on the problem and the problem itself defining ways in which the theories must grow.

I hope I have also communicated to you the excitement of applying social psychological theory to a problem area like cancer. Although this is not an easy kind of research to conduct, either logistically or emotionally, it has combined for me the intellectual pleasure that comes from grappling with some of the thorniest issues in social cognition with the emotional satisfaction that comes from beginning to understand a problem of such profound human significance as cancer.

REFERENCES

Abrams, R. D., & Finesinger, J. E. Guilt reactions in patients with cancer. *Cancer*, 1953, *6*, 474–82.

Brickman, P., Rabinowitz, U.C., Coates, D., Cohn, E., Kidder, L., & Karuza, J. Helping. *American Psychologist*, in press.

Bulman, R. J., & Wortman, C. B. Attributions of blame and coping in the "real world": Severe accident victims react to their lot. *Journal of Personality and Social Psychology*, 1977, *35*, 351–63.

Heider, F. *The psychology of interpersonal relations.* New York: John Wiley, 1958.

Janoff-Bulman, R. Characterological versus behavioral self-blame: Inquiries into depression and rape. *Journal of Personality and Social Psychology*, 1979, *37*, 1798–1809.

Meyerowitz, B. E. Personal communication. Los Angeles, March 1980. (Meyerowitz is now in the Department of Psychology, Vanderbilt University, Nashville, Tennessee.)

Thompson, S. C. A complex answer to a simple question: Will it hurt less if I can control it? *Psychological Bulletin*, 1981, *90*, 89–101.

Weisman, A. D. Coping with an untimely death. In R. J. Moss (ed.), *Human adaptation.* Lexington, Mass: D.C. Heath, 1976.

Wortman, C. B., & Dunkel-Schetter, C. D. Interpersonal relationships and cancer: A theoretical analysis. *Journal of Social Issues*, 1979, *35*, 120–55.

RESEARCH HIGHLIGHT

BURNOUT: THE LOSS OF HUMAN CARING

In recent years, the number and range of services offered by the helping professions have greatly increased. More and more opportunities exist for people to seek and obtain help, protection, cure, education, or special treatment of some kind for the problems that they face. The professionals they turn to are often highly skilled in such areas as law, medicine, social welfare, and counseling. But more than simple application of skill is expected from these professionals. The people who seek their help expect them to be personally concerned. The helping professionals are asked to be warm and caring, on the one hand, and objective, on the other. If they fail to meet these high expectations and treat their patients or clients in ways that are considered indifferent, rude, or even dehumanizing, people are quick to criticize them and complain about the individuals who staff society's service institutions.

Ellen says she is burned out. She is angry and frustrated, feels impotent and incompetent. Her morale and her self-image are low. "I feel like my soul is dying," says Ellen. "I can't look straight in my clients' eyes anymore. I've become cold, uncaring, and no longer interested in working with losers. All I want to do is quit my job, and yet I feel trapped." How did this sensitive, caring, and committed young woman get burned out? And why does it happen to so many people in the various health and social-service professions?

There are many situations in which people work intensely and intimately with other people. They learn about people's psychological, social, and physical problems, and they are often called upon to provide personal help of some kind. Such intense involvement with people occurs on a large-scale, continuous basis for individuals in various health and social-service professions. Hour after hour, day after day, these professionals must *care* about many other people, and our research indicates that they often pay a heavy psychological price for being their brother's keeper. Constant or repeated emotional arousal is a very stressful experience for any human being and can often be disruptive or incapacitating.

And yet, in the large and steadily growing literature in these fields, very little attention is given to the emotional stresses experienced by the professional. One of the main reasons for this seems to be the traditional client-centered orientation shared by these professions. The focus is almost exclusively the client, the patient, or the person who, in some other way, receives services. Within this framework, the professional is viewed as merely the provider of services, whose role and existence are defined by the presence of the clients and are justified only as long as he or she continues to serve, help, and provide. However, the stresses experienced by the professional are very real and have a tremendous impact.

In order to perform their work efficiently and well, these professionals may defend themselves against their strong emotions through techniques of detachment. Ideally, they try to gain sufficient objectivity and distance from the situation without losing their concern for the person they are working with. However, in all too many cases, they are unable to cope with this continual emotional stress, and *burnout* (a total emotional and physical exhaustion) eventually occurs. They develop negative self-concepts and negative job attitudes, lose all concern or emotional feeling for the people they work with, and come to treat their clients in detached and even dehumanized ways.

PROJECTS

Name _____

Date _____

13.1: ASPECTS OF DEPERSONALIZATION

Almost all of us have experienced being processed by some large institution, such as a hospital, a school, a service agency, or a military unit. During such an experience, we feel like numbers or objects rather than people. In short, we feel depersonalized. What factors contribute to this sense of depersonalization? Think about one of your own depersonalizing institutional experiences, and try to identify, as concretely as possible, what caused you to feel that way.

1. How did *physical* aspects of the institution contribute to your depersonalization (e.g., identical equipment or uniforms for everyone, long corridors that make it difficult for people in their offices to see anyone else)?

2. How did *procedural* aspects of the institution contribute to your depersonalization (e.g., rules that restricted what you could say or do, long waits)?

3. How did *interpersonal* aspects of the institution contribute to your depersonalization (e.g., lack of eye contact, use of form letters)?

4. What changes would you recommend to reduce the depersonalization experienced by an institution's clients or patients?

Name _____

Date _____

13.2: WHAT DO I DO THAT I WOULD RATHER NOT DO, AND WHAT DO I NOT DO THAT I WOULD LIKE TO DO?

We all get overly involved in doing things we do not like, things that keep us from doing what we do like. Culture and society emphasize and reward certain activities and therefore are partly to blame. The self can be seen as having two parts: One is verbal, communicative, future-oriented; the other is nonverbal, physical, present-oriented. Modern Western society, with its emphasis on competition, work, and achievement, thus encourages one aspect of the self at the expense of the other, especially for the college student. The goal of this exercise is to explore the effect of that emphasis on your choice of activities and on the way you feel about your choices, and consequently on your stress and ability to cope with stress.

A. Indicate three things that you would like to do more often in your life.

   1. _____

   2. _____

   3. _____

B. Indicate three things that you would like to stop doing as much as you do and perhaps even hate doing.

   1. _____

   2. _____

   3. _____

C. Explain briefly why you do not do enough of A and do too much of B.

_____

_____

_____